as often as they enforced a racist regime. Maintaining laws against miscegenation was hard work. The racial regime was cruel and harsh and violent, but it was never robust enough to achieve its apparent goal of sexual segregation."

—Hendrik Hartog, professor emeritus, Princeton University

"A creative, insightful, thoroughly researched history. Told through the gripping stories of countless couples fighting to preserve their unions, Schumaker shows how their resistance led to a surprising level of toleration for interracial cohabitation while also documenting its limits in stark terms. Not only did authorities repeatedly criminalize those relationships and penalize some couples severely; the white men who governed the segregated South protected their own wealth and diminished that of African Americans by relentlessly denying the inheritance claims of Black members of interracial families. Through Schumaker's deft narratives, interracial marriage becomes a way to understand anew the intersection of individual experience and the social order."

—Michael Grossberg, professor emeritus, Indiana University

Praise for
Tangled Fortunes

"For generations, Mississippi politicians thundered about raci
but experience on the ground was always more complicated. In
velous synthesis of legal and social history, Kathryn Schuma
beneath the rhetorical surface, exposing the complex, shifting
tion of race, sex, and marriage in the Magnolia State."

—James T. Campbell, author of *Middl*

"This deeply researched, beautifully written book uncovers a f
history that changes how we see the Jim Crow South. As Sch
shows, legal efforts to police the color line did not eliminate in
marriage. Following the compelling stories of those couples a
efforts to keep their families together, this book reveals the pos
of human agency and the limits of formal law in dictating the
everyday life. This is a must-read."

—Laura F. Edwards, Princeton Ur

"*Tangled Fortunes* is a brilliantly researched and surprising work
torical reconstruction. Schumaker illuminates how multiracial f
survived and sometimes flourished across a century of Mississippi
from Reconstruction until the dawn of the civil rights era. The b
and ugliness of the racial regime and of white supremacy are never
ten, but the Mississippi Schumaker reveals, filled with hesitant leg
and frustrated prosecutors, and couples and families that insisted
ing lives on their own terms, is quite different than the Mississi
thought we knew. Couples sometimes hid in the deep shadows of tl
or their lawyers mobilized formalisms and contradictions to escape
ecution and imprisonment. But sometimes they lived in quiet but a
open rebellion, and local communities colluded with interracial co

KATHRYN SCHUMAKER

TANGLED FORTUNES

The HIDDEN HISTORY *of*
INTERRACIAL MARRIAGE
in the SEGREGATED SOUTH

BASIC BOOKS
New York

Basic Books

Hachette Book Group

1290 Avenue of the Americas, New York, NY 10104

www.basicbooks.com

Printed in the United States of America

First Edition: January 2025

Published by Basic Books, an imprint of Hachette Book Group, Inc. The Basic Books name and logo is a registered trademark of the Hachette Book Group.

The Hachette Speakers Bureau provides a wide range of authors for speaking events. To find out more, go to hachettespeakersbureau.com or email HachetteSpeakers@hbgusa.com.

Basic books may be purchased in bulk for business, educational, or promotional use. For more information, please contact your local bookseller or the Hachette Book Group Special Markets Department at special.markets@hbgusa.com.

The publisher is not responsible for websites (or their content) that are not owned by the publisher.

Print book interior design by Amy Quinn.

Library of Congress Cataloging-in-Publication Data

Names: Schumaker, Kathryn, author.
Title: Tangled fortunes : the hidden history of interracial marriage in the segregated South / Kathryn Schumaker.
Description: First edition. | New York : Basic Books, [2025] | Includes bibliographical references and index. |
Identifiers: LCCN 2024013281 | ISBN 9781541605312 (hardcover) | ISBN 9781541605336 (ebook)
Subjects: LCSH: Interracial marriage—Mississippi—History. | Interracial marriage—Law and legislation—Mississippi—History. | African Americans—Legal status, laws, etc.—Southern States. | Common law marriage—Southern States. | Racially mixed families—Southern States. | Inheritance and succession. | White supremacy (Social structure)—Mississippi.
Classification: LCC E185.62 .S38 2025 | DDC 306.84/50976—dc23/eng/20240403
LC record available at https://lccn.loc.gov/2024013281

ISBNs: 9781541605312 (hardcover), 9781541605336 (ebook)

LSC-C

Printing 1, 2024

For Matthew

CONTENTS

Mississippi, ca. 1910, showing counties and cities of note (credit: Kate Blackmer).

PROLOGUE

Ralphine Burns was living an otherwise quiet life when the sheriff arrived to arrest her. On that spring day in 1924, she was recovering from the birth of her baby boy, Clarence, who was not yet three weeks old.[1] A seamstress by trade, Ralphine owned her own home on Grant Street in Natchez, Mississippi, a little more than a mile from the towering bluffs that overlooked the Mississippi River.[2] She was forty-one years old and had been born and raised in Adams County, where she brought up her own nine children.[3] But in the eyes of the law, there was nothing respectable about Ralphine and her family. The sheriff was here to take her away from her children on the charge of "unlawful cohabitation."[4]

This was not Ralphine's first encounter with the Adams County sheriff or the judge. Fifteen years earlier, she had faced possible jail time after being accused of the same crime. That time, the prosecutor eventually dropped the charges.[5] Now, the district attorney once again alleged that Ralphine had long lived with a man who was not her husband. Ralphine was Black, and her partner, William Sanders Dean, was white.[6]

According to the enforcers of Jim Crow justice, theirs was an illegal interracial union.

For eighty-seven years, the state of Mississippi outlawed interracial marriage. From 1880 to 1967, the state joined much of the rest of the United States in prohibiting Black people and white people from establishing legal family ties that crossed the color line, and it sought to sever them at every turn.[7] Laws prohibiting interracial marriage were at the heart of Jim Crow, the legal regime designed to reinstate white supremacy across the former slaveholding South. But such prohibitions were not restricted to the South: many western and midwestern states also codified racial inequities by adopting laws prohibiting interracial marriage.[8] By the late nineteenth century, states forbade white people from marrying Asian Americans and Native Americans, too. By the early twentieth century, most states, at one time or another, had prohibited people from marrying across the color line.[9]

The regulation of interracial sex and relationships had long been used to define race in the United States, and, specifically, to fuse together Blackness and slavery. The earliest prohibition on interracial marriage, forbidding unions between Black enslaved men and free white women, dates from Maryland in 1664.[10] But something changed in the 1860s. The end of slavery threatened to level the races. In the same year that Abraham Lincoln issued the Emancipation Proclamation, 1863, white supremacists invented the word "miscegenation" to lend a scientific veneer to the concept that interracial sex was unnatural, warning that it could obliterate racial distinctions entirely.[11] Laws prohibiting interracial marriage after the Civil War therefore sought to protect white supremacy in the absence of slavery. These laws were crucial to perpetuating racial inequities, as they attempted to assign all people to various racial categories: white, Black, "Mongolian," or "Indian," for example. In doing so, these laws helped perpetuate the idea that racial classifications were scientific, sensible, and enforceable.[12] The idea of whiteness as "pure"— that a white person could have no African or Native American or Asian ancestors—was the central fiction of the whole scheme.[13] Laws governing marriage were essential to reproducing whiteness by perpetuating the idea that only white women could give birth to white babies, yet the very language of these laws pointed to a complicated history of interracial sex and families.[14] In Mississippi before 1890, the law classified a person with "one quarter or more" blood quantum of African ancestry as Black.[15] In 1890, lawmakers wrote into the state constitution a stricter one-eighth blood quantum of African ancestry in their quest to create an impenetrable fortress of racial segregation.[16]

Or, at least, this is what they claimed to do.

Ralphine's story does not end the way you might expect. Although she and her partner, William, were prosecuted twice for unlawful cohabitation, the couple ultimately emerged from this saga with their family intact. By the time Ralphine and William were arrested in 1924, they had been together at least a decade, and probably more than two. They hired a lawyer to defend themselves and arrived in court prepared to fight back. On November 19, 1924, the case went to trial.[17] The state called three witnesses: two white men, both carpenters and likely William's coworkers, and one of their neighbors, a Black woman named Susannah House.[18] The jury found them guilty of unlawful cohabitation, though neither was sentenced to serve any time in jail. The judge fined William $100 and Ralphine $25.[19] But the couple was not willing to give up so easily.

Their lawyer appealed their convictions to the Mississippi Supreme Court. In 1925, the justices overturned the jury's verdict. While the prosecutor had introduced evidence that the couple lived together, the justices noted that the district attorney had not proven that Ralphine was a Black woman. As evidence, they cited witness testimony that Ralphine's children appeared to be white.[20] Ralphine and William were free to return to their home on Grant Street, untouched by the police or the courts. This is what they did. After William's death in 1939, Ralphine is noted in the Natchez City Directory as the widow of "Wm. S. Dean."[21]

Ralphine and William's legal saga is the story of a couple committed to keeping their family together and steadfast in refusing to allow the state to police their private lives. But it can tell us something about the law as well. The Adams County courts could not be called "soft" on crime. In 1908, a year before Ralphine was first charged with unlawful cohabitation, her brother, Clarence, had been convicted of burglary and sentenced to serve seven years in the state penitentiary, Parchman Farm. He was alleged to have stolen a single earring and $2.85 in copper pennies.[22] Something else was driving the lax treatment that Ralphine experienced in the Adams County court, particularly given that she and William beat the case at the height of the segregation era.

Anti-miscegenation laws were the center of the Jim Crow legal and social order. When slavery was abolished, not only did states pass and enforce new laws prohibiting interracial marriage, but white supremacists used violent means to threaten those engaged in interracial relationships. Southerners defended lynching Black men as a means of protecting "white womanhood," even though most Black victims of mob violence were not actually accused of rape.[23] It was not that interracial sex did not happen. Even the earliest colonial laws prohibiting interracial sex were gendered, revealing a desire to police the sexuality of white women that went hand in hand with efforts to ensure that the children of enslaved Black women were slaves, regardless of who their fathers were.[24] After emancipation, white men raped Black women with little fear of consequence, as they had under slavery—even though rape was a capital crime.[25] It was no secret in the South that white men could and did seek out Black women as romantic and sexual partners, even when it was against the law. According to one historian, the "much-traveled sexual backroad between the races was clearly marked 'one-way.'"[26] Relationships between white men and Black women have therefore often been described in two ways: as illicit consensual encounters or as rape.[27] Neither was likely to result in a criminal charge. It was only marriage that was off-limits for interracial couples, and only formal marriages that were prosecuted. Or so conventional narratives have held.[28]

This book argues that those conventional narratives are wrong. Interracial relationships, including marriages, were in fact surprisingly common in the heart of Jim Crow.[29] Ralphine and William's story might seem extraordinary. And it was in some respects—they defied Jim Crow to keep their family together, and against great odds they succeeded. And yet, as an interracial couple in Jim Crow Mississippi, they were hardly alone. Ralphine and William used a strategy that many interracial couples before them had employed to avoid the heavy hand of Jim Crow law: they intentionally did not obtain a marriage license. Had they done so, the license could have served as evidence to charge the couple with violating the legal prohibition on interracial marriage, punishable by a sentence of up to ten years of hard labor at Parchman Farm.

Even without a license declaring them husband and wife, Ralphine Burns and William Dean were married. Their long-standing union produced many children. It was openly known in Natchez. Ralphine called herself "Mrs. Dean."[30] This was not an illicit relationship. Even the criminal charge reveals its openness: their conviction was for "unlawful cohabitation"—the offense of living together, something husbands and wives did. To some degree, their relationship was protected by its very informality. In living together without obtaining a marriage license, they were able to go about their lives without interference from the state, from nosy neighbors, or from anyone else—most of the time.

In many states, couples were not required to obtain marriage licenses. Efforts to require licensing ran headfirst into a long history of Americans marrying privately, in venues ranging from churches to homes. The legitimacy of marriage did not exclusively derive from a document issued by a court clerk. It was, instead, dependent on the consent of the man and woman who wished to be husband and wife. Though common law marriages are sometimes treated as relics of an earlier era, they were widespread and important well into the twentieth century.[31] As late as 1941, twenty US states recognized common law marriages as valid, including South Carolina, Georgia, Florida, Alabama, Mississippi, and Texas.[32] Common law marriage persists today in a handful of states.[33] The willingness of courts and legislatures to recognize informal unions reflected a desire to encourage marriage paired with practical concerns. Many couples did not seek marriage licenses because they could not afford the fees. A minister may not be available to preside over a ceremony. Or a couple might be unable or unwilling to travel to a courthouse to obtain a license. There were all kinds of reasons that a marriage license might seem unnecessary or inconvenient or might be lost. Across the South, when county courthouses burned or flooded, they often took local records with them.[34] When the children or widows of common law marriages found themselves embroiled in inheritance disputes with other family members, courts typically recognized their claims to inherit. Marriage and family law undoubtedly played an important role in structuring the gender and racial order of the South.[35] But for many people, a license was not necessary to make a marriage.[36]

And yet legal prohibitions on interracial marriage did not only jeopardize would-be husbands and wives. Jim Crow also denied their children the right to be recognized as legitimate. Born outside of wedlock, the law marked them, in its cruel language, as "bastards." The British common law, which most states adopted into their own codes of law after independence, labeled illegitimate children as *filius nullis*. Translated to English, this made them "the children of no one." States openly discriminated against children born out of wedlock. This was felt especially keenly at the end of life, when property was passed from one generation to the next, as states had long excluded illegitimate children from inheriting property from their fathers.[37] In Mississippi, children were first in line to inherit when a person died without a will. Grandchildren were next, then widows.[38] Illegitimate children, however, could only inherit from their mothers.[39] White men were those most likely to own property in the South during the Jim Crow era. Their biracial children had much to lose.

Ralphine's family deeply understood the stakes of interracial inheritance. She had her own tangled family tree. Ralphine's father was the son of a white man, William Burns Sr., and a Black woman, Rachel Burns. William enslaved Rachel, and he emancipated her and their six children at some point before 1842.[40] When William died unexpectedly in 1849, he left no will behind.[41] His brother, Andrew Burns, traveled from New Jersey to settle the estate, and he promptly attempted to sell Rachel and her children—his own nephews and nieces—back into slavery. A white lawyer, Charles Lacoste, intervened and negotiated with Andrew, successfully persuading him to leave the family be. (Charles likely had special sympathy for Rachel's plight, as his own common law wife, Delia, was Black.)[42] Rachel and her children escaped this perilous situation with their freedom, but they did not inherit anything of William's estate.[43] Had they been white, the property would have been theirs, and Andrew Burns might not have ever set foot in the state of Mississippi.[44] Ralphine's father had personally suffered the consequences of laws prohibiting the recognition of the biracial sons of white fathers. It cost his family dearly.[45]

Ralphine and William's long-standing union reflects another key aspect of Jim Crow: the primary purpose of segregation law was *not* to separate white and Black people. Though iconic photographs from the era tell a story of the separation of every aspect of life for Blacks and whites—"colored" toilets; "whites only" railway cars and lunch counters; segregated schools—this was just one facet of Jim Crow.[46] The conventional narrative of segregation as a system of complete racial separation is just as incorrect as the idea that interracial relationships did not occur. The static, totalizing view of Jim Crow ignores the many ways that white and Black people encountered one another on a daily, often intimate basis.[47] Black women raised white children. Black and white children could not attend the same schools, but they could play together when they were small.[48] Some Black domestic workers lived in the homes of their white employers, cooking in their kitchens, serving their dinners, nursing the sick, and caring for the elderly.[49] This closeness was a feature of segregation, not a flaw. It was interracial intimacy—especially the treatment of Black workers as servants and caregivers—that made it possible for white people to wield power over Black southerners daily.[50] It is not unusual to find multiracial households in the census, though Black members of white-headed households are often identified as cooks, servants, or laborers.

True separation could have led to Black autonomy and independence, which were fundamentally at odds with the aim of white supremacy.[51] (Witness the fate of Tulsa's Black Wall Street, burned to ashes, or the countless Black homes, churches, and businesses destroyed by rampaging mobs in the nation's many race massacres.)[52] The purpose of segregation law was always to place white people in positions of power above their Black neighbors, employees, or even those people who were complete strangers. White people reaped immeasurable benefits from the everyday subjugation of Black people. Among the most obviously tangible were the grossly inequitable allocation of tax dollars to the public schools reserved for white children and the exploitation of underpaid Black labor in homes, fields, and factories.[53]

Propping up this system was the ability of white southerners to make and enforce the law for everyone else—and the murderous violence they could inflict on Black people who dared resist.[54] The mantra of "separate but equal," as articulated in *Plessy v. Ferguson*, the infamous 1896 US Supreme Court decision, was the lie on the lips of every segregationist. Jim Crow was not a cohesive legal regime mandating separation, nor was it a mere reflection of southern "tradition" and culture. It was antithetical to any concept of equality.

Interracial families could avoid prosecution for two primary reasons. The first was that in Mississippi the laws governing family life were complicated and sometimes ambiguous. Marriage is both a public institution and a deeply private relationship between two people.[55] Even as the state forbade interracial couples from marrying, officials could not dictate what people did behind closed doors, away from the view of prying eyes. Couples could consider themselves married without ever seeking legal recognition. The second reason was that almost all the interracial families described in this book were headed by white men and Black women. White supremacy was inextricable from the gender politics of the Jim Crow South. For a Black man to take a white wife was a violation of white men's authority over white women and children—a clear example of a Black man "getting out of his place." White men did not encounter the same challenge to their power if they had Black common law wives. A Black woman and a white man living under the same roof did not pose the same threat to white supremacy. Indeed, observers might expect such a man to employ the services of a Black housekeeper and thus easily explain away such domestic arrangements without questioning where each person slept at night. Reflecting the gendered aspects of white supremacist ideology, neighbors might gossip that a Black woman was a white man's "concubine," which both disparaged her reputation and disqualified her from being seen as a wife.

It was not all white people who stood equally atop the racist hierarchy. Jim Crow functioned to protect the authority of white men above all others, including white women. Marriage itself created a hierarchy in the home that was used to justify sex discrimination. In the nineteenth century, advocates for women's rights faced a formidable foe in the form of marriage law. The common law concept of coverture deprived women of legal personhood once they married and justified depriving them of everything from property ownership to the right to vote. Unshackling women from coverture took more than a century of struggle.[56] Into the 1970s, the legal afterlife of coverture continued as women struggled to gain access to everything from home loans to birth control independent of a husband.[57] White women could vote after the ratification of the Nineteenth Amendment in 1920, but in most southern states, they could not serve on juries and were largely excluded from legislative office. Alabama, Mississippi, and South Carolina barred women from serving on juries until the 1960s.[58] For most of the twentieth century, southern law preserved power for white men in the family and public lawmaking institutions. The first Black woman legislator was not elected to the Mississippi Legislature until 1985, just one year after that same body belatedly ratified the Nineteenth Amendment.[59] The use of poll taxes and literacy tests disfranchised Black men and women alike, and even many poor white men, including William Dean.[60]

White men wrote the laws; white men enforced the laws. And during the Jim Crow era, the white men who governed the state were as committed to patriarchal governance as they were to supposed white racial superiority. White women benefited from and many actively championed both causes, as the twin commitments of white supremacy and patriarchal rule were mutually reinforcing. They worked hand in hand to deprive Black people of political power, property, fair wages, and many of the trappings of freedom.[61] They shored up the privileges of white manhood, especially in shielding the domain white men had long considered their own: the home. Many elite white southern men who ruled Mississippi believed strongly in the right of white men—even those from humble backgrounds, such as William Dean—to choose their own sexual, romantic, and domestic partners. At the same time, the labyrinth of interracial relationships that had underlaid slavery meant there were few white men who would invite scrutiny of the "purity" of their own family trees.

These histories are rarely simple. No matter how many or few records a person leaves behind, their intimate lives will always be shrouded to some extent. The history of interracial relationships in the segregated South entails much that cannot be known from the records that remain. Yet it is not an impossible task to recover pieces of these hidden histories. Interracial families sometimes appear in the records of criminal courts, as Ralphine Burns and William Dean did, charged with "unlawful cohabitation." Other interracial couples appear openly in the census. Reading these records alongside one another can help trace the contours of enduring intimate relationships. In rural Franklin County, Albert Bunckley and Lucinda Sanders lived under the same roof in 1900, though Albert is identified as her "boarder." In 1910, he is recorded as living next door. That year, Lucinda had ten living children; the oldest had been born in 1887—seven years after the Mississippi Legislature outlawed interracial marriage. The children's father was Albert Bunckley.[62] Albert and Lucinda had a decades-long relationship that produced at least fourteen children, but the couple was not charged with unlawful cohabitation until 1913. They were convicted. Albert was sentenced to serve four months in the county jail; Lucinda's sentence was half as long.[63]

Other stories unravel not in criminal courts but in the comparatively mundane chancery courts, in wills, land deeds, and disputes over property. Some men planned ahead, leaving property to their biracial children and providing for their Black wives in their wills. Such was the case of August Bourgeois, a white man, whose relationship with Alice Slade, a Black woman, lasted more than three decades and produced three sons. After August Sr. died in 1910, his son August Jr. filed his will in the Hancock County Chancery Court, which bequeathed his home and eighty acres of property to "my sons, August Bourgeois Jr., Joseph Franklin Bourgeois, and Albert Bourgeois." The will did not name Alice as his wife, but it did offer her security, noting, "It is also my will that Alice Slade shall enjoy the use of my home as long as she may live. My property must not be divided until after her death."[64] But when men died without wills, it was exceedingly difficult for Black women and their children to inherit property that should have been theirs.[65] Inheritance was one place where segregation law remained robustly enforced. Generational wealth is one of the key ways that people provide security for their spouses, children, and grandchildren. For people who had formerly been enslaved, the importance of property ownership to freedom was particularly salient.[66] Courts regularly refused to acknowledge the claims that Black family members made against the estates of dead white men. In doing so, they often erased the existence of interracial family bonds entirely.

The commonality of common law marriages between white men and Black women was intentionally forgotten, in part, because segregationists became more aggressively defensive about Jim Crow and its many vulnerabilities. Hysteria supposedly generated by fears of interracial sex between Black men and white women rose during World War II and crested as the Black Freedom Struggle coalesced in the 1950s and 1960s.[67] A favorite line of segregationists was that desegregated schools would inevitably lead to "miscegenation"—the implication being that nothing could be as antithetical to southern values. One of segregation's core weaknesses was the fact that, as much as white supremacists ranted about the "threat" of interracial sex and marriage, they often tolerated the crossing of the color line—if those relationships involved white men and Black women.

It is tempting to imagine law as a force structuring society, like the wood frame upon which a house is built. Ordinary life does not always follow the contours laid out by the law. Instead, the law is more like a blueprint than a solid frame; the building only resembles it inasmuch as the builders endeavor to make it so. Law is not only made in the halls of legislatures and in cavernous courthouses; it is made every day, influenced as much by culture as by what is inscribed in the lawbooks.[68] People do not always follow the law; those tasked with enforcement sometimes neglect their duties. And laws can sometimes be vague. What seems like a straightforward statement—Mississippi outlawed interracial marriage—does not, then, translate into "People did not form families that crossed the color line." As an abundance of evidence from the nineteenth and twentieth centuries shows in the chapters that follow, this statement is false. Instead, what unfolds when we look at the evidence is a story about how the law on the books does not always translate to practice on the ground.

Tangled Fortunes focuses on Mississippi—arguably the state where the color line was most violently enforced—where the rigid separation of white and Black was an illusion, and where the concept of white racial purity was at once a white supremacist fantasy and a useful political bludgeon.[69] Legal prohibitions on interracial marriage operated to protect white wealth more effectively than they prevented white men and Black women from forming lasting partnerships. At the same time, this is not to argue that such relationships were acceptable *everywhere*, in Mississippi or in other states. The toleration of interracial common law marriages was highly dependent on local circumstances and politics, and not every state validated informal marriage. Within these confines, some couples found ways to carve out space to remain together. Most often such families were treated as open secrets in their communities, often subject to disapprobation but not always to legal prosecution. Interracial couples might be cast out of respectable society, but this did not necessarily mean they were sent to the penitentiary.

Laws prohibiting interracial marriage sought to harm families by treating them as criminal; they were also used to deprive children and widows of their rightful inheritances. They sometimes forcibly separated husbands and wives through incarceration or banishment from the state. As with any marriage, the intimacy that defined these interracial unions was often out of the view of prying eyes, known in its fullness and meaning only to the two parties to the union. In this sense, this history is destined to be incomplete. Whether Ralphine Burns and William Dean loved each other, we cannot know with certainty. But what is obvious from the record is a long history of struggle, marked by the persistent efforts of ordinary people to protect their families even in the face of formidable opposition.

CHAPTER 1

INHERITANCES

MARY ANN AND LEVIN

When Levin Dickerson died on February 2, 1871, he left behind a large estate amid some of the most profitable farmland in the United States. His cotton plantation was nestled in the flat, fertile expanse of the delta that stretches between the Mississippi and Yazoo Rivers. On paper, he died a bachelor. But on the eve of the Civil War, Levin also claimed ownership of eighty-two enslaved people who ranged from six months to seventy-five years old, including a woman named Mary Ann and her son and daughter, Oliver and Susan, born in 1858 and 1860, respectively.[1] Levin was the biological father of Mary Ann's children. After the war, Mary Ann, Oliver, and Susan stayed with Levin; they were only parted by his death. Although the couple never procured a marriage license, in July 1871 Mary Ann's lawyer filed a petition asking the court to recognize her as Levin's legal wife, making Susan and Oliver his legitimate children and therefore his direct heirs.[2]

It may come as little surprise that the judge of the Coahoma County Chancery Court refused to grant the petition. Judge Edwin Preston Harman had the pedigree of a typical southern lawyer. The son of a wealthy plantation owner, Harman was also former adjutant in the Confederate Army and had been severely wounded at the siege of Knoxville.[3] Chancellor Harman denied Mary Ann's request, instead allowing Levin's nearest white relatives—his brother, Pete Dickerson, and Pete's son-in-law William Brown—to take possession of the plantation. The profits of the valuable harvest would be reaped by white hands.[4]

But Susan and Oliver's saga did not end there. Their lawyer appealed the court's ruling, and in the autumn of 1873 the Mississippi Supreme Court ruled in favor of Mary Ann and Levin's children, declaring that they were Levin Dickerson's true heirs.[5] In their decision, the justices of the state's highest court determined that the relationship between Levin and Mary Ann was a legal marriage. Though they had been born into slavery, in 1874 Susan and Oliver Dickerson inherited Levin's plantation.[6]

This was not just a reversal of fortune for these two young people. Before emancipation, there would have been no question that enslaved children could not inherit, regardless of who their father was. Mary Ann and Levin's relationship might have taken on many of the features of a marriage—living together, raising children, and perhaps even sharing a sense of genuine affection—but the law would have never recognized it as such. The court's 1873 ruling in *Susan Dickerson et al. v. W. N. Brown* signaled the vast changes sweeping across the landscape of the South. Emancipation meant that ties of blood and affection would no longer be denied solely on account of race. A decade before, Susan and Oliver had been classified as property. Now they inherited land that would secure their futures.

How could it be that two children could come, by decree of the state supreme court, to inherit the very plantation on which they had been born into slavery? Emancipation and the Reconstruction era transformed the lives of ordinary Mississippians—especially people like Mary Ann,

Oliver, and Susan Dickerson. This dramatic development required more than the end of slavery. The change that allowed this inheritance to come to pass was nothing short of a revolution in how the law treated families.

THE SURRENDER OF GENERAL ROBERT E. LEE AT APPOMATTOX Court-house on April 9, 1865, sounded the death knell for the Confederacy. Though slavery was all but dead, it was not yet clear what the end of enslavement would mean for the 4 million freed men, women, and children in the South.

For women like Mary Ann, emancipation was a fork in the road. When she claimed her freedom, she pondered a future that was not hers alone. There were monetary concerns, of course. Unless she fled the county, supporting herself would be difficult without resorting to the same kind of work enslaved people had done on plantations before the war. But it would be difficult to set out on her own without funds or a clear prospect of well-paying work elsewhere. Reuniting with family would make the transition to independence easier, and freedpeople sometimes traveled hundreds of miles to reunite with long-lost spouses, parents, and children. Mary Ann did not have just herself to consider. If Levin recognized Susan and Oliver as his daughter and son and resisted letting them go, Mary Ann could have faced an impossible choice: leaving to claim her independence or staying to remain with her children.[7] Black women who remained on the plantations where they had been enslaved were vulnerable to the same sexual abuse at the hands of white men that they had suffered under slavery.[8]

In her lawsuit Mary Ann was insistent that she had not been coerced into the relationship or into staying.[9] The choice, she claimed, was hers alone. Looming over the lawsuit was the fact that slaveholders often raped and sexually abused the people they enslaved.[10] An entire corner of the market in human traffic catered to the desires of white men to purchase "fancy girls" marketed for their physical beauty and sexual attractiveness.[11] These women and girls were often themselves fair-complected owing to the long history of interracial sex and rape. It is doubtful that

Mary Ann had a meaningful choice in 1855.[12] But to legitimate their children, Mary Ann had to claim that she consented.

Her argument was bolstered by the fact that she had not fled the plantation even when she had become a free woman. By July 1862, Union troops had secured a stronghold upriver in Helena, Arkansas.[13] The Dickerson plantation was less than a dozen miles from the Mississippi; it was perhaps twice that distance to Helena. In the Mississippi Delta, some enslaved people ran away to Union lines when they could, seeking freedom.[14] Rumors would have coursed through plantations, spreading word that the Union Army was near. At some point, either during or after the war, Mary Ann resolved that she and the children would stay. A few years later, she bore a third child, a boy they named Samuel.[15]

Before Mary Ann became free, her relationship with Levin could not have been a legal marriage. The law of slavery prohibited enslaved people from having the ability to consent or contract to marriage.[16] Enslaved people formed lasting unions, but they had no legal protections from being separated. Even members of the state's small free Black population could not find a right to marry within the state's code of law, which explained that marriages could only be formalized between "free white persons."[17] An 1865 state constitutional convention, led by whites and attended by ex-Confederates, begrudgingly amended the existing state constitution to abolish slavery and left in place language establishing that "all free men, when they form a social compact, are equal in rights."[18] One delegate identified the rights of freemen as "the right of personal security, and of personal liberty, and the right of property"—though they clearly understood this language did not establish "social and political equality."[19]

Surely, after emancipation, Black southerners could at least be legal husbands and wives to one another. Making Black men and women into legal husbands and wives had clear benefits in the eyes of white lawmakers. White politicians loathed the prospect of impoverished Black women and children becoming dependent on community support.[20] This anxiety was not limited to the South. Northern states had their own vagrancy laws criminalizing "idleness" and requiring the poor to work.[21] If the marriage of freedmen and women was legalized, the financial support of wives and children would become the responsibility of Black men. And with few employment opportunities, these men and their families would be more likely to remain on the plantations where they had been enslaved—now as "free" workers.

Whether a Black person could marry across the color line posed a separate question. Not all couples were willing to wait to find out how the state legislature would answer it. George D. Stewart and Mary E. Olive were married in Natchez, Mississippi, on April 15, 1865, less than a week after Lee's surrender. Natchez had been under Union Army control since 1863, and Mary and George were both teachers employed by the Freedmen's Bureau.[22] Mary was a twenty-five-year-old white woman, and the couple's marriage certificate noted that George was twenty-three years old and "3/4 white," the son of a white man and a woman who had both white and Black ancestry.[23]

Although George and Mary faced no major obstacle to marriage, the early years of their union witnessed existential threats—first, from the state legislature, and when that did not drive them apart, from white vigilantes. In the autumn of 1865, in his address to the first session of the Mississippi Legislature to convene after the end of the Civil War, Governor Benjamin Humphreys struck a tone that was at once conciliatory toward the states of the Union and hostile to the free Black men and women of Mississippi. Declaring that the people of the state accepted the abolition of slavery "in good faith," Humphreys announced a legislative agenda focused upon controlling the lives and labors of Black people and preserving the white republic. Many white supremacists assumed that Black people would remain dependent on whites to safeguard their lives and interests. This meant legislating inequality, but Humphreys also insisted that it required separation. "Race purity" was crucial to all, he reminded the legislature. "The purity and progress of both races require that caste must be maintained; and intermarriage between the races forbidden. Miscegenation must be the work of other climes and other 'people.'"[24]

When the new legislature convened in November, its members immediately set to work devising this new "caste" system.[25] The laws they crafted wrote new forms of racial discrimination into Mississippi law. They looked to the North for inspiration, borrowing heavily from midwestern and northeastern states' so-called Black laws, which regulated the movements and labors of free Black people.[26] The legislature criminalized vagrancy (that is, the offense of being without work) and forced Black children into "apprenticeships" under whites.[27] The new laws passed in Mississippi became known as the Black Codes for their racist restrictions on Black Mississippians. Other states soon followed suit, adopting Black Codes of their own.[28] These laws were not just about work. They defined family, with a notable focus on marriage.

This legislative agenda sought to sever any familial ties that might exist between Black and white Mississippians and prevent others from forming them in the first place. The Vagrant Act criminalized "living in adultery or fornication with a freedwoman, free negro, or mulatto." It also labeled "all white persons" found "associating with freedmen, free negroes, or mulattoes on terms of equality" to be vagrants. Black vagrants could be fined up to $50 and jailed for up to ten days; the penalty for whites was harsher: up to a $200 fine and six months of incarceration.[29]

The legislature also embedded new regulations of Black families in the Act to Confer Civil Rights on Freedmen. The law extended limited civil rights to Black men and women, including the right to marry. But it went a step further: the law declared that "all freedmen, free negroes, and mulattoes, who do now and have heretofore lived and cohabited together as husband and wife shall be taken and held in law as legally married" and made the children of such unions legitimate.[30] Though this clause at last legalized Black family bonds between husbands and wives and between parents and children, not all welcomed the automatic assumption of the obligations of matrimony. For many women, white or Black, marriage was the only contract they would make in their lives. Some Black women chafed against its strictures, in which their husbands controlled their wages, their children, and even their sexuality, much like slaveholders had.[31] To some, marriage seemed like simply trading one form of bondage for another.[32] Informal marriage practices among ex-slaves allowed couples greater freedom to separate and remarry, or reject marriage altogether.[33] Many other states in the former Confederacy passed similar laws. To freedmen and women, there were certain benefits of the new law: it made children of those unions legitimate, meaning they would inherit the property their parents accumulated.

The legislature was also careful to proscribe interracial marriage, which it made into a felony punishable by life in prison. Mary and George Stewart now faced an uncertain future and the threat of criminal prosecution. The new law also defined Blackness: a person "descended from a negro to the third generation" was Black, even if "one ancestor of each generation may have been a white person."[34] This was the state government's acknowledgment of a truth that later legislators would deny: that many Mississippians had mixed ancestry. As the state's legislators at the time were aware, many Black Mississippians had complicated family trees with as many white ancestors as Black ones, or even more white ancestors than Black ones.[35]

These legislators were not really concerned with interracial sex, though the Black Codes did criminalize interracial cohabitation for the first time in the state's history. What concerned lawmakers was the possibility that blood ties that crossed the color line could become legal familial bonds. Many formerly enslaved people had white fathers, grandparents, half-siblings, and cousins. Should these ties become legal relationships, the consequences of this shift would transform southern households. It was not just personal relationships that would be made anew, but very material questions of fortunes like those of Levin Dickerson.

In December 1865, the Thirteenth Amendment became part of the US Constitution. Abolition was the law of the land. This was achieved with no help from Mississippi, which stubbornly refused to ratify the amendment until 2013.[36] But the tumultuous and transformative Reconstruction era was just getting started.

In Washington, Radical Republicans were increasingly distressed by the kid-glove treatment President Andrew Johnson was offering to the states of the former Confederacy. They castigated the Black Codes passed by southern legislatures, which defied the Republican ethos of free labor.[37] They worried that the work of abolition would be undone by laws that offered rights and privileges to white people only, creating an underclass of Black people who lived in a system that mirrored slavery. Without establishing the citizenship of freedpeople, southern state legislatures would run roughshod over the Thirteenth Amendment.

In early 1866, Senator Lyman Trumbull of Illinois introduced a federal civil rights bill aimed at addressing these specific concerns. It wrote national birthright citizenship into law for the first time in history.[38] Purposely targeting the Black Codes, the bill focused squarely on establishing the rights of formerly enslaved people.[39] It declared that all citizens had the same right "to make and enforce contracts, to sue, be parties, and give evidence, to inherit, purchase, lease, sell, hold, and convey real and personal property, and to full and equal benefit of all laws and proceedings for the security of person and property, as is enjoyed by white citizens."[40]

As Congress debated the new law, which eventually would become the Civil Rights Act of 1866, some white Mississippians began to panic. They feared that the federal law would void the Black Codes that distinguished between the rights of Black people and white people. Did the equal contract rights mentioned in the Civil Rights Act extend to marriage? If so, did it give Black people the right to marry white people? "Shall the negro intermarry with our daughters, and take an equal place in our household?" asked the *Vicksburg Journal* ominously. "The civil right bill says that he shall."[41]

Mississippians were bound to find out. Congress passed the law on March 13. Though President Johnson vetoed it two weeks later, this proved no obstacle: Republicans had enough votes to override the veto, and the Civil Rights Act became law on April 9, 1866.[42]

But laws do not enforce themselves. Interracial couples cohabited regardless of the law, and some sought marriage licenses. Whether officials would interpret the civil rights bill to legalize interracial marriages depended on local circumstance. Some refused, claiming the federal law was unconstitutional. Such was the predicament faced by Arthur and

Faraby Beddenfield, who unsuccessfully sought a marriage license in August 1866. Arthur, whom the newspaper described as "black as the ace of spades," and Faraby, a white woman, lived together and wanted to ensure that their union was legal. They had known each other for years—Faraby explained that Arthur had been enslaved on her father's plantation. They wanted to marry, she said, because they were in love.[43] The newspaper reported that, after seeking the license, the pair had been jailed. Nancy Hurd, a white woman, was also arrested for "unlawful cohabitation with a negro"—a charge that was levied after she, too, attempted to procure a marriage license.[44]

Elsewhere, judges simply seized the authority to determine the federal law's scope. Mollie Furlow, a white laundress, and Ben Leslie, a Black veteran of the Union Army, were indicted for "unlawful cohabitation" on June 7, 1866. Mollie and Ben were arrested just after daybreak on June 12, stirred from their shared bed. The Hinds County *Gazette* documented their relationship with lurid interest. "The man was a very black, sprightly and impudent negro" whose intellect was "a little more than ordinary." He was "very imperious and gruff in his conversation with her, while she is very affectionate and obedient to him." The reporter was careful to note Mollie's unwomanly features and her ignorance: "She is not possessed of any of those attractions which adorn her sex, and seems to be extremely illiterate."[45] The message was barely veiled: Black men would take advantage of vulnerable white women if they could.

Mollie and Ben both pled innocence and denied that their relationship was intimate. During the trial, the state's star witness was a man identified as "Mr. Derryberry," whose testimony described "the woman sitting in the negro's lap with her arms around the negro's neck, and his arms around her waist." Derryberry had taken a good look inside "their shanty" and determined there was only one bed inside. Another witness, Mr. Nolly, testified that he lived a hundred yards from their home and had seen them together nearly every day. He explained that he had observed "many evidences of a strange intimacy between the accused parties." A third witness described seeing someone under the covers of Mollie's bed, and, "upon turning down the cover, . . . found it to be a big black negro."

Two other witnesses also testified that they had seen the pair share a bed.[46]

Mollie and Ben's lawyer objected to the charges, arguing that it was unclear what they were being changed with. Was it fornication? Adultery? Or some other form of "unlawful cohabitation"? He pointed to the new civil rights bill as evidence that the charges should be thrown out, arguing that "in contemplation of law there can be marriage between a negro or freedman and a white woman, and the mere fact that a negro or freedman and a white woman dwell and cohabit together is no proof of unlawful cohabitation." Indeed, it might be evidence of marriage. Mollie and Ben's lawyer said the indictments flew in the face of "the gist of the civil rights bill" recently passed by Congress.[47] Judge John Watts disregarded such arguments because, the newspaper explained, he rejected the constitutionality of the law. Mollie and Ben were convicted by the jury and sentenced to serve six months in the county jail and pay a $100 fine.[48]

The question raised in the trial of Mollie Furlow and Ben Leslie was a crucial one. Many—probably most—couples in Mississippi did not obtain marriage licenses because they were not required to do so. Common law marriage was not only tolerated; by some (though not all) nineteenth-century judges it was celebrated as bringing order to society.[49] The 1866 Civil Rights Act, in ensuring that Black and white southerners had equal rights to contract, implied that interracial couples could consent to marry, regardless of whether they sought a marriage license.

In 1865, Elizabeth Duke, a white woman, gave birth to a daughter, Julia. Elizabeth's partner, a Black man named Nelson Salter, was not her husband. Like many other couples of their era, especially those who were poor or uneducated, Nelson and Elizabeth did not obtain a marriage license. By the end of that year, their union had been explicitly outlawed by the Mississippi state legislature via the Black Codes. Like the Stewarts, Nelson and Elizabeth remained together despite the dubious legality of their relationship. They had another daughter, Maggie, in or around 1869—further proof that they remained a family.[50] In September 1869, Nelson and Elizabeth were charged with unlawful cohabitation in Wayne County, in the far southeastern part of Mississippi. But, unlike other interracial couples, they were not convicted. According to contemporary news reports—the courthouse in Wayne County burned in 1892, and the fire consumed virtually all its records—Nelson and Elizabeth produced a marriage license as their defense.[51] But was an interracial marriage lawful? The attorney general of the state gave an opinion stating that he believed it was.[52]

This decision changed the couple's lives. Nelson and Elizabeth's marriage endured. By 1880 they had added two more daughters to their brood, and they now shared a home with their twin baby granddaughters, who were born to Julia in late 1879.[53] The federal Civil Rights Act stood as a shield against those who would attack any interracial relationship. Nelson and Elizabeth wanted to be married. And, thanks to the work of Congress, they got their wish.

FAMILIES LIKE THE SALTERS AND THE STEWARTS ARE EASY TO FIND IN the historical record because they captured the attention of newspaper editors, who often flogged the issue of "miscegenation" in order to attack Reconstruction-era governments as illegitimate.[54] These editors relished stories of couples where the men were Black and the women were white. "Miscegenation" made for good headlines.

These editors paid considerably less attention to intimate relationships between white men and Black women. On plantations across the South, the law of slavery dictated that a Black woman's sexuality was never fully her own. Americans openly commented on the practice of "concubinage" as endemic to slavery. But viewing interracial sex and relationships through a binary of consent or coercion oversimplifies the lives of Black women, who, though they might have faced limited choices, held some power over their own sexualities and desires.[55] Some slaveholders, including Vice President Richard M. Johnson, treated Black women as wives, even though enslaved women had none of the legal obligations or protections that white wives had.[56]

According to Mary Ann Dickerson, her affection for Levin was real. The couple never sought a marriage license because, she said, they were not required to do so. Instead, they engaged in an exceedingly common practice: informal marriage. In the nineteenth century, judges often heard cases where no marriage license existed or a formal ceremony had not been held. As jurist James Kent wrote in his influential *Commentaries on American Law*, "No peculiar ceremonies are requisite by the common law to the valid celebration of the marriage."[57] All that was necessary was the couple's mutual agreement to live together as husband and wife.

Prior to the Civil War, the Mississippi Supreme Court had explicitly validated common law marriages.[58] Most states did the same, including slave states such as South Carolina, Georgia, Kentucky, and Texas.[59] After emancipation, southern state courts continued to uphold these unions. In 1869, the Alabama Supreme Court affirmed that "a marriage good at the common law, is to be held a valid marriage in this State."[60] Even in Louisiana, which was not a common law state, owing to its French colonial history, the courts recognized informal marriages as valid. In an 1833 opinion, the Louisiana Supreme Court wrote that "cohabitation as man and wife, furnishes presumptive evidence of a preceding marriage."[61]

The courts were willing to declare cohabiting couples to be legally married for many reasons, not least of all because by doing so they reduced the number of single mothers and illegitimate children who might rely on taxpayer support. Favoring marriage helped ensure that children would inherit their parents' property even if evidence of a public ceremony could not be found. In the cotton South, generational wealth in the form of land and slaves was crucial to protecting the status of elite whites. White men sat atop this hierarchy of race and sex, governing their plantations as patriarchal fiefdoms.[62]

And yet legislatures treated these men with suspicion, concerned that they might seek to make affectionate attachments to enslaved women and children into legal family ties. Men who enslaved their own biological children often did not adopt views that were radically abolitionist, as the case of Thomas Jefferson very clearly shows. (Sally Hemings, the enslaved half-sister of Jefferson's dead wife, bore six of his children.)[63] But some white men did seek to free their family members and provide for them. In the decades preceding the Civil War, as they fended off abolitionist attacks on slavery, state legislatures made it exceedingly difficult for slaveholders to emancipate enslaved women and their biracial children or to leave them property.[64]

This system of slavery, which tolerated and enabled interracial sex, created a clear problem for the post-emancipation world. Slavery had drawn the divide that enabled white men to have Black children without the need to worry that those children could make claims as their heirs. Emancipation changed all of this. In this new world, the children born to slaveholders and enslaved women had the right to inherit and own property. Next to be transformed was the institution of marriage itself.

ON TUESDAY, JANUARY 7, 1868, A NEW CONSTITUTIONAL CONVENTION began in response to new demands from Congress regarding the seceded states' return to the Union. One hundred delegates met in Jackson, Mississippi. Most of the men were white, and more than half of the men at the convention had been born and raised in the South. Although the state had a majority Black population, only sixteen delegates were Black men.[65]

The convention was dominated by Republicans, and not only because Black men had been allowed to vote, per the requirements of Congress. Democrats, who sneered that the entire endeavor was illegitimate, mostly refused to participate at all. As John R. Lynch, an influential Black Republican, later explained, the radicals who controlled the party "took the position that no respectable white Democrat could afford to participate in an election in which colored men were allowed to vote." If they conceded to partake in the biracial convention, this "contamination" of their politics "would be unwise if not dangerous."[66] Critics derisively called these Republican-dominated Reconstruction constitutional conventions "black-and-tan" conventions, a name borrowed from the coloration of various canine breeds. (The label worked a double insult—it not only deemed the delegates "dogs," but also threw suspicion on the whiteness of any man who attended such a gathering.)[67]

Delegates lambasted the previous Mississippi constitution, which had created a system of two-tiered rights and favored large plantation owners with the least burdensome tax rates. It had preserved the position of wealthy white men atop a society governed to keep them powerful and prosperous at the expense and by the labor of all others. The newly elected convention president, Alston Mygatt, declared, in his opening remarks, "This hour brings to a final end that system that enriched the few at the expense of the many—that system that hindered the growth of towns and cities, and built up large landed aristocracies— that system that discouraged agricultural improvements, and mechanic arts—that destroyed free schools, and demoralized church and State, has come to an end."[68]

The tone had been set, but the delegates remained divided on some key questions. The convention had many Radical Republican delegates, but there were conservatives present who were less interested in revolutionizing Mississippi society. Many balked at the idea of universal male suffrage, backing either a racial qualifier—which they claimed "nine-tenths" of the other states had—or property and education tests that would ensure that most Black men remained politically powerless.[69]

On the fourteenth day of the convention, the Committee on the Bill of Rights presented its draft to the delegates. The draft bill of rights had thirty-one provisions. It abolished the death penalty—which previously had been applied for a wide range of offenses, including property crimes such as grand larceny—and prohibited the compensation of former slaveholders for their losses in human capital. It banned property and education requirements for electors and forbade qualifications of race or color for jurors.[70]

Among the most hotly contested issues was whether this colorblind constitution would legalize interracial marriage. George Stovall, a delegate from Carroll County, introduced a measure that would inscribe a prohibition of interracial marriage into the state bill of rights. The measure was much harsher than the existing unlawful cohabitation law. As justification, Stovall announced to the convention, "Whereas, the fact has been demonstrated by physiologists, and long since settled as an axiom in science, that the progeny resulting from an intermarriage between the white and black races, are very liable to a character of hereditary diseases" that were "most destructive to human life." He concluded "that the general intermarriage of the two races occupying the South, will inevitably result in the destruction of both, and it should be the settled policy of all good men of both races, who desire the perpetuation and prosperity of their respective races, to discontinue such commingling."[71]

A Black delegate, Mathew Newsom of Claiborne County, countered Stovall's proposal by raising the stakes. Rather than simply prohibiting marriage, Newsom argued that the constitution should punish *all* those who engaged in interracial intimacy. His proposed amendment would target "all persons of this State living in a state of concubinage and miscegenation," adding that couples convicted of miscegenation "shall be confined in the State penitentiary, at hard labor, not less than five years nor more than ten years, and be forever incapable of voting at any election in this State, and from giving testimony in any court of justice."[72] This proposal was far more punitive than the one originally proposed by Stovall. In addition to the five to ten years of imprisonment "at hard labor," it extended the proposed punishment to include disfranchisement. Those convicted would also lose the right to testify in court.

By including "concubinage," Newsom specifically targeted white men who engaged in informal relationships with Black women but who refused to accept the obligations of marriage and fatherhood. A ban on interracial marriage alone would leave in place the system that protected white men's sexual prerogative. By raising the stakes, he bet that the entire provision outlawing interracial marriage would lose. Newsom's amendment took square aim at the sexual prerogative of white men.

If there was any doubt about the subtext of Newsom's proposal, others made it clear. Another Black delegate, Doctor Stites, suggested an amendment that offered a plain statement of their intent: "That white men living with and cohabitating with females of color, except under and by virtue of the rights of marriage, are guilty of a greater crime than that of adultery." His proposal further stipulated that the state legislature should be compelled to draft "such laws as will prevent the spread of such crime, and shall impose a fine and imprisonment on such guilty white men, or disqualify them from the rights of citizenship."[73]

By a narrow margin, the convention voted to table the measure. The anti-miscegenation provisions died at the convention. They did not make it into the new state constitution.

Another Black delegate, Thomas W. Stringer, offered the only clause on marriage that survived into the final constitution. He proposed that the convention add language giving legal status to all cohabiting couples in the state. This would bestow upon the state's freedpeople the same rights and obligations of matrimony that they had been denied under slavery. The provision declared "that all persons who are now, and have heretofore lived and cohabited together as husband and wife, shall be taken and held, in law, as legally married, and their issue shall be taken and held as legitimate for all purposes in law, and that concubinage and adultery are prohibited in this state."[74]

The delegates crafted one of the most racially progressive constitutions in US history. The new Mississippi constitution wiped away previous distinctions of class and color. It enfranchised all men over the age of twenty-one—two years before the Fifteenth Amendment attempted to accomplish the same task for the rest of the nation.[75] It established the state's first public school system.[76]

The constitution also included a revised version of Stringer's proposed language regarding marriage. The final draft of the constitution declared, "All persons who have not been married, but are now living together, cohabiting as husband and wife, shall be taken and held, for all purposes in law, as married." At the same time, the constitution made it clear that this was not an endorsement of a cohabiting free-for-all. (This was the 1870s—not the 1970s.) The constitution clarified that "the legislature may punish adultery and concubinage."[77] But those couples who "cohabited as husband and wife" were legally wed.

The 1868 constitution went through two rounds of popular voting. In the first round, the constitution was narrowly rejected owing to a controversial clause that would have disfranchised former Confederates. But after the national elections of 1868 affirmed Republican control of Congress—and ushered out the presidency of Andrew Johnson in favor of war hero Ulysses S. Grant—Congress agreed to allow Mississippi voters to again consider the constitution. The "objectionable clauses" disfranchising white Confederates were separated out to allow for discrete votes. The marriage clause remained. Voters approved the new constitution in November 1869. On December 1, 1869, the radical Mississippi constitution took effect.[78]

The stakes were high. In the very early morning of July 19, 1868, when the night was dark and still, Mary and George Stewart were awakened from their slumber. Four white men stood at the door, beckoning George into the darkness. George later testified that the men lured him out of his home under false pretenses before seizing and dragging him 500 yards from the house. The men accused George of being a member of the Union League, a Black self-defense organization formed to counter the violence and terror of the Ku Klux Klan. When George refused to reveal the organization's "password," the men forced him to his knees and told him to "say his prayers" and prepare to die. As they poured coal tar over his head, Stewart wrestled himself free and escaped into the night as one of the men fired shots at his fleeing form. The shooter missed.[79]

George Stewart's assailants were charged before the Vicksburg Military Commission for conspiracy and attempted murder. The tribunal found two of the men not guilty. The other two were found guilty of a lesser charge of "conspiracy to assault with intent to outrage and injure" and were sentenced to serve one year at hard labor in the state penitentiary at Jackson.[80] The *American Citizen*, a Canton newspaper, reported on the tribunals as an example of the abuses of military rule over the South. It omitted the detail about George Stewart's alleged involvement with the Union League and instead reported (mistakenly) that his offense was being a white man married to a Black woman—in fact, it was George who had African ancestry. The editor expressed deep sympathy for the accused men, who, it conceded, had "acted heedlessly" in their response to "the contempt which the man [Stewart] had exhibited for the community in which he had come to reside, and in responding to the demands of a sense of offended decency which the intelligent blacks themselves must have shared." The attempted murderers were "worthy and useful citizens, honorable, trustworthy, courageous men." The prison sentences imposed on the men were, in the *American Citizen*'s view, "'cruel and unusual' and immeasurably disproportionate to the offense."[81] The military tribunals, it said, were unconstitutional.

It is not clear whether these men targeted George Stewart because he was married to a white woman, because he was allegedly a member of the Union League, or because he taught Black children. The most likely answer is that their violent fury was a reaction to all three. But the attempted murder did not end Mary and George's marriage. The 1870 census records George and Minnie Stewart, both schoolteachers, residing in Natchez.[82] After George's death, Mary filed for a pension as his widow.[83] In the face of legal precarity and violence, the Stewarts did not part ways. They found some protection in the law. Their struggles reveal how some families fought to remain together, despite the high costs.

THE NEW STATE CONSTITUTION GRANTED TO MANY COHABITING COUples across the state the status of being legally married the instant it became law—regardless of whether they knew it. And, of course, it mattered a great deal whether couples were legally married or not. It gave a widow a claim to part of her dead husband's estate. It gave children the presumption of legitimacy—making them heirs to their parents' fortunes. It ensured that men could be held financially responsible for their wives and children. The colorblind language of the provision raised alarm among those who disapproved of interracial relationships. The *Vicksburg Herald* charged that the marriage provision was "born of the spirit of hate and malignity which actuated many members of the Constitutional Convention" who crafted the provision "as a legal cloak for miscegenation."[84]

Republican politicians were not finished wiping away the vestiges of the old system that allowed white men to take Black women as sexual companions without making them wives. In June 1870, seven months after the new constitution's ratification, the state legislature repealed the 1865 law prohibiting interracial marriage along with the rest of the Black Codes, including the section of the Vagrant Act that criminalized interracial cohabitation.[85] Making good on its word, the legislature left in place the race-neutral unlawful cohabitation law.[86]

By 1871, all references to race and color had been stricken from state law regarding marriage. Couples who lived together "as husband and wife" in 1869 were legally married, regardless of the racial identity of either party. The Radical Republican legislature sought to equalize families and remove racial barriers to the rights and obligations of matrimony. This legal transformation of the family was not limited to Mississippi. During Reconstruction, interracial marriage was legal in every Deep South state except Georgia. In places where it remained illegal, including the Upper South states, couples sometimes found ways around the law, including by invoking the 1866 Civil Rights Act. In North Carolina, for example, one interracial couple successfully argued that the state should acknowledge their union.[87] The passage of the federal Civil Rights Act, the ratification of the Fourteenth Amendment, and the new state constitutions all offered hope to people who sought to defend family ties that crossed the color line.

Not everyone was pleased by these developments. Mississippi newspapers breathlessly reported on interracial couples who obtained marriage licenses. In 1872, they covered a case from the Mississippi Delta town of Sardis, where James Rogers, a white man, and Martha Ubanks, a Black woman, were jailed for unlawful cohabitation. When the couple was brought before Judge E. S. Fisher, they requested that he remedy the situation by marrying them.[88] He agreed, and the case was dropped.[89] The status of interracial couples who cohabited without obtaining marriage licenses, however, was subject to disagreement among and between politicians, judges, lawyers, and ordinary people. The line between common law marriage and "unlawful cohabitation" was a special source of contention. Many Mississippians disagreed about what made cohabitation into a legal form of marriage, and not all cohabiting couples wished to be burdened with the obligations of matrimony.

Mississippi state law criminalized fornication and adultery—the crimes of having sex outside of marriage—only within the guise of its law prohibiting "unlawful cohabitation." This misdemeanor law was far less punitive than the Black Codes–era prohibition on interracial marriage. Those convicted of unlawful cohabitation could be fined up to $500 and sentenced to up to six months in jail, though they might face significantly lesser penalties.[90] These charges could be used to punish interracial couples where district attorneys and juries were motivated to do so even if the couple wished to be considered married, as happened to James Rogers and Martha Ubanks. The unlawful cohabitation law remained on the books after emancipation and the ratification of the 1868 constitution.[91] The law was technically colorblind. It forbade persons of any race or color from unlawfully cohabiting. But as in other states in the South, unlawful cohabitation charges were used to punish so-called miscegenation even where the law did not explicitly forbid sexual relationships between people of different races.[92]

The legislature did amend the unlawful cohabitation law to accommodate the marriages that the new state constitution formalized. It read, "The penalties of this article shall not apply to any man or woman, who, at the time of the adoption of the present constitution of this state, were, and had been living together as husband and wife, although they may not, in fact, have been married, according to law."[93]

THIS WAS THE LEGAL LANDSCAPE UPON WHICH MARY ANN DICKERSON launched her fight to secure Levin's estate for their children. In it, her lawyers argued that Susan and Oliver were Levin's legitimate daughter and son and should therefore inherit his plantation. This dispute would prove to be a pivotal test of the resiliency of the law's colorblindness.

The lawyer representing Mary Ann's children filed a suit in the Coahoma County Chancery Court alleging that Levin's brother, Pete Dickerson, and his son-in-law William Brown had conspired to "cheat and defraud" his clients by presenting themselves to the court as Levin's legal heirs. Pete coveted Levin's plantation, which was considerably larger than his own. Its 2,600 acres produced a cotton crop worth an estimated $40,000 each year.[94] As minors—Oliver was fourteen years old and Susan twelve—the children could not file a suit on their own.

But Mary Ann had the crucial support of several men from Friars Point, who backed her lawsuit, and one of them, Campbell Flagg, a landowning Black man, had filed the suit on the children's behalf as their "next friend."[95]

The lawsuit did not deny that Mary Ann, Oliver, and Susan had been enslaved. It also did not assert that Mary Ann and Levin had ever held a formal marriage ceremony, even after emancipation. Instead, the lawsuit relied upon the 1868 state constitution and its transformation of marriage bonds. By living together in 1869, the couple had become legally wed. There was no formal marriage conducted between Levin and Mary Ann because, the complaint explained, "at the time when their intercourse commenced marriage between a white man and colored woman was prohibited by law." Nonetheless, Levin cared for Mary Ann "with all the ardor and devotion of a true lover[,] and while the laws of the state forbid the solemnization of the marriage rites between them, they were married in heart and by the laws of nature and of love." Proof of the legitimacy of their union was that Levin was faithful to Mary Ann and "remained true in his love," and that he "never attempted to marry any woman of his own color after the commencement of his intercourse with [Oliver and Susan's] mother."[96]

Further proof of the legitimacy of their union was the fact that Levin had trusted Mary Ann to keep the keys to the store. She had her own bedchamber, as was common at the time, but slept with the father of her children "in his bedchamber two thirds of the time." And, the suit explained, Levin had always recognized Susan and Oliver as his children, and they "continued to honor and obey him as their father until the day of his death."[97] Just as importantly, the complaint argued, Levin and Mary Ann both knew about the ratification of the new constitution and its provision making cohabiting couples husband and wife. Indeed, it claimed on the children's behalf, "their father joyfully embraced this opportunity of doing justice to her, who had been so many years the partner of his bosom[,] and to the children of his loins[,] and after he had seen the provisions of the constitution and knew the effect of a continuance of his intercourse with their mother." Indeed, Levin "rejoiced that a public ceremony of marriage would be unnecessary."[98] None of this persuaded the chancellor, who denied the children's claim.

Two lawyers handled the appeal for Mary Ann and her children: Alexander Hamilton Handy and Hamilton H. Chalmers. They made a formidable legal team. Handy was a former chief justice of the previous iteration of the state supreme court, the High Court of Errors and Appeals.[99] Chalmers had briefly practiced law before the war and had become a judge to replace his brother, James, when James had left the bench to join the Confederate Army.[100] James, a brigadier general, had been one of the leaders of the Confederate regiments that had massacred surrendering Union soldiers at Fort Pillow. Amid the outrage that followed the slaughter, he had proudly noted that the Confederates had "taught the mongrel garrison of blacks and renegades a lesson long to be remembered."[101]

Hiring these lawyers to argue the case was likely a strategic choice. Before emancipation, Handy had been a vocal defender of slavery.[102] The brothers James and Hamilton Chalmers were Democrats—both of them would eventually participate in the bloody overthrow of Reconstruction in Mississippi.[103] In 1876, Hamilton Chalmers would be elevated to the Mississippi Supreme Court bench. But in 1871, it was not yet clear that Democrats would regain control of the state, and the electoral environment of Mississippi suggested that Republicans might prevail. Men like the Chalmers brothers, looking to shore up a role in state politics, faced a choice: either rejecting all campaigns as illegitimate—as some Democrats did—or working within the current Republican landscape. It seems that Hamilton Chalmers, at least, hedged his bets. Regardless of why they took the case, the appellate attorneys for Mary Ann and her children were part of the state's conservative political class—they were not "scalawags," certainly not Black—and this positioned them to argue a delicate case with force and authority in a way that would appeal to the judges on the bench. For the lawyers themselves, on the other hand, the case may have represented little more than a paycheck.[104]

The three state supreme court justices were all appointees of Republican governors. They were not radicals, and having conservative lawyers argue for a broad reading of the 1868 constitution may have influenced their receptivity to Handy and Chalmers's arguments. Friars Point was an exceedingly small town, even by Mississippi standards. It was also a place where many residents were politically connected. David F. Alcorn, the white sheriff of Coahoma County, was another man listed as one of the sureties of the children's appeal.[105] Alcorn was a cousin of US senator James L. Alcorn, a Republican and leading figure in Reconstruction politics, who also hailed from Coahoma County.[106] There is no evidence to show that Levin Dickerson was himself politically connected, but it could not have hurt to have Alcorn's cousin on their side.

In the appeal, Chalmers stated, "It is admitted by us that the intercourse was criminal, and the marriage void in its inception. But this was solely by reason of the incapacity of the woman." After the ratification of the 1868 constitution and the repeal of the anti-miscegenation law, Mary Ann and Levin were free to choose one another as husband and wife. Chalmers wrote, "It is alleged that both parties earnestly desired that it should be a marriage, valid in law, as it was in love, and that they cherished each other, and lived and cohabited together as husband and wife."[107] The fact that they remained together even after Mary Ann became a freedwoman was evidence that their relationship was a common law marriage. She could have chosen to leave; Levin could have cast her out of the home. But the couple remained together, which was proof of their mutual consent.

The appeal noted that Mary Ann was Levin's widow and that she was therefore possibly entitled to dower in the estate.[108] The British common law had long recognized the principle of the "widow's thirds"—a practice that set aside a portion of a dead husband's estate for his wife so that she would not be thrust into poverty or (this was especially important for the aristocracy) be forced to marry. The "widow's thirds" shored up the propertied elite in England, ensuring that wives who outlived their husbands would not be thrown into desperate poverty by callous eldest sons.[109]

All the same, the primary parties to the lawsuit were Susan and Oliver, who as Levin's children had the best claim as his direct heirs. Mary Ann's situation was more complicated. She had now married a Black man, and her new husband, a blacksmith named Jackson Clifton, lived near the Dickerson plantation.[110] Widows who inherited property could lose their dower right if they remarried. (The law presumed that the new husband should bear the burden of support for his wife.) Because Mary Ann and Clifton were married by the time the appeal was underway, it likely made the most sense to make the claim exclusively on behalf of the children, who had a clear, compelling argument to inherit Levin's estate.

THE DICKERSON CHILDREN'S APPEAL TO THE MISSISSIPPI SUPREME Court rested upon the argument that the state constitution no longer recognized class or color. As Chalmers explained, there were "no blacks and no whites in this State, in contemplation of law. The State only knows its citizens, as her children, and recognizes no difference between them." The provision that declared cohabiting couples to be married did not and could not apply solely to Black people. The brief declared, "There is not in the constitution, nor in the whole body of the new Code, the slightest allusion to white men or to black men as such. All laws apply to all; all rights belong to all."[111]

William Brown's lawyer took the opposite tack. Sexual relationships between Black women and white men could never be legitimate, he argued. Such pairings were "shameful," and it would be a "gross absurdity" to recognize them as legal marriages. Mary Ann Dickerson was Levin's "colored concubine," and nothing more. Interpreting the constitution to say that interracial couples could be legally married, he said, "would have the effect to convert the concubinage and moral turpitude of the parties into the binding force of legal marriage and virtuous cohabitation, without their consent, in derogation of public decency, decorum and good manners."[112] Chalmers countered this argument by pointing out that white men frequently cohabited with Black women. "Indeed," he wrote, "it might be argued, that this provision was intended to apply more especially to whites than blacks."[113]

In October 1873, the Mississippi Supreme Court sided with Susan and Oliver Dickerson. By choosing to remain together when the new constitution was ratified, Mary Ann and Levin became legally married. The chancery court should recognize their claim as valid. When the new constitution was ratified, and the couple became legally married, their children became Levin Dickerson's legitimate heirs. On the point of the "shamefulness" of interracial marriage, the court explained, "As a question of policy or propriety, people may differ, but this is a view of the case which the court cannot entertain. They can only declare legal rules. Matters of taste and propriety, like this, the people must determine for themselves, within the established laws."[114] If interracial common law marriage should be illegal in the state, it would have to be prohibited by the legislature. This was not the work of the courts.

In *Dickerson*, the state supreme court justices were much more interested in encouraging marriage than they were in imposing racial restrictions onto a race-neutral document. Moreover, the court emphasized that marriage existed for the public good—not for individual fulfillment. Indeed, it did not really matter whether Mary Ann and Levin loved each other. If they openly cohabited as husband and wife while the constitution was ratified, they were legally wed, and the court had an obligation to the people of the entire state to recognize them as such. The majority opinion explained, "If, practically, a man and woman recognize each other as . . . husband and wife, though they attempt to restrict the operation of the law upon their relation, the law should hold them" to the obligations of marriage. In fact, the justices explained, "public policy requires this, the peace of the community requires it, the good of society demands it—to be married persons, unless some statute has rendered the observance of some form of marriage necessary." For the justices, the case was not really about slavery, or even about interracial marriage; instead, it was about the power of the state government to decide who was and was not married.[115]

PERHAPS THE BIGGEST MISTAKE THAT WILLIAM BROWN'S LAWYER made was in assuming that the court would *never* see an interracial relationship as being legitimate. His lawyer made no effort to argue that Mary Ann and Levin had not lived together. He did not deny that Levin was the father of Susan and Oliver. This, of course, lends even more credence to the children's lawsuit: their cousins did not contest the relationship because they all knew about it. Perhaps William's lawyer could not imagine a world where anyone would consider such a relationship to be meaningful and legitimate. Certainly Pete and William did not care what Levin's wishes were or whether he wanted to protect his own children and provide for them after his death.

The *Clarion-Ledger* of Jackson, Mississippi, published the full text of the *Dickerson* decision, along with an editorial note deriding the court's decision to make "the alleged illegitimate offspring of a colored woman" the heirs of Levin Dickerson. Under the headline "A Strange Case with a Moral," it warned white men that "while the good they do is oft interred with their bones, the sins they commit, live after them." Levin's "sins" were his biracial children. The editor wrote, ominously, that "the decision throws the sanctity of the marriage tie around the beastly degradation of concubinage, and says with King Lear, 'let copulation thrive.'"[116]

In 1874, the chancery court granted Susan and Oliver's guardian, Campbell Flagg, control over the estate.[117] The inheritance ensured that when they came of age, the siblings would maintain independence from white people. A quarter century after they prevailed in the state supreme court, they still lived in rural Coahoma County. Oliver was a cotton planter, and he owned his land mortgage-free. As an independent farmer, he could support his growing family. He lived on his farm with his wife and five children, who attended school. They did not have to work in the fields for wages, as other Black children did. Oliver and his family lived just down the road from his sister, Susan, who also owned her own farm.[118]

Mary Ann's victory ensured that her children would not face a future of poverty and deprivation. But this outcome was far from certain. Just six months after siding with Susan and Oliver Dickerson, the state supreme court rejected the effort of another Black woman to be identified as the widow of a white man. In *Madora Rundle v. G. G. Pegram, Adm'r.*, the court declared that Madora Rundle's relationship with her alleged common law husband was not a marriage, and therefore his white daughter was his sole legal heir.[119] The same justices that awarded the Dickerson plantation to Susan and Oliver disparaged Madora's relationship as a form of "adulterous intercourse." As the case of Madora Rundle shows, judges had the tools to discredit relationships between Black and white Mississippians even when the language of the law was racially neutral. Madora's legal defeat sounded a warning bell that any gains made during Reconstruction would have to be vigorously defended.

The decade that followed the *Dickerson* and *Rundle* cases would prove this to be true. The state constitution recognized interracial marriages, and judges had begun to validate familial relationships that crossed the color line. Resistance to this new reality would not be fleeting or easily overcome, especially as a full-scale effort to overthrow Reconstruction took root across the South. Indeed, the struggle to protect interracial familial bonds had only just begun.

CHAPTER 2

STRATEGIES OF SURVIVAL

ALBERT AND CARRIE

Albert Talmon Morgan claimed to have loved Carrie Highgate even before he set his eyes upon her. Both were recent migrants to the South, lured to Mississippi by a shared desire to deliver on the postwar promise of freedom and equality. Albert was among the tidal wave of Radical Republicans swept into state office following the enfranchisement of Black men. Carrie was a twenty-one-year-old schoolteacher. He was visiting one of the state's newly established schools in Jackson when he overheard Carrie leading her pupils in a stirring rendition of the abolitionist anthem "John Brown's Body." He was white and she was Black, but by the end of their first meeting, Albert declared that he had fallen "head over heels in love with her."[1]

The feeling was mutual. Albert had been born in Wisconsin, joined the Union Army, and then served as a delegate to the 1868 constitutional convention that legalized all common law marriages.[2] Carrie was born free in Upstate New York, and after her brother Charles perished from battle wounds just a week before the Confederate surrender at Appomattox, she had traveled south to teach freedpeople.[3] Albert admired Carrie's industriousness and her faultless reputation in Jackson.[4]

Albert and Carrie were wed on August 3, 1870. They exchanged vows in a small ceremony at a friend's home in Jackson before a Black preacher, the Reverend J. Aaron Moore.[5] Moore was a fellow Republican member of the legislature and, alongside Albert Morgan, one of the delegates to the 1868 constitutional convention.[6] The wedding captured the notice of Democratic newspapers, whose editors relished the opportunity to associate Republican politics with interracial sex.[7] Despite the derision and publicity surrounding their wedding, Carrie's family did not object. Her sister, Edmonia Highgate, wrote to her friend, the famous abolitionist Gerrit Smith, that Carrie and Albert had "their share of disagreeable things to contend with owing to the prejudice against the two races inter marrying," but that they "are however so admirably suited to each other that they are happy."[8]

THEIR MARRIAGE WAS LEGAL, BUT THREATS ABOUNDED, AND ALBERT and Carrie's newlywed bliss would be short-lived. Critics of the new Republican state government would make "miscegenation" and "amalgamation" rallying cries against the multiracial democracy that Reconstruction finally established in the South. These new governments and their constitutions—including the radical 1868 Mississippi constitution—remained in a precarious position, vulnerable to overthrow by electoral fraud and outright violence. This was a lesson the Morgans learned personally. Four years after their wedding, Carrie and Albert would have to flee the state as white supremacists launched a murderous campaign that would become the model for others who sought to overthrow Reconstruction and reinstate white rule.[9]

Interracial families like theirs faced a harrowing landscape in the last decades of the nineteenth century as the state legislature and the courts became more openly hostile to their existence. If state legislatures invalidated interracial marriages once again, these families would lose all their legal protections. Widows and children would no longer inherit. Husbands and wives would have no right to live together undisturbed by threats of violence or prosecution. The gains made by Black southerners, including their right to keep their families together, had to be relentlessly defended from outside attacks. Some interracial couples found ways to survive; others would not be so fortunate.

IN 1884, ALBERT MORGAN SELF-PUBLISHED A MEMOIR OF HIS TIME AS A politician and lawyer in Reconstruction-era Mississippi in the hope of setting the record straight about his bloody exit from the state. In 1874, Albert had newly been elected sheriff of Yazoo County. In his telling, the

Carolyn Highgate Morgan (Angela Morgan Papers, 1861–1957, Bentley Historical Library, University of Michigan).

Albert Talmon Morgan (Angela Morgan Papers, 1861–1957, Bentley Historical Library, University of Michigan).

previous sheriff—unwilling to concede his post—led a mob that attacked Albert, who killed the man in self-defense.[10] Democrats made Albert infamous as a cold-blooded murderer.[11]

Clearing his name was not the only task. Albert also wanted to rewrite narratives about the defeat of Reconstruction and the rise of Jim Crow politics. Namely, he sought to correct the presumption that white Mississippians cared deeply about interracial sex and marriage. No one was more prone to the supposed vice of "miscegenation" than slaveholders, and "under the old slave codes, the line between the races varied according to the whim, caprice, or interest of the slaveowner." Slaveholders crossed "the line" with impunity, even as they relied upon a firm belief in racial difference to justify slavery. Albert also implied that the state legislature had changed the law to accommodate the resulting growing class of fair-complected children of enslaved women, as slave owners sometimes sought to legitimate their sons and daughters and bring them into respectable white society. As he explained of the state legislature's adoption of the 1857 law demarcating the line of Blackness at one-quarter blood quantum of African ancestry, "The last change fixed it where it proved, as was no doubt intended, most convenient for a large and by no means disreputable class of the best citizens of the State." Barely veiling his assertion that many of the state's white bourgeoisie had African ancestry, he wrote that the legal change "proved a great blessing, I am certain, to several of the most high-toned and honorable ladies and gentlemen of Yazoo."[12] Albert alleged that among Carrie's pupils at the Black school in Jackson were "so many unrecognized children of 'first citizens of Mississippi,'" including "children of Governors, United States Senators, members of Congress, of the 'High Court of Errors and Appeals,'" and virtually every other political office in the state.[13] White men were long-standing practitioners of the "amalgamation" they now disparaged.

Although Mississippi Republicans had repealed the state's Black Codes, written a new and egalitarian constitution, and ratified the Fourteenth and Fifteenth Amendments, the new legal order they had created was fragile. Black Mississippians held an electoral advantage against whites, and with the support of less than one-third of white voters, the party could successfully win statewide elections and local contests in Black-majority counties.[14] This electoral landscape made the radical 1868 state constitutional convention possible, and it also meant that Black lawmakers and their white Republican allies could control the governorship, the legislature, and many county and local offices. But their power only held so long as Black men could vote.

The tenuous triumph of Republican politics faced threats from those who opposed the equality of the races. Foremost among them was the Ku Klux Klan, which spread across the South after its 1866 founding, taking root in Mississippi communities.[15] Masked vigilantes terrorized Black voters and families, burning schools for Black children and murdering Republicans.[16] The Klan's purpose was unquestionably political: its members sought to defeat the Republican Party and restore white Democratic rule. In Mississippi, the Klan was most powerful in the eastern counties, where Black people made up a smaller percentage of the population and held less political power.[17] A year after he presided over the wedding of Carrie and Albert Morgan, the Reverend J. Aaron Moore was nearly killed in a Klan attack on a Meridian courthouse. He hid under the body of a murdered judge, playing dead. When they realized he had escaped with his life into the woods, Klan members burned his home.[18]

Hooded riders made a special point of harassing and beating interracial couples for violating the unwritten law against interracial sex and marriage—especially Black men who married white women.[19] They also harassed and assaulted Black women who cohabited with white men. Congressional hearings held in 1871 into Klan violence laid bare this campaign of violence. Betsy Lucas, a Black woman living in Noxubee County, was terrorized for living in "open and notorious adultery" with a white man, Robert Jackson.[20] In the spring of 1870, a dozen masked Klansmen arrived at the plantation and dragged Betsy out of the house. They "put a rope around her neck, a bridle-rein, and whipped her, and gave her a certain number of days to get away," a Black witness testified to the joint committee. Though the men wore disguises, Betsy easily recognized their voices.[21]

Betsy was not their only victim. A white Noxubee County lawyer, James Rives, explained that four Black women were targeted for living with white men "as their concubines." Rives explained that the Klan only acted because a grand jury had failed to indict the couples for adultery or fornication. As the defect in the law that forced the Klan into action, he cited "a recent decision made by our supreme court declar[ing] that it was not a violation of the statute unless the parties had lived together as man and wife."[22]

Indeed, Mississippi did not criminalize interracial sex or any other kind of casual sexual relationship. While the offense might fall under a statute prohibiting "fornication" (that is, an unmarried couple having sex) or adultery in other states, Mississippi only criminalized "unlawful cohabitation." A judge from Mississippi's seventh district, A. Orr, explained that Klan members acted when the law was insufficient to punish offenders of what he termed "the unwritten common law of the white man of the South." The Mississippi state code did not "adequately" address the crime of a Black man bragging about having sexual intercourse with a white woman. The offender, the judge explained, had to be "whipped."[23]

Witnesses also testified that it was common knowledge that the federal Civil Rights Act had invalidated the Black Codes prohibition on interracial marriage. Rives explained that he also knew of a white "Federal soldier" named Smith who "married a Negro woman in this town." Another local white man was, like Robert Jackson, targeted by the Klan for cohabiting with a Black woman. In response, he made their union legal by finding a Black preacher to wed them.[24] But on its own, the law could not protect Betsy Lucas and Robert Jackson or other interracial couples who faced violence or prosecution. Some Mississippians remained committed to the idea that interracial relationships were socially and culturally transgressive, violating the spirit if not the letter of the law.

Klan members were furious that juries had declined to indict interracial couples. Some prosecutors aggressively levied charges of "unlawful cohabitation" at interracial couples. The success of this approach depended on the jury. L. D. Shadd and Fannie Crawford were charged with unlawful cohabitation in Hinds County in 1875. After a daylong trial, the jury declared the couple not guilty.[25] But a different Hinds County jury found against another couple, Henry W. and Mary Kinard, when they were tried together a few years later. Henry, a white man, and Mary, a Black woman, had been together since 1868—a year before the ratification of the state constitution legalized interracial common law marriages. Over their decade together, Mary gave birth to three sons. But on January 17, 1879, a Hinds County grand jury indicted Henry and Mary together for unlawful cohabitation.[26] Four days later, the sheriff arrested Henry, who posted bond.[27]

The Kinards' case reveals how prosecutors weaponized the vague language of the state's law to punish interracial couples and deny them status as common law husbands and wives. When the case went to trial, the couple found themselves before Judge Solomon S. Calhoon, a Confederate veteran who had little sympathy for their situation. Henry and Mary pled not guilty, and they were tried together.[28] Erwin Barlow, a former employee of Henry's, was the star witness for the state. Erwin had an axe to grind. He had worked on Henry's farm since January 1878 and lived near the couple's home, which he claimed to visit often. But in November of that same year, Henry had Erwin arrested, and Erwin served twenty-five days in the county jail. After he was released, he reported to county officials that Henry was unlawfully cohabiting with Mary, and it was his testimony that sealed the couple's fate at the trial.[29]

In his testimony, Erwin painted a picture of true affection between Henry and Mary. Damningly, he claimed to have seen the pair "in bed together, undressed, with said Mary stroking said H. W. Kinard's whiskers." Though he did not catch them "in the act of copulation," Erwin was certain that the relationship was sexual. He had heard it straight from the source, testifying that Henry "told him in the year 1878 that Mary was his wife." Mary had three "mulatto" children, whom Henry affectionately called "his boys."[30] Another witness for the prosecution was far more ambivalent about Henry and Mary's relationship. Edmond Falconer claimed not to know whether the relationship between the two was romantic or sexual, though he acknowledged that the pair had lived together since 1869.[31]

This detail—that Henry and Mary's relationship predated the ratification of the 1868 constitution—should have given them ample cover to beat the charge of unlawful cohabitation. But the witnesses who testified in their defense gave no clear explanation of whether the relationship was a common law marriage. Mary and Henry's witness Shed Donaldson knew Erwin and, like him, worked for Henry. But Shed claimed Henry and Mary never shared a bed. He knew this to be a fact because he was their boarder and slept in the same bedroom with them: Mary and Henry in their own beds, while Shed slept on the floor. He did, however, testify that he had seen Henry affectionately "caress" Mary's sons and call them "his boys."[32] James Bell testified that he had known Henry and Mary for years but had not ever seen "anything of the relationship of husband and wife between them."[33] Henry's brother, William, testified to the same, claiming that Mary was in fact Henry's employee, working as a "cook, washerwoman and field hand."[34]

What the jury was meant to make of this is not clear. Henry and Mary's lawyer seemed intent on arguing that, although they shared a home and children, the couple was not "unlawfully cohabiting." He seemed more confident in proving to the jury's satisfaction that the pair did *not* have an ongoing sexual relationship than he did in establishing that their relationship was a common law marriage. If anything, his defense strategy relied on discrediting Erwin Barlow. The Kinards' lawyer introduced four witnesses who all testified that Erwin, the state's star witness, was a known liar who had a bad reputation in the community.[35] The charge was simply revenge for Erwin's own arrest and stint in jail. As one witness put it, Erwin Barlow "will not tell the truth and is unworthy of belief."[36]

But Erwin's spotty reputation did not matter to the jury, which voted to convict Henry and Mary Kinard anyway. The court sentenced Henry to the maximum penalty of six months in the county jail. Mary, on the other hand, was sentenced to serve just one day.[37]

The instructions given to the jury illustrated the muddy legal definition of unlawful cohabitation. It was not enough for the state to prove that Henry and Mary had a sexual relationship that resulted in the births of three sons. The crime was not found simply in illicit sex, even between a master and a servant living under the same roof. The judge instructed the jury that they should find Henry and Mary guilty of unlawful cohabitation if they believed "beyond a reasonable doubt that the defendants lived together at any time within the last two years as man and wife without being actually married," but that it was also not necessary that they believe the defendants "habitually sleep together in the same bed." Instead, the crime of unlawful cohabitation was defined by the conditions that "the parties should live together under the same roof and that sexual intercourse be habitual between them as between man and wife, that is, as upon recognition between them of his right to habitually refer to her for the gratification of his passions and a habitual yielding of her person to him for this purpose."[38]

The ruling in the Kinards' case may seem confused and contradictory. But it borrowed its language from an unlawful cohabitation suit dating back to the early years of Reconstruction—one that would be cited repeatedly in cases involving interracial couples. Joe Carotti operated a railroad hotel and saloon in Holly Springs, where among his employees was a servant named Mary Wilson. Joe leased the hotel from the Mississippi Central Railroad in 1866. His business was bustling, but he also had a rather busy personal life. When Joe and Mary were jointly indicted for unlawful cohabitation in 1867, several men were eager to share their stories about Joe Carotti's amorous adventures.

Henry Ormesby, an Irish merchant, was determined to see Carotti punished. Someone—perhaps Henry—wrote "anonymous letters of a scurrilous nature" to authorities of the Mississippi Central Railroad accusing Joe of having "illicit intercourse" with Mary. According to Henry, Joe had demonstrated such little discretion that he had personally witnessed the pair in the act of copulation through hotel windows. The men were already feuding before the unlawful cohabitation case: Henry operated a saloon out of his home, so perhaps he felt that Joe was stealing his customers.[39] The anonymous letter to the railroad may have been a ploy to get the company to revoke Joe's lease. (John McGuirk, an employee of the railroad, investigated the accusations, assembling a group of men to test whether Henry could have witnessed what he said he did.

The report deemed Henry's tale "impossible": "A person standing up in said room by the window might perhaps expose to view the head and breast from said Ormesby's house, but not the remainder of the person," McGuirk concluded.) A jury convicted Joe of unlawful cohabitation, but upon appeal, the Mississippi Supreme Court reversed his conviction. It did not matter to the court whether the pair had had sexual intercourse once or even a few times. Instead, what mattered was whether they lived together as married couples did without accepting the obligations of marriage. Mississippi law, the court reiterated, did not criminalize casual sexual relationships outside of marriage.[40]

The confusing language the judge offered the jury in the Kinards' case—that unlawful cohabitation was when a couple acted as "man and wife," with the man exercising "his right to habitually refer to her for the gratification of his passions"—was drawn verbatim from *Carotti v. State*. In its opinion in *Carotti*, the court had explained that in addition to a habitual sexual relationship, the couple must live together in a manner that was "openly notorious . . . as if the conjugal relation existed between them." This was not an offense committed in private, or under the cover of night. The crime was one committed toward the *state*—not toward each other. The problem was that unlawfully cohabiting couples rejected the strictures of marriage. Such couples lived together "without incurring those obligations and responsibilities which attach to the married state."[41]

The perplexing thing about Mary and Henry's conviction is that they did not seem to be skirting the obligations of marriage. And the 1868 state constitution loomed over the Kinards' trial. Several witnesses testified that the Kinards had lived together for more than a decade—since 1869, specifically. The Kinards' lawyer asked the court to instruct the jury that if they believed Henry and Mary "were so dwelling together during the whole of the year 1869 then they were lawfully married by the constitution of the State."[42] Such a finding would require the jury to acquit the couple and instead acknowledge that their relationship constituted a legal marriage. But Judge Calhoon refused.

Henry Kinard immediately appealed his conviction. In his brief to the Mississippi Supreme Court, his attorney explained that the ratification of the 1868 constitution made the pair "husband and wife" and argued that they "cannot, ten years afterwards, be punished for performing their duties as law-abiding citizens."[43] But T. C. Catchings, the Mississippi attorney general, defended the couple's conviction on the basis that the marriage provision of the 1868 constitution was "designed to protect innocent persons"—specifically, those who "by reason of their former condition, had not been legally married."[44] The "former condition" he alluded to was slavery—implying that the state constitution was *not*, in fact, colorblind. He implied that the constitution only protected couples who had previously been enslaved.

In 1879, the state supreme court ruled against Henry Kinard, upholding his conviction for unlawful cohabitation. The decision was written by associate justice Hamilton H. Chalmers, who, just six years earlier, had successfully argued that Mary Ann and Levin Dickerson's interracial relationship was a legal marriage before the same high court on which he now sat.[45] From this vantage point, Chalmers denied the same legitimacy to Henry and Mary Kinard that he had argued to grant the Dickersons. Notably, in his opinion upholding the Kinards' conviction, Chalmers did not cite *Dickerson* at all.

The ruling was brief but to the point: the relationship between Mary and Henry was not a marriage. The couple had lived together in a relationship of "concubinage."[46] Stunningly, the court did not deny that their union had taken on the qualities of a marriage. It was long-lasting, produced children, and was not hidden from public view. But as Henry's "concubine," Mary could not be Henry's wife. Although interracial marriage was legal, their relationship was not. Instead of returning home to care for their boys, Henry and Mary went to jail.

The deciding factor for the supreme court was Mary's racial classification. Just by invoking the term "concubinage," Justice Chalmers resurrected terminology used to describe sexual relationships between white slaveholders and the Black women they enslaved.[47] These were relationships of profound inequality. "Concubinage," specifically, boiled down complicated intimacies into a system of exchange revolving around sex. Such relationships were certainly not marriages. This sleight of hand allowed Justice Chalmers to justify differential treatment for interracial and same-race couples. Indeed, Chalmers's opinion treated the Kinards' relationship with open disdain. He did not even bother to name Mary. Throughout the decision, he called her merely "a negro woman," as if her name mattered less than her racial classification.[48]

MUCH HAD CHANGED BETWEEN 1873, WHEN THE MISSISSIPPI SUPREME Court declared the Dickersons to have had a legal marriage, and six years later, when it denied the Kinards the same status. The state's Black majority had not assured Republican dominance in politics. Even when Republican lawmakers were triumphant in the early 1870s, the party was riven by factional battles. Republican US senator James L. Alcorn was a former slaveholder and Confederate who, despite his political affiliation, was not hesitant to court the votes of white supremacists. Alcorn announced his bid for the governorship in 1873. Black Republicans distrusted Alcorn; in the election of 1873, some supporters backed an opponent, Adelbert Ames, as governor. Ames prevailed. (The historian Eric Foner noted that "even Alcorn's plantation hands voted against him.") Alcorn remained in the Senate.[49]

Then the political winds shifted against the entire party. The Panic of 1873, a financial crisis followed by years of economic depression, drew national politics away from a focus on Reconstruction in the South. And amid the election of 1874, white supremacists launched what they euphemistically termed a "political revolution" in Mississippi.[50] It was indeed a revolution, in the sense that Democrats led a coup that overthrew biracial democracy. It was also a blood-soaked endeavor.

Justice Hamilton H. Chalmers had been one of the participants and beneficiaries of this revolution. In 1881, two years after he ruled against Henry Kinard, Chalmers penned an article titled "The Effects of Negro Suffrage" for the *North American Review* laying out his commitment to white supremacy. In the article, he described Black people as "a hopeless minority" that was "destitute alike of property, education, or morality." Black voters, he explained, robbed white men of "the rulers of their choice."[51] Chalmers reminded readers that political equality of the races would lead to other forms of intermingling, embellishing his condemnation of Black suffrage with a reference to the sexual threat that Black men posed to white women: "How many years must elapse before some elegant and accomplished negro will lead out the mistress of the White House to a state dinner, or an American President be glad to wed his daughter to a millionaire whose face is as black as his diamonds may be glittering?"[52] Of course, as Chalmers knew all too well, many interracial liaisons in the South resulted from the actions of *white* men. He left this part out of his screed.

But Mississippi already had competing precedents that provided a basis on which the justices could build two standards for lawfulness: common law marriage and unlawful cohabitation. The court's rulings in *Carotti* and *Kinard* did not mean that the state's high court was souring on the validity of common law marriage. In the very same term that the justices affirmed the Kinards' conviction, it heard another case invoking the 1868 constitution. A widow was claiming that her union, never formalized, was a common law marriage. But this case had an important difference: the couple was white.

Susan and Bryant Adams fell in love and were first engaged in the early 1830s, but his family disapproved of the match. Bryant married another woman and was widowed, and then he married again. And yet Bryant and Susan continued their relationship in adultery. Bryant moved Susan into a house on his plantation, where she bore his children. His wife was furious and left him. The couple never filed for divorce.[53] Bryant and Susan absconded west from North Carolina, ultimately ending up in Tishomingo County, in Mississippi's northeast corner. There they kept the secret of their scandalous past until Bryant's death in 1878. Their relationship remained adulterous until the death of Bryant's wife in 1867. When Susan claimed to be Bryant's legal widow, one of his sons from his second marriage sued for control of his father's estate, claiming that the union between Susan and Bryant was never legal. Justice Chalmers wrote the majority opinion in *Adams v. Adams*, and he declared the relationship between Bryant and Susan Adams to be a legal marriage. Though it had begun with adultery and, arguably, bigamy, this did not matter. Although the marriage clause in the 1868 constitution "was undoubtedly intended principally to apply to our colored population," Hamilton conceded, "it embraces all who fall within its provisions."[54] And so the court declared Bryant and Susan's relationship to be a common law marriage, making Susan his widow and heir.

The decisions in *Kinard* and *Adams* indicated that "unlawful cohabitation" held a different meaning for interracial couples than for same-race couples, or at least for white people. The justices had already begun a process of separating informal marriages, categorizing interracial ones as illicit while offering the protection of law to same-race couples like the Adamses. The state legislature would make the next move to criminalize interracial relationships.

A six-year campaign of violence, voter intimidation, and fraud had disfranchised many Black men and led to Democratic victories in state and federal elections.[55] When a biennial session convened in 1880, repealing the gains Black Mississippians had made during Reconstruction was on the agenda. The legislators also targeted interracial marriage. The new code of laws declared that the "marriage of a white person and a negro or mulatto or person who shall have one-fourth or more of negro blood, shall be unlawful."[56]

This new law struck at the heart of the 1868 constitution. No longer was the state's marriage law colorblind. And yet the language of the law itself was rife with problems of enforcement. Many enslaved people had had mixed ancestry, and after emancipation, some of those people had married white partners. Newspapers regularly referred to Carrie Highgate as a "mulatto"—a term used to describe a person of mixed white and African ancestry. Were Carrie and Albert Morgan's children legally Black or white? The children of interracial unions often straddled the color line in this way. They might meet the blood quantum definition of whiteness. And, of course, many of the children of interracial marriages had fair skin and could adopt white identities.

This was not even the largest obstacle to enforcement of the law prohibiting interracial marriage. The law further declared that interracial unions "shall be incestuous and void."[57] Incest, of course, had a very specific meaning: a sexual relationship between persons related within a certain degree by blood or kinship. It also had an archaic meaning, "adulterous," and it is likely that the bill's authors intended for the law to classify interracial marriages as impure and taboo.[58] Lawmakers may have also sought to make interracial cohabitation and sex punishable in the same way that the law treated incest. Surely they did not intend to declare only those interracial marriages that were also incestuous to be void (one imagines such a phenomenon would be exceptionally rare). Courts could sentence individuals convicted of incest to terms of up to ten years in the state penitentiary. Regardless, it seems that in the 1880s, when this law was in effect, no one tested whether an interracial marriage had to also be "incestuous" to be void.

The law also said nothing about common law marriage. As Henry and Mary Kinard knew all too well, "unlawful cohabitation" was a misdemeanor offense. It was significantly less punitive than the marriage law. Predictably, in the wake of the 1880 law, many interracial couples simply did not obtain marriage licenses. Such relationships fell into a legal gray area. The legality of their unions—if they were tested in court—would be left to the discretion of prosecutors and juries. This left cohabiting couples vulnerable to prosecution, even if they considered themselves married. At the same time, as many couples would discover in the intervening decades, the line between lawful and unlawful cohabitation was not always clear.

Mississippi courts continued to use unlawful cohabitation charges to prosecute interracial couples. Hattie Brown and Mark Stewart lived in Yazoo County, where their relationship was not much of a secret. They were jointly indicted for unlawful cohabitation in 1884. The couple hired a lawyer, who requested that Mark and Hattie be tried separately. This was a strategy to cast both in more favorable light—if the couple was not tried together, it would not be obvious that theirs was an interracial relationship. Should it be clear that Mark was white and Hattie was Black, they feared that the jury would convict them regardless of the strength of the prosecutor's case. The judge denied their request.[59]

Hattie and Mark were tried together, as Henry and Mary Kinard had been. Not only could the jury see that the defendants were an interracial couple, but the district attorney seized the opportunity to grandstand about the perils of miscegenation. Their lawyer protested and asked the judge to instruct the jury that Mississippi did not explicitly criminalize interracial sex, but the judge refused. This point mattered for Hattie and Mark's defense, as they lived in separate houses. Witnesses at the trial nevertheless stated that Mark was "frequently seen at the house of Hattie Brown and in her bed"; especially damning was the evidence that "Hattie Brown had two mulatto children whom Mark Stewart had been heard to call his children." The jury convicted them.[60]

Together Mark and Hattie appealed their conviction to the Mississippi Supreme Court. The pair employed two lawyers, both white men from Yazoo City: J. C. Prewett and T. H. Campbell. Both men were active in Democratic politics. It also seems they had both a professional and personal interest in the topic of marriage. The men, both bachelors, had also served as president and vice president of the Yazoo Valley Mutual Benefit and Hymeneal Association—a mutual benefit society "for unmarried people."[61] Prewett and Campbell claimed that the court should have granted the request to try Mark and Hattie individually, as "trying them together resulted greatly to the prejudice of the defendants." They were not on trial because their relationship crossed the color line. The only offense they had allegedly committed was "unlawful cohabitation"—theoretically a race-neutral crime.[62]

In April 1887, the state supreme court handed down its ruling in *Stewart and Brown v. State of Mississippi*. Unsurprisingly, the court sided with the state and upheld their joint conviction. The justices refused even to chastise the district attorney for lecturing the jury on interracial sex, declaring, "We do not perceive that his appeal to the jury in regard to miscegenation or his denunciation of the same was improper or unjust to appellants."[63] According to the justices, Hattie and Mark were justly ridiculed and shamed.

This ruling offered prosecutors reassurances that they could use unlawful cohabitation to charge interracial couples even if they did not live together. And it offered them another powerful weapon: racial prejudice. The ruling established that district attorneys could lecture juries about the perils of "miscegenation" even though interracial sex was not a crime and unlawful cohabitation was race-neutral. It offered the supreme court's stamp of approval to grandstanding district attorneys, clearing the way for them to unleash vitriol against interracial couples.

By the 1880s, both the legislature and the courts took a belligerent stance toward interracial marriage. This did not mean, however, that those couples whose relationships preceded the 1880 law parted ways. Nor did it mean that Black women and white men did not continue to form intimate partnerships. While the marriage law may have deterred couples from seeking marriage licenses in the first place, the penalty for unlawful cohabitation simply was not harsh enough to act as a broad and effective deterrent for many couples. In the 1880s, prosecutors regularly charged couples with unlawful cohabitation. They also learned that juries and judges did not always share their enthusiasm for such prosecutions.

Courts often handed out sentences that were far below the maximum possible. And those who were accused found ways to challenge their convictions. Frank Cox, a white farmer in Lincoln County, lived with a Black woman, Fannie Collins, for years—starting at least as early as 1880, when the census recorded them as part of the same household.[64] Despite the risk of prosecution, Frank and Fannie remained together. In 1884, a Lincoln County jury found Frank guilty of unlawful cohabitation and sentenced him to the maximum penalty allowable by law: six months in the county jail and a $500 fine. Fannie, in contrast, received a thirty-day sentence and a fine of just $1.[65] But a week later, the judge ordered that Frank's sentence and judgment be set aside, and that his sentence be postponed until the court's next term, so long as Frank posted a $200 bond.[66] The following term, the court again postponed the sentence, "pending good behavior."[67] The newspaper did not note, however, whether Fannie received the same treatment.

As in this case, charges of unlawful cohabitation did not typically result in particularly harsh fines or sentences. The 1884 spring term of court in Batesville, a town in the Delta, witnessed at least eleven people dragged before the court on unlawful cohabitation charges. Among them, Jim Lofton and Addie Metcalf were fined just $5. Harriet Hitch was fined $10 and sentenced to serve one day in jail—nowhere near the harsher penalties available at law. Such results were on par with other morals-based crimes. (A man convicted by a jury of "profanity" also received a $10 fine.) Two couples received $20 fines apiece and one day in jail.[68] Two years later, Andrew Purdy received the most severe sentence of the 1886 May term of court: a $25 fine and ten days in jail. Two other women received lighter sentences, including one who served no jail time at all.[69]

It is not clear whether individuals were charged because of their race or for some other reason. It is possible that these Batesville couples were not prosecuted because they fell into different racial classifications, as newspapers frequently singled out instances of "miscegenation." In the Warren County Circuit Court in Vicksburg, a local newspaper reported with interest on the June 1885 indictment of a Black man, Warren Ware, for unlawful cohabitation with a white woman named Susie Jeter. The case, the newspaper noted, was the "first case of the kind that has appeared upon the dockets of the Court for years."[70]

In some cases of same-race couples, those charged avoided convictions by agreeing to marry.[71] The Batesville prosecutions show how many people preferred accepting a fine to being saddled with the obligations of matrimony. In other instances, as was the case with Mary and Henry Kinard, unlawful cohabitation was used to punish people who had committed other kinds of offenses—such as sending a vindictive, loose-lipped employee to jail.

It seems that some legislators were not happy with the law. In 1888 both houses of the state legislature considered bills that would amend Mississippi's unlawful cohabitation law.[72] Introduced by Senator James W. Barron, Senate Bill 282 would have amended the law to clarify "what language shall be sufficient in bills of indictment for unlawful cohabitation."[73] The Senate Judiciary Committee, after considering the bill, recommended against passing it, and in early March the Senate indefinitely postponed debating it.[74] The law remained vague—and prosecutors remained ready to use it.

In 1882, the GRENADA SENTINEL, based in Grenada, Mississippi, published the horrifying story of the "maniac" Captain Thomas Kirkman, a man of great honor who had committed unspeakable atrocities. Sometime between midnight and daybreak on Friday, August 4, Thomas took an axe and brutally murdered Narcissa Hurd, a Black woman, and her four children, including her five-month-old baby. He then injected himself with an overdose of morphine. The story was a "fearful shock," given Thomas's upbringing as a gentleman who was "well-born, well-raised, and carefully educated."[75] He was a member of the executive committee of the county Democratic Party.[76] The Clarion-Ledger, in its coverage of the tragedy, which it called "a chapter to the criminal history of Mississippi that will never be forgotten," noted that Thomas was "finely educated, brave and cultivated, with an extensive connection among the best families in the South."[77]

Initially, the newspaper blamed jealousy brought on by Thomas's relationship with Narcissa, with whom he had cohabited for years. Reports noted that Thomas had fathered Narcissa's children. His madness was compounded by financial troubles that plagued him in the months before the murders.[78]

But just a week later, the Sentinel's editor wrote a meditation on the appalling crime that cast the blame not on Thomas's financial woes or his possessive nature, but instead on interracial relationships writ large. "The tragic end of Capt. Tom Kirkman," the editor wrote, deserved more than a passing mention. Thomas was born with "early advantages" that "would have enabled him to win distinction in any branch of professional or literary labor that he might have chosen." In the editor's view, "the great mistake of Capt. Kirkman's life, was in not marrying and throwing around him all those moral helps and restraints, which a pure, sensible, loving wife never fails to command." Instead, he had "lavished the wealth of his affections upon an uneducated negress without the sanctions of wedlock, thus violating the commands of God, the laws of his country, and the customs of society." His sense of reason had been dethroned by the choice he faced: either leaving the children, "with his own blood circulating in their veins, to struggle in life as best they could, or living with them in utter poverty and disgrace." These were the "distracting thoughts of this unfortunate man as he horrorscoped the future of that sleeping woman and children around whom his affections were playing like laughing devils; and why should we wonder at the tragic end?"[79]

The column ended with a warning to other white men who considered taking Black wives: "Young white men, the colored women may unwittingly drag you down, but with all of your pride and rising intellect, you cannot elevate them to the plane from which you have fallen."[80] The editor did not seem to doubt the affection Thomas had for Narcissa and their children. Indeed, it was this forbidden love that had led to his downfall, a tragedy for all involved. The editor of the *New Orleans Times-Democrat* concurred, noting that Thomas felt "tender regard for the woman and children," but that he would "rather see them dead" than leave them to face the cruel future that awaited them.[81]

This framing of the murders as a dual tragedy—the downfall of a respectable white man and the brutal murders of his partner and biracial children—fit squarely in the literary tradition of the "tragic mulatto." The grooves of this narrative were already well-worn by the 1890s; the Kirkman tragedy fit easily into this trope, allowing commentators to neatly explain how a man with such impeccable personal and professional credentials could commit such a horrific act.[82] Thomas could envision no happy future for his own children, and so death was preferable. He might have been written as a character in a Southern Gothic novel, but he was very much a real person, and the violence he inflicted on his own partner and children ended their stories in one of the worst ways imaginable.

When Thomas Kirkman murdered Narcissa and their children, interracial marriage had only been illegal in Mississippi for two years. Prior to 1880, their relationship had not only been legal but may well have been a legal marriage. The "tragic mulatto" trope lifted responsibility from the state legislature for destroying families and lives with legislation, and most importantly, it shielded Thomas Kirkman from the sole blame for his actions. His crimes were instead an object lesson about the deadly consequences of interracial romance.

On February 5, 1890, a new constitutional convention began—the third in twenty-five years. The purpose of the convention was to reestablish white supremacy.[83] As one white man explained, it fell to the current leaders to save future generations from having to resort to "shot guns in their hands, a lie in their mouths, and perjury on their lips, in order to defeat the negroes."[84] Better to legalize their disfranchisement and save white people the trouble. The delegates were also inspired by a brewing agrarian revolt, which threatened to unite poor white farmers with Black Republicans in a coalition that could wrest back control of the state legislature from white Democrats.[85] Across the South, biracial political coalitions of Black and white populists were threatening the Democratic stranglehold on southern states.[86]

On Tuesday, August 12, 1890, the convention was called to order. The delegates chose a Hinds County circuit court judge as the president: Soloman S. Calhoon.[87] This was the very same Judge Calhoon who had sentenced Henry and Mary Kinard to jail for unlawful cohabitation in 1879. Calhoon was already enmeshed in Democratic politics before his appointment to the circuit court in Hinds County, a path likely eased by his personal association with William McWillie, a one-term member of the US House of Representatives whose plantation was near Calhoon's childhood home. Calhoon read law and was licensed to practice at just eighteen years old. In 1858, he was the founding editor of the *Yazoo Democrat* before serving as private secretary to then governor McWillie and as secretary of the Mississippi Democratic Convention.[88] In 1861, he enlisted in the Confederate Army, becoming a lieutenant colonel. When he returned to Mississippi after the Confederate surrender, Calhoon married McWillie's daughter, Margaret.[89]

Calhoon was open in his embrace of white supremacy. In a speech months before the convention began, he offered up his view that "Negro suffrage is evil" and that "the only sweeping and certain remedy" was to remove universal male suffrage from the state constitution.[90] Calhoon saw himself as an architect of the new political order, proposing a plan for government with an electoral college system to choose all state legislators, judges, and the governor. The idea was so anti-democratic that it raised the ire of other delegates, who called it "oligarchic" and a plain violation of the US Constitution, which guarantees to every state a "republican form of government."[91] (Other delegates were less critical, with one stating that he was in favor of any plan to "insure white supremacy.")[92]

In a speech on the convention's first day, Calhoon declared that Reconstruction had led to catastrophe. The blame lay solely with Black Republicans. Calhoon had a simple solution to the problem. He declared, "The ballot system must be so arranged as to effect one object." This "object," he explained, must be disfranchisement, "for we find the two races now together, the rule of one which has always meant economic and moral ruin," and "another . . . whose rule has always meant prosperity and happiness, and prosperity and happiness to all races."[93] In Mississippi, the white man must govern.

This was not their only aim. The 1890 constitution also tightened the state's prohibition on interracial marriage, and in doing so, it redefined race. The constitution drew the definition of Blackness at one-eighth blood quantum of African ancestry. In its next session, in 1892, the state legislature followed suit by amending the law prohibiting interracial marriages. The new law would prohibit intermarriage between "a white person and a negro or mulatto or person who shall have one-eighth or more of negro blood" while also making it illegal for white people to marry persons of "Mongolian blood"—a class that was entirely left out of the 1880 law, reflecting a recent increase in Chinese migration to the state.[94] The legislature at last replaced the legal language of "incestuous and void" with "unlawful and void." Notably, neither marriage provision mentioned Native Americans. This change meant that the children of interracial couples were more likely to be classified as Black than white. It also made it more difficult for a white person to marry someone with African ancestry.

In addition, the legislature turned to the enormous blind spot in its prohibition of interracial relationships: common law marriage. In its new 1892 code of law, it adopted a measure stating that "marriage shall not be contracted or solemnized unless a license shall first have been duly issued, and such license shall be essential to the validity of a marriage."[95] Together, the new laws governing interracial and common law marriage took square aim at those couples who continued to cohabit in defiance of the law. Together, they stripped existing interracial families of any legal recognition they might seek.

Not everyone was happy with this change. The editor of the *Vicksburg Evening Post* remarked on this "remarkable" piece of legislation, calling it "very dramatic and severe" to prohibit *all* common law marriages. The editor noted that even those marriages celebrated in churches before entire communities would be "void," making "the whole ceremony . . . worthless" without the proper documentation.[96] The children of any such union would be illegitimate. Newspapers around the state reprinted the critical article.[97] The editor of the *Clarion-Ledger* was one of the few that defended the change.[98] But the late nineteenth-century experiment in requiring marriage licenses was short-lived. By 1904, the Mississippi House of Representatives had passed a bill reauthorizing common law marriage by a two-thirds majority, though the measure failed in the Senate.[99] In 1906, the repeal of the 1892 marriage license requirement had enough support in both chambers to become law.[100] That same year, the legislature kept "Mongolians" on the list of persons prohibited from intermarrying with whites.[101] Nowhere in the public debates over marriage licensing did anyone mention race.

DESPITE THE RAMPANT HOSTILITY TOWARD INTERRACIAL COUPLES, THE legal reforms of the 1890s did not deter all such relationships. Records show that many carried on as they had before, though they often disguised their relationships as those of employer and employee. Men could also find ways to protect their partners and children financially. Such was the case of Matilda Gibson, a Black woman, and John McAlpine, a white man, who had been together since at least 1870, when the census-taker first recorded them as sharing a home in Claiborne County. John was a retail merchant; Matilda was described as his cook. Despite Matilda's appearance as a domestic worker, she was John's wife. Matilda was described as "Black," but her two sons, Harry and Lee, were designated "mulatto"—indicating that they had white parentage. The boys had been born after emancipation, in 1865 and 1868.[102] Their father was John McAlpine.

By the time the census-taker came calling again in late June 1880, the state legislature had outlawed interracial marriage. Matilda and John dutifully put up appearances. Matilda and her children told the census-taker that they lived next door, probably in a house on the same property. In the ensuing decade, Matilda had given birth to at least two more children, daughters named Salena and Maria.[103]

Matilda and John were not parted until John's death in April 1894. In 1881, a year after the Mississippi state legislature declared unions like theirs to be illegal and void, John had drawn up a will. It provided for Matilda and the children after his death, ensuring their security in a world that was hostile to interracial families and especially to Black wealth. John's will was filed in the Claiborne County Chancery Court after his death thirteen years later. In it, John declared that he did "give, bequeath and devise to Matilda Gibson and her heirs all [his] Real and personal Estate," which included his entire plantation comprising hundreds of acres of land—some of which he had purchased in 1876 from Jefferson Davis as the latter divided up his own brother Joseph's estate.[104]

John did not refer to Matilda as his wife. The children—*their* children—were identified only as "her heirs." John also designated Matilda as his executrix, and she took over the operation of the plantation in the spring of 1894.[105] Matilda hired their son Lee to work as foreman on the plantation.[106]

Even carefully laid plans could go awry. Although John attempted to protect Matilda and their children, his death occurred amid an economic crisis that pushed farmers across the United States into debt. The nation was gripped by a punishing economic depression. Cotton prices tumbled to less than a third of what they had been in 1870, selling for the meager sum of just seven cents a pound.[107] Matilda purchased supplies for the plantation and her family at M. Kaufman & Son in Port Gibson, which sold everything from meat to molasses, soap, suspenders, and shoes.[108] The profits from Matilda's plantation in 1894 and 1895 did not cover the debts she incurred for seed and supplies.[109] The 1894 crop fell short by $100; the loss was almost double the following year, when Kaufman's firm bought the cotton for just eight cents a pound. By the autumn of 1899, when prices began to recover, it was too late. Creditors had foreclosed on the inherited cattle and lands.[110]

But all was not lost. Although John's will did not name Matilda as his wife, the appraiser's report on the estate listed several items on Schedule B, "exempt property set aside for the widow and children to which they are entitled by law." This included two mules named Maria and Rhody, a wagon and harness, two cows, all the "farming implements," and the household furniture. Before his death, John had transferred ownership of other properties to Matilda, too—ones that were out of reach of his creditors. Although their sons, Harry and Lee, were identified as Gibsons, in adulthood they adopted the surname McAlpine.[111] When their widowed sister, Salena, fell ill in the autumn of 1904 and drew up her own last will and testament, she appointed her mother, Matilda Gibson, and her brother Harry McAlpine as the executors of her estate and the guardians of her three young children.[112]

True to her word, Matilda raised Salena's children, who were aged ten, eight, and seven when their mother died in 1905. Salena had requested that the children all attend school, and by 1910 all three could read and write. The oldest, Ezra, worked in a grocery store. It seems that Matilda was able to devote her time to raising up her grandchildren in part owing to one crucial fact: she was a homeowner. Matilda owned the home she had lived in on Flower Street in the small town of Port Gibson.[113] Even sixteen years after John's death, the census identified her as widowed. It does not appear from the census record that Matilda ever remarried. If they were ever prosecuted for unlawful cohabitation, it does not seem to have made any difference. Matilda and John's union endured.

Even Henry and Mary Kinard stayed together, defying the Mississippi Supreme Court's ruling that their relationship was illegal. More than two decades after *Kinard v. State*, H. W. Kinard appears in the 1900 census. He shared his home with a Black woman, whose name is given as Mary Jackson. Mary is described as Henry's "housekeeper," but she is almost certainly his wife, and probably the same Mary Kinard with whom he was arrested more than twenty years earlier. The couple had moved away from Hinds County, the site of their prosecution. Kinard now rented a plantation in Washington County in the Mississippi Delta.[114]

There is more evidence that this is the same Henry and Mary Kinard. At the time the Kinards were charged in 1879, the couple had three sons. In 1900, there are two young adult men in the Kinard household, William and Charley, who are both identified as Black. There seems to have been some confusion with the census-taker, who first described both young men as Henry's sons but then scrawled "boarder" over "son." Despite this, the young men shared their father's surname. Charley's birthday is given as March 1878—less than a year before his parents were charged with unlawful cohabitation. The couple's third and oldest son, Alex, lived next door with his wife. The family was a blended one; Alex's wife, Henrietta, had had several other children prior to the couple's marriage. Their union had produced one child: a baby girl they named Mary, just like her grandmother.[115]

These families did not go unnoticed by their contemporaries. Former congressman John R. Lynch had a storied career as one of the most prominent Black Republicans in the Reconstruction era. Lynch's political career had begun in 1870 when he was elected to the Mississippi House of Representatives; soon after, he was chosen by his peers in the state legislature as the first Black Speaker of the House. In 1872, he was elected to the US Congress.[116] Lynch had experienced a firsthand view of how white supremacists used fraud and intimidation to win elections, including his own contested campaign against the brother of Justice Hamilton H. Chalmers, James R. Chalmers, in 1880 that spurred a congressional investigation.[117] He also knew that a tremendous gap yawned between Mississippi law and the lives of ordinary people. Indeed, Lynch was well acquainted with the contradictions of southern laws governing race. His mother, Catherine White, had been enslaved near Vidalia, Louisiana, and his father, a white man, had been an overseer. But Lynch rejected the notion that the relationship between his parents was one of concubinage, insisting it was defined by genuine mutual affection.[118]

By the first decade of the twentieth century, white historians had written off Reconstruction as a disaster, saying it was an era in which corrupt and inept "Negro rule" led to the catastrophic mismanagement of southern states.[119] Lynch's book, published in 1913 as *The Facts of*

Eminent Colored Men.
HON. JOHN R. LYNCH,
OF MISSISSIPPI.

Representative John Roy Lynch, 1884 (John Wesley Cromwell, Library of Congress, Prints and Photographs Division).

Reconstruction, rebuked these historians and their interpretations of the politics of the era. But this was not the only intervention on the agenda. In the last third of the book, Lynch spent an entire chapter dwelling on a rather unusual and sensitive conversation he had had with another prominent Mississippian in 1884. Lynch had visited the office of the newly appointed secretary of the interior, Lucius Quintus Cincinnatus Lamar—a Democrat and former US senator who had penned the Mississippi Secession Ordinance—to congratulate him on his new post.[120] This was not Lynch's primary motive for the visit: he had come to plead on behalf of two public servants who faced dismissal from their posts in the Interior Department's pension bureau, a white lawyer and a Black doctor.[121]

The men, Lynch explained to his readers, had been dismissed because they were both married to women who fell into a different racial classification from their own. While the Black doctor was allowed to retain his position, Lamar was insistent that the white lawyer must go. The man was a Mississippian, and his marriage to a Black woman was well known in the state. Lamar could not risk inflaming passions about "amalgamation."[122]

But Lynch was not dissuaded. In his book, he claimed that his rebuttal to Lamar went like this: Both men knew that white southerners often had Black wives, and that this was accepted practice in their home state. Lynch wrote that he told Lamar, "For no one knows better than you do, Mr. Secretary, that this alleged opposition to amalgamation is both hypocritical and insincere." Lamar and Lynch both knew that "local sentiment in our part of the country tolerates the intermixture, provided that the white husband and father does not lead to the altar in honorable wedlock the woman he may have selected as his companion of his life, and the mother of his children." By this point, Lynch was clearly as invested in educating his readers on the social mores of Jim Crow as in recounting the precise wording of their conversation. He continued, "It is only when they marry according to the forms of law that the white husband and father is socially and otherwise ostracized."[123]

"Such unions," Lynch continued, "are known to exist, and yet are presumed not to exist. None are so blind as those who can see but will not see."[124] In short, interracial common law marriages were an open secret in Mississippi. Despite Lynch's attempt to intercede on his behalf, the man—whom Lynch did not name, citing the delicacy of the public servant's position—was fired and moved his family to Kansas. Lynch lost track of the family, though he noted that he suspected "that, like thousands of people of the same class, their identity within the colored race has long since ceased and that they have been absorbed by the white race, as I firmly believe will be true of the great mass of colored Americans."[125]

Although Lynch treated the identity of the civil servant as if it were a secret, he was speaking of none other than Albert T. Morgan, who had fled with his family from Mississippi amid the Democratic coup ten years earlier. By 1884, Albert was living in DC, where he again became the subject of a political attack that ended his career in the federal government. The 1884 election restored a Democrat to the White House for the first time since the Civil War. By the time he was fired from federal service, Carrie and Albert had five children.[126]

Some have questioned the veracity of this exchange, especially as it is quoted verbatim in both *The Facts of Reconstruction* and Lynch's later memoir.[127] Time and memory almost certainly colored Lynch's recollection of his conversations with Secretary Lamar as he sat down to recount them decades later. But precision was not the point. In these passages he was plainly attempting to reveal another truth: the hypocrisy of southern whites who claimed that the color line was inviolable and that white men never had Black wives.

It was true, too, that the Morgans' children adopted white identities. Albert Jr. married a white woman in Indiana (where interracial marriage was illegal) and lived the rest of his life as a white man.[128] Their daughter, Lucia, also married a white man.[129] Angela Morgan became a prolific writer and poet most notable for her pacifist works. Obscuring her family's roots in Reconstruction-era Mississippi, Angela invented an alternate family history, claiming to be the daughter of the distinguished-sounding "Alwyn Morgan and Carol Baldwin Morgan," even though she stayed close to her mother.[130] The triumph of Jim Crow forced the Morgan children to set aside their father's radical vision of social equality to pursue the privileges of whiteness in the world outside the South.

Those families that remained faced difficult circumstances. The law was no longer on their side. Marriages that had once been legal were now declared void. But these changes did not mean that every interracial couple parted ways or that white men abandoned their Black wives and biracial children. Not all interracial families left Mississippi or the South. They had ties to their communities, and often to the land. Like Matilda Gibson and John McAlpine, and Henry and Mary Kinard, they found strategies of survival that allowed them to go about their lives despite the political hysteria over miscegenation. The path ahead would not be easy, and they would not find their relationships untested—especially when money was at stake.

CHAPTER 3

CONCUBINES AND WIVES

MARY AND WILLIAM

The news arrived via telegram: "W. A. Covington died 2 PM to-day."[1] It was too late to catch the evening train south from Memphis to Bolivar County, so Mary Covington had to wait and take the morning train to the family plantation in the Mississippi Delta.[2] Things would soon get even worse for the grieving widow. Mary learned that William had left no will behind when he died in 1892. Like many other farmers of the era, he instead left a pile of debt.

Mary and William Covington had been together for nearly three decades—a union that produced eleven children. William owned 640 acres of land situated among the bayous and the rich Delta soil of Bolivar County, about five miles east of the county seat at Rosedale. In the decade before he died, William Covington had taken out loans of roughly $30,000 from a Memphis cotton firm owned by Godfrey Frank.[3] Frank advanced money to planters and operated a store not far from the Covington plantation that sold furniture and other goods on credit.[4] William Covington had not yet settled his debts. Unable to pay off loans he had secured in the 1880s, he had consolidated his debts by mortgaging his plantation to Godfrey Frank in 1889.[5] In the months after William's death, Godfrey Frank moved to foreclose.

Mary faced the prospect of losing her home to a creditor who she argued had misrepresented how much William truly owed the firm.[6] Under ordinary circumstances, she would have been allowed to reserve part of the estate as it went into foreclosure. Mississippi law protected debtors' children and widows from creditors.[7] But Mary and William's was not an ordinary marriage: as Mary was Black and William was white, his creditors sought to deny that she had ever been a wife at all.

Then came a new headache for Mary. A white cousin from Tennessee, J. H. Dickey, declared himself to be William's true heir, staking his claim to the Covington plantation. Dickey did not deny that Mary and William had had a long-standing relationship, but he argued that Mary was merely William's "concubine." Their children were illegitimate and, like their mother, not entitled to inherit anything of William Covington's estate.[8]

Mary's position was not all that unusual. Her relationship with William had traversed the 1870s, when interracial marriage was still legal. Like many other couples, they remained together after the legislature voided their union. Yet even if everyone conceded that the legislature could void legal marriages, the question remained unresolved: Could lawmakers invalidate the legitimacy of a child born in wedlock? At the time of their births, many of Mary's children were the legitimate sons and daughters of William Covington. No one could make a stronger claim to their father's estate, will or no will.[9]

The prohibition of interracial marriage kept wealth in white hands. It also served the fiction that southerners did not practice "amalgamation." The children of interracial unions posed a threat to both of these things. To admit that, for a decade, Black women and white men could enter into marriages on equal footing, and that some communities continued to tolerate interracial families, the courts would have to confront the legacies of the democratic revolution that accompanied Reconstruction, transforming everything from the legislature to the most intimate aspects of home life. The Covington case was a test of how far the court would be willing to bend both history and law to the cause of white supremacy.

IN 1894, MARY COVINGTON SAT DOWN TO GIVE A DEPOSITION. MARY could not write—when sending notes to friends and family, she dictated them.[10] Like so many other people who had been born into slavery, she did not leave a written record. Other people would try to have their say about Mary and her relationship, remaking her history to fit their own purposes. But when she was called upon to give her deposition, she had an opportunity to tell her own story, without interruption from lawyers.

It began like this: Mary met William when she was enslaved on the Niles plantation in Bolivar County. She had been born into slavery in Tennessee, where she was the property of a young woman named Margaret Humes. In 1852, Margaret married Joseph Warren Jenkins Niles.[11] At some point before the war, Margaret decided that Mary should be moved from Tennessee to the Bolivar County plantation. Mary was only in her early teens, but she already had a child: a six-month-old infant named Robert Martin. A year or two passed before Niles hired William Covington to work as an overseer on the Bolivar plantation. This was how Mary and William met, and their intimate relationship began soon after. Mary gave birth to a baby girl, whom they named Octavia. But their daughter did not survive to see her first birthday, and Mary lost a child before she turned twenty years old.[12]

By July 1862, the Union Army had established its stronghold in Helena, Arkansas, upriver from Bolivar County on the Mississippi. As she had done before the war, Margaret Niles decided once again to separate Mary from her family by moving her back to Tennessee. But Mary did not remain enslaved for long. She learned of the Emancipation Proclamation, issued just months after she was forcibly separated from William.

73

One of her first acts of freedom was to formalize their union. "I regarded myself as being a free woman," Mary explained of her decision to wed William on the streets of Nashville in 1863.[13]

With the war moving east from the Mississippi River, Mary and William returned to Bolivar County to find work. Their early years together were not easy. They were poor, and others criticized their marriage. Mary's brother and parents did not want her to live with a white man.[14] And in May 1868, William and Mary were indicted in the Bolivar County court on a charge of unlawful cohabitation.[15]

The prosecution aroused local interest. Even though the Covington estate dispute occurred decades later, witnesses who had been present recalled the day of the trial in their depositions. A Black preacher and justice of the peace recalled that the courthouse was packed with eager onlookers.[16] One of the jurors, J. B. Griffin, said Covington privately made a personal appeal when the men saw each other on the street. "Old fellow, do what you can for me," was how Griffin remembered William's plea.[17] The jury deadlocked, and the case against Mary and William was eventually dropped.[18] One of the observers noted that the judge instructed the jury about the recent constitutional convention and its implications for marriage.[19] Mary explained that this was the reason for the couple's second wedding ceremony: when they confirmed their intent to be husband and wife, the district attorney declined to continue prosecuting the pair.[20]

They could not yet afford to buy their own place, so the couple rented and worked for wages. Mary cooked in the kitchen of Dr. Niles, and William went back to work supervising the men and women working in the cotton fields. They leased a home on the plantation of Campbell Brown, an area that locals referred to as the "Brown deadening."[21] (A "deadening" was land cleared for cultivation by cutting rings in the bark of trees, which killed the trees and made them easier to remove—essential in the process of planting cotton in the densely wooded Mississippi Delta.) From here, Mary explained, she and William worked their way to independence, spending Mary's wages on a horse.[22] Eventually, they earned enough to buy property on the Brown deadening, the land that was now subject to the contest between Dickey, Frank, and Mary and her children. There, they built a small two-room house.[23]

Mary and William had a pressing need to increase their financial security: their family was growing. Mary gave birth to twin boys named William and Robert in December 1864, but Robert died just four days later.[24] Two daughters followed: Cornelia in 1866 and Emma in 1868.[25] The 1870s offered a decade of respite. This was especially true for Mary, who had known suffering and loss in her youth. Interracial marriage was legal, lifting the threat of prosecution. Mary had babies at roughly two-year intervals, and all of them survived infancy.[26] William earned enough money to buy land. They furnished their home with goods purchased from the Carson's Landing Frank & Co. store.[27]

Soon they had six children at home, and Mary and William wanted to send them off to school. The local options—segregated and seasonal to accommodate child labor in the fields—left much to be desired. Mary and the children moved to Helena, Arkansas, so that the oldest three girls, Cornelia, Cora, and Eva, could enroll in Southland College.[28] While Mary had gone north to Tennessee and claimed freedom, northern missionaries had journeyed south. Among them were a pair of white Quakers who had founded an orphan's asylum, which eventually became Southland—a haven for Black southerners seeking a high-quality education for their children.[29] Helena was not far from Bolivar County, about sixty miles upriver from Rosedale via steamboat. Southland was the only place within a reasonable distance that Mary and William could send their children to receive a high school education.[30] Eventually, Mary and the children relocated to Memphis.[31]

In the evidence Mary presented, much of the way William cared for her and their children was quantified in dollars and cents. Mary described how William had paid an Irish physician, Charles Agar, to deliver their twin sons, Robert and William.[32] Witnesses who knew the couple in Arkansas explained that Mary took in boarders, but William handled the finances.[33] A local gunsmith noted that William set aside $750 each year for the "maintenance" of Mary and the children in Arkansas.[34] But his support was not merely financial. Mary's sister Mariah Slaughter described a family headed by two parents who were devastated by the deaths of their children. William buried their children on the plantation in a family plot; he ringed the plot with fencing to keep cattle and other intruders out.[35]

Lewis Stubblefield, a landowning Black farmer who visited the Covington plantation to spay hogs, testified for Mary, noting that William called her his wife.[36] Stubblefield, like many other Black residents of Bolivar County, had been involved in politics in the 1870s and 1880s. White efforts to disfranchise Black voters and shut them out of politics were less successful in majority-Black counties like Bolivar than in majority-white ones.[37] The sole Black delegate to the 1890 convention was Isaiah Montgomery, who also happened to be the convention's sole Republican. A few years before the convention, Montgomery had settled land offered to him by an agent for the railroad in Bolivar County. In the late 1880s, he helped found the all-Black town of Mound Bayou, which was roughly twenty miles east of Rosedale.[38] He was not, however, an effective advocate for Black political rights. Montgomery also served on the convention committee on the franchise, which suggested the literacy test that would become the cornerstone of white political rule in the Jim Crow era.[39]

Bolivar County was therefore somewhat of an anomaly in the Delta. Like other counties, it had a Black majority. It also had its share of Black landowners and a Black-owned bank in Mound Bayou.[40] Mississippi's second Black US senator, Blanche K. Bruce, had launched his political career in Bolivar County when he was elected sheriff and tax assessor in 1871.[41] Bruce was not born or raised in Bolivar County, but he relocated there in search of economic and political opportunity during Reconstruction. He also owned and operated a large plantation, though by the 1890s he had relocated to Washington, DC.[42] Other Black Mississippians also held on to land they acquired, either as free people prior to the Civil War or in its wake.

Bolivar County may have seemed a more promising place for William and Mary to bring up their children compared to other counties in the state, especially in the eastern half. Black landownership was common, if not necessarily widespread, and the majority-Black population had kept the Ku Klux Klan and other white vigilantes at bay when they targeted Black property owners.[43] But with the triumph of white supremacist state politicians, no place in Mississippi was ever fully safe for a family like the Covingtons.

THE 1880s BROUGHT A SLEW OF NEW CHALLENGES TO THE COVINGTON household. Increasingly, lynch mobs murdered Black Mississippians with impunity. Agricultural crisis heightened tensions between Black and white farmers, with renewed violence, especially against Black men who held on to economic independence.[44] Any foothold Black residents of Bolivar County had found in land, property, and power in the decades following Reconstruction was at risk.

Personal tragedy also befell the Covingtons. In 1881, their thirteen-year-old daughter, Emma, died.[45] And in January 1882, it began to rain upstream in the Ohio River Valley. The downpours were unrelenting that winter, swelling tributaries of the Mississippi and sending huge volumes of water cascading south toward the Delta.[46] The Mississippi River began to rise, coming perilously close to topping the levees by February.

By early March, the levees could not hold. Floodwaters rushed through crevasses that opened in Bolivar County. A Rosedale resident told a Memphis newspaper that some buildings in the town were under ten feet of water. "About twenty acres of the levee north of the place is left intact, and upon the narrow space are collected five hundred negroes with mules and cattle. The mules are running about frantic for want of food, and the negroes subsist by killing and eating the starving cattle," E. H. Moore explained of the miserable scene of suffering. "The country below here is a sea, with a little knoll or island here and there, upon which human beings and domestic animals are crowded."[47] The floodwaters poured into the Mississippi and Arkansas Deltas, drowning people and livestock, inundating fields and towns, and displacing tens of thousands of residents. Measurements north of Bolivar at Helena,

Arkansas, and south at Vicksburg showed that the Mississippi River remained above flood stage for more than 100 days that spring.[48]

Mark Twain, in his autobiographical *Life on the Mississippi*, published soon after the floods, noted, "This present flood of 1882 will doubtless be celebrated in the river's history for several generations before a deluge of like magnitude shall be seen." The river, at some points, was "*seventy miles wide!*"[49] Twain's words were prescient. The flood was one of the worst in decades. The scope and scale of the catastrophe that spring would not be surpassed until the devastating flood of 1927.[50] The Mississippi River had long claimed the Delta as its floodplain. In the 1880s, it did so again and again, year after year. The floods were an inevitable consequence of efforts to pen up the enormous, powerful river and clear the land for cotton. The old forests that had covered the plain had soaked up water, but the clearing of the fields for agriculture made the soil less able to absorb floodwaters.[51] The following two springs were also marked by flooding, but none as severe as 1882.

Whether Covington's plantation was inundated entirely, in part, or not at all, these years were financially difficult for the family. The floods forced farmers to plant crops later than usual, risking a poor harvest. It was the next year, in 1883, that Covington first took the loans from Godfrey Frank, setting his family on a collision course with the cotton firm over unpaid debts a decade later. In 1886, he took out two life insurance policies that would be paid out to Godfrey Frank in the event of his death—likely a hedge against his family losing everything to creditors if he died before he could repay the mortgage.[52]

Mary and William again faced tragedy when their four-year-old son, Thomas, died in 1885.[53] But the plantation did well enough that William sent Mary and some of the children to Arkansas in 1887.[54] Three of the older girls were in school, and the three youngest stayed home with her. William may have had another reason to send Mary and the girls away. If Mary lived in a separate household in Arkansas, rather than cohabiting with William, the family might be less likely to attract unwanted attention from neighbors, or—worse yet—the district attorney.

MARY'S EVIDENCE ABOUT THE COUPLE'S MARRIAGE WAS NOT LIMITED TO her own words or to the stacks of depositions from those who knew her. Among the artifacts of their family life she presented to the court was the family Bible, which was inscribed with the birth dates of the children. It also contained the dates of the deaths of their deceased sons and daughters, including Octavia, Robert, Emma, and Thomas, and, finally, of the children's father, William Sr., in 1892.[55]

Mary also presented a sheaf of letters William had written in the final years of his life. They are full of the mundane details of everyday life on the farm, but they revealed how heavily William's financial anxieties weighed on him. One year, too much rain. Another, too little. In January 1891, William wrote to his daughter Cornelia, who had married and moved away, that the cotton prices were so low he was anxious about "what on earth will happen next." He signed off affectionately, "May God bless you is my prayer accept my love and think and pray for me often; my love to you and Mr. Miller [Cornelia's husband]."[56] But he was not destitute. In December 1891, just a month before his death, William shipped a cow to Cornelia and her husband, who were living in Stuttgart, Arkansas.[57]

The witnesses for Mary and the children were primarily Black residents of Bolivar County, who spoke openly of their relationship. They confirmed that Black neighbors considered the couple to be married and gossiped about whether the children would inherit the Covington estate upon William's death.[58] N. L. Glass, the Black preacher and justice of the peace, recalled that other Black residents had commented on William's affection for Mary, noting "how kind he treated Mary and the children." It "was often said that he could not treat a white woman any kinder," Glass said.[59] William Johnson listed numerous Black residents of the county who knew of the relationship, including former US senator Blanche K. Bruce.[60] Johnson said Bruce had recounted an exchange he had had on the train with William, who was on his way to Memphis to see Mary and the children at the time.[61] Mary's lawyers unsuccessfully attempted to have Bruce deposed in the case.[62]

White people also testified that William and Mary were married. Many of the witnesses lived in Arkansas and had met the Covingtons while doing business with the family. That Mary and William were an interracial couple was well known in Helena.[63] William, it seems, liked to socialize over a glass of whiskey or beer, as did many of his white neighbors.[64] Fred Braker, a plasterer, recalled that William had told him that the couple had been married in 1863.[65] William had told him this because, Braker explained, "I thought it strange that a white man should have a black wife."[66] Another witness, J. W. Fulton, had also discussed the legality of the union with William. "I asked him how he evaded the law in living with Mary Covington and he told me he had had her so long the law made them man and wife."[67]

Elkanah Beard, the former president of Southland College, was another white witness who testified for Mary. Beard recalled meeting William Covington when he had come to Helena to visit his children. Beard noted that William had paid the girls' tuition and sent money for their clothing, medicine, and other necessities—financial support that many of the other students at the school lacked. William referred to the girls as "his daughters" and to Mary as his wife in his correspondence with Beard.[68]

Albert McGee, a cousin of Mary's who had worked for the Covingtons in the 1870s, explained that he recalled only one instance of Dickey visiting the family. It was the spring of 1872. "He stayed only one night," McGee recalled, and Dickey had protested when the children sat with them at the supper table. Mary had given birth just two weeks prior. In her period of confinement, she stayed in bed.[69] "Mr. Dickey got mad and said 'William I don't like this,'" McGee recounted. William refused to send his children away from supper. He thought "just as much of his children" as Dickey "did of his." William told Dickey if he was uncomfortable, he should leave at daybreak.[70] Dickey did just that.

Another white witness, Charles Trumper, met William while he was traveling to Arkansas to see the family. Trumper was a carpenter, and he recalled with clarity the day he had met William Covington. It was in December 1888—on the day before the *Kate Adams* steamboat disaster.[71]

The ship was carrying nearly 200 passengers when it disembarked from Arkansas City on its way to Memphis, but halfway through its journey north, a spark lit some of the cotton bales aboard. The ship's crew frantically tried to smother the flames, but to no avail—the fire swept through the steamer as terrified passengers leapt into the cold currents of the Mississippi River. Many made it to shore, but confusion reigned about how many died in the fire or drowned. Major newspapers, including the *New Orleans Times-Picayune* and the *New York Times*, mistakenly reported that William Covington was among the victims of the conflagration.[72] "Mrs. Fields is positive that W. A. Covington, a planter and merchant of Rosedale, Miss., perished in the flames. She thinks he must have been suffocated in his stateroom, as he was aboard, and nothing has been seen or heard from him since the disaster," a report in the *Chicago Inter-Ocean* explained.[73] The boat did not keep a list of passengers, and it seems that other passengers did not realize William had disembarked the boat at Helena in the darkness of the early morning, a few hours before disaster struck.

Perhaps Trumper remembered the meeting because William Covington was reported in newspapers across the nation as missing and presumed dead. But William was very much alive in Arkansas, spending Christmas with his wife and children. Trumper called on the Covingtons at William's invitation. Later, he had been a guest in the Covington home in Stuttgart after Mary and the children moved there. William visited when the rhythms of the planting and harvesting seasons allowed. Trumper recalled socializing with other white people hosted by William, who supplied a "pony keg of beer."[74]

He recalled that William had informed him that he and Mary had been legally wed "shortly before the war broke out," but that William also "spoke of his troubles he had about her for having her as his wife." Trumper recalled that "he said that if he had made a mistake it was no ones [*sic*] business but his," and that "he had her for his wife, the children were his and that he would stick to her and the children until the last."[75]

Trumper also offered another piece of the puzzle, helping to explain why Covington's affairs remained unsettled prior to his death: William had a plan that would secure the safety of his family after his death. He wanted to sell the Bolivar County plantation to pay off his debts. With the remaining funds, he planned to buy 400 acres near Pine Bluff, Arkansas, where Mary and the children "would have no trouble after his death about his property."[76] William died before he could see it through.

J. H. DICKEY'S LAWYERS ARGUED THAT THE COURT SHOULD DISREGARD all of this testimony and evidence that William and Mary Covington were ever married. They argued that Mary's Blackness made her unsuited to the role of a white man's wife, even when such a marriage was legal. The facts of the case were merely "characteristic of the relations between a white man and his colored mistress," which shared no qualities with "the married relation, except the facts of cohabitation and the births of children."[77] Indeed, they claimed that "to establish a marriage between a white man of wealth and a negro woman and former slave is one of the strongest illustrations that can possibly be presented of the dangers to estates" that were meant to be protected by the law prohibiting interracial marriage.[78]

The witnesses for Dickey were a mix of people who knew his mother in Tennessee and white neighbors who knew the Covington family in Mississippi. Other white plantation owners in Bolivar County knew about Mary and William's relationship and their children. But they insisted that Mary was *not* William's wife. She was a "kept woman" or his "concubine." The distinction between the two categories was clearly based on race. The witnesses agreed that William and Mary's relationship was sexual, that it produced children, and that she "kept house." But whether her housekeeping work was evidence of her status as a wife or as a servant was less clear. At one point, a witness who insisted that the couple was not married stumbled over his explanation of Mary's status, noting that he had "always seen her doing just as other men's wives would do in reference to everything pertaining to the house."[79]

This slip was telling—many men expected their wives to take on most, if not all, of the domestic duties and to manage the household. The comment that Mary did for William "just as other men's wives would do" could be seen as evidence of their marriage. The white witnesses for Dickey implied that doing domestic tasks and having children made a white woman a wife, but these same characteristics made a Black woman a servant or a concubine. They distinguished what made a marriage legitimate was not based on the relationship between the two people, but on their racial classifications. In their minds and in their testimony, they created a two-tiered system that justified denying interracial couples the status of being a family even if the couple's relationship was founded in mutual consent and affection. They also inadvertently revealed how racial prejudice could allow some interracial couples to avoid prosecution under the draconian marriage law. White people assumed a Black woman living with a white man was a servant—not a wife.

Dickey's lawyers also focused on the evidentiary trail. The Davidson County court clerk in Nashville could not produce a marriage certificate from 1863.[80] Moreover, a life insurance policy William took out indicated that he was not married.[81] Dickey's witnesses were also divided on whether public knowledge of Mary and William's relationship hurt William's social status. Several of the witnesses testified that William did not try to conceal it, which hurt his ability to retain respectable standing in white society.[82] It also, it seems, troubled his business at times. At least one employee insisted that he would not work on the Covington plantation if Mary and the children were present.[83]

Jacob Frank, Godfrey Frank's brother who had also been a partner in the Frank & Co. firm at Concordia in the 1880s, testified that William was an "unmarried man" and that Mary was merely his "servant."[84] She was, as he explained, "by me and the community at large regarded as the concubine or kept-woman of W. A. Covington."[85] This, he admitted, hurt William's reputation among white people. "Because of the fact that he kept such a negro woman as his mistress or concubine, he was not so far as I know invited into the homes of his friends and acquaintances," Frank explained.[86] He said that William confessed to him "deep regret and concern because of the unfortunate attitude in which he was placed with his friends and neighbors, arising from his illicit intercourse and connection with the woman Mary," and sought advice on "the best course to pursue so as to free himself from the criticisms of his neighbors and friends."[87] Frank resisted the idea that Mary and the children were "family" to William. He "never saw" William and Mary "treat each other as husband and wife."[88]

Another white planter from Bolivar County insisted on the same. Yes, everyone knew that William and Mary had an intimate relationship. But Mary was "generally regarded as his concubine," he explained, adding that he would not have believed that the couple was married even if he had heard it from William Covington himself.[89]

Another witness for Dickey had worked for Covington in the years when Mary and the children lived in Arkansas. J. R. Peterson had worked for both William Covington and Godfrey Frank. He said he regularly carried mail to and from the post office addressed to Mary—but always to "Mary Richardson," not "Mary Covington." He also relayed a story in which William had heard a rumor that Mary had been unfaithful, adding that William had flown into a rage over it. "He told me that he was going to Memphis; that he had heard through one of his girls, that 'the damn bitch' was keeping another man, and he was going to see about it, and if she was, 'she would never get a god-damned cent of his money.'"[90] This exchange supposedly took place around Christmas, just a month before Covington's death.

Peterson shared other details about the circumstances of William's death. William had been sick; when Mary finally arrived at the plantation on the train from Memphis, she asked Peterson whether he knew of a will. "She said that he was the father of all those children, and she felt that she and those children ought to have the property," he recalled of their conversation.[91] Despite his low opinion of Mary, and his insistence that she was not William's legal wife, Peterson did not seem eager to see Dickey prevail in the suit. When asked if he had any interest in the result of the litigation, Peterson said, "I have got my preferences, and that is that the negro should have it, because Mr. Covington would have wished them to have it."[92]

MORE DETAILS ABOUT MARY AND WILLIAM'S STRUGGLE TO KEEP THEIR family together emerged from other depositions, sometimes inadvertently.

One white witness recalled overhearing a conversation between William and Maranda Hanna that took place over a late dinner around the time the Covingtons were charged with unlawful cohabitation in 1868. Hanna "asked him how he got out of his indictment, and he told her by representing that he was married," the witness told the lawyers. (When asked if she had a preference in the suit, she was as candid as Peterson had been about the outcome, noting that she wished "to see the white folks get it.")[93]

Another witness was a member of a grand jury in 1872. William Arnold was a justice of the peace in Bolivar County. He had also served on a grand jury sent to investigate allegations of unlawful cohabitation. Arnold explained that they had visited the Covington plantation, but, upon the advice of the "carpet-bagger" district attorney, the couple was not indicted. "We did not indict because District Attorney Clark said that he thought—that because of some National Law, he thought they ought not to be indicted." Arnold further clarified that the district attorney specifically "considered them married according to that National law."[94] This is likely a reference to the 1866 Civil Rights Act, which some had interpreted to encompass an equal right to marry regardless of race.

James McGee, Mary's brother, recounted a day in December 1869 when William Covington returned from Maranda Hanna's. He carried a newspaper to show Mary. McGee recalled that William "told her that he had found something that would give them satisfaction—both of them. He read it to her, and told her that he didn't suppose that there would be any more trouble at all. That they would be considered as man and wife under the present constitution."[95] According to McGee, Robert Martin—Mary's oldest son—was present.[96] This was, in Mary's recollection, the third moment that the couple was wed.

AFTER EACH SIDE'S LAWYERS PRESENTED REAMS OF EVIDENCE TO THE Bolivar County Chancery Court, the judge made a devastating determination for Mary and her children: their testimony should be excluded from the case because they were "interested parties" to the suit and therefore likely to give false testimony.

Mary's lawyers appealed the decision to the Mississippi Supreme Court, and the justices accepted her appeal. In March 1900, the court sided with Cornelia and Mary Covington when it handed down its decision in *Frank v. Covington*. As William's alleged child and widow, Cornelia and Mary's testimony should have been allowed. Their interest in William's estate only existed after his death, when they became his alleged heirs. This ruling did not necessarily guarantee that they would receive anything from the estate or even be considered his heirs—it just ensured that their depositions would be included in the evidence weighed by the Bolivar County Chancery Court when it determined the outcome of the litigation over the Covington estate.[97] But it was a win for Cornelia and her siblings, who moved to Chicago in the 1890s.[98] Sometime after she gave her deposition and told the court her life story, Mary Covington died, and Cornelia and her husband took in the youngest children.[99] Mary would not see the outcome of her yearslong struggle to ensure that her children would be recognized as their father's heirs.

In the months after the state supreme court's decision, lawyers for both the Covingtons and Dickey gathered new depositions and evidence, which they submitted to the chancellor. Judge Allen McCaskill Kimbrough, who overheard the case, was a resident of Greenwood, Mississippi. Kimbrough was wealthy and well-connected politically. Judge Kimbrough's Gulf Coast summer home was just a half-mile down a sun-bleached white shell road from the home of former Confederate president Jefferson Davis. The association was both personal and professional: Kimbrough served as the lawyer for Davis's widow, Varina.[100] The Kimbroughs' winter home in Greenwood was next door to the home of James K. Vardaman.[101] As Kimbrough oversaw the Covington case, Vardaman was the editor of the *Greenwood Commonwealth*, having twice unsuccessfully run in the Democratic primary for governor. Vardaman ultimately prevailed in 1903 owing to a change in the primary law that empowered voters, rather than a convention, to choose the Democratic nominee. His incessant race-baiting helped tip the balance in his favor.[102]

Kimbrough shared Vardaman's profoundly racist views that undergirded his opinion that Black and white people could never be equal. In 1913,

Kimbrough's oldest daughter, Mary Craig, married the famous muckraker and socialist Upton Sinclair. Toward the end of her life, Craig penned an autobiography in which she recounted her childhood on the family's plantation. Many of the Black people her family formerly enslaved had stayed close, working as tenant farmers and household employees, and Craig noted that she had called them all "aunt" or "uncle" out of respect. Craig uncritically described her mother's obsession with her "blue blooded" lineage and her father, Judge Kimbrough's, views on race, particularly how he "deplore[d] the 'natural defect in the blood of the Negro' which made him shiftless and averse to responsibility."[103] Kimbrough ran the plantation like a fiefdom, as "on the plantation, Papa's will was the law. These were 'his' Negroes," she wrote.[104] Craig recounted "discovering" a young Black child, whom the family took in as a servant. Though they claimed to adopt the child, he was not treated as a white son would have been. Craig explained, "The child made himself a member of the family, and was the liveliest of all the youngsters, half-servant and half-pet."[105] Mary's words revealed how many white Mississippians could imagine relationships to Black people as being at once familial and profoundly inequitable.

On February 23, 1901, Judge Kimbrough handed down his opinion in the *Covington* dispute. Kimbrough, himself the father of ten children, did not mince words in describing the relationship of Mary and William Covington. "W. A. Covington was a single or unmarried man at the time of his death," he wrote, and "he had never been married either to the said Mary Covington or Richardson, or any one else." Mary and William did have "carnal knowledge" of one another, but the relationship was "immoral and unlawful in its inception and so continued." The couple did not "mutually assent to the marriage relation" as defined by the 1868 constitution, "nor did they ever regard each other as man and wife." Their children were therefore "illegitimate," leaving J. H. Dickey as "the true and only heir at law of the said W. A. Covington, deceased."[106]

The ruling disparaged the relationship between Mary and William, not only as it reflected Kimbrough's personal views about interracial relationships but also in how the facts of the case mirrored the judge's own life. Mary Craig Sinclair, his own daughter, wrote in her memoir that her mother "did not love him, but she admired him," and in return, he tried "to give her everything that money could buy."[107] To Craig, her father's financial support of her mother was a sign of the soundness of their enduring bond and his devotion as a father and husband. And yet William Covington's support of his own large family, his devotion to Mary, and his efforts to give his children an education far superior to his own were not evidence of a familial bond between him and Mary and their children.

The ruling bent reality to paint this picture of Mary and William's relationship. By describing their relationship as "immoral and unlawful," Kimbrough erased a full decade of Mississippi history in which interracial marriage was not only legal but sanctioned by a state constitution ratified by popular vote. Nor was the fact that the Covingtons had been investigated by a grand jury but not prosecuted evidence that their relationship was a marriage. Instead, Judge Kimbrough implied that it revealed the shortcomings of the jury and prosecutor. Never mind that William could have abandoned his family after the failed prosecution. The immense weight of all the evidence that William not only recognized and supported his children but loved and cherished them did not matter. Judge Kimbrough cast them into illegitimacy and robbed them of their inheritance simply because they were Black.

The judge viewed the history of the Covingtons' relationship through the lens of Jim Crow law as if it was inevitable. His decision had profound consequences not only for Cornelia and her siblings but for all the children born in the era when interracial marriage was legal. Judge Kimbrough showed how easy it was to deny the claims of the legitimate sons and daughters of white men—so long as those children had Black mothers. The court could simply deny that a white man and a Black woman could have ever been legally married. The children of interracial marriages were, by default, illegitimate. The 1870s were simply an unfortunate aberration in an unbroken chain of history in which Black and white people could not form families. This history had nothing to do with the present.

As CORNELIA TOOK HER LEGAL BATTLE TO THE STATE SUPREME COURT, other states were grappling with similar questions of race, family, and history. Indeed, she may have followed one local case with particular interest: the saga of another Black woman, Maria Evans Laurence, whose life and current predicament resembled that of the Covingtons. The story unspooled in Chicago, where Cornelia and her siblings lived.[108] Maria's common law husband, a white dentist, died in 1891. The couple had been together for decades. And, like William Covington, Henry Laurence died without leaving a will. Local newspapers avidly covered the story; even the *Dziennik Chicagoski*, a Polish-language paper, printed a story about the case.[109] The *Chicago Chronicle* described it in a front-page headline reading, "Strange Romance of Courtship and Marriage in the Cities of the South."[110]

Maria Evans Laurence appeared in the court of Judge Theodore Brentano to be recognized as the widow of Dr. Henry Laurence. She was there to claim her dower right—her "widow's thirds"—in Henry's estate. Like Mary Covington, she brought a bevy of witnesses with her. Maria told the court that Henry's brother had cast her out of the home she had shared with her husband and into the streets after his death in 1891. Henry had an estate valued at $100,000—worth millions in today's currency—and Maria had been left destitute.[111] The couple had been together for more than twenty years, but they had never obtained a marriage license. Maria asked the court to declare her Henry's widow.

The story that Maria told in her quest to claim status as Laurence's wife may not have been all that surprising to readers of the *Vicksburg Commercial Herald*, which printed an article it called "A Romantic Story" with the subtitle "Negress Who Claims to Have Been the Lawful Wife of White Men of Wealth and Culture."[112] Certainly, it would not have surprised Cornelia Miller or her siblings. Maria's story had begun fifty years earlier, in 1840, when she had been an enslaved woman set for auction in Yazoo County. She was sixteen or seventeen years old at the time, born into slavery in Adams County, Mississippi. The story was told as a romantic tale, in which slavery played the role of the lovers' foil. A white man named John Evans "fell in love" with Maria and vowed to "secure her freedom and then marry her." (Reports of the trial were careful to comment on Maria's "rare beauty.")[113]

But Evans was penniless. It took him seven years to save up, Maria claimed, but in the end "he was true to his dark-skinned sweetheart." John saved up $1,000 to purchase Maria's freedom from a slaveholder in Kentucky. He then took her to Cincinnati, where, she claimed, the two married. They returned to Yazoo and then, eventually, moved to New Orleans following the Civil War. It was there that Maria met her second husband, the dentist Henry Laurence. The couple took in Henry as a boarder and, after John died in 1867, Maria and Henry began a romantic relationship. They moved to Chicago ten years later.[114]

What likely shocked readers—and perhaps steeled Cornelia Miller's resolve—was its ending: Maria prevailed in the trial court. In late 1895, the jury heard evidence about Maria and Henry's enduring relationship. The *Chicago Inter-Ocean* reported that Henry had introduced Maria as his wife to Mrs. Agnes Dennison. Mrs. Louise Smith recalled how Maria nursed Henry when he was in ill health, "and that during the time the doctor gave a number of evidences that the colored woman was his wife." Maria Harvey, a nurse, testified that Henry "appeared to be very happy" in his wife's company.[115] For part of their relationship, Maria was the one with funds, and at times she served as his benefactor. With the money and property she had inherited when John Evans died, Maria kept Henry financially afloat.[116] Henry's white relatives countered that they did not acknowledge Maria as his wife and, therefore, she could not be legally recognized as his widow.[117]

The jury sided with Maria. When a *Chicago Tribune* reporter visited Maria at home after the court ruled in her favor, she explained that her victory was about more than her bank account. "I wanted the money, of course, although the fact that I had beaten Mr. Lawrence's [*sic*] relatives would have been almost as much satisfaction to me," she explained. Maria was upset that his family had turned her out into the street after her husband's death, leaving her impoverished for the first time since she had been enslaved fifty years before. "Those people who opposed me knew they didn't tell the truth," she said. But she took the high road, noting, "Yet I can't hate them for it."[118] Judge Brentano reflected that he was "asked to either consider the complainant as a concubine or a servant." But he concluded that the jury got things right. "I do believe that he recognized this woman as a helpmeet during life and I think in equity that she was his legal wife."[119]

Maria's triumph was short-lived. The Illinois Supreme Court eventually overturned the jury's ruling, refusing to recognize the couple's bond as a common law marriage. They privileged the testimony of Henry's white family members, concluding that Maria "occupied the position of a servant or a housekeeper,—not of a wife."[120] Henry Laurence is interred in Oak Woods Cemetery, on Chicago's South Side. At the end of her life, Maria ended up in the Cook County Infirmary.[121] Maria outlived Henry by twenty years. Her body was not interred next to Henry's. Maria's body was likely buried in an unmarked grave, or, as sometimes happened to unclaimed bodies, donated to medical science.[122]

Like Cornelia Miller and her siblings, Maria was denied an inheritance that would have been hers had she been white. These are not only tragic stories. They are examples of how quickly and effectively the memory of the era in which interracial marriage was legal was erased. The laws prohibiting interracial marriage had not torn apart Mary and William Covington or Henry and Maria Laurence. In life, they could navigate hostile law and politics. And, notably, neither Judge Kimbrough nor the justices of the Illinois Supreme Court denied that these were intimate relationships. It was in death that they could not avoid the sentence that the courts would pass upon their relationships. Mary and Maria were not allowed to be widows. They were labeled the servants and "concubines" of white men. By denying that they were ever married, the courts revealed one purpose of so-called anti-miscegenation laws. These laws did not prevent the formation of interracial families. They did not prevent the births of biracial children. What they did was ensure that white wealth would remain in white hands.

CHAPTER 4

"THE LAW IS A GRINNING CORPSE"

CHARLES AND ELLA

In December 1907, the editor of the Port Gibson *Reveille* reported on a "moral movement" developing in the city. Turnout was less than the organizers had expected, but nevertheless, "the hundred men present went away deeply impressed by the forceful argument against the one great sin which, if allowed to go unchecked, promises to undermine the social system of the south."[1] That sin was of course "miscegenation."

More than twenty-five years after the state legislature outlawed interracial marriage, some southerners remained fixated on the "problem" of interracial sex and relationships. At the Port Gibson meeting in 1907, Justice of the Peace Harris Dickson took the stage and gave a rousing "appeal for Anglo-Saxon purity," then offered printed questionnaires to the audience, encouraging attendees to conduct their own independent investigations into interracial liaisons that they could present to the circuit court grand jury.[2] The gathered men anointed themselves the Port Gibson Law and Order League, but the only law that concerned them was the prohibition on unlawful cohabitation. It was the only legal tool that early twentieth-century prosecutors and courts had to punish interracial couples who lived together but chose not to marry.

The league was infuriated that the police, juries, and courts were doing nothing to prosecute and punish cohabiting couples. The police and aldermen, meanwhile, chided the leaguers for the absurd level of surveillance they expected. No one argued that white men did not continue to live with Black women. But they fundamentally disagreed about who was responsible for enforcing the law—or whether policing other people's private lives was even desirable. Their conflict centered on one of the main problems segregationists faced into the twentieth century. White men made the law. They sat on the juries that were tasked with indicting and convicting alleged offenders. White men were also prime beneficiaries when juries declined to convict. It was not concern for Black women's interests that allowed interracial families to survive into the Jim Crow era, but instead the right of white men to govern their own homes.

A POSTAGE-STAMP-SIZED TOWN SITUATED HALFWAY BETWEEN VICKS-burg and Natchez on the Natchez Trace, Port Gibson had a proud reputation as the jewel of southwestern Mississippi. Residents boasted of the town's impressive architecture, ranging from stately colonnaded homes set amid leafy streets and bursting garden beds to the Temple Gemi-luth Chassed, a Moorish Revival–style synagogue topped by a brick-red onion-shaped dome.[3] It was, as a sign welcoming visitors to town explains, a place that General Ulysses S. Grant allegedly proclaimed "too beautiful to burn" amid the Union Army's battle for Vicksburg.[4]

Yet rumors abounded that, when it came to the willingness of residents to look the other way when white men consorted with Black women, Port Gibson was the "worst town in the whole state."[5] There is also evidence of a certain amount of leniency in the treatment of local white men charged with unlawful cohabitation with Black women. In the months immediately following the meeting of the Law and Order League, a white man named George Emerick pled guilty and received a ninety-day jail term for the charge, followed by a pardon from the governor after sympathetic residents circulated a petition in his support.[6] Six months later, a jury declined to convict a married white man, Joseph Regan, and a widowed Black woman, Kittie Harper, of unlawful cohabitation.[7] The pair's acquittal provoked the fury of the presiding judge, John N. Bush, who launched into an extended lecture on this "crime that threatens our whole country." "I am rather surprised, gentlemen, at your verdict," Bush scolded the jury, claiming that he had never seen "a stronger case of circumstantial evidence in my life." He turned it back on the jury, chiding, "Gentlemen, are you going to put your approval on any such conduct as that?"[8]

The men of Port Gibson were not alone in fretting about the inadequacy of the law to prevent or punish interracial cohabitation. In the decades since Mississippi had outlawed interracial marriage, the legal system of Jim Crow had spread through states from Maryland to Texas. The fervor for so-called anti-miscegenation laws was not limited to the South. By 1900, more than half of all states had laws prohibiting interracial marriage, including Oregon, California, Nebraska, and Indiana.[9]

But an important shift had occurred. In the early twentieth century, some argued that the primary threat to white racial purity no longer came from Black men. Upon his retirement from the bench in December 1907, former US congressman and judge Thomas Norwood of Georgia gave a speech castigating the white men of the South for their failure to adhere to the color line.[10] "The white man alone is responsible" for the neglect of the rule of law, Norwood argued. "He alone makes our laws. He alone enforces our laws. He it is who forbids by law marriage between his race and the negro, though the latter have but one-eighth of negro blood." The white architects of the law brazenly ignored the color line that they themselves constructed. As Norwood thundered, "He commands the negro not to transgress the law, but he, the lawmaker, steps over the line and wallows with dusky Diana with impunity."[11] The lawbreaking that marred southern communities made anti-miscegenation laws dead letters. And worse—the lawlessness of white men made a mockery of the entire legal system. "We forbid marriage between the two races, and we make it a crime for them to associate. But," Norwood warned, "the law is a grinning corpse."[12]

Norwood's rage could hardly be suppressed. In his view, the solution to the "crime of miscegenation" had to be dual: Black men who crossed the color line must be lynched. White men must be imprisoned. "Draw a dead line between the races. Tell the negro, when he crosses it the penalty is death. Tell the white man, when he crosses it the penitentiary is there." He concluded with a flourish: "Arrest this incipient miscegenation! It is the neglected crevasse that broke the bank, when we see the resistless flood rushing on its course of inundation and ruin."[13]

James K. Vardaman had just finished a term as governor when he published Norwood's speech in the pages of his new magazine, *Vardaman's Weekly*, in the spring of 1908. While other Mississippi newspapers gave brief reports about the talk, Vardaman reprinted it in full, devoting nearly five full pages of the magazine to the transcript. Vardaman was himself a vocal racist who made anti-Blackness central to his political campaigns. He advocated for the repeal of the Fifteenth Amendment, which prohibited states from restricting the right to vote on the basis of race, and he used the first issue of *Vardaman's Weekly* to call for the end of Black public education in the state.[14] His opposition to political rights for Black men, he later explained, came from his belief "that political equality for the colored race leads to social equality. Social equality leads to race amalgamation, and race amalgamation to deterioration and disintegration."[15] In his view, interracial sex would lead to the downfall of the South. Of course, on the campaign trail, Vardaman cast "race amalgamation" as a future threat caused by Black political power and federal intervention into state affairs—not a reflection of reality in places like Mississippi, where the white man's law triumphed.

Vardaman's path to the governorship had been paved by more than his racist rhetoric. He was a beneficiary of the reform of Mississippi's electoral system, which had historically favored the wealthy planters of the Delta through a convention system that allowed Democratic Party leaders to choose slates of candidates.[16] Having fended off the threats of third-party politics by the early twentieth century, the Democratic Party consolidated its power but also faced new conflicts within its own organization.[17] These were resolved, in part, by allowing voters to choose in primary elections. At the same time, Democrats raised poll tax requirements and limited party membership to whites alone—yet another step toward eliminating the influence of Black voters.[18] (The concept of the all-white primary would not be ruled unconstitutional by the US Supreme Court until 1944.)[19] Vardaman represented a different class of white men. Though he came from wealth, he aspired to capture the votes of "rednecks," campaigning directly to raucous crowds.[20] He was a Progressive in the sense that he embraced government intervention to better the position of white Mississippians—particularly the lower classes. A national movement that encompassed politicians from both political parties at the turn of the century, Progressivism targeted society's ills: poverty, drunkenness, and vice. Progressives desired government solutions to these problems, guided by expert advice.[21] Their enthusiasm for scientific expertise led many of them to embrace eugenics as a "racial science," and this stance fueled their enthusiasm for segregation and the prohibition of interracial marriage.[22]

Mississippi Progressives had their differences. Mississippi governor Edmond F. Noel, who held office from 1908 to 1912, insisted that the state was required to provide separate schools for Black children. Vardaman, who had preceded Noel in the governor's office, complained that Mississippians should not "squander" tax dollars on Black children.[23] Vardaman's Progressive hodgepodge of a platform embraced improvements to public education (for white children, of course), an end to the brutal convict lease system, the complete disfranchisement of Black men, and an enthusiastic embrace of lynching. Southern Progressives were concerned with policing morality, arguing that all forms of interracial sex and relationships were forms of degeneracy that the state could and must police. Vardaman took this position even further during his campaigns by endorsing the white mobs that lynched Black men for allegedly raping white women.[24]

But Vardaman and other Progressives ran up against the long history of white men having dominion over their private lives—including their choice of romantic, domestic, and sexual partners. In this sense, many southerners viewed interracial cohabitation as a private issue: so long as it was white men doing the cohabiting with Black women and the relationships did not take the form of illegal marriage, the public should not police it. The idea that not all things should be subject to public debate likely accounted for the response to the charges against George Emerick and Joseph Regan in Port Gibson. Both men were farmers in their sixties who had white wives and large families.[25] Their relationships with Black women appear to have been extramarital affairs. George's and Joseph's actions were therefore not offenses against society but against their wives and children. Perhaps some members of the jury found it distasteful that the prosecutor aired these white couples' dirty laundry in open court for all of Claiborne County to see. If Port Gibson truly was "the worst town in the whole state," perhaps some feared that their own family secrets might be unearthed next.

Thus the "moral" movement against miscegenation that swept cities and towns across southwestern Mississippi faced continual resistance. This was not just a battle to "purify" white society. It was a war to determine what was properly a matter of public interest. Port Gibson was not the first town to form a league dedicated to exposing and punishing interracial relationships. That distinction went to Vicksburg, where the city's elite, including the local sheriff, police chief, and various lawyers, judges, and businessmen, gathered in July 1907 to announce the formation of an Anti-Miscegenation League. Organizers boasted that several hundred white men turned out for their first meeting. The newspaper noted approvingly that they were joined by "a number of negro men who pledged the white men their cooperation in their efforts."[26] The cooperation of Black men was essential for those who argued that the prohibition on interracial relationships benefited everyone—Black or white.

The editor of the *Vicksburg American* reported on the new organization with approval. He opined, "It is folly to talk and write of 'white supremacy,' 'race purity' and the like while a condition is winked at, the very existence of which makes our high-flown declarations the very spirit of farce."[27] The implication was clear: white men continued to have relationships with Black women, and the courts were struggling to indict and convict offenders. In early July 1907, Judge Theodore Birchett instructed a grand jury of sixteen men to bring forth charges on three pressing crimes: gambling, carrying concealed weapons, and miscegenation. The last was the "root of the race trouble," Judge Birchett explained. "White men in this community were living with negro women," he declared. "This was a crime and the whole community was scandalized." "The mulatto" was a particular "source of trouble."[28] (The judge did not clarify whether he meant the children of these interracial unions or the women themselves, though the presence of a class of racially ambiguous children did not make the color line seem more rational.)[29]

Two and a half weeks later, the grand jury had done nothing to address the problem of miscegenation. In a statement full of palpable disappointment, the grand jury reported that it was "unable to secure evidence sufficient to bring an indictment against any one." Locals were unwilling to give evidence about illicit interracial couples to the court. Some concluded that the law could not be relied upon to regulate this sensitive part of life. The *Vicksburg American* declared it was the private citizen's duty to ostracize those who engaged in interracial relationships. "It is possible to make it impossible for a man to live in a community without a resort to the power of the courts to eject him," the editor explained. "The crime of miscegenation must be made so odious that no man will dare to insult his fellows by committing it."[30] Neighbors should use scorn and shame to push white men to end their relationships with Black women.

The inability of the Vicksburg Anti-Miscegenation League to secure the convictions of interracial couples itself caused a scandal. Throughout the forested hills of southwestern Mississippi, newspapers spread gossip that the leaguers had uncovered illicit liaisons between Black women and prominent white men but could not persuade anyone to testify. White supremacists had disfranchised Black voters and policed Black men through lynching, but they struggled to control the behavior of other white men.

ALTHOUGH EFFORTS IN VICKSBURG WERE FRUITLESS, JUDGE MOISE Wilkinson presided over successful attempts to indict interracial couples in Natchez. Wilkinson was born in Amite County sometime after the Civil War. His father was a former slaveholder. Wilkinson's background as part of the wealthy, landed elite placed him in opposition to the growing discontent spreading through rural Mississippi communities in the 1890s. Amid a deepening economic crisis, tenant farmers rebelled. Amite County was a hotbed of "Whitecap" activity in the 1890s, and this may have informed Wilkinson's views on the importance of law and order. The Whitecap movement formed, in part, in response to the dramatic rise in timber prices that made Black-owned lands more valuable in the final decades of the nineteenth century. Although the vigilante Whitecappers terrorized their Black neighbors, they also targeted white merchants— including Jewish shop owners—who seemed overly amenable to doing business with Black farmers.[31] In Mississippi and Louisiana, white men formed Law and Order Leagues to put down Whitecap insurgencies in Amite County and other locales. Wilkinson stood apart, in the words of one newspaper, as "especially vigorous in the enforcement of the criminal law, and offenders convicted in his courts have little to hope for in the way of leniency."[32]

Formerly a major center of the slave trade, Natchez had a long history of interracial sex and relationships. As one historian blithely noted in a chapter titled "Amusements, Vice, and Desires" in a book on antebellum Natchez, "Of course, with the presence of so large a slave population miscegenation was common and may have contributed to less organized prostitution than in river towns farther north."[33] At the same time, Natchez also had the largest community of free Black people in Mississippi before emancipation, and many of these men and women had white fathers and enslaved Black mothers.[34] Perhaps the most well-known Black resident of Natchez, William Johnson, was likely the child of the white slave owner who emancipated him.[35]

The district attorney eventually persuaded the grand jury to indict at least thirty-five people during the spring and fall sessions of the Adams County Circuit Court in 1909. Some were indicted as pairs, while others were charged individually. It is not always clear who was charged with whom, and some names are missing from the extant record entirely. But overall, these were not youthful offenders. Most of the people charged with unlawful cohabitation were older, with some in their sixties and seventies. Many had children. These were mostly not secret affairs, but long-standing relationships that were likely well known within the community. Some were marriages.

One of the first men arrested was Charles Zerkowsky, the American-born son of Polish Jews who immigrated to the United States before the Civil War.[36] The city's Jewish community had roots in the mid-eighteenth century, when Natchez fell under the control of the Spanish Empire.[37] Charles's father, Aaron Zerkowsky, worked as a peddler; some of his sons followed him into the retail trade and opened their own businesses, operating as the Zerkowsky Brothers.[38] Like many Jewish southerners, by the early twentieth century the Zerkowsky family was largely assimilated into southern white society. Alongside Charles's business dealings, he was also extensively invested in real estate.[39]

According to official records, Charles was a lifelong bachelor. The census regularly recorded him as living with his siblings, including his unmarried brother Seaman. But the district attorney argued that Charles was unlawfully cohabiting with a Black woman. In April 1909, Charles was arrested along with his alleged partner, Ella Carter.[40] Among the witnesses subpoenaed in the case was Charles's brother Sam Zerkowsky.[41]

Although he was the only one charged in 1909, Charles was not the only member of his family to have a Black partner. His brother Seaman had an eight-year-old biracial son named Joseph Zerkowsky. Joseph lived with his mother, Savannah, and her husband of five years, Willie Washington.[42] Joseph's descendants identified Seaman as his father. Sometime after his relationship with Savannah ended, Seaman fathered two children with another Black woman, Mattie Holmes, though they were not arrested or charged in 1909.[43]

Nap Lisso was another of the men caught in the dragnet. Called a "prominent traveling man of Natchez," Nap—short for "Napthalia"—was a salesman for Natchez firms, traveling to sell their products. He, too, was a member of the city's Jewish community, and his family's roots were in New Orleans. Nap was probably an associate of the Zerkowskys, as he had connections to grocery wholesalers in Chicago (perhaps Nap himself was the link). In 1899, he married a Jewish woman from New Orleans, but tragedy struck just two years after the wedding. Nap was widowed after his wife, Mathilde, suffered a blood clot after surgery.[44] At some point after Mathilde's death, Nap pursued a relationship with Christine Williams, a Black woman. They were both arrested and charged with unlawful cohabitation in the spring of 1909.[45]

Both Port Gibson and Natchez had significant populations of Jews in the early twentieth century. The fact that two of the more high-profile men arrested for unlawful cohabitation were Jewish raises the question of whether they were targeted specifically because of their Jewishness. Southern Jews inhabited an uneasy position on the white side of the color line. The law declared them white, though socially and culturally, they were often marked as outsiders and faced discrimination.[46] Their position, like that of others who skirted the margins of whiteness, such as Italians and Slavs, plainly exposed the problematic nature of the very idea of whiteness.[47] The lynching of Leo Frank in Georgia in 1915 reflected an outpouring of antisemitic vitriol that would fuel the founding of a new iteration of the Ku Klux Klan, exposing broader anxieties about race and sex in the South.[48] Their Jewishness may have influenced the decision of the district attorney to target them. At the same time, by prosecuting them for cohabiting with Black women, the court in one sense affirmed the whiteness of men like Charles Zerkowsky and Nap Lisso.

Many of the men who were charged were not Jewish, however. The arrest and prosecution that captured the most public attention was the trial and conviction of policeman William Paul and his alleged partner, Emmaline Miller. William, a fifty-five-year-old white man, had served as a police officer in Natchez for nearly three decades. He and Emmaline, a forty-three-year-old Black woman who worked as a cook, were indicted together for "unlawful cohabitation," and on Wednesday, April 21, 1909, they pled not guilty to the charge.[49]

William and Emmaline were tried later that same afternoon. Theirs was the first unlawful cohabitation trial held before Judge Wilkinson in the Adams County Circuit Court that spring. The jury initially could not decide on a verdict in the case. But after a day and a night of deliberations, they found both William and Emmaline guilty.[50] It seems that some jurors were unsure about convicting the pair, prolonging the deliberations. William Paul was sentenced to three months in jail and assessed a $200 fine. Emmaline Miller's fine was smaller—only $75—but her jail sentence was twice as long. William's efforts to gain a new trial were rejected by the court.[51] Despite his conviction, he remained a sympathetic figure to many local whites, who circulated a petition imploring Governor Noel to pardon him.[52] There was not, evidently, a similar effort to gain a pardon for Emmaline.

With this victory under his belt, the district attorney continued his quest to indict and prosecute interracial couples. But despite dozens of arrests and charges, William Paul and Emmaline Miller would be the only couple charged with unlawful cohabitation in 1909 and 1910 to serve any time in jail. The same day the jury pronounced William and Emmaline guilty, they heard another unlawful cohabitation trial. This time, they found the defendants, J. N. Ratcliff and Mamie Joseph, not guilty.[53]

The prosecutions continued during the last week of April and into May. Five people—three women and two men—were arrested and charged on Friday, April 30, 1909. These indictments included William Sanders and his partner, Mamie Godbolt; another couple, Caleb Weir and Ella Stanton; and a woman named Carrie Rowan, whose partner, Henry Hunter, was also later charged.[54]

Natchez was a small town. Many of these couples knew one another, and it seems likely that they socialized amongst themselves. Ella Stanton and Carrie Rowan were next-door neighbors on Woodlawn Avenue.[55] The women were also identified as the respective heads of their households. Ten years earlier, Carrie and Henry Hunter had lived together on Orleans Street in Natchez, suggesting that their relationship may have been long-standing. He was identified as her "boarder" in that census.[56]

In 1920, Caleb Weir and Charles Zerkowsky owned neighboring homes on Liberty Road.[57]

While some of the couples did not appear to have children, others had large, growing families. William Sanders, a white butcher, was fifteen years older than his partner, Mamie Godbolt, who described herself as a laundress. Mamie was a homeowner, and her home was, in fact, probably William's as well. (He is conspicuously absent in the census.) At the time of their arrest, the couple had seven children. Mamie would soon become pregnant with their eighth child, a baby named John who was born in February 1910.[58] Mamie and William had been together since the mid-1890s, when their first child, Martha, was born.[59] Their relationship began in the years after the ratification of the new state constitution and the decision of the legislature to prohibit common law marriage. Neither of these developments prevented William and Mamie from forming a partnership that, by 1909, had already lasted a decade and a half. By prosecuting Mamie and William for unlawful cohabitation, the district attorney sought to break up a family.

Mary Dent, a "mulatto" woman in her late sixties, was also arrested in May.[60] She was charged alongside her longtime partner, retired ferryboat captain Lawrence H. Clapp.[61] They, too, had been together for at least a decade. In 1900, Clapp lived with a Black woman named Mary Garrett, who—just like Mary Dent—was born in Mississippi to parents from Virginia and Maryland. Their ages differ by ten years, and Mary Garrett was identified as widowed in 1900.[62] But given their shared first name and similar family histories, it seems most plausible that Mary Garrett and Mary Dent were the same person and that Mary and Lawrence's relationship was at least a decade long.

IN THE WAKE OF THE FIRST TWO TRIALS, SOME OF THOSE FACING INDICTMENTS chose to plead guilty to unlawful cohabitation rather than subject themselves to a public trial. Henry Hunter pled guilty on April 22. He was fined $150 and received a six-month suspended jail sentence pending good behavior.[63] (Presumably "good behavior" meant no longer cohabiting with Carrie Rowan.) The next day, R. Lee Parker, a butcher, likewise pled guilty. His fine was $100, and he too received a six-month suspended sentence.[64] His partner, Cora Poter, received the same suspended sentence and a $25 fine.[65] On April 29, Nap Lisso pled guilty and received a $150 fine along with a suspended six-month jail sentence.[66]

The prosecutions dragged on into the autumn term of court. Carrie Rowan pled guilty on October 12 and received a $50 fine.[67] Six other individuals did the same that day, including Mamie Godbolt and William Sanders, who received $50 and $150 fines, respectively.[68] The following day, Lawrence Clapp and Mary Dent pled guilty and received their fines.[69] All those who pled guilty had their jail sentences suspended pending good behavior.

By autumn, the district attorney had lost some of his enthusiasm for prosecuting interracial couples. In October, the court declined to pursue the charges against some of those charged, including Charles Zerkowsky, Caleb Weir, and Ella Stanton.[70] One couple pled not guilty, and the jury declined to convict them.[71] By April 1910—a year after the district attorney began his crusade to prosecute interracial couples—the court had dropped the charges or stayed the prosecutions of eleven accused individuals.[72] By the autumn term of court that year, unlawful cohabitation cases had virtually disappeared from the court's docket.

Though they made headlines, these unlawful cohabitation prosecutions do not seem to have derailed the lives of those accused of engaging in interracial relationships. Amid his legal struggle, Charles Zerkowsky continued to do business in Natchez, and it does not appear that his public reputation suffered greatly even as the charge was publicized. Indeed, Charles seems to have become more prominent as a local business and civic leader after his very public arrest. His campaign to encourage farmers to diversify their crops amid the boll weevil crisis led the local newspaper to dub him the "Peach Tree King of Adams

County."[73] R. Lee Parker likewise appeared to retain his position in the city's business community. The two men went on to serve together on the Natchez Chamber of Commerce.[74]

Even the state's governor foiled the plans of so-called race purists. In May 1908, much to the outrage of the Vicksburg Anti-Miscegenation Leaguers, Governor Noel issued a pardon for R. F. Wilson, who had pled guilty to "unlawful cohabitation" in Leflore County. Wilson, a white man, and his Black partner, Katie Jones, had been driven from Greenville before being arrested and charged in Leflore County. Wilson's brother, "mortified" by the prospect of a trial, pled guilty on his behalf, and the judge assessed a fine of $300 and sentenced Wilson to serve thirty days in the county jail.[75] Wilson attempted to withdraw the guilty plea, but the court refused, and the state supreme court later upheld the lower court's ruling.[76] "We feel that a deadly blow has been struck at the enforcement of law by the man sworn to enforce it," a letter to the editor of the *Vicksburg Herald* complained.[77]

But only white men received mercy from the governor. In November 1908, the mayor of McComb joined more than forty other signatories in a petition sent to Governor Noel on behalf of Susie Perkins, a white woman who had been sentenced to ten years in prison following her marriage to a Black man in 1905.[78] Susie Perkins, the petition explained, was an "ignorant creature" who had been fooled by a light-skinned Black man, Charles Martin. Charles, a schoolteacher, "was reported to be white, and visited in the homes of white people in the community." They had not suspected his Blackness. Charles allegedly enticed Susie to travel to Louisiana with him, where they were married. The petition claimed that he "deserted" Susie when his racial identity was exposed, leaving her alone to face a decade of incarceration.[79]

The truth is almost certainly more complicated. Charles did flee once the couple faced charges. Susie could claim naïveté as her defense.[80] But as a Black man, Charles could make no such claim to ignorance of Mississippi law and custom. At the same time, we do not know whether Charles identified as Black or, for that matter, had any African ancestry. But even if the allegations were false, Charles surely knew the penalty a Black man faced when accused of having a sexual relationship with a white woman: death by lynch mob. Fearing for his life, Charles fled the county. He was recaptured in early 1908, but again escaped before trial.[81] Given his propensity to slip away from the law's reach, one wonders if Charles, like Susie, had the sympathy of some locals. Perhaps not everyone was convinced he was in the wrong.

Susie Perkins alone faced punishment for their joint transgression of the law. There were very few white women incarcerated at the Oakley penal farm, the state prison for women.[82] When the McComb mayor petitioned for a pardon on Susie's behalf, he expressed sympathy toward a white woman and her plight. Having a relationship with a Black man did not necessarily place her beyond the bounds of respectable white womanhood. The penitentiary was no place for a lady.

Among the other signatories of the petition was J. B. Webb, the former district attorney who prosecuted Susie's case. Webb also wrote separately to plead for clemency. Rather than focusing on Susie's ignorance, he wrote that he believed she should never have been convicted. "It was impossible for me to prove that he had more than 1/8 negro in him," Webb explained of Perkins's husband, Charles Martin. "My best information was that he was either 1/16 or 1/32 negro. Whether he ever goes to trial or not makes no difference; he cannot be convicted, because of this fact." He had long advocated, he explained, for "let[ting] Susie go free."[83] The women's warden and chaplain at the penitentiary also wrote in support of the petition. Judge Wilkinson wrote against clemency, labeling Perkins "a common prostitute."[84]

The petition was unsuccessful. Susie Perkins stayed in prison, diligently working Sundays to accrue time against her sentence. At some point, she was transferred to Parchman, the massive penal farm in the Delta.[85] She was finally released on November 26, 1912. Marrying Charles Martin had cost her seven years of hard labor.[86]

WITH THE INCREASE IN UNLAWFUL COHABITATION PROSECUTIONS after 1907, the Mississippi Supreme Court received a slate of appeals from convicted couples and individuals. One of these cases came from Port Gibson, where Judge Bush and the district attorney James D. Thames had not given up on prosecuting Black women and white men. The case revealed the willingness of the supreme court to invalidate convictions when prosecutors played fast and loose with the rules of evidence.

On June 28, 1909, a circuit court grand jury in Port Gibson brought an indictment against Charles Cade and Ella Killian for unlawful cohabitation. Charles, a divorced forty-year-old white butcher, was rumored to have taken up with Ella, a Black woman in her early twenties.[87] Charles was arraigned the next day and the judge set the trial for June 30, just two days after the original indictment was issued.[88] Ella was in Memphis, supposedly to be treated by a doctor for an unspecified medical issue. The state's lawyers implied that, having caught wind of her impending arrest, she had fled the city to avoid prosecution, calling the timing of her illness "convenient." Charles hired a lawyer who seemed a worthy adversary of District Attorney James Thames: Charles S. Thames, his brother.[89] Charles Thames was familiar with unlawful cohabitation prosecutions. In June 1908, he had been the district attorney pro tempore who unsuccessfully prosecuted Joseph Regan and Kittie Harper.[90] (His brother was absent at the time.)

Despite Ella's absence, Judge Bush allowed James Thames to continue with the prosecution. The witnesses did not, however, make his task easy. Three of the five witnesses called by the state were Ella's Black neighbors, and they all denied knowing anything about a sexual relationship between the couple.[91] District Attorney Thames, exasperated with one neighbor, Cary Murry, who claimed to know nothing, asked, sarcastically, "You are the most ignorant negro in the world, ain't you?" (Cary dutifully replied, "Yes, sir.")[92] DA Thames painted a picture for the jury: Black people would not incriminate their own. Cary, he implied, was feigning ignorance to protect Ella. The two white witnesses were both reluctant to state what they knew about the relationship, though DA Thames prodded Tom Rowan into admitting that Charles had referred to Ella as "his woman."[93] The district attorney, stymied by his witnesses, argued the case to the jury directly, labeling Charles Cade a "traitor to his race" and Ella Killian a "negro wench"—though he frequently used an even more offensive racial slur to describe her. It is "disgusting and shameful and outrageous," he told the jury. "Here is a man that goes down and absolutely attacks every sacred relation of home life and is bedding up with a negro woman and making her to all intentions, his wife."[94]

Following his brother's racist tirade, Charles Thames objected to the remarks and—anticipating an appeal—requested that the stenographer ensure that the entire speech was printed in the trial record.[95] He also objected to other arguments the district attorney made. Namely, that the jury could convict a man based on their hunch. Moreover, it was not enough even if the jury believed "occasional acts of sexual intercourse" had taken place—the law specified that the pair must also cohabit.[96]

The jury deliberated until the next day, when they returned with a verdict of guilty.[97] The judge handed Charles Cade the maximum penalty allowed by law: six months in jail and a $500 fine.[98]

Charles's lawyer appealed his conviction. In the spring of 1910, the Mississippi Supreme Court reversed the lower court's decision, noting that the district attorney had not given Charles enough time to find and call the most important witness: his alleged lover, Ella Killian. Even if they were indicted together, the couple deserved the presumption of innocence. Charles had the right to call witnesses for his defense.[99] In June, District Attorney Thames brought a new unlawful cohabitation charge against Charles Cade. This time, the jury acquitted him.[100]

Anti-miscegenationists were dealt another blow when the Mississippi Supreme Court voided a conviction from the Gulf Coast. Louis P. DeJean, a white Pascagoula businessman, and Eva Lewis, a Black woman, were convicted of unlawful cohabitation in January 1914. Louis was sentenced to five days in jail and a $500 fine; Eva's sentence was thirty days, and her fine was $5.[101] Unlike in Charles Cade's case, the district attorney had no shortage of nosy neighbors willing to testify to what they had seen and heard at the cottage that Louis and Eva shared in Long Beach, a coastal village outside Gulfport where a malaria-afflicted Louis sought out the restorative sea breezes.[102] (Louis insisted to the court that Eva was merely his live-in employee.)

One neighbor, R. J. Burgdorf, was so desperate to know the intimate details of the relationship between Louis and Eva that he once burrowed into the crawl space under the cottage in the dead of night and lay there for hours "to try to hear what was going on between them."[103] R. J. testified that he saw Louis greet Eva affectionately and that the couple ate supper at the same table. He told the jury that he witnessed Louis wrap his arms around Eva as he taught her to shoot roman candles on Christmas day. Louis took Eva out to the wharf to see the Gulf, in plain view of everyone. After Christmas, Eva appeared in a sumptuous white fur coat—no doubt a token of Louis's affection.[104] The animosity between the neighbors was mutual. R. J. claimed that he had watched one evening as Louis beckoned Eva into the backyard, where he told her, "I want to learn you how to shoot a gun to defend yourself." Eva took her practice shots at R. J.'s fence.[105]

Louis's lawyer argued in his appeal that the couple had been convicted based on prejudice—not on evidence. The justices wrote that the judge had allowed inappropriate questions from the prosecutor that maligned Louis's reputation and prejudiced the jury. Louis had testified in his own defense, and the prosecutor used his cross-examination to make numerous lurid accusations, all of which Louis denied. The prosecutor alleged that, just a week after Louis's wife died, his father-in-law had caught him in bed with Eva. He asked if it was true that Eva had been "horsewhipped" and driven out of Pascagoula and that the Elks Club had expelled Louis. Was it not also true, the prosecutor needled, that Louis's son had repeatedly attempted to get Louis to end the relationship, and that, upon one of the son's visits to Louis's home, Eva had "shot at him through the door"?[106]

All of this proved to be too much for even the state's supreme court justices. The state attorney general insisted that "district attorneys cannot be to [sic] zealous in stamping out this source of evil, and the zealous performance of their duty should not be held as a ground for a reversal of the case," but the justices did not agree.[107] The prosecutor had created a "prejudicial error" that merited a new trial.[108] But it does not appear that Louis DeJean was retried for the crime of unlawful cohabitation: he died of "apoplexy" less than a year after his conviction was reversed by the court.[109]

In both the *DeJean et al. v. State* and *Charles Cade v. State* cases, a lack of evidence posed a major problem, even when juries voted to convict. Witnesses' reluctance to share the intimate details of their neighbors' personal lives was difficult to overcome. The men who testified against Louis DeJean and Eva Lewis were neighbors in Long Beach, where the pair was new to town. Louis and Eva's associates in Pascagoula did not testify. Louis's son did not attend the trial or serve as a witness. And even Tom Rowan, the Port Gibson town marshal, was reluctant to confess what he knew about Charles Cade's private life. Knowledge of "unlawful cohabitation" required familiarity with a person's regular living arrangements. The people best suited to give this kind of testimony were those who were closest to the people charged with crimes—such as Louis DeJean's son, or Charles Cade's Black partner, Ella Killian.

Their silence speaks loudly, but not necessarily clearly. Local white people allegedly whipped and scorned Eva Lewis for her living arrangements. How she felt about being Louis DeJean's partner, the court record cannot say. The same is true for Ella Killian, Charles Cade's partner, who fled before his trial. Anxious to protect Ella, Charles likely encouraged her to go. Louis DeJean's son, for his part, seemed less sympathetic to his father's situation than unwilling to associate with the entire affair—the trial included.

DESPITE A SLEW OF GUILTY PLEAS, THE EFFORTS OF ANTI-miscegenationists in Natchez do not seem to have been a rousing success. Their arrests did not have much of a lasting effect on Mary Dent or Lawrence Clapp. In the 1910 census, taken the year after the couple pled guilty, Mary and Lawrence were recorded as living together. The census identified her as his "companion."[110]

Charles Zerkowsky and Ella Carter's relationship also endured despite their prosecutions. After his death in October 1930, Charles's executors filed his will. The document was signed a month prior to his death. It seems that Charles was aware that the end was near, and he had spent some time in a sanitarium. Charles bequeathed a building on O'Brien Street to Ella—the same woman with whom he had faced unlawful cohabitation charges more than twenty years earlier. Ella, who lived in the building, was also to receive $1,500 in cash. (In comparison, he left a fifth of that sum to his synagogue, the Congregation of B'nai Israel.) To ensure that Ella's inheritance would be protected, the will instructed the executors—his brothers—to pay Ella's share of the estate first. Then the congregation could take its funds. After that, his siblings would split what remained of his land and other assets.[111] The will created a hierarchy of those whom Charles Zerkowsky sought to protect most after his death, with Ella Carter first in line. The brothers respected his final wishes. On March 26, 1931, Ella received her inheritance.[112]

There is more evidence that interracial relationships were tolerated to an extent in Natchez, even in the post–World War I era. As part of his research for his book on twentieth-century Natchez, Jack Davis conducted interviews with locals. Many recalled the existence of interracial families as late as the 1930s despite the law prohibiting their existence. Charles Moritz, a Jewish man, and his Black wife, Dorcas Walker, had an enduring bond. Moritz recognized his biracial children and grandchildren until his death in 1930. Walker died the same year.[113] Although Charles and Dorcas maintained a strong bond in life, they were separated in death. Charles was buried in his family's plot on Jewish Hill in the Natchez City Cemetery; Dorcas was buried in a segregated section reserved for the graves of Black people.

Not everyone stayed. Other couples and families left Natchez. Following his unlawful cohabitation charge, Nap Lisso moved to Chicago, where he worked as a grocery wholesaler. In 1917, he formally married Christine Williams, with whom he had been charged with unlawful cohabitation eight years earlier.[114] Perhaps Nap and Christine moved to Chicago so they could wed without interference. After Christine's death in 1929, Nap remarried, this time to Carrie Washington.[115] The pair received a marriage license in Indiana, where interracial marriage was prohibited by law. In 1930, they are both identified as white in the census, though her name is given as "Carita"—a name suggestive of Latin ancestry.[116] They lived on 111th Place, a racially mixed neighborhood mostly occupied by homeowners on the city's far south side, close to the Indiana border. Two of the houses near them were occupied by interracial couples. Nap Lisso died and was buried in Chicago in 1937. After her husband's death, Carrie was identified as a Black woman.[117]

Perhaps no couple defied the sanctimonious "race purists" more than William Sanders and Mamie Godbolt. Despite their very public arrests and charges, the relationship between them was long-lived, spanning several decades. The couple grew old together. Although Mamie and William were recorded as living separately in 1910—the year after their unlawful cohabitation indictments—the 1920 census found the family once again united under the same roof. In that year, they lived with six of their children: Rose, Willie, Charles, Anthony, Ida, and Laura. The census-taker conveniently identified Mamie as a "housekeeper" rather than William's wife. Their family continued to grow after their convictions. In 1920, their youngest child, Laura, was not yet two.[118]

The family was still together ten years later, though they briefly moved away from Natchez. According to the 1930 census, the family had moved north to a rural part of Warren County. Mamie is no longer the supposed housekeeper. Instead, she is identified as William's sister—even though the census identifies the two as being of different races. Mamie and the children are labeled as "Negro," while William is racially classified as white. But the children are identified by the census-taker as William's, and they are all given his surname. There are also several very young children who are likely William and Mamie's grandchildren—two three-month-old baby girls, Mamie and Melia; three-year-old Louisa; and a baby boy, Silas.[119]

Mamie and William eventually returned to Natchez. In 1940, they lived with two of their adult children, Philomena and Anthony, on Claiborne Street. By this time, Mamie was in her sixties and William in his mid-seventies. But there is one notable change in the way the census-taker identified the family in 1940: all the people in this household were now called "white."[120] It is likely that this classification did not reflect the consensus of the community. In the 1941 city directory, Philomena is identified as "colored."[121]

The example of Mamie and William is remarkable, even as the existence of interracial families in Natchez was not. The pair kept their family together despite the law declaring their marriage illegal. By the 1940s, they lived in an intergenerational household full of children. We do not know what the neighbors thought or whether they cared. And while we cannot know what brought Mamie and William together—whether convenience, true affection, or something else—we do know they fought to remain together even in the face of legal prosecution. While the law sought to void their partnership, the challenges of enforcement allowed them to remain together over many decades, building a life and a family in the shadow of Jim Crow.

CHAPTER 5

"ONE DROP"

ANTONIO AND CLARA

In the early decades of the 1900s it was not particularly unusual for law enforcement officers to arrest or charge consenting adults with intimate crimes such adultery or fornication. Legislators wrote these laws to regulate a community's morality, and in the early twentieth century every state had a version of such laws on the books. Adultery and fornication laws were seen as tools to protect married men and women from the threat of seduction and to insulate children from the tragedy of divorce and destitution. The threat of being criminally charged discouraged men and women from having sex outside of marriage, or at least pushed them to legalize their unions if a woman became pregnant out of wedlock. Fornication and adultery laws therefore protected the institution of marriage—most of the time.[1]

In October 1912, however, the district attorney of Hancock County, Mississippi, used Mississippi's morals law to destroy families rather than protect them. He instructed a grand jury to consider indicting six married couples on charges of adultery.[2] No one disputed whether these couples were married. No one alleged infidelity on the part of either husbands or wives. Some of these couples had been married for decades. Several had been wed by Catholic priests. Others registered their unions with the county clerk. The problem was race.[3] Hancock County officials alleged that these unions were illegal because they violated the state's law prohibiting interracial marriage.

Bay St. Louis had the same long history of slavery and interracial sex as the rest of the state, but it differed from places like Natchez and Port Gibson in that it was strongly Catholic, reflecting its long colonial French and Spanish history. It was home to many recent immigrants from Southern Europe, who arrived carrying their own ideas about race, religion, and family. All of this would make the color line difficult to enforce. The state legislature used a blood quantum definition of whiteness, a concept that was distinctly American.[4] But as the histories of the interracial families in Bay St. Louis reveal, it was not a concept that all Mississippians accepted, including Antonio and Clara Grandich.

Bay St. Louis is a small town on Mississippi's Gulf Coast. In 1910, it had a population of just over 3,300 people.[5] It is the seat of Hancock County, which borders Louisiana to the west, where the Pearl River wends its way along the state line and spills into the Gulf of Mexico. Gulfport and Biloxi lie to the city's east. In 1912, New Orleans was a short train ride west from Bay St. Louis via the Louisville and Nashville Railroad line. The city itself spans the western peninsula at the mouth of the bay from which it takes its name. In the early twentieth century, Bay St. Louis was home to people who mostly made their livelihoods in the warm waters of the Gulf Coast surrounding the city. By then it already had a thriving industry in tourism; its population tripled in the summer as visitors sought a seaside refuge from the unrelenting southern heat and humidity.[6]

On Christmas Day in 1913, President Woodrow Wilson sought out the restorative Gulf breezes as he and his family vacationed in an antebellum mansion at Pass Christian, just across the mouth of the bay.[7]

The six couples charged with adultery had lived in or around Bay St. Louis for decades. There was little mystery about their ancestry. The women were all members of sprawling Catholic families with deep roots in the county, and some of their ancestors had been among the first French settlers in the region. They had been born and raised in Hancock County, and their parents, siblings, aunts, uncles, and cousins lived nearby. Three of the women charged with adultery were sisters. Clara Grandich, Mary Brighenti, and Victoria Remetich were the daughters of Vincent and Louisa Covacevich, who themselves were longtime residents of Hancock County. Vincent had immigrated to the United States in 1859 from the Austrian Empire—he identified himself as Slavic—and he married Louisa Jourdan in 1875.[8] Louisa was a good match for Vincent: she was the one with property. Although most of the records from the settlement of her father's estate have been lost, a land dispute with the Southern Pine Company includes receipts showing that Louisa paid property taxes on 800 acres of land north of Bay St. Louis that she inherited after Victor Jourdan's death.[9] The land was part of a large homestead claim that her French grandfather, Noel Jourdan, had once held as a settler in Hancock County.[10] Noel owned plantations in both Mississippi and St. James Parish, Louisiana, where he held dozens of people in slavery until his death in 1845.[11] Some of that land became his son Victor's property, and eventually it passed to Louisa.

Vincent and Louisa had seven children together, but only four survived into adulthood: their daughters Clara, Mary, and Victoria, and one son, Victor.[12] Each sister, like their mother, married a European immigrant. The Covaceviches and their daughters were all parishioners at Our Lady of the Gulf, which served Catholics of all racial classifications.[13] (The lone Covacevich son, Victor Jr., escaped the notice of the grand jury, although he had married a white woman. When his sisters were indicted for adultery in 1912, Victor and his wife, Louise, were already living in New Orleans.)[14]

Our Lady of the Gulf Catholic Church, overlooking the Gulf of Mexico in Bay St. Louis, 2016 (photographer: Carol M. Highsmith; Ben May Charitable Trust Collection of Mississippi Photographs in the Carol M. Highsmith Archive, Library of Congress, Prints and Photographs Division).

Unlike inland parts of the state, where the struggle for land and cotton—or, in the early twentieth century, the timber industry—dominated the economy, Bay St. Louis was an attractive place for sailors, who could make a living working on the water rather than in the fields. The brackish waterways along the coastal fringe of southern Mississippi nurtured rich oyster beds, feeding a nationwide boom in the early twentieth century when Americans' appetites for the bivalves were seemingly limitless. In towns and cities across the United States, oysters could be purchased inexpensively, fresh or canned, shipped in from the Northwest, the Chesapeake, and the Gulf Coast.[15] Oystering was so profitable that it spurred a boundary dispute between Louisiana and Mississippi; the resulting lawsuit was ultimately settled by the US Supreme Court in 1906.[16]

When sailors first arrived in Bay St. Louis, they found it to be a city that was very much a part of the world of New Orleans. Socially, politically, and geographically, it was closer to New Orleans than to the state capital at Jackson. In the early 1900s, New Orleans mayor Paul Capdevielle, who spent months each year at his summer home, caused a scandal in Bay St. Louis when he wielded his political influence to back a Black postmaster over two white women.[17] But despite its proximity to New Orleans, Bay St. Louis was under the jurisdiction of Mississippi and its legal system of white supremacy. Immigrant men may have been Catholic; they may hail from Southern or Eastern Europe; they may have arrived on American shores with no money to their names. Mississippi law offered them something of immense value: whiteness.[18]

The claims of some of these immigrants to full political, social, and economic rights would be contested. New Orleans and elsewhere along the Mississippi Gulf Coast convulsed with violent conflict between native-born Protestant whites and their foreign-born neighbors in the late nineteenth century. The olive skin, dark hair, and devotion to Catholicism of these immigrants marked them as suspiciously foreign even as state and federal law classified them as legally white. In Louisiana and Mississippi, Italian peasants labored side by side with Black workers as field hands on cotton and sugar plantations while native-born whites shunned such labor as unsuitable.[19] Immigrants from Southern and Eastern Europe had few choices, as they were frequently poor and illiterate. Many of them worked menial jobs. Opponents of immigration often likened Italians and other "ethnics" to African Americans, labeling them as uneducated, dirty, and prone to criminality. Anti-immigrant rhetoric increased to a fever pitch in the 1890s, with native-born whites disparaging Italians as anarchists, or as members of criminal syndicates with ties to the mafia. In 1891, after a jury declined to convict eleven Italian men accused of murdering the city's police chief, a New Orleans mob broke into the jail and lynched them before they could be released.[20] The problem was widespread, with Italians being lynched from Mississippi to Florida.[21]

Antonio Grandich likely found himself on the margins of whiteness when he arrived in Bay St. Louis. Perhaps this helped nurture his kinship with families like the Covaceviches who held their own contested claims to whiteness. As people who did not fit neatly into the racial categories created by law, European immigrants at times openly defied the color line, refusing to choose between whiteness or Blackness. Indeed, inter-marriages between immigrants and Black southerners were not isolated to Bay St. Louis. In other Gulf states, Italians sometimes obtained mar-riage licenses to wed their Black partners into the twentieth century.[22]

Such vagaries of local culture and politics had little to do with the racial classifications imposed by the US Census Bureau. The bureau iden-tified six categories into which all persons would be sorted for counting: White, "Negro," Indian, Chinese, Japanese, and "All other"—a cate-gory mostly made up of Hawaiians, Koreans, Filipinos, and "Hindus."[23] Census-takers were instructed to differentiate between persons who were "evidently full-blooded negroes" and "mulatto," which the guidelines explained "includes all other persons having some proportion or percepti-ble trace of negro blood."[24] Within the classification for whites, they were to carefully distinguish between "Native-born" white people and those of "foreign birth," and between those with two foreign-born parents and those of "mixed parentage." The scrupulous attention to immigrants and their place of nativity reflected national anxieties about the millions of migrants who arrived in the United States in the late nineteenth cen-tury, which ultimately justified the restrictive federal immigration law of 1924.[25] The census-takers who arrived at the doorsteps of the Covacevich sisters in the summer of 1910 identified them, their husbands, and their children as white.

Antonio Grandich immigrated to the United States in the early 1880s.[26] He and Clara Covacevich were wed in October 1889.[27] We do not know what, if anything, Antonio knew about Clara's family before they were married or whether this information would have mattered to him. At the time, the law prohibiting interracial marriage was relatively new, and it drew the color line at one-quarter blood quantum of African ancestry. Perhaps he did not question Clara's family history at all. But in 1900, the census clearly identified Clara's father, Vincent Covacevich, as "white," and her mother, Louisa Covacevich, as "Black." Clara's sister

Victoria and her husband George Remetich lived next door to her parents in 1900. The census-taker identified them, too, as an interracial couple that year. Although George was white, Victoria and their son, Victor, were both racially identified as "Black."[28]

George hailed from the Adriatic. He had been born in the coastal region of Dalmatia—which was then controlled by the Austrian Empire and is today part of Croatia—in 1873. At the age of twenty-three, he had set sail from the port city of Trieste, arriving in New Orleans. At some point, he made his way to Bay St. Louis, where he met Victoria. They were married by a priest at Our Lady of the Gulf Catholic Church in Bay St. Louis on July 21, 1898, just two years after his arrival in the United States.[29] Their oldest daughter, Clara, was born the following spring. She was baptized at Our Lady of the Gulf, where Clara and Antonio Grandich served as her godparents.[30] The Remetiches had two more children, Vincent and George, in the following years.[31] (In 1918, perhaps as a result of the scrutiny put on foreign nationals with ties to an enemy nation during World War I, George Sr. applied for naturalization.)[32] Mary, the third Covacevich sister charged with adultery, married an Italian immigrant from Bologna, Ildebrandi Brighenti.[33] Ildebrandi—who was also called Henry—arrived in the United States in 1885, and the couple wed in 1900. They had three daughters, and Ildebrandi worked as a boat engineer.[34]

The other couples charged with adultery, the Pouyadous, Melitos, and Eurissas, were not close relations to the Covaceviches, though they also had deep roots in Hancock County. Mary and Victor Pouyadou had five children. Mary was the daughter of Peter Favre and Margaret Raboteau and a descendant of Simon Favre—a French settler who had fathered children with multiple women, establishing the surname as one of the most common in Bay St. Louis. (A newspaper article describing a 1991 family reunion dutifully noted the hundreds of pounds of fried chicken, potato salad, and baked beans consumed by his gathered descendants.)[35] Simon Favre had been born in Mobile in colonial French Territory in 1760.[36] Over the course of his life, France, Spain, Great Britain, and the United States had fought for territorial control over the valuable ports that

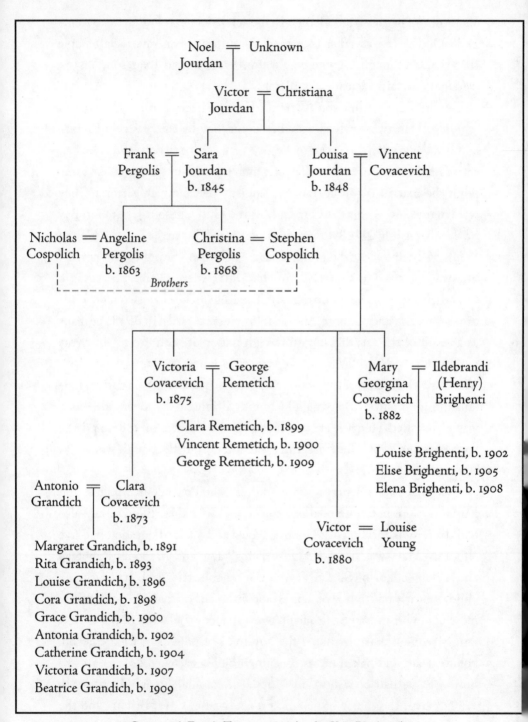

Covacevich Family Tree, ca. 1912 (credit: Kate Blackmer).

studded the Gulf Coast. Favre, like many other French residents, had made a life and career triangulating between warring European empires, Native nations, and the United States. Fluent in Chickasaw, Choctaw, and the pidgin Mobilian language, he had taken advantage of the shifting political winds to act as an agent to Native tribes, becoming an indispensable interpreter.[37] He had also helped the Spanish and Americans negotiate treaties with the Choctaw. His father, Jean-Claude Favre, who was possibly himself the métis child of a French trader and his Choctaw wife, held a huge tract of land at the western edge of present-day Hancock County along the border of the Pearl River. Like other white men on the old American frontier, Simon Favre eventually turned to the most profitable pursuit available: slavery. By the end of his life, he had enslaved dozens of Black men, women, and children on his Mississippi plantation. He was also the father of at least thirteen children by three women: six sons and daughters born to his white legal wife, Celeste Rochon; at least six children born to a Choctaw woman, Pistikiokonay; and one son born to a Brazilian slave-trader named Rebecca Osten.[38] Notably, in his last will and testament, Favre bequeathed his thousands of acres of land to his white children and his illegitimate son with Osten. His half-Choctaw children received nothing.[39]

Unlike the other couples who were identified as white, the 1910 census identified both Mary and Victor Pouyadou and their five children as "mulatto."[40] Victor, the only man investigated for adultery who was not an immigrant, had been born in Mississippi. While there was apparently no doubt about Mary's racial classification, in the 1900 census Victor had been classified as white.[41] The census also placed him in his aunt's home on St. George Street that year, though Mary—despite identifying herself as married—is recorded as living with her parents two blocks away. All the people in the Favre household were racially identified as Black.[42]

The two other women investigated by the grand jury, Georgeann Melito and Lena Eurissa, were descended from another sprawling Catholic clan. Saverino Melito, who was called "Sam," left Italy for the United States with his parents and brothers in the early 1890s. He married Georgeann Spadoni in Louisiana in 1898 when she was just fifteen years old.[43] Within a few years, they welcomed their first daughter, Pauline. Like many other Italians in the Deep South, Sam worked as a grocer, selling fruits and vegetables to support his wife and their growing family, which eventually included five daughters. Two other children died in infancy. At the time that Sam and Georgeann were charged with adultery, their youngest daughter, Josephine, was barely a year old.[44]

Georgeann's mother was Mary Victorine Cospelich, a daughter of Peter and Adele Cospelich, who had thirteen children together. Georgeann's father, George Spadoni, was an Italian immigrant who became a naturalized American citizen in 1882.[45] Another of Peter and Adele's daughters, Marie Magdalene, married an Austrian immigrant, Matthew Eurissa. Their daughter Lena—Georgeann's first cousin—was also charged with adultery in 1912. Lena and her husband, Willis Fulton, were newlyweds, having been married for fewer than six months.[46]

Adele and Peter Cospelich, Georgeann and Lena's grandparents, had been married on February 26, 1871, in Hancock County.[47] At the time of their wedding, the couple already had at least six children. The late timing of their wedding may have been the result of two factors: Adele had likely been enslaved prior to 1865, and the Mississippi state legislature repealed its prohibition on interracial marriage in 1870. Three of their children, Victoria, Peter, and Victor, were born before emancipation. It is not clear from the records whether Adele was enslaved by Peter. Either way, the wedding was a formality; Adele and Peter had clearly been together for years. In the following years, the family continued to grow. John was born in 1872, and twins Oliver and Olivia, the babies of the family, were born in 1876. For at least a decade following their wedding, their marriage was legal in Mississippi, regardless of Adele's racial classification.[48]

The story of the Cospeliches offers a glimpse of how ordinary people experienced the rising tide of Jim Crow laws that washed over the state after 1875. Adele and Peter's relationship began under slavery, when it was not possible for a Black woman and a white man to legally be wife and husband. Like Mary Ann and Levin Dickerson and William and Mary Covington, Adele and Peter remained together despite the dubious legality of their union. They had other things to attend to—children, especially. When interracial marriage became legal, Adele and Peter took advantage of the change. They did not know at the time of their wedding that the state legislature would make their marriage illegal again ten years later. They may not have cared anyway, given that their relationship had begun under such conditions.

Peter and Adele may have believed that the 1880 law, which only prohibited marriages between white persons and persons with "one quarter or more" blood quantum of African ancestry, did not apply to them—either because they were already married or because they viewed the blood quantum as offering sufficient leeway for some white men, like Peter, to remain married to women who had African ancestry. Or perhaps they did worry about the status of their union. The 1880 census described Peter, Adele, and all their children as "mulatto," even though Peter was legally white.[49] Whether this is a consequence of the census-taker classifying Peter alongside his wife and children for expedience, or because someone in the family misled the census-taker to hide that theirs was an interracial marriage, it is not possible to say.

Adele was Peter Cospelich's second wife. Peter had lived in Hancock County for most of his adult life. He appears in the 1840 census as the head of a household of two adult white men and is described as a Spanish immigrant (a later census identifies his birthplace as Italy); it reports that he worked as a carpenter on a ship and served as the head of a large household. There were nine men and three women in the home.[50] The women were likely his first wife, née Harriet Hays, and their two daughters. Harriet and Peter were no longer together after 1853; they either divorced or—more likely—Harriet died. By 1857, Adele had given birth to Victoria, her and Peter's eldest daughter.[51] Their delayed marriage—fourteen years after the birth of their first child—indicates that there was a reason they were unable to marry earlier. Perhaps Harriet was still alive and, as a Catholic, Peter was unable to remarry despite being divorced or separated. The most obvious reason for their arrangement, however, was Adele's race and her legal status.

From there, the Cospelich family tree becomes even more complicated. The children of Peter and Adele married on both sides of the color line. While their daughters, Mary Victorine and Marie Magdalene, married immigrant men from Europe, two of Peter and Adele's sons married sisters: John Cospelich wed a "mulatto" woman, Clara Sabatier, in 1895, and two years later, his baby brother Oliver married Clara's sister Rita. Stephen and Nicholas also married sisters, Christina and Angeline Pergolis, respectively. The Pergolis sisters were the daughters of Sara Jourdan, another daughter of Victor Jourdan. Their aunt was Louisa Covacevich; Clara Grandich served as the witness at the wedding of Stephen and Christina.[52] Another Cospelich son, Peter Cospelich Jr., married into the Favre family. After his first wife, Elizabeth Favre, died, Peter married a white woman named Emma Mitchell. Their census classifications defy Jim Crow logic. The 1900 census listed Emma as Peter's white "housekeeper," while Peter and his children are classified as "Black."[53] But the following year, Peter and Emma traveled to New Orleans, where they wed. In 1910, the census-taker identified Peter as white and Emma and their son Theodore both as "mulatto."[54] By 1920, Emma was widowed and living in New Orleans. In this census, she and everyone else in her household are white.[55]

The Cospelich children remained close-knit despite the complications of racial classifications. In 1900, a widowed Adele was living with two of her adult daughters: her eldest, Victoria, and youngest, Olivia. Some of her grandchildren also lived in the home. The census identifies everyone as "Black." Nearby lived Adele's sons Oliver, Stephen, Nicholas, and John with their families. They, too, are identified as Black.[56] In 1910—just two years before two of her granddaughters, both classified as white women, would be charged with unlawful cohabitation—Adele was identified in the census as "mulatto."[57]

THE STORIES OF THESE FAMILIES DEFIED COMMONSENSE UNDERSTANDings of how the color line operated in Mississippi. And yet their lives were not all that unusual. The couples charged with adultery constituted only a few of the local families with connections that crossed the color line. Even into the twentieth century, interracial marriages were not uncommon in Bay St. Louis. Some were openly identified in the census despite the state's anti-miscegenation law. Individuals' racial classifications often shifted from census to census, raising the question of whether the effort to categorize people as white or Black had anything to do with how these families saw themselves. Certainly a man's whiteness or Blackness mattered for things like voting, and it should have mattered in regard to who was allowed to marry whom. But many of these Bay St. Louis families seem to have had their own sense of the social order in which family and religion played more important roles than arbitrary racial classifications. A binary division between Black and white did not suit their lives or their reality.

Indeed, Charles Strong, the census-taker, seemed bewildered by some of the household arrangements in Bay St. Louis as he went door to door in June 1900. The racial classification of Joseph Cospelich is illegible; whatever was first written was then overwritten with a heavier hand. Joseph's wife and children, in contrast, are clearly racially classified as "Black."[58] The census-taker also appeared confused by Charles Cade, who was initially described as "white" but later corrected to "Black." (Earlier censuses describe Charles as "mulatto," so it is likely that he appeared to be white. Perhaps he answered the door first, and it was his Black family that gave him away.)[59] Richard Optime, a white man, and his Black wife, Hettie Valsin, were initially described as making up two separate families. But someone corrected Strong, who changed Hettie's status from head of her own household to "wife" to indicate her relationship to Richard. The couple, who were both over the age of fifty and thus past their childbearing years, seemed unconcerned by the potential consequences of identifying their marriage as illegal.[60]

Others were less brazen. In 1910, August Bourgeois, a sixty-year-old white man, lived with Alice Hayden, a Black woman who was described as his "housekeeper." This was a ruse. Both August and Alice were identified as "widowed," and they also lived with Alice's three children, the oldest of them named for his father, August. The three boys were aged eighteen, fourteen, and thirteen, and they all worked alongside August Sr. in his lumber business.[61] The couple's relationship began around 1880, after the death of August's first wife. Their oldest son, August Jr., married Mary Wilhelmina Cospelich, a woman whose lineage tied together two of the largest interracial families in Bay St. Louis. Her paternal grandparents were Peter and Adele Cospelich. Her maternal grandparents were Victor and Christiana Jourdan. Mary Wilhelmina's aunt was Louisa Covacevich, the mother of Clara and the grandmother of the Grandich girls.[62]

With generations of local women marrying white immigrant men, the children of these unions did not seem to question their own ability to marry whomever they pleased—within some bounds. There was a long history of interracial marriage in Hancock County, as in the rest of the state. In Bay St. Louis, the African ancestry of many families was distant, with generations of white men marrying women with mixed ancestry. These families may not have held the same social status as other white families, but they were part of a community with many other people who had histories just like theirs. Many of the men who had immigrated from Italy and Austria did not seem concerned with the legal or social conventions of Jim Crow. Their children became even more distant from those ancestors who were racially identifiable as Black. These couples were not breaking with tradition as they chose to get married, even if others might question the legality. Henry Leduc, the parish priest at Our Lady of the Gulf in the late nineteenth century, had been born in France, and he was evidently willing to preside over the weddings of many of these couples.[63] It was Jim Crow law with its blood quantum rule that was attempting to impose something new on the long-standing practice of interracial relationships in Hancock County.

The outcome of these adultery cases is probably lost to history. The records of the local circuit court were destroyed at some point, either when Hurricane Camille made landfall at Bay St. Louis in August 1969 or when Hurricane Katrina sent a devastating twenty-eight-foot storm surge through the town in 2005.[64] The local newspaper does provide some insight into the couples' fates. In March 1913, the *Sea Coast*

Echo reported that the cases were "passed to the grand jury," but it did not identify whether the grand jury issued indictments. The grand jury noted, in its letter concluding its business for the spring term of court, "In certain instances we have had great difficulty in getting at the truth on account of the reluctance of witnesses to testify. In fact, we have been handicapped by the difficulty in getting witnesses to tell what they knew about occurrences which we were investigating."[65] If this note applied to the unlawful cohabitation cases, the grand jury may have declined to indict the couples owing to a lack of evidence.

Or perhaps the district attorney decided to drop his pursuit of the charges. If a couple *did* marry as white people and the marriage was later contested, it was difficult to prove a person's exact racial ancestry. This was a problem that plagued any state attempting to legislate race or ethnicity using the blood quantum measure, and problems of racial classification were certainly not limited to Bay St. Louis.[66] Using a one-quarter rule of African ancestry only required knowledge of a person's grandparents, who would likely be part of a community's living memory. Though, if any of those people had mixed ancestry, suddenly the racial math became much more complicated. The smaller the blood quantum, the more difficult it was to determine conclusively the racial identities of people three or four generations back, who were usually long dead. A one-drop rule that classified anyone with African ancestry as Black created an impossible standard of knowledge, considering the paucity of records of people who were enslaved. Even post-emancipation census records did not create consistent or reliable records of racial classifications.

The marriage licenses for Hancock County did not specify the race of either the bride or the groom until the 1920s.[67] In order to enforce Mississippi's marriage law, the state had to find ways to prove that an individual met the standard of one-eighth "blood quantum" of African ancestry. By the time the state charged these six couples with adultery, it was not even clear that they had violated the Mississippi anti-miscegenation law. Even if local authorities felt that the couples should not be allowed to marry, they could not, if pressed in court, necessarily prove that these individuals had broken any laws.

Unlawful cohabitation and marriage laws were not the only way to punish interracial families. The editor of the local newspaper followed these cases with careful interest. Charles Moreau was both the founder and the owner of the *Sea Coast Echo*; he was also the chair of the school board trustees.[68] Charles had been born and raised in New Orleans and had made Bay St. Louis his home in the early 1890s.[69] Faced with the difficulties posed by the marriage law, he and the other trustees decided to pursue a second approach to the "problem" of mixed-race families in Bay St. Louis. On October 16, 1912, they called a special meeting to determine whether the children of Sam and Georgeann Melito, Ildebrandi and Mary Brighenti, George and Victoria Remetich, and Antonio and Clara Grandich were "of the colored or Ethiopian Race, and therefore ineligible to enter at or attend" the city's white school. The trustees determined in this meeting that, in fact, the children were members of the "colored race." They therefore ordered the superintendent to refuse them admission to school.[70] Such a practice was not unusual. As one historian explains, "All it took for a family's children to be barred from the white school was for one neighbor to charge another with having 'negro blood.'"[71]

The measure targeted only four of the six couples that had been investigated for adultery. The other two did not have children in the white school. Lena and Willis Fulton had only recently been married, and the Pouyadou children were consistently classified as "mulatto" in the census and likely attended the segregated Black school.[72] Their oldest daughter, Hazel, had been noted as "colored" when she received her First Communion at Our Lady of the Gulf the previous June.[73] In contrast, the children of the Grandich, Brighenti, Remetich, and Melito families had always attended the white school.

Antonio and Clara were horrified by this development. It was one thing to attack their marriage, but now local officials were targeting their children. The Grandiches considered themselves and their daughters to be white people—they were not, in their own view, "colored." Their daughters Cora, Grace, Antonia, and Catherine belonged in the white school. They decided to pursue every legal avenue available to them to ensure that the girls would be readmitted to their school—a process that would take years, ending with a ruling from the Mississippi Supreme Court.

The Grandiches hired an attorney from Gulfport, George Dodds, to represent them in their lawsuit against the school trustees. Dodds filed a petition for a writ of mandamus, a court order that compels a public official to do something—in this case, they wished the court to require the superintendent to readmit the girls to the white school. In October 1914, a local jury found against the Grandich family and for the trustees, who argued that Christiana, "the wife of Victor Jourdan, a white man living in St. James, La., and great-grandmother of the children in question, was a full-blooded negro woman."[74] But the circuit court judge, Joseph I. Ballenger, set aside the verdict and ordered a new trial.

The Grandiches now hired a new lawyer, J. A. Leathers, who filed another petition for a writ of mandamus in 1915. Although the Grandiches were the principal plaintiffs, George and Victoria Remetich served as sureties in the suit. Each of the four families held a shared interest in the outcome of the case: if the Grandiches prevailed, it was likely the other children would also be allowed back into the white school. In the petition, the Grandiches made a forceful argument that denied any African ancestry. The children "were all white," although the petition conceded that they might have "a slight strain of the Indian or red race in their veins." The school trustees' order banishing the Grandich girls from the white schools caused "them irreparable damage" and subjected "them and their children to the humiliation and disgrace of being classed and looked upon as members of the colored race without any of the rights and standing to which the white race and their children are entitled under the Laws and customs of the State of Mississippi."[75]

Four days before the term of court was set to begin on the first Monday of October 1915, a Category Four hurricane made landfall at Grand Isle, Louisiana, and traveled north through New Orleans, sending damaging winds and devastating storm surges flooding through Gulf Coast communities. Nearly all the homes and buildings in Grand Isle were destroyed, and a twelve-foot storm surge flooded through Bay St. Louis.[76] Hundreds of people died, though the toll could have been much higher:

the United States Weather Bureau in New Orleans used its nascent storm prediction methods to send boats out to warn residents of the danger.[77] Court finally resumed three weeks later, and the judge permitted the lawsuit to proceed. At the next term of the circuit court in March 1916, the case was heard before Judge James H. Neville and a jury of twelve white men. All of the evidence that was presented concerned the racial identity of a woman who had been dead for six decades and had never set foot in Hancock County: Clara's grandmother, Christiana Jourdan.

The Covacevich women wanted to tell their own story. Clara's mother, Louisa, was first to take the stand. Clara and Antonio's lawyer politely asked Louisa to remove her bonnet, explaining that he wanted the jury to be able to hear her more clearly. But, of course, the bonnet did not cover Louisa's mouth—it was tied around her hair. The jury, the lawyer hoped, would notice its texture: something he was sure would make her whiteness obvious. Such tactics were commonly used when a person's racial identity was contested in court, because it encouraged the jury to rely on their own perceptions rather than other, possibly inconvenient, evidence.[78] Louisa Covacevich's body was as much the subject of her testimony as her memories were, which was key to the Grandiches' case, as it quickly became clear that Louisa knew very little about her own family history. But what she did know, she told the jury, was that she had Native American ancestry. She was not Black.

Louisa testified that she had been born to Victor and Christiana Jourdan in St. James Parish, Louisiana. The Jourdans had had twelve children, Louisa said, and she was the baby. When asked about the color of her mother's skin, she testified that she could not remember; her mother, Christiana, had died when Louisa was only two years old. But she knew that her father was French and her mother was "Indian." She knew little of her mother's family, only of an uncle named Baptiste; she knew him to be "pure Indian" because he "never wore pants"—only a strip of deer hide. The lawyer asked Louisa to show the jury her ankles so that they might inspect the hue of her skin. Louisa played up her supposed Native heritage, explaining that in her youth, "I exposed my skin by having a good time by sporting, shooting and hunting, and that is the reason I am skinned up and brown like I am today." Louisa then spoke directly to the jury, explaining, "Now, gentlemen, look . . . a white person can be exposed to the weather and get tanned so much as I do." (The lawyer gently chided his witness, reminding her not to "argue the case.")[79] But she had made her point: the proof of her heritage was right before their eyes. The school board's lawyer was incredulous. At the previous trial, Louisa had testified that she had no knowledge of any of her relatives, and she had certainly made no mention of an "Indian" named Baptiste. Louisa clarified that a childhood friend had explained the relation to her in the time since the trial. "I knew not at the time but I know now," she told the jury.[80]

Clara Grandich testified next. During her testimony, Antonio sat in the audience with the couple's two youngest daughters. Clara pointed her family out to the jury, ensuring that the jurors would see the girls with their own eyes. She explained that her husband was a white man from Austria and that the couple had been married "as white people" before a justice of the peace in Hancock County. Their older children had all attended the white school in town. It was only the younger children who were turned away.[81] The consensus of the community, she implied, had *always* been that Clara and her children were white people.

The school board's lawyer declined to interrogate Clara and chose instead to press Louisa on the story she had told about her past. He recalled Louisa to the stand and quizzed her about her sisters—a tactic that forced her to admit that she had relatives on the other side of the color line. Two of her sisters had married "colored men." Clara's lawyer, on cross-examination, sought to deflect concern about Louisa's ancestry by setting the blame for her sisters' marriages on her father. As he put it, "Were you in any way responsible for your sister having married a negro?" No, she was not responsible for this breach of the color line, she responded, explaining that, instead, "My father was."[82]

Determined to offer up proof that the Grandich girls had African ancestry, the attorney for the trustees, E. H. Gex, traveled to St. James Parish, Louisiana, to find people who had once known Christiana and would testify about her past. He returned with a pile of depositions.

St. James Parish straddles the Mississippi River upstream from New Orleans. The rich soil made the plantations some of the top sugar producers in the state. Celine Clouatre, who also grew up in St. James Parish, explained that she had seen but never spoken to Christiana Jourdan, but she remembered her as a woman whose skin was "very dark" and who wore her hair tied up in a handkerchief. Christiana was, Celine thought, "more a colored than a white woman."[83] At the same time, Celine acknowledged that the community had recognized Christiana as Victor's wife. Lucien Thibodaux, a peddler from St. James Parish who had occasionally sold his wares at the Jourdan plantation, explained that Christiana was a "colored" woman "who pretended to be the wife of Victor Jourdan." He labeled her a "griff," a term for a person of mixed white and African ancestry.[84] Another white man from the parish, Camille Blouin, also testified that he understood that Christiana was a "colored" woman, as her skin was the hue of a "gingy cake."[85] Camille explained that he knew that Christiana was considered to be "colored" because the church was segregated, and she and her daughters sat on the Black side (Victor did not attend Mass).[86] The lawyers also deposed a man who had been enslaved by Victor Jourdan, Nora Francoise, who had been born in 1843, just a few years before Louisa's birth. Christiana was Black, he explained, but her skin was "a little lighter than 'gingy cake' color," and she had "straight hair hanging down her back."[87]

The trustees' lawyer was determined to have as many people as he could, both white and Black, state on the record that Christiana was Black. The lawyer for the Grandiches, in contrast, did not seem terribly concerned with descriptions of Christiana's color. He focused instead on the ambiguities—her skin tone, whether her hair was straight, whether the witnesses knew that Native Americans lived in the woods near the plantations of St. James Parish. He banked on the jurors questioning, either implicitly or explicitly, whether one could really know Christiana's ancestry. Curiously, neither the lawyers nor the people they questioned seemed concerned with whether Christiana was enslaved.

And other residents of St. James Parish stated in their depositions that Christiana was not considered "colored." A white woman, Marguerette

Robinson, had been raised in New Orleans but spent each summer in St. James Parish, where she had met Christiana and her children. Marguerette explained that she had first seen Christiana when two of the Jourdan children received their First Communion. Christiana, she explained, was an "Indian woman." Her father was Baptiste Sauvage—a notable difference from Louisa's testimony, which identified Baptiste as her uncle.[88] (She clarified that she knew he was "pure Indian" because he had long black hair and wore only a shirt, "never pants.") Christiana had straight "dove black" hair and "red" skin, Marguerette recalled. The Jourdans owned slaves; Christiana and her children lived in the house, where servants and enslaved women tended to their needs. Christiana had died when Marguerette was still a child, perhaps nine or ten years old, in 1852 or 1853.[89] Her mother, she said, had attended the funeral. Although the school trustees' attorney repeatedly implied that someone had bribed Marguerette into giving this testimony, her responses revealed an intimate knowledge of the plantations of St. James Parish in the years preceding the Civil War. She identified the Jourdan plantation as lying between those owned by Francois Bourgeois and those owned by Leon Arseneaux, which the census confirms. (Although Victor is identified in the census, Christiana is not listed among the people who lived in his home.)[90]

Jules Dugas, who had also grown up in St. James Parish, gave a deposition in the case. Jules had been born free before the Civil War, the child of a white father and a Black mother. Speaking about his youth, he said, "I did not think I was colored at that time, because I was raised in the white folks house."[91] Jules also remembered Victor and Christiana Jourdan, and in his recollection, Baptiste Sauvage had been Christiana's uncle—not her father—though Baptiste visited the Jourdan plantation often.[92] Dugas noted that he knew that Christiana was a "pure Indian" woman by the marks on her skin: she had a thin blue tattoo on her face and another on her wrist, which looked like they had been drawn by a pencil, and she wore a ring in her nose.[93]

The depositions from St. James Parish both helped and hurt the trustees' case that the Grandich girls were "colored." Many of the witnesses recalled that Christiana was a "colored" woman, but they also all testified to her light complexion, which suggested that she also had white ancestry. Christiana was not a "full blooded negro," as the trustees had alleged. Even if the jurors believed these witnesses and agreed that Christiana was "colored," extending the logic of the 1890 constitution to her grandchildren created a new problem: the blood quantum. The color line in Mississippi was detailed only in the marriage law, which drew the line between white and Black at one-eighth blood quantum. How much African ancestry the girls had made for impossible racial arithmetic.

One might assume that the jurors would not care about the actual answer, perhaps believing that any African ancestry was evidence of a person's inherent Blackness. A history of an enslaved woman bearing the children of a white slaveholder certainly would not have surprised them. This was the story of so many Black women in the South. Indeed, Christiana's husband probably did enslave her. Even if he treated her as his wife, if she was enslaved they could not have been legally married. Their children had lived through the transition from slavery to freedom, and when Christiana's daughter married a white immigrant from Austria in the 1870s, their union was legal regardless of whether the bride had African ancestry. Even after the legislature passed a ban on interracial marriage in 1880, the law only prohibited the intermarriages of white people with persons who had "one fourth" blood quantum of African ancestry, allowing women like Louisa to claim legal whiteness. In either case, it does not appear that anyone had challenged the legitimacy of Louisa's marriage in the nineteenth century. With each successive generation, Christiana's daughters and granddaughters became more distant from their African forebears, a break made starker when Christiana died while Louisa was so young. Louisa never had the chance to ask her mother about her parents or her past. To calculate such blood quantums in court, a person needed to know a history that was, quite simply, unknowable.

But, of course, Mississippi's color line pretended that such calculations could be made. That somehow, people alive in the present could identify the parentage of people born three generations before them, including babies born enslaved, so many of whom had white paternity. Knowledge of these things was most often passed down through families, seldom leaving a written record. The census did not even bother to record the first names of adults who were enslaved, much less provide details about their family ties. If court officials wanted to enforce the blood quantum system, they faced a difficult task if jurors expressed any skepticism. Christiana, by many accounts of people who knew her, had mixed ancestry. Her daughter Louisa also had a white father, as did her granddaughter Clara. Even by the testimony of the trustees' own witnesses, the daughters of Antonio and Clara fell below the one-eighth quantum. If the court applied the legal rule, the girls were legally white—or at least white enough to marry another white person. Their appearance, too, suggested their whiteness, raising the barrier to certainty even further.

The jurors sided with Antonio and Clara. The girls were white. Perhaps they were persuaded by their appearances. Or perhaps they felt there was enough doubt about Christiana's parentage to let the past lie. The Grandiches considered themselves to be white people, and they rejected a notion of one-drop racial inheritance. The jurors may have been further troubled by scrutinizing the family's past so closely. After all, there were many other families like the Grandiches in Bay St. Louis. Ruling against the whiteness of one family might open questions about other people on that side of the color line, inviting unwanted scrutiny of family trees. The court issued the writ, forcing the superintendent to readmit the Grandich girls to the white school.[94]

WITHIN DAYS, THE TRUSTEES FILED AN APPEAL TO THE MISSISSIPPI Supreme Court, which the court agreed to hear. Their appeal ignored the racial math imposed by the state constitution. Instead, it argued that "as a result of the alleged negro blood in Christina [*sic*] the Great Grandmother of the Grandich children, . . . the Grandich children are of the African or colored race, and that therefore they are not entitled under the constitution and laws of this state to admission to the white public schools."[95] The appeal suggested that a different rule might be applied to school attendance—one that was stricter than the marriage law. The case presented a fraught question: Could a white couple have Black children? Was it possible for a person to be too Black to attend a white school, but eligible to marry another white person? It strained the logic of racial segregation to grant as much. And yet the Grandich case turned upon such determinations of race, blood, and descent.

The state supreme court's ruling in *Moreau v. Grandich* sought to put these questions to rest. On the inheritability of Blackness, the justices looked next door for guidance from the Louisiana state courts. In 1909, that court had issued a ruling in which it attempted to clearly define each racial category, from "Negro" to "mulatto," "griff," and "octoroon." The court ruled that a person might not appear to be a "negro" but could still be "colored." It was not simply skin color or hair texture or the shape of one's nose that determined race. Instead, to be Black was to be descended—no matter how distantly—from someone who had African ancestry. And for such people, who might not be classed as "negroes," there was a meaningful term to describe this racial category. As the Louisiana court ruled in *State v. Treadway*, "That word is the word 'colored.' The word 'colored,' when used to designate the race of a person, is unmistakable, at least in the United States. It means a person of negro blood pure or mixed; and the term applies no matter what may be the proportions of the admixture, so long as the negro blood is traceable."[96]

"Traceable" did impressive work here. It lifted the burden of proving that race was in any meaningful sense determined by appearances. Skin color did not matter. Instead, it was any ancestry that could be "traced." With its borrowing from *Treadway*, the Mississippi Supreme Court moved to adopt a "one-drop" rule of African racial inheritance. It did not matter how many white ancestors a person had, so long as there was traceable Black ancestry. The Grandich children were legally Black. They could not attend the white school. The ruling made no determination, however, about the legality of their parents' marriage.[97]

THE GRANDICH FAMILY LEFT BAY ST. LOUIS IN THE AFTERMATH OF the state supreme court's ruling. Antonio's health had declined in recent years, and he died on April 9, 1918. He was buried in Cedar Rest Cemetery in Bay St. Louis, just blocks from the Gulf of Mexico.[98] His widow and daughters moved to New Orleans, where they lived in a house on Broad Street in the Seventh Ward. Four of the older girls found work in a confectionary. Cora and Grace worked as clerks, while their younger sisters Antonia and Catherine wrapped candies. Louise, their older sister, worked as a maid.[99]

Regardless of the Mississippi Supreme Court's declaration that the Grandich girls were Black, they identified as white women the rest of their lives. The oldest of Clara and Antonio's daughters, Margaret, married a white man, Warren Cobb, in the early 1910s. By 1920, the couple and their two daughters lived in a small Seventh Ward home a few blocks from Margaret's mother and sisters.[100] Rita, the second oldest, also married a white man. Her husband, Julius Davis, worked as a dock foreman for Standard Oil in Baton Rouge. The couple took in boarders while Rita raised their daughters.[101]

Many of the descendants of these families left Bay St. Louis for places where their ancestry would not be known. The Melitos left for Los Angeles, where Sam continued to work as a grocer, selling fruits and vegetables. Their daughters married, and the Melito family grew to include grandchildren. Sam died in October 1945, just a month after the Japanese surrender ended World War II. He and Georgeann had been married for fifty-six years despite the best efforts of Mississippi officials. Georgeann outlived her husband by nearly three decades, and she died on July 4, 1973. They left their difficult past behind in Mississippi. Their grandchildren knew nothing of the story of their past or about Georgeann's contested racial identity in their lifetimes.[102]

Some members of the Covacevich family stayed. Ildebrandi and Mary Brighenti remained in Bay St. Louis after their children were excluded from the white school. They remained married, and the census in 1920 identifies them as an interracial couple. All their children are identified as "mulatto."[103] This did not prevent them, too, from crossing the color line. The Brighentis' daughter Helen married a white man in New Orleans.[104] By 1940, she had divorced and returned to Bay St. Louis.[105] Helen worked as a forewoman in a Works Progress Administration sewing room, and she shared a home with her grandmother Louisa Covacevich.[106] Louisa, Helen, and everyone else in the house was identified racially as white in 1940. Officials in Bay St. Louis tried to impose a sense of racial order on the city's residents for decades but never completely succeeded in their quest. Although they targeted individual couples, their ultimate purpose was to correct a whole community that, they believed, had allowed people to cross the color line with impunity for far too long. But even with their various bureaucratic and legal tools, they could not erase the long history of interracial marriage, nor could they resolve the racial ambiguities that endured through the generations.

CHAPTER 6

MYTHS OF RACIAL INTEGRITY

RALPHINE AND WILLIAM

World War I veterans returned home to a nation convulsed by its own internal battles. The Red Summer of 1919 witnessed dozens of brutal episodes of mob violence. The bloodiest incident took place near the Arkansas Delta town of Elaine, where a shootout between hostile whites and attendees of a Black sharecroppers meeting sparked rumors that Black men planned to murder white plantation owners. White men and federal troops flooded into the area, where they massacred Black residents, killing perhaps hundreds of people.[1] In many cities, strikes gripped industries as workers embraced militant action. Meanwhile, the influenza pandemic was still sweeping through communities.[2] In the Mississippi Delta, the boll weevil decimated cotton crops.[3] Amid this tumult, the Second Ku Klux Klan grew in strength and influence, calling its followers to defend the nation against the threat of "mongrelization" with its battle cry of "one hundred percent Americanism." The organization's revival was bolstered nationally by the popularity of eugenics ideology, which provided a fatally flawed path toward a better, supposedly "healthier" society. It offered scientific solutions to the problems of poverty that plagued the South. Eugenics ideas infused political debate, bridging older notions of scientific racism with the modern era of segregation.[4]

The growing popularity of eugenics marked another struggle in the efforts of white supremacists to enforce the color line. The reality of life for ordinary Mississippians, however, reveals just how difficult this struggle remained into the 1920s. White men and Black women continued to cohabit in communities across the state. Interracial cohabitation continued to serve as a point of public debate and political concern. Even as they flogged the myth of white "racial purity," white politicians, judges, and juries grappled with the long-standing practice of white men believing they had the right to govern their own private lives. Into the 1920s, the legal regime of Jim Crow generated political and legal debates about race, marriage, and family that remained unsettled even in a decade better remembered for the triumph of eugenics policies and the resurgence of the Ku Klux Klan.

A KEY STUMBLING BLOCK TO WHITE SUPREMACIST CAMPAIGNS TO EFFECtively enforce anti-miscegenation laws was the law itself. In the 1920s, the old statutes remained on the books: the one-eighth rule of Black racial inheritance allowed for some people with African ancestry to legally marry whites, and unlawful cohabitation remained a misdemeanor offense. The Mississippi Supreme Court's decision in *Moreau v. Grandich* confused rather than clarified the color line. It applied the one-drop rule for school attendance even as the state's constitution and legislation continued to rely on the one-eighth rule for marriage. And the court's ruling in *Moreau* would not enforce itself.

The one-drop rule was always a white supremacist fantasy, but it was a useful one for segregationists. For those who favored hard racial categories and were looking to bolster their argument that segregation was beneficial to all peoples, the pseudoscience of eugenics offered a bounty of justifications. Lothrop Stoddard, an American eugenicist with a Harvard PhD who styled himself an expert on race and civilization, wrote books that became pillars of white supremacist eugenics thought. His 1921 book, *The Rising Tide of Color*, celebrated the conquest of Asia, Africa, the Americas, and Australia by European and American colonizers, demarcating white "political rule" over nine-tenths of the globe from the "rising tide" of people of color. World War I was Stoddard's modern "Peloponnesian War," a conflict that risked the survival of white civilization by pitting European nations against one another.[5]

Stoddard wrote extensively on eugenics theories; he also allegedly joined the Massachusetts Klan.[6] His books shaped the organization's intellectual justifications, lending the veneer of science to the Klan's racist principles. Stoddard's 1923 book, *The Revolt Against Civilization: The Menace of the Under-Man*, claimed that the price of allowing intermarriage would be the inevitable decline of American civilization—the most advanced the world had ever seen. Stoddard described "African negroes" as "congenital barbarians" who, as a class, were unable to independently develop or contribute to the rise of civilizations. He warned that if "interbreeding occurs" between whites and such lower races, "the racial foundations of civilization are undermined, and the mongrelized population, unable to bear the burden, sinks to a lower plane."[7] Stoddard argued that "for civilization to arise at all, a superior human stock is first necessary; while to perfect, or even to maintain that civilization, the human stock must be kept superior."[8] In other words, Americans must keep the white race "pure" or risk losing everything. It was a clarion call for extremists.

Eugenicists also created problems for the system of racial segregation. It was important that those focused singularly on the Black/white divide not read these books too deeply. Stoddard focused as much of his disdain on the "lower classes" of European immigrants as on Black people, grouping Italians, Poles, Russians, and Greeks together as "inferior" in intelligence and racial stock.[9] (The titular "revolt against civilization" in the book was the Bolshevik revolution in Russia.) In states with racial classification laws, these "undesirable" immigrants from Southern and Eastern Europe fell on the "white" side of the color line. For Stoddard and other northeastern Klansmen, the theories provided an important foundation, supporting their twin projects of immigration exclusion and racial segregation. For Mississippians, the problems were more apparent and immediate: to make whiteness meaningful, they had to draw the line somewhere.

In the view of eugenicists, the stakes of maintaining white racial purity could not have been higher. Some Mississippi politicians eagerly embraced such ideas. As James K. Vardaman wrote in *Vardaman's Weekly* in 1921, "I would rather the white race would die in one great heap than that it should pollute its blood with the dark blood of the negro."[10] Vardaman was obsessed with "amalgamation," as he called it, frequently referencing Madison Grant's 1916 book, *Passing of the Great Race*, as the authority on the "negro question."[11] Eugenics treatises were widely available to suit the cause of white supremacy.

Yet this embrace of eugenics principles could not square with reality, even in states where legal segregation was the rule. While the Klan may have captured the discourse, many white Mississippians remained ambivalent about strict enforcement of the color line. Perhaps most surprisingly, during the 1920s Mississippi's courts and legislature backed away from strict adherence to the one-drop rule. Publicly, white Mississippians shouted their dedication to white racial purity to the nation and the world. Politicians staked their claim to power on a rigorous, violent defense of segregation. Privately, however, interracial families went about their business, doing what they could to avoid attracting the harsh public gaze. And in the 1920s the profound contradictions of Jim Crow again broke through the surface. Even as the Klan and eugenicists found their devotion to the supposed cause of white racial purity embraced by politicians and ordinary people, all the challenges of enforcing racial segregation remained in place, as stubborn as ever. Not everyone was willing to let eugenics dictate their private lives— especially some white men.

EARLY ONE MORNING IN APRIL 1919, MOLLIE KEMP, A BLACK WOMAN, and J. W. Morrison, a white man, were roused from sleep by the deputy sheriff of Humphreys County.[12] Mollie and J. W. were both poor itinerant laborers. They followed the work, harvesting cotton or picking up other odd jobs in the rural Delta. Mollie hoed in the fields or worked as a cook. J. W. sometimes worked as a logger. The couple lived with Mollie's young daughter in a rented house in Belzoni, a town of 2,000 people on the Yazoo River that served as the county seat.[13] When the deputy sheriff arrived at their doorstep early that morning, J. W. claimed he needed to go get his mules, but he instead slipped away. He was finally arrested three days later.[14] J. W. posted bond for himself and for Mollie, and they were free until their trial.[15]

The indictment alleged that the couple's relationship had lasted for three years, and it accused the pair of "lewdly and unlawfully" cohabiting "in adultery."[16] Mollie and J. W. hired a local white attorney, Thornton E. Mortimer, to defend them, and the case was tried in Belzoni on May 1 before a jury of twelve white men. Numerous witnesses testified about knowing the pair, and most conceded that they often worked together and were seen in the same house. The jury found them both guilty. They were each sentenced to serve sixty days in the county jail and pay a $300 fine. Both were less than the maximum penalty available at law.[17]

Mollie's appeal, filed with the state supreme court by her lawyer John A. Sykes, rested on an important technicality. Sykes argued that the judge had improperly allowed the district attorney to cross out the words "in adultery" that followed the indictment for "unlawful cohabitation" after the trial had ended—once the district attorney realized that he had not proven in court that either J. W. or Mollie were married to other people. No witness was even *asked* during the trial about the marital status of either defendant. Seeing the problem the wording of the indictment presented, the judge simply crossed out the words, leaving only a general charge of "unlawful cohabitation." This allowed Mollie's lawyer to argue that the indictment was therefore flawed, as neither Mollie nor J. W. had a spouse. Crucially, a judge did not have the authority to modify an indictment without the approval of a grand jury. In March 1920, less than a year after their conviction, the Mississippi Supreme Court agreed with Mollie's lawyer.[18] The justices overturned her conviction for unlawful cohabitation and sent the case back to the local circuit court to determine whether the couple would be tried again.

The problem with the prosecution of Mollie Kemp was not just a matter of sloppiness—the motivation for charging the couple had never, at its heart, been about their interracial relationship. The indictment made no mention of either party's race. The charge was a pretext to the real cause of concern: a witness testified that another Black cotton worker, Jerry Lindsay, claimed that Mollie Kemp had "beat him out of his cotton" and "never settled fair and square."[19] Before Mollie and J. W. were indicted for unlawful cohabitation, Jerry had already filed suit in court alleging that Mollie owed him money.[20] Another Black man, Paul Hudson, testified that Jerry had ratted out the pair to the sheriff to pressure Mollie to settle the suit and pay him what he believed he was owed. Paul explained that Jerry had tried to press him to back his campaign against the couple. But Paul, who did not want to be involved, had told Jerry he "didn't know anything about that."[21] The indictment seems to have been less about a desire to punish the pair for their relationship than about wielding the unlawful cohabitation law to discipline Mollie Kemp for the alleged theft.

The decision by the district attorney to charge the pair does reveal an interest in enforcing the law. But the witnesses made this difficult to do. The district attorney interrogated a range of men, both Black and white, including the white owner of a cotton plantation where Mollie and J. W. sometimes worked and the white operator of a cotton mill in Belzoni. While these white witnesses were evasive about whether Mollie and J. W. slept in the same house, Jerry Lindsay insisted that he knew they cohabited. But there was a problem with Jerry's testimony—he had not actually witnessed the pair sharing a bed.[22]

Had the district attorney been motivated to do so, he could have ensured that the indictments were correct. But there was evidently not a great deal of thought put into prosecuting this relationship, even though it was a clear example of the so-called crime of "miscegenation." The white witnesses seemed particularly reluctant to tell the jury what they knew about the intimate life of J. W. Morrison, even though one of them had lived next door to Mollie for years.[23] The jury, for its part, seemed more interested in charging the pair based on their general reputation as a couple than in acknowledging the facts of the case. They felt that Mollie deserved to be punished, and the substance of her crime seemed to matter less to them than one might expect.

All these elements were familiar to observers of other unlawful cohabitation cases. Neighbors and acquaintances were often reluctant to testify about defendants' private lives. Indeed, it was often the white male witnesses who made the district attorney's job difficult. The prosecution thus followed the well-trod path of pursuing interracial couples who had lived together for years, but who then, as a consequence of some other conflict, had suddenly been put into the limelight, subject to having their personal lives scrutinized. As an exasperated circuit court judge in Vicksburg complained, "I know this practice has been going on for a long time; but continuous violation of the law does not repeal it."[24] After the state supreme court invalidated Mollie and J. W.'s conviction, Delta newspapers did not note whether the couple was tried again.

MOLLIE KEMP AND J. W. MORRISON WERE NOT THE ONLY INTERRACIAL couple prosecuted in Mississippi in the decade following World War I. The rise of the Second Ku Klux Klan and its growing influence in the early 1920s seems to have sparked a stronger interest in enforcement of the law in certain parts of the state.

The Klan was reborn in the wake of the popular 1915 silent film *Birth of a Nation*, which portrayed hooded riders as the saviors of the white South during Reconstruction. This iteration of the Klan had even vaster ambitions than the First Klan's focus on racial terror in the South.[25] In 1921 and 1922, Klaverns spread across the state. Limited to "white, Protestant men," the Second Klan's influence was far greater than the First Klan's had been during Reconstruction. It was a national phenomenon headquartered in Indiana. The Second Klan embraced the enforcement of Prohibition, condemned Catholics and immigrants as anti-American, and vilified socialists and anyone with politics that fell too far to the left.[26] Klansmen in the 1920s also targeted Black people as unequal and unfit for full citizenship and brayed about the dangers of "amalgamation," as they had during Reconstruction.

The Klan's influence was felt in Mississippi legislation that reflected a hardline public position on interracial marriage. Former Progressive governor Edmond F. Noel, who had strong support from the Klan, proposed a new law that would make it a crime to speak in favor of the legalization of interracial marriage.[27] The law sailed through both houses of the state legislature in 1920 without a single dissenting vote.[28] The current governor, Lee M. Russell, approved it on March 25, 1920.[29] In its final form, the law declared that any "person, firm, or corporation who shall be guilty of printing, publishing or circulating printed, typewritten or written matter urging or presenting for public acceptance or general information, arguments or suggestions in favor of social equality or of intermarriage between whites and negroes, shall be guilty of a misdemeanor."[30] Notably, the maximum penalty—six months in jail and a $500 fine—was the same that could be levied for unlawful cohabitation. A person who simply spoke in favor of interracial relationships could face the same punishment as J. W. Morrison and Mollie Kemp. The law made white racial purity the official position of the state government. Merely speaking about interracial relationships was as bad as actually engaging in one.

No legislator expressed concern that the law might conflict with First Amendment protections of speech and the press. Nor would the legislators have worried that the US Constitution prohibited this kind of law, despite its obvious muzzling of speech. Even Congress had passed laws blatantly infringing on First Amendment rights, restricting the speech of pacifists and socialists through the Espionage and Sedition Acts during World War I.[31] Indeed, the Mississippi law followed in a long line of state legislatures policing speech aimed at the promotion of Black rights. It was not until 1925, in *Gitlow v. New York*, that the US Supreme Court established that the First Amendment even applied to the states.[32] The Mississippi law was just one among a wave of laws restricting speech rights, including the federal wartime acts. Mississippi, for its measure, added its own sedition acts in 1920, making it a felony for any person to advocate "in print or verbally" for the "overthrow of the Constitution or government of the United States or the Constitution or the government of the state of Mississippi, by violence."[33] There was irony embedded in this law: a violent overthrow of biracial democratic rule and the suppression of Black voters had paved the way for the writing and ratification of the 1890 Mississippi constitution, a fact that delegates openly celebrated at the time.

The Klan made its messaging unavoidable. Mississippi Klaverns engaged in publicity campaigns to drum up public support, ensuring that local newspapers reported on the sums of money they donated to the needy. Each article was followed by a statement from the recipient praising the Klan for its benevolent gesture. Natchez Klan No. 2 presented $500 (though only $200 in cash and the rest a promissory note) to the repair fund for the Protestant Orphans Home.[34] The King's Daughters Home in Brookhaven received $1,000.[35] A Klavern paid the taxes of a widow in McComb.[36]

Klan members also held even more ostentatious displays of their messaging. On July 4, 1922, they paraded through the streets of Jackson. Hundreds of men marched in their white hoods, chanting, "AMERICA FOR AMERICANS," and "WE STAND FOR FREE SPEECH, FREE SCHOOLS, FREE PRESS." (We can assume their message was not in opposition to the legislature's recent work to criminalize speech endorsing "social equality" or interracial marriage.)

With or without donning white hoods, many Mississippi politicians embraced venomous language about the threat of what they called "racial amalgamation." When Congress debated the Dyer Anti-Lynching Bill in 1922, Mississippi representative John E. Rankin took the opportunity to warn that such a law would "encourage the negro brutes in their attacks on the defenseless white women of the country." The anti-lynching bill was in fact "a bill to encourage rape," he ranted, as "the shadow of the negro criminal constantly hangs . . . like the sword of Damocles over the head of every white woman in the South."[37] He praised the southern states as the "greatest bulwark of Anglo-Saxon civilization in the Western Hemisphere." Reciting the white supremacist canard that the races had always been separate, he continued, "God forbid that the line of cleavage between the white man and the negro in this country should ever be broken down! If it should be, then America, once proud America, would soon find herself sinking hopelessly into the implacable mire of mongrelization."[38]

Rankin's demagogic politics might have been useful for putting supporters of the anti-lynching bill in a defensive position—few politicians openly embrace a "pro-rape" stance—but it offered a dramatic disconnect from the lives of ordinary Mississippians, who lived in a world that was complicated by the long-standing open secret of interracial families in their midst. Rankin's emphasis on Black men conveniently avoided the fact that white men—such as J. W. Morrison—continued to cohabit with Black women in the South, frequently crossing the color line with impunity.

White Mississippians argued among themselves about the proper way to address this problem. Members of a missionary society in Hattiesburg attempted to rally support for a petition to the state legislature to elevate the penalties for unlawful cohabitation.[39] The Jackson police department announced a "crusade against unlawful cohabitation" in 1922.[40] The same year that Rankin made his abhorrent comments about rape, a circuit court judge in Lincoln County complained that "one of the most hateful things in the Southland is the cohabitation of white men with negro women." The judge lectured the impaneled grand jury because, in his view, "We lack the courage, the manhood to report it." He reminded the men that they were "under oath" and instructed them to "do our duty though the heavens fall."[41]

By 1924, the Klan was powerful enough to control the Democratic state convention held in Jackson on May 30. The influence of the White Knights was felt keenly by all attendees. The Klan met secretly the night before the convention to endorse former governor Noel as the convention's chairman, and he was elected as temporary chairman the next day on a platform of "the enforcement of all laws" and "especially the liquor laws."[42] But the Klan's influence was not unchallenged. At the convention, former US senator LeRoy Percy condemned the Klan, arguing that its supporters had expelled the delegations from the only two anti-Klan counties: Washington (Percy's home) and Warren, which included Vicksburg. Percy castigated Noel for appointing "well known" Klansmen to the committee on credentials. He proclaimed that the convention was not an exercise in democracy, but instead a "klavern of the Ku Klux Klan."[43]

Percy provided an ideal foil for the Klan. He rejected the extremism of Vardaman, who had unseated him from the US Senate in a 1912 primary election.[44] Despite their shared backgrounds from wealthy white families, Vardaman claimed the mantle of populism while painting Percy as an elite who was overly accommodating to Black people. Percy was in many ways emblematic of the paternalist racism that infused the so-called "Bourbon" politics that dominated the Delta counties, which had Black majorities but where whites controlled most of the land and wealth. Percy's stance was not hardline enough for some white supremacists. To make matters worse, his wife was Catholic.[45] Percy was exactly the kind of politician that Klan members loathed: he was allegedly overly indulgent of Black people, insufficiently vocally racist, and held questionable moral positions. Klan members believed Percy and his ilk had too much influence in state politics. In the early 1920s, they seemed poised to claim victory.

THE KLAN HAD A VISION OF MISSISSIPPI THAT, IF PUT INTO ACTION, would require a stark departure from the state's complicated racial history. The same spring that the Klan wrested control over the state Democratic convention, the Adams County Circuit Court in Natchez again became a focal point of the long-standing battle for white men to assert their right to choose their own partners, regardless of racial classification.

From the spring of 1924 until the spring of 1925, grand juries indicted a dozen interracial couples. Judge Robert L. Corban presided over the Adams County Circuit Court with R. E. Bennett serving as the district attorney. Charges began rolling out in April, as the grand jury, made up of nineteen white men, issued a lengthy list of indictments. They heard testimony from 125 witnesses over a week, taking a special interest in vice crimes. The *Natchez Democrat* reported on the grand jury's work in euphemistic terms, noting, "Certain alleged offenses against the moral code which heretofore have been passed up on account of evidence being more or less based on suspicion have been investigated and indictments returned."[46] While politicians like Rankin blustered about the alleged crimes of Black men, the newspapers handled the indictments in Adams County with considerably more delicacy. It referred to the cases as "unlawful cohabitation" charges and made no reference to the vastly more inflammatory term of "miscegenation." All the accused men in these cases were white and all the women were Black.

These indictments seemed to reflect the political climate of the state and the influence of the Klan. Morals offenses such as bootlegging, gambling, and interracial cohabitation once again intensely aroused the interest of the court, as happened during the Progressive Era. The indictments issued by the grand jury were mostly for morals offenses—especially liquor violations and interracial cohabitation—though there were also a smattering of charges of other crimes, including embezzlement, burglary, and assault. Most of the jury's work that session was in trying and convicting people for liquor-related offenses. Four people were fined for possessing illegal stills, while seven received jail sentences for possessing alcohol.[47]

Fritz Meyer and Ella Ford were among the first couples indicted for unlawful cohabitation.[48] The indictment alleged that "Fritz Meyer, a man, and Ella Ford, a woman, late of the County on the 24th day of March 1924 . . . did willfully, lewdly, and unlawfully cohabit together, and have habitual sexual intercourse with each other . . . the said Fritz Meyer and Ella Ford not being then and there lawfully married to each other."[49] Notably, the indictment did not say anything about Fritz, a German immigrant, and Ella, a Black woman, being an interracial couple. Instead, as in the prosecution of J. W. Morrison and Mollie Kemp, it focused on the fact that they were unmarried.

The district attorney subpoenaed three witnesses to testify before the grand jury. Two of the witnesses were white: William Wilson and his son, Otis, lived on a farm down Liberty Road from Fritz and Ella's home. Tom Hays, a Black farmer, also lived nearby. Christian Meyer—probably Fritz's brother, as they were both born in Germany—also lived nearby. Fritz and Ella had lived together for at least four years by the time they were arrested. The 1920 census captured the pair living together in a house on a farm in rural Adams County owned by Ella Ford, where Fritz is identified as her "boarder."[50] If there was more to the relationship than this, the census does not say. The district attorney believed that Fritz was more than just a renter on Ella's property. The pair pled not guilty.[51]

Ella and Fritz were not cowed by the indictment. Instead, they fought back, hiring two local white lawyers, Charles Engle and Ernest Brown. The attorneys presented a demurrer that protested the indictments on behalf of all the couples charged with unlawful cohabitation, focusing on the sort of evidence required by law. They objected to the nature of the charge, noting that the indictments failed to identify whether the unlawful cohabitation had occurred in "adultery or fornication," and also noted that "the crime charged in the indictment is one of which time is of the essence." Without proof that the cohabitation was "habitual," the couples could not properly be charged under the law.[52]

In a surprising move, Judge Corban agreed with the defendants' attorneys, effectively dropping the unlawful cohabitation charges against some of the couples indicted by the grand jury.[53] But the district attorney, Bennett, was not prepared to allow Fritz and Ella to go free. He filed an appeal on the ruling with the Mississippi Supreme Court.[54]

The Mississippi Supreme Court agreed to hear the case of *State v. Meyer and Ford*. In their brief to the court, Fritz and Ella's lawyers argued that the indictment alleged that the couple cohabited and had illicit sexual intercourse on only one day: March 24, 1924. Previous cases made it clear that for cohabitation to be unlawful, it had to be sustained over a longer period of time. An unmarried couple engaging in sexual intercourse for a single day—even if the man was white and the woman was Black—did not constitute unlawful cohabitation as Mississippi courts had long interpreted it. The state still lacked a fornication law that would make any form of interracial sex illegal. The indictment "charges a condition that is impossible in fact," the brief argued.[55] "This court has always held that to constitute the offense, the habitual sexual intercourse must extend over or through a specified period of time, that is for some months, weeks or at least some days."[56]

In its ruling in *Meyer*, the state supreme court made an important change in how it would interpret the offense of unlawful cohabitation. The justices declared that time was *not* "of the essence" and the indictment's failure to identify an extended time period of "habitual sexual intercourse" was not fatal to the case.[57] Ella Ford and Fritz Meyer would have to face the charges. Fritz eventually pled no contest. The court assessed him a $50 fine, but he was not sentenced to serve any time in jail.[58]

Ralphine Burns and William Dean—called "Willie" in the indictment—were tried on November 19, 1924. Three witnesses testified: two white carpenters, Joseph S. Burns (no relation to Ralphine) and William Bennett, and one of Ralphine's neighbors, a Black woman named Susannah House.[59] Susannah was combative in her testimony, refusing to testify that she knew Ralphine was Black. When asked about the race of Ralphine and William's children, she testified that the children were as "white as the district attorney."[60] Ralphine's children were fair; her son, Clarence, was a redhead. But Ralphine's family had roots in the antebellum free Black population of Natchez, so her ancestry was not buried very deep. The jury of twelve white men heard the case and judged the pair to be guilty on the same day.[61]

The trial of Ralphine and William likely influenced the other couples charged. Several pled no contest and received fines. Peter Burns and Lizzie Stampley, who had a yearslong relationship that produced two sons, also pled guilty.[62] Peter paid a $100 fine; Lizzie was fined only $25.[63] Neither faced any jail time. Peter and Ralphine were not related, but they may have known one another. In 1880, a four-year-old Peter had lived in his father's boardinghouse just a few doors down on Pine Street from the home of Ralphine's father, William Burns Sr.[64]

When the court convened for the spring term in March 1925, it went to work resolving the final cases from the year before. J. M. Crawford and Millie Brooks had their charges dropped.[65] On April 3, 1925, the district attorney dropped the charges against seven more people, including Seaman Zerkowsky and Mattie Holmes.[66] As in 1909, the enthusiasm for prosecuting interracial couples eventually faltered, and the court moved on to other business.

RALPHINE BURNS AND WILLIAM DEAN CHALLENGED THEIR CONVICtions, contending that the state had not proved that they were unmarried. Of course, the district attorney probably assumed that he need not make such a case: it was obvious to the jury that all of these couples were being tried because the women were Black and the men were white. They could not legally marry in Mississippi.

Or could they? The lawyers for Ralphine and William raised two important points for their brief in the appeal: that the state had not demonstrated that the pair was not married, and that the state had not demonstrated that Ralphine was legally Black. "This fact was nowhere proven by the district attorney or attempted to be proven," the brief explained. "It is a fact that cannot be proven by mere profert for the reason that the shades of color vary so among different members of the white race that one cannot distinguish the race under certain circumstances and with certain individuals."[67] In other words, the district attorney could not simply assert that Ralphine was Black. He needed to prove it with evidence.

And the Mississippi assistant attorney general, Harry M. Bryan, agreed with Ralphine and William's lawyers. As Bryan explained in the state's brief to the court, "We reluctantly believe that the record does not show that the charge of the indictment was fully sustained."[68] He continued, "It is only by inference that it could be concluded that one of the parties was white and the other a negro. This being true, we cannot adopt a miscegenation theory which would relieve the state from actually proving that they were not married." This argument is instructive. Although the unlawful cohabitation law was race-neutral, Bryan's argument effectively said what many people knew: it was used to target interracial couples. But if the district attorney had not shown that Ralphine was Black, a key element necessary to convict her was missing. This might have been obvious to the jurors, but it was not a clear part of the trial record. Without this evidence, *because* they openly cohabited and had a large family, Ralphine and William's relationship was arguably a marriage.

On June 1, 1925, the Mississippi Supreme Court overturned Ralphine and William's convictions. The ruling rested on the basis that the state had not proven Ralphine's Blackness as a fact. Susannah House's testimony was cited as evidence of Ralphine's possible whiteness or—at the very least—her racial ambiguity. In short, at the trial, "there was a total failure to prove that the woman was of other than the white race." Altogether, the court wrote, "There is not one scintilla of evidence tending to prove that these defendants were not married to each other." Instead, "on the contrary, the circumstances, declarations, and actions of these parties come dangerously close to establishing a common-law marriage."[69] The Mississippi Supreme Court stopped short of declaring that Ralphine and William's relationship was a legal marriage, but the ruling implied as much, sending the case back down to Adams County Circuit Court.

If he wished to do so, the district attorney could have tried Ralphine and William again, but there is no evidence that he did. There were no further charges of unlawful cohabitation in the following years.[70]

THE STATE LEGISLATURE WAS WELL AWARE OF THE PROBLEMS THE ONE-eighth rule was causing for prosecutors. Just one year after the Mississippi Supreme Court had vacated Ralphine and William's conviction, members of the legislature moved to address the blood quantum problem of the state marriage law. If the state continued to rely on the one-eighth rule of racial inheritance, people like Ralphine Burns—not to mention the mixed families of Bay St. Louis—could use their racial ambiguity to their advantage. Some members of the legislature demanded a far stricter definition of whiteness.

For guidance, they looked to other states. A different standard was championed by eugenicists in Virginia, which had now adopted its infamous 1924 Racial Integrity Act. This law employed the so-called one-drop rule of racial inheritance, declaring that any African ancestry made a person Black, regardless of skin color. The Virginia law aimed to be as stringent as possible. Lawmakers in other states could follow along, close the blood quantum loophole, and make the one-drop rule the new standard. Theoretically, this rule could further empower anti-miscegenationists to target those individuals whose ancestry was the subject of whispers and rumor. The law was paired with another law engineered by eugenicists to test the legality of forced sterilization of the "feebleminded." Together, these two laws put Virginia at the vanguard of state efforts to legislate race and sex in ways that would promote and protect "white civilization."[71]

On the first day of the state legislative session in January 1926, Representative Bernard Guion of Yazoo County introduced a new law that mirrored the Virginia Racial Integrity Act, redefining whiteness according to a strict one-drop rule.[72] The Virginia law was not written by the Klan. Instead, it was drawn up by white elites who argued that racial science could solve the "race problem" once and for all. Before 1910, Virginia's blood quantum law had been more liberal than Mississippi's, using the "one quarter" rule for Blackness; the law had then been revised to define anyone with more than one-sixteenth blood quantum of African ancestry as Black. The new Virginia law went even further: a "trace" of Black blood defined a person's race. As John Powell, a founder of the Anglo-Saxon Clubs of America, explained, "One drop of Negro blood makes the Negro."[73]

Unlike the Mississippi state constitution, which had proved so problematic with its one-eighth rule, Guion's proposed law would expressly prohibit marriage "between a white person and anyone other than a white person, or a person with no other mixture of blood than white and the American Indian." A white person could have "no trace whatsoever of any blood other than Caucasian." White persons could, however, have a "trace" of Indian ancestry and retain their whiteness. The law also set the blood quantum of American Indian ancestry at one-sixteenth, just as the Virginia law had done.[74] This so-called Pocahontas exception protected some of the wealthy and influential descendants of Pocahontas's marriage to John Rolfe from being classified as anything other than "white."[75]

Guion's measure had the backing of Mississippi governor Henry Whitfield, who expressed support for the bill in his message to the state legislature in February 1926. Whitfield alluded not only to the existence of interracial sex in his address but also to the problem of the color line and the racial indeterminacy of people of mixed descent, making oblique reference to the both the *Moreau v. Grandich* and *Dean v. State* cases. Whitfield declared, "Within recent years in operation of school lands, in questions of descent and marriage, this problem has become a complex one in the state. In my opinion the barriers should be so clearly defined that no court or executive officer could make any mistake in formulating an opinion or making a decree in any question arising where mixed blood of an individual might constitute a legal question." In his view, the law should resolve any uncertainty. As he explained, "There is a [solemn] duty that the white race owes to itself to preserve its blood in its strictest integrity."[76]

But Whitfield was careful to couch his concerns in rhetoric about the threat of outsiders. He explained that it was not "native Mississippians" who threatened the color line. Rather, it was "people of all races" who could come to Mississippi, bringing their dangerous ideas about interracial marriage with them. In other words, immigrants threatened the state's racial order. As Whitfield explained, "Many of these will not have the racial ideas that native Mississippians have and if some precaution is not taken to prevent it there is a danger that to some extent racial barriers may be broken down."[77]

Whitfield's speech went even further than the text of the law. He raised the issue that had long helped create problems in the enforcement of the unlawful cohabitation law: the state still lacked a law specifically criminalizing interracial sex. Whitfield declared, "I further recommend that a law be enacted visiting severe penalties on any white person who indulges in any sex relation with a member of the colored race." It was here that he finally gestured toward concerns about the predilections of the state's white men. "We have emphatically stated to the negro race that they must remain on their side of the social line," he said. "I think we ought to state with equal emphasis that white men would not cross the line into the negro domain."[78] The issue of interracial sex, however, proved to be less popular with legislators than the proposed marriage law. Despite Whitfield's endorsement, the legislature did not even consider a law prohibiting interracial sex during its session in 1926.

Like many of his predecessors, Whitfield blamed white men for breaching the color line. He lamented, "Much of the trouble which we have in the state of Mississippi between the races results from the utter disregard that a certain element of white men have for negro women, and I hope the legislature will enact legislation that will as far as possible prevent low grade white men from disregarding the rules of virtue and violating the sanctity of the race."[79]

Whitfield's words did not go unnoticed outside the state. Indeed, the *Chicago Defender* printed the text of his entire speech, calling it "one of the most sensational confessions ever made by the chief executive of a state."[80] Two key things connected Black Mississippians to their friends and family who fled north: the Illinois Central Railroad and the Chicago *Defender*. The *Defender*, though published in Chicago, was a lifeline between Black people in Mississippi and in Illinois.[81] Its editors crowed over the governor's admission that white supremacy was rife with hypocrisy, and white so-called racial integrity a farce. But despite the rise of the Second Ku Klux Klan, and despite the problems of enforcement presented in the Natchez cases, Guion's "racial integrity" bill did not pass. The legislature declined to adopt the one-drop rule and instead kept the old marriage law in place.

The state legislature did not record most of the verbal debates over proposed laws, so we cannot know precisely what motivated all opposition to the one-drop rule. But there is one piece of evidence that indicates that some members felt uncomfortable with the potential consequences of classifying *anyone* with African ancestry as Black. Representative Gideon Brown of Jasper County was the sole member of the legislature who put his opposition to the racial integrity law on the record. Brown was a lawyer in the small town of Bay Springs, so perhaps he was more attuned to the specificities of law and potential problems of enforcement than his colleagues.

Brown's vote was not symbolic, he explained. Instead, he was concerned with the consequences for other white people of moving the color line so dramatically. For him, it was personal. "Mr. Speaker," Brown explained, "I voted against this Bill for the reason, in my opinion, it divorces my wife from me without any court decree, from a court, competent to grant divorces, and without legal cause or any other cause."[82] It seems that Brown believed that either he or his wife had African ancestry, even though they were both legally white. And he was not afraid to admit as much before his colleagues in the Mississippi House of Representatives.

At the time of the debate over the racial integrity bill, Gideon Brown was in his fifties. He had been married for decades to his wife, Emma. Gideon and Emma Brown were both identified as white people in the 1920 census.[83] Indeed, Emma had always been identified as white whenever the census-taker had arrived at her door. When she died in 1951, the *Clarion-Ledger* ran a brief obituary—an honor reserved for white people.[84] Gideon and Emma had been married for more than thirty-five years. Both had been raised in Jasper County—a rural part of the state east of Jackson that never topped more than 20,000 inhabitants—and had lived their entire lives there. Their families' histories would have been the subject of local knowledge and, possibly, gossip. Both of their families farmed, and Gideon and Emma grew up in the post-emancipation era. Gideon was born in 1870 and Emma was three years his junior. They married after Emma turned eighteen, and the couple had four children.[85]

It is possible that the "problem" with Gideon's marriage originated with his wife's side. Emma's parents were named James and Mary Ainsworth. The Kelly Settlement of Forrest County, Mississippi, near Hattiesburg, was home to many families with mixed Black, white, and Native heritage, including a branch of the Ainsworth family.[86] Many of these Ainsworths could trace their family trees back to Sampson Jefferson Ainsworth, a white man, and Martha Ann Ainsworth, a Black woman he enslaved. Emma's father, James, was likely related to Sampson Ainsworth, though the exact relationship is not clear from the census. Many Ainsworths had intermarried with the descendants of Newton and Rachel Knight, who were southern Mississippi's most well-known interracial couple. These facts could possibly implicate Emma's father, but at the same time, Emma's mother, Mary, had ambiguous parentage as well. In the 1900 and 1910 censuses, Mary is called "Mariah," and in 1880 she is given the initials "M. L."[87] Her birthplace is reported alternately as Mississippi and Alabama. She is difficult to identify in the census before 1880.[88] But it is possible that Emma's mother had African ancestry and that this accounts for the difficulty of tracing her lineage prior to Reconstruction. Emma was the oldest of eleven children born to James and Mary/Mariah. Her parents had moved to Texas in the early 1900s, where they identified as white people for the rest of their lives.[89]

No other members of the legislature were willing to commit their opposition to the law to the record. But in the end, some must have been persuaded, either by Gideon Brown's speech or by other unstated concerns. Guion's law failed to get the support it needed to pass both houses, ultimately faltering in the Mississippi Senate.[90]

Just one year before the failure of Guion's bill, Judge W. H. Clark proclaimed, at the Fourth of July festival and opening of the new Rankin County Courthouse in Brandon, that "the omniscient creator has prohibited the amalgamation of the black and white races through history for a period of 10,000 years. They have been thrown together but they have never mixed so that the identity of the one was lost in the other. They have never met on the basis of social equality or through the amalgamation process."[91] Even white supremacists knew that this was a lie. They needed only to look around them, or, for a judge, at the docket book of his court. As a Methodist preacher complained of the "unspeakable and monstrous crime of miscegenation" in a 1922 sermon, "We have plentiful evidences of all sizes upon the streets of Vicksburg." The preacher concluded his diatribe on the subject thus: "If God had intended a cream-colored race, he would have made them so in the beginning."[92] This was not the end of efforts to tighten the color line. The Mississippi House of Representatives again considered the "racial integrity" bill when it convened for the 1928 legislative session. Representative Bernard Guion again introduced it.[93] And just as in 1926, the bill failed.

The debate over the bill, captured by the *Clarion-Ledger*, was heated. When Representative Henry Clay Hamblen of Greenville questioned Guion about the enforcement provisions of the bill, Guion was indignant. "What do you want to know for?" Guion asked. "Do you want to marry a negro?" (One can be almost certain that rather than "negro," he used a slur that the paper opted not to print.) Hamblen was not cowed by Guion's sneering question. Instead, he took to the podium to explain his personal opposition to the bill, which was grounded in

Portrait of unidentified Mississippi woman with her children, showing the range of complexions within one family, ca. 1920 (John E. Rodabough Papers, Manuscripts Division, Archives and Special Collections, Mississippi State University Libraries).

its possible sweeping effects on the state's social order. "And I wish to add that I know lots of white negroes, whose negro blood has almost entirely been breeded out of them, who are just as good, just as clean and a good deal more intelligent than the gentleman from Yazoo"—a scathing insult lobbed directly at the bill's author, Guion. Hamblen proposed an amendment to the law that would eliminate its enacting clause, making it a dead letter. The amendment passed; the bill did not. Once again, the Mississippi Legislature had considered, debated, and rejected a measure that would have inscribed a one-drop rule of racial inheritance into law.[94]

DESPITE THE LEGISLATURE'S UNWILLINGNESS TO ADOPT A ONE-DROP rule, it took a stand on so-called social equality, targeted at the Republican Party and the current occupant of the White House, in the following year. In 1929, the Mississippi Senate adopted a resolution condemning President Herbert Hoover for hosting Illinois representative Oscar De Priest—the only Black member of Congress—and his wife for tea at the White House. The incident signaled Hoover's support for "social equality," and the Senate held "strong hope that the president and his wife will hereafter regard and respect the feelings of the white people of the south in refraining from such social acts as would be interpreted as a recognition of social equality which we are compelled to consider as inimical to the welfare, racial purity and preservation of all the white people of our great nation." In explaining his support, seemingly blithely unconcerned about the legislative debates over the color line that had taken place in the same building just a year earlier, state senator W. B. Roberts declared that a white man inviting a Black woman into his residence "is the revival of a thing we settled in the south at the end of the reconstruction days."[95] But, of course, this was a falsehood, and one that his own colleagues had discussed in recent sessions.

Former governor Edmond F. Noel, the Klan's spokesperson in the legislature, died in late July 1927. Governor Whitfield died soon after that of an illness. His replacement, a "law and order" Democrat named Dennis

Murphree, served less than a year. Representative Guion also died, from a sudden attack of "indigestion," in September 1928, just months after his second defeat in the battle for a harsher "racial integrity" law.[96] Murphree was trounced in the Democratic primary by Theodore Bilbo, who castigated Murphree for calling out the national guard to protect Black prisoners from a lynch mob.[97]

Despite the insistence of some white Mississippians that they valued white racial purity, the records of the legislature and the courts reveal that the "problem" of the color line was anything but settled in the 1920s. The debates over the proposed "racial integrity" act died with Guion. As the agricultural depression of the 1920s spiraled into global financial catastrophe in the 1930s, Mississippi legislators had other major problems to confront. Cotton prices had fallen in the 1920s and bottomed out by the early 1930s. Since World War I, Black Mississippians had begun fleeing north to cities such as Chicago, Milwaukee, and Detroit in search of better economic opportunities for themselves and their families. Although northern cities were deeply segregated, they allowed the Black migrants to create and maintain a measure of independence that white Mississippians fervently sought to deny them.[98] The importance of maintaining control of property was even more crucial for Black people as the nation fell into the Great Depression and families of all racial classifications struggled to keep themselves fed, clothed, and sheltered. Economic crisis bred radical politics, both on the right and the left. The next decades would bring new threats to southern-style white supremacy—including growing scrutiny by outsiders.

CHAPTER 7

EXILING THE PAST

PEARL AND ALEX

Pearl Mitchell Miller's husband said she had left Mississippi of her own accord. She had departed the state in the 1920s and settled in Chicago, where Alex Miller later joined her. The couple eventually purchased two side-by-side rowhouses on Chicago's South Side, just a few blocks from Lake Michigan.[1] Pearl and Alex lived comfortably as landlords, renting to various families and individuals who lived in the flats of the two buildings.[2] The rents kept them secure during the Depression: among Pearl's possessions was a fur coat.[3] When she died in 1945, aged just forty-eight, Pearl owned property in Jackson, Mississippi, as well as Chicago.[4]

But Pearl's niece, Eddie May White, vehemently disagreed with this account. In Eddie May's version of the story, her aunt had been forced to leave her home in Jackson by order of the Hinds County Circuit Court.

Pearl and Alex had been indicted for unlawful cohabitation, and to avoid facing trial and possible jail time, the couple had agreed to leave the state. Pearl was a Black woman, Eddie May explained, and Alex was a white man. Only in Chicago could they legalize their union, which they did— many years later—in 1939.[5]

Various records from her life identify Pearl as Black (the 1910 census), as "mulatto" (the 1920 census), and, after 1930, as white.[6] Once again, arguments about Pearl's race were really arguments about inheritance— specifically, the contested ownership of three residential lots in Jackson. Pearl had written a will before she died, but it only discussed the land the couple owned in Chicago. It said nothing about the Jackson properties. One of these was the home on South Roach Street that Pearl had lived in before she left for Chicago. Now, Pearl's half-brother, James Lucks, lived there, as did a handful of other tenants. Alex Miller accused James and Eddie May of collecting the rents on the properties and spending it rather than turning it over to him, as they should have.[7]

The legal fight over Pearl Mitchell Miller's estate would play out during a fraught time for the court. In the late 1930s and through the 1940s, the US Supreme Court issued a series of rulings challenging basic tenets of segregation law. In 1944, it ruled the all-white primary—a key tool of disfranchisement—unconstitutional. In response, during the 1946 election campaign US senator Theodore Bilbo of Mississippi claimed that "white civilization" was under attack, and that Black voting would inevitably lead to "interbreeding and intermixing" and "the mongreliza-tion and destruction of both races."[8] Bilbo incited a campaign of violence against Black voters so outrageous that it nearly derailed his Senate career (he died facing multiple Senate investigations for both anti-Black vio-lence and corruption).[9] He was an extremist even among segregationists, but these developments nevertheless troubled the claims of moderates that segregation law was beneficial to both white and Black southerners.[10]

State and local challenges to Jim Crow law abounded during these decades. In a 1949 case that captured national attention, the Missis-sippi Supreme Court justices heard the appeal of Davis Knight, who had been convicted in the lower court of violating the law prohibiting interracial marriage. Both cases—the fight over the Miller estate and the Knight appeal—required the justices to confront the state's history of interracial marriage. The inheritance dispute over Pearl Miller's property captured much less attention than Davis Knight's case, but it laid bare the truths about interracial marriage in Mississippi: that white men continued to marry Black women well into the twentieth century. Racist politicians could shriek about the dangers of "amalgamation" all they liked, but the courts would still have to deal with the legacy of interracial marriage amid growing threats to Jim Crow.

IN SOME WAYS, THE CASE SEEMED CLEAR-CUT. PEARL'S WILL LEFT ALL OF her property to her husband. At the same time, it included an ambiguous clause that gave Eddie May White and James Lucks an opening to make their claim to the Jackson property: "It is my wish that my husband is to have no other claim, right or title to any other property that I may own in the United States, except the properties specifically mentioned in this will."[11] James, Eddie May, and Charles Young—Pearl's nephew, who was also part of the lawsuit—interpreted this wording as evidence of Pearl's desire to see her family members in Jackson inherit her properties there, even if she had not explicitly said so. By excluding "any other property," Pearl meant for her brother and extended family to have the land in Jackson after her death.

Eddie May and James contended that Alex had no title to the property, even as Pearl's widower. Pearl and Alex's relationship was illegal in Mississippi, and the relationship had begun with Alex and Pearl "unlawfully and illicitly" cohabiting in Jackson. As an interracial couple, the pair could not have been legally wed in Mississippi. The state's law also declared that any interracial couple that went out of state to marry and returned to Mississippi would face up to ten years at Parchman Farm.[12] Therefore, "if any marriage was contracted or undertaken to be contracted in Chicago," their lawyer argued, "such could never be lawful, or be recognized in the State of Mississippi."[13] Alex could not be Pearl's widower; therefore, he was not her heir—at least in the state of Mississippi.[14] The property should go to Pearl's closest living relatives: her half-siblings and their children.

Initially, Alex Miller insisted that his wife was not a Black woman. As Louisa Covacevich had done decades before, he identified a fictional Native American ancestor in Pearl's family tree to distract from concerns that she may have had African ancestry. Alex claimed that Pearl had been born in Copiah County, Mississippi. "The mother of Pearl Mitchell was an Indian by the name of Maria Cox," and her father was "a prominent white man" named "Dr. R. M. Mitchell."[15] Sixteen years before the litigation over Pearl's estate, "it became necessary" for her to "offer evidence to prove her parentage and race." (Why this was necessary, Alex's lawyer did not say.) At that time, two men had submitted affidavits saying that Pearl's mother was Native American and her father was white.[16]

But this story was not consistent with other evidence—including the petition Alex Miller presented to the Cook County Probate Court following Pearl's death, which clearly identified James Lucks as Pearl's half-brother and one of her surviving kin.[17] Moreover, Eddie May and James's lawyer dredged up the records from the Hinds County Circuit Court showing that Pearl and Alex had been arrested and indicted for unlawful cohabitation in November 1923. Eddie May White's story about Pearl's decision to move to Chicago was true. After Pearl and Alex's indictment, their lawyer had struck a deal with the district attorney: if Pearl left Mississippi, the state would drop the charges. She departed in December. Alex joined her in Chicago the following February. In November 1924, the case was "nolle prossed"—dismissed—as the district attorney declined to pursue the charges.[18] Pearl never returned to Mississippi or to her former home on Roach Street.

By the time the chancery court heard the case, Alex Miller had abandoned the defense that Pearl had no African forebears. His lawyers conceded that Pearl was a Black woman. Faced with the records from the circuit court, Alex admitted that he had violated "Section 459 of the State's criminal law"—which criminalized going out of the state to marry—but nevertheless was asking for the "benefit of Section 470, of the State's civil law, pertaining to Descent of property as between husband

and wife." Alex Miller was willing to admit he married a Black woman as long as property was at stake.

In June 1947, Hinds County chancellor Vincent J. Stricker issued his ruling. Given the wealth of evidence about Pearl and Alex's past, he declared that Pearl was a Black woman, and that her marriage to Alex was illegal in the state of Mississippi. The unlawful cohabitation indictment had sent Pearl and Alex "into exile," after which they could not return to Mississippi without risking conviction and a ten-year sentence at Parchman Farm. "In this state such a marriage is void by law, and is an offense against Nature and Government," the chancellor declared.[19] Chancellor Stricker's logic was simple: Pearl and Alex's marriage was "void and criminal" in Mississippi, and it could not be used to give Alex preference as Pearl's heir over her blood relatives.[20] Stricker rejected the notion that their relationship could be validated by another state's law, disparaging Illinois's acceptance of interracial marriages. He explained that "certainly the descent and distribution of property in this state cannot be controlled or influenced by the miscegenous customs and practices of the State of Illinois."[21]

The chancellor concluded with an appeal to higher law. This was not just a question of property rights. It was a matter of morality. "Are we to measure the difference between right and wrong in this State by the social and moral standards of the State of Illinois, and deprive those who are guilty of no wrong here of their property according to those standards?" Stricker wrote. "I think not. And surely not in this Court."[22] Chancellor Stricker had no respect for Pearl and Alex's marriage, and neither did the state of Mississippi. The court ruled in favor of James Lucks, Eddie May White, and Charles Young.[23] The Jackson properties were theirs in equal share. But not for long.

ALEX MILLER WAS NOT SATISFIED TO ALLOW PEARL'S FAMILY TO inherit her Mississippi estate. He already controlled the Chicago properties, but he felt entitled to Pearl's Jackson lots. He appealed the chancery court's ruling. One year later, in June 1948, the Mississippi Supreme

Court sided with Alex, declaring him to be Pearl Miller's sole rightful heir. Newspapers covered the suit, calling it the "first" of its kind in "the state's history."[24] It was certainly not the first case in which the state supreme court had validated an interracial marriage or allowed property to pass across the color line. It was extraordinary, however, for the Mississippi Supreme Court to uphold an interracial marriage sanctified elsewhere.

In their appeal brief to the state supreme court, Alex's lawyers had conceded the legality of Mississippi's law prohibiting interracial marriage, but also emphasized that Pearl and Alex were no longer citizens of the state of Mississippi, and that they were therefore free to legally marry in Illinois once they established residence there. This was important because they could invoke a higher law than Mississippi's: the United States Constitution. The principle of comity flowed from the Constitution's Article IV, which dictated that states should give "full faith and credit" to the "public Acts, Records, and judicial Proceedings of every other State."[25] Comity was central to the American system of federalism. Each state had its own laws governing marriage, separation, and divorce. Typically, states treated a marriage contracted in another state as valid. This allowed couples to move across state lines without worrying about having to remarry. It also allowed a divorce granted in one state to be effective in others.[26] This was the genesis of Nevada as a divorce destination. Its laws governing divorce were the least onerous of any state, drawing aggrieved couples from coast to coast. They only needed to remain in Nevada for six weeks to establish residency before petitioning for a divorce. After that, they could return home, unmarried. A divorce granted in Nevada would be respected in, say, New York, where it was famously difficult to end a marriage.[27]

Laws governing interracial marriage complicated the concept of comity. If Pearl and Alex had the right, as citizens of the state of Illinois, to marry, and this marriage was valid so long as they remained residents of that state, the principle of comity implied that they might claim to be married in states where their union was illegal. Courts had long held that there were exceptions to comity for marriage—specifically for incestuous or polygamous marriages and those that defied public policy.[28] Mississippi law clearly did not fully extend comity to interracial marriages, because it threatened couples who returned to the state even for one night with incarceration at Parchman. The Hinds County judge and district attorney had effectively exiled Pearl from her home state for the rest of her life. The principle of comity, if extended to all cases of interracial marriage, would invalidate Mississippi's efforts to punish couples like Alex and Pearl.

These were not questions that the Mississippi Supreme Court justices wanted to answer fully when they accepted Alex Miller's appeal. Instead, they threaded the needle of interracial marriage law carefully, separating criminal from civil law. The justices did not want to declare that a marriage that was celebrated in another state would be respected by Mississippi courts under any circumstances. Doing so would undermine the entire body of law prohibiting interracial marriage. But unlike Chancellor Stricker, the high court justices seemed interested in ensuring that Alex Miller would inherit even though Pearl's will could be read to imply that she desired her blood relatives to have the property. They could find a loophole to let Alex's claim through, but it had to be narrow enough to exclude most other claims.

In an opinion authored by Chief Justice Sydney Smith, the Mississippi Supreme Court declared that the marriage between Alex and Pearl was valid *because* they never returned to Mississippi. They therefore had not violated the letter or the spirit of the marriage law, as the "manifest and recognized purpose of this statute was to prevent persons of Negro and white blood from living together in this state in the relationship of husband and wife."[29] As the couple had accepted the terms of their exile, the court would acknowledge the validity of their Illinois marriage after Pearl's death.

One wonders what might have unfolded had the genders of the actors been reversed. It seems far less plausible that the justices would have sided with a Black widow seeking to inherit her dead white husband's estate after the couple fled the state, or with a Black widower of a propertied white woman. The ruling seemed to rest on assumptions about both race and sex.

The Mississippi courts had long denigrated Black women as "concubines" to subvert the claims they might try to make as the widows of white men. Violence was used to deter Black men from marrying white women. Yet the court had no qualms about making Alex Miller into Pearl's widower. To inherit Pearl's property was his entitlement as a white man.

THE LAWSUIT OVER PEARL MILLER'S ESTATE UNFURLED IN THE YEARS following World War II. The war's effects were cascading across the globe, troubling the politics of Mississippi and other southern states. While Southern Democrats had formed an important and influential part of Franklin Delano Roosevelt's New Deal coalition, the gathering clouds over Europe signaled trouble for segregationists. After Hitler consolidated power in Germany, his Nazi regime crafted legislation that bore a striking resemblance to Jim Crow laws. Indeed, the Nazis carefully studied and emulated American segregation laws, including those defining race and prohibiting interracial marriage.[30]

Black activists frequently and loudly connected the fight against fascism abroad with the struggle for Black freedom at home, as the *Pittsburgh Courier* did most directly in its "Double V" campaign.[31] Amid the Depression, a resurgent labor movement and Black migration out of the South threatened the death grip white landowners and employers had on the region's workers. Labor organizers launched an effort to unionize Black tenant farmers and workers.[32] Civil rights lawyers made headway in cases involving Black laborers in the South who were held in peonage, arguing that these men and women were subjected to conditions akin to slavery.[33] A. Philip Randolph, the head of a Black union, successfully pressured Roosevelt into issuing an executive order prohibiting defense contractors from discriminating in hiring based on race. Randolph's proposed March on Washington, scheduled amid FDR's efforts to gain support for the Allies, threatened to create a publicity nightmare for the president.[34]

After the Allied victory, the brewing Cold War put even more pressure on the United States to project its image as a global beacon of freedom. Black veterans returned to their southern homes having risked their lives in service to their country and demanding equal rights. In response, white people brutalized and lynched Black veterans across the South. Maceo Snipes, for example, was murdered for casting his vote in a Georgia election.[35] This did not deter all Black veterans from attempting to exercise their rights or joining civil rights organizations. Their wartime experience and the brutal treatment Black veterans received upon returning to their southern homes steeled the resolve of some men. Many of them became civil rights leaders in the 1950s and 1960s, including Medgar Evers, Amzie Moore, and Aaron Henry in Mississippi.[36]

Civil rights activism spiked during and after the war. The NAACP increased its membership nearly tenfold during the war years.[37] Newly flush with cash, the organization could widen its efforts to expand its courtroom challenges to *Plessy v. Ferguson* and other rulings that had bolstered racial segregation. During and after the war, this litigation strategy began to pay dividends. In 1938, the NAACP Legal Defense Fund (LDF) won its first major higher education case when the US Supreme Court ruled that states offering public graduate programs to white students must offer similar educational opportunities to Black students.[38] The LDF funded the successful challenge to the all-white primary—a key tool for excluding Black voters who could pay poll taxes and pass the literacy tests—in the 1944 US Supreme Court decision *Smith v. Allwright*. Two years later, the LDF scored another major victory with the Supreme Court's ruling in *Morgan v. Virginia*, in which the court declared that states could not require racial segregation in interstate bus travel.[39] In 1950, the justices decided two higher education cases concerning civil rights, ruling that the separate and unequal treatment of a law student, Heman Sweatt, and of an education graduate student, George McLaurin, violated the Fourteenth Amendment of the US Constitution.[40]

After Roosevelt died in office in 1945, his successor, Harry Truman, took a bold public stance on civil rights. While the Democratic Party had always been the party of white supremacy in the South, nationally it was the party of the New Deal. Franklin Roosevelt's landslide victory in 1932 had inaugurated a new era marked by Democratic politicians who were being elected by a coalition that included Southern Democrats and, increasingly in the 1930s, Black voters outside the South. In 1948, Truman caused an uproar when he issued an executive order desegregating the military. Legislators in southern states viewed these national developments with growing alarm. When the national Democratic Party added civil rights to its party platform, Southern Democrats walked out and formed a new political party: the States' Rights Democratic Party, otherwise known as the "Dixiecrats."[41] The Mississippi Legislature adopted a resolution in January 1948 denouncing proposed federal civil rights legislation, including "an anti-lynching act, an anti-poll tax act, a fair employment practices act, an act forbidding segregation, and other acts of this same character and devious purpose," which the resolution claimed were "aimed at nothing less than the subjugation of the sovereignty of the forty-eight states of the union."[42]

Across the South, white politicians increasingly embraced extremist positions during and after World War II.[43] Mississippi's noisiest champion of "white purity" was US senator Theodore Bilbo. A Vardaman acolyte who had studied demagoguery at the feet of the infamous "White Chief," Bilbo blended fervent Progressivism and virulent racism. Before the 1930s, his focus had been enacting Progressive reforms. But by the early 1940s, Bilbo had pivoted to become the political face of southern white supremacy.[44]

Bilbo's political career had begun more than three decades earlier in the Mississippi Senate. It began, as it ended, embroiled in scandal. Among Bilbo's points of consistency was his imperviousness to the public opprobrium that followed. In 1910, Bilbo—then a relatively unknown member of the state Senate—was accused of accepting a cash bribe to change his vote in the caucus for US senator from James K. Vardaman to LeRoy Percy. The state Senate held an investigation in the spring of that year into the affair, which allegedly took place at an establishment of ill repute in south Jackson owned by Mamie Stamps, a Black woman.[45] Mamie ran an assignation house, where couples could rent rooms to engage in various illicit activities. In other words, she traded in secrecy and discretion. No doubt this was what made her establishment an attractive place to conduct other illegal business.

It is perhaps not surprising to modern readers that white Mississippi politicians were familiar with a place like Mamie Stamps's assignation house, but it is remarkable how blithely Bilbo himself explained his knowledge of her business before the entire Mississippi Senate.[46] Like many other Mississippi politicians, he had mastered the dual nature that was so common to southern state politics. He was a Baptist Bible school teacher who was fired from his first job after being accused of having an affair with a student.[47] His extramarital affairs were poorly kept secrets.[48] (Perhaps he had one at Mamie Stamps's place—one critic labeled him a "frequenter of lewd houses.")[49] Bilbo was cruel and callous toward his wife, and his marriage eventually ended in divorce.[50] But this distinction between his persona in the public sphere and the reality of his private life did not seem to trouble him, nor did it dull his political shine among his fervent supporters. Bilbo admitted to taking the bribe, claiming his motivations were only to expose the briber.[51] The Mississippi Senate failed to expel Bilbo by one vote, though the body then voted in favor of a resolution requesting his resignation. It declared that Bilbo was "unworthy of belief" and "unfit to sit with honest, upright men in a respectable legislative body."[52] The bribery scandal thrust Bilbo into the political spotlight. It did not, however, dent his ambitions or hinder his success. The following year, he was elected lieutenant governor. A biographer called this his "real political birth."[53] In 1915, Bilbo won the governorship.

Bilbo had a particular strain of racist views, which he employed more and more once elected to national office. His supporters were, in the words of another white Mississippian, "the sort of people that lynch Negroes."[54] By the 1940s, Bilbo was openly identifying as a member of the Ku Klux Klan and vocally supporting lynching. He was a fervent advocate of the removal of Black people from the United States, as well as for colonization efforts that would send Black Americans to the West Coast of Africa.[55] He was thoroughly separatist in his advocacy for white supremacy. In 1947, just before his death, he self-published his treatise on racism. Titling it *Take Your Choice: Separation or Mongrelization*, Bilbo argued that the solution to the "Negro problem" was their expulsion from the United States.[56] After his death, the Mississippi Legislature passed a resolution praising Bilbo for having "worked unceasingly and often alone to preserve Southern customs and traditions and in doing so sought to preserve the true American way of life."[57] Even with the triumph of Bilboism, Mississippi was still a state of contradictions. And, as was evident in *Miller v. Lucks*, its court system was forced to contend with the state's complicated past.

BILBO BROADCAST HIS MESSAGE ABOUT A WHITE RACE UNDER SIEGE into a state where white people understood—even if they did not believe it could happen—that white supremacy was subject to challenges from multiple angles. These internal and external threats to white supremacist rule in Mississippi and other southern states did not push politicians to moderate their stances. Many adopted a virulent and violent full-throated defense of the subjugation of Black people.

The antipathy to Black people not only infected politics but also spread through the state's criminal justice system. Willie McGee was one victim of this turn. He was arrested and charged with raping Wiletta Hawkins, a white woman, in November 1945. Wiletta told police that she had been assaulted by a stranger who had broken into the room where she slept. In the darkness of the night, she could not see her attacker. But Wiletta was certain the man was Black.[58] Willie McGee was arrested, and his trial took place just one month later. The jury deliberated for less than three minutes before declaring him guilty. As with other Black men accused of raping white women, his sentence was death.[59]

Willie's trial was plagued with irregularities. He confessed to the crime only after being beaten by the police who interrogated him. The judge had refused to grant his lawyers' request to have the trial moved to another county owing to fears he could not get a fair trial with local men as jurors. After the Mississippi Supreme Court granted the appeal and ordered a new trial, he was convicted again. This time, the jury took eleven minutes to declare him guilty.[60]

Willie was tried a third time in 1948. He testified at this trial, explaining that his two previous confessions were beaten out of him. This time, though, the Mississippi Supreme Court was not sympathetic to any of his lawyers' claims that he had not received a fair trial. His lawyers appealed to the US Supreme Court, claiming a range of federal rights deprivations, but the justices did not agree to hear his petition. They tried appealing to both state and federal courts, including another petition to the US Supreme Court in 1950. All these efforts failed. Among Willie McGee's defenders was Bella Abzug, a leftist attorney from New York, who argued that the relationship between Willie and Wiletta was consensual.[61] Protesters from around the country traveled to Jackson to gather at the capitol. Forty-one of them were arrested, and as a condition of their release they were told to leave the state.[62]

On the evening of May 7, 1951, state officials strapped Willie McGee to a portable electric chair at the Jones County courthouse. Crowds milled about outside the building, eager to witness his death. No women were allowed inside, so some white women brought chairs to sit in outside. Officials positioned chairs before the crowd of white men who had gathered, all eager to witness Willie McGee's death. Five minutes after the clock struck midnight, the executioner administered the first shock. Five minutes after that, Willie was pronounced dead.[63] When word reached the hundreds gathered outside, the crowd cheered.[64]

The vicious response to Willie McGee's conviction fits squarely within midcentury resistance to civil rights reforms. Outwardly, white Mississippians had never been more defensive about their historic commitment to white supremacy. They had good reason to be worried. Even as the courts pointed out the many defects in the legal color line, segregationists blamed civil rights activists and "outside agitators" for encouraging miscegenation. Doing so required embracing the historical fiction of racial integrity.

LESS THAN SIX MONTHS AFTER WILLIE MCGEE'S ARREST IN NEARBY Laurel, Mississippi, Junie Spradley and Davis Knight were married in the spring of 1946. He was a twenty-one-year-old veteran of the navy, and Junie was just eighteen. The couple held their ceremony on April 18 at City Hall in Ellisville in Jones County, where they were wed by the town's mayor. They received a marriage license, which was filed in the "white" marriage registration book kept by the court clerk.[65] Junie's mother was present. The mood was buoyant. The happy couple left the courthouse to begin their life together.[66]

Two years later, on June 22, 1948, the Jones County sheriff arrested Davis for violating Mississippi's law prohibiting interracial marriage. According to one reporter, "a committee of women" who had called on the district attorney was responsible for Davis's indictment. Upon their advice, the district attorney called Junie and her mother into his office, where he informed them that he had been told that Davis was "part Negro," and that if this was true, and he had "one-eighth Negro blood," they could not "live together in Mississippi." Junie insisted that Davis was a white man—he even had military records to prove it. The district attorney then appealed to Davis's father, Otho Knight, who presented two of his daughters as evidence that the entire family was white.[67]

Faced with the couple's refusal to leave or separate, the district attorney decided to prosecute Davis alone. The arrest warrant issued by the court cited two offenses: "miscegenation" and "unlawful cohabitation."[68] The indictment accused Davis of being "a Negro or mulatto male person, with 1/8 or more of Negro blood," who had "wilfully and feloniously and unlawfully" married a white woman.[69] In December, Davis was tried before a jury of twelve white men. The jury convicted him and sentenced him to serve five years at Parchman Farm.[70]

In one sense, the prosecution of Davis Knight fits neatly within the narrative that white southerners adhered to a "one-drop" idea of Black racial inheritance and that they would not tolerate interracial relationships between white women and Black men. But Davis's case is in many ways a peculiar example of a prosecution of an interracial couple.[71] Among the curious facts of the case was that the couple encountered no difficulty in obtaining a marriage license. When asked whether he doubted that Junie and Davis fell into different racial classifications, the mayor later said the thought had not crossed his mind.[72] He had signed the license, and it had been filed with the county clerk, who also had not questioned whether Davis was a white man. She testified at the trial that she had not felt the need to do so, as he had come in "with a crowd of white ladies." The mayor who married Junie and Davis was, in her view, "unquestionably a white man," so there had been no reason to doubt his approval of the match.[73]

It was no secret that Davis Knight was a descendant of Newton and Rachel Knight, who are perhaps the most famous interracial couple in Mississippi history. Newton Knight's Unionism has been the subject of multiple books and a 2016 feature-length film, *The Free State of Jones*, starring Matthew McConaughey.[74] Even in the 1940s, the Knight family was well known in Jones County, and their complicated family tree would not have been a mystery to local residents.[75] Despite having African ancestry, many descendants of Rachel and Newton did not identify as Black, including Davis's father, Otho, who identified as a white man.[76] As part of a tight-knit community, many Knights occupied an uneasy space, where they identified as white but were labeled "White Negroes" (or vastly more offensive terms) by others.

The only real question presented at the trial of Davis Knight was the racial identity of Rachel Knight, Davis's great-grandmother. Given his many white ancestors, whether Davis had a sufficient blood quantum to make him Black depended on whether Rachel herself had mixed ancestry. But by 1948 Rachel had been dead for nearly six decades.[77] At the trial, Davis's lawyer, Quitman Ross, leaned into the unknowability of Rachel's race, attempting to emphasize the absurdity of the blood quantum rule. When Tom Knight, one of Newt Knight's white sons, testified about Rachel's racial identity, the prosecutor asked him to describe her "percentage of Negro blood or mixture of Negro blood," and Ross objected, saying that no one could "capably answer that question." The judge allowed the question, noting that Tom could "give his opinion" as to Rachel's blood quantum.[78]

Tom's cross-examination was belabored by two things: First, his hearing loss meant he struggled to understand what the lawyers were saying. And second, he was exceptionally reluctant to discuss a thorny point in his family's history, as his own siblings had married across the color line. Rachel's son Jeff had married Tom's sister Molly. His brother Madison had married Rachel's daughter Fannie.[79] Molly Knight was Davis's paternal grandmother, and Jeff Knight was his grandfather. Molly and Jeff's son Otho was Davis's father, whom Tom identified as sitting in the courtroom.[80] D. H. Valentine, a witness for the state, explained that the general assumption in Otho's community was that "he was a Negro." And Otho's son Davis was likewise "a Negro, mulatto Negro."[81] Otho Knight, of course, disagreed with this assessment.

D. H. Valentine claimed to have extensive knowledge of the Knight family, including Rachel's appearance. He confidently described her "kinky hair, a flat nose, [and] big thick lips," though he admitted on cross-examination that he had been born the year *after* Rachel died.[82] Many witnesses relied on social characteristics to determine Rachel's racial classification. Other characteristics of the Knight family placed them outside the bounds of white respectability. Valentine claimed that he had "never visited their home" because he had been "raised better."[83]

Another witness for the prosecution explained that Jeff Knight, Davis's grandfather, "was always classed as a Negro." Ross's objections to this testimony, which relied on witnesses' "opinions" about the racial identities of long-dead people, spurred the judge to dismiss the jury. The judge conceded, "The Court doesn't think you can show how much Negro or how much White blood a man has in him by mere reputation, but this being a charge of miscegenation," he would allow "any proof . . . as to how he was considered, whether White or Negro." At the same time, the judge said, "the Court doesn't hold it would be conclusive as to how much Negro blood or White blood he had in him, but it is evidentiary as to intent."[84]

Ross had an interesting exchange with another witness, Wiley McHenry, when he quizzed him about the racial reputations of Davis's father and grandfather. Ross wanted to pin down what, exactly, made a person a "negro" in the minds of his fellow Mississippians. He asked Wiley, "And it's generally true that any person who is known or thought to have Negro blood in them, whether it is little or much, is considered a Negro by White people in the South, isn't it?" Wiley replied, "No, no, not necessarily." He clarified that if people accused a man of being "a Negro," "you could look at a man and tell if it is true or not." Ross said, "You mean any person who has any negro blood in him, enough that you can tell it?" To which Wiley replied, "That's right."[85]

This was part of Ross's larger strategy in proving Davis Knight's innocence. Ross was careful to ask the white witnesses such questions as, "Every person who is known to have any Negro blood in them, no matter how little it is, if it's known they are considered by all White people you know as being Negroes, aren't they?" This question was intentionally framed. Ross wanted to underscore the distance between the informal opinions of white people about who was Black and who was not and the letter of the law, which used the strict blood quantum rule. By demonstrating that white people used the one-drop rule regardless of whether a person was legally Black, he undercut their ability to accurately determine who was or was not Black according to law. As one witness told Ross, "I'm no blood analyzer."[86] But this was the catch: the concept of the "blood quantum" was itself nonsense. Therefore, there could be no actual "blood analyzer."

The racial classification of Davis's mother, Addie, likewise posed a problem for the prosecution. One witness, when asked about her, insisted that she must be Black because she lived with Otho.[87] When Ross pointed to Otho's wife sitting in the courtroom, another witness explained that he "couldn't say she is a negro" just based on observation alone.[88] Even in court, under oath, the one-drop rule could not withstand scrutiny.

Moreover, not every white person agreed about whether Davis had any African ancestry. One of Ross's key witnesses was a white physician. J. W. Stringer testified that he had seen Rachel Knight as a child, but that in his opinion she did not look Black. "She looked more like an Indian to me," he told Quitman Ross.[89] Indeed, Stringer explained, he had not previously heard the Knights described as "Negro"—but instead as being of "mixed blood." And that, he thought, could have meant "mixed with Indian." Stringer further said that when he had visited the Knights' home, he had eaten with them at their table, waited upon by "Negro servants" who had taken their own meals in a side room.[90] The prosecutor was irate with this testimony. He pressed Stringer on whether he had ever heard anyone else say that the Knights had Black ancestry. "I have as much right to my opinion as they have," Stringer replied, when asked about others' opinions on Davis's racial classification. When asked about Jeff Knight's physical features, Stringer replied that he had observed that Jeff had "a normal human nose" and "normal human lips."[91] An opinion about someone's race was just that: an opinion. Not a fact.

Henry Knight, another of Davis's witnesses, also cast doubt on Rachel's racial classification. While he did not deny that she had African ancestry, Henry explained that Rachel was "creole and Indian." Her skin color was "ginger cake"—evidence of her own mixed ancestry.[92] Another white witness likewise testified that Rachel was "ginger-cake colored." Her skin tone was, he said, "about the color of a Choctaw Indian."[93] The state's case rested on the idea that Rachel was a "full blooded Negro"—if she herself had European ancestry, then Davis Knight fell outside of the marriage law's one-eighth blood quantum rule.

Quitman Ross then submitted yet more evidence of Davis's racial indeterminacy: his honorable discharge papers from the US Navy, which showed that he had been inducted on July 2, 1943, at Camp Shelby in Mississippi as a white man. Davis Knight was honorably discharged from service on January 6, 1946, just four months before his wedding to Junie Spradley.[94]

The jury did not buy Quitman Ross's arguments about racial indeterminacy. They convicted Davis Knight of violating the state law prohibiting interracial marriage and sentenced him to five years of hard labor at Parchman Farm.[95]

THE *CHICAGO DEFENDER* CROWED ABOUT THE IMPLICATIONS OF THE Davis Knight case for all white southerners. Reporting on Davis's conviction and his appeal to the Mississippi Supreme Court, the story wryly observed, "Skeletons in the ancestral closets of many southern white families gibbered and clattered their ancient dry bones together this week in fear and trembling" amid Davis's appeal.[96] Observing from a safe distance, the *Defender* argued that the case threatened to expose the hypocrisy of segregationists.

Even within the Mississippi courts, others quietly shared their doubts about Davis's conviction and the problems it posed to Jim Crow. Quitman Ross appealed the conviction to the Mississippi Supreme Court, where he found the support of an unusual figure: the assistant attorney general of Mississippi, George H. Ethridge.

Upon reviewing the case, Ethridge argued that the high court should overturn Davis Knight's conviction and order a new trial. Ethridge wrote a brief focusing on the gap between the state's witnesses and the actual language of the state law. The witnesses had insisted that racial classifications in the state were based on the one-drop rule, but this did not reflect the law itself. Quitman Ross's insistent questioning of each witness about how they defined a "Negro" paid dividends in the appeal. Even when the justices had applied the one-drop rule in *Moreau v. Grandich*, this had only applied to schools—the marriage law remained unchanged. It was written into the 1890 state constitution. Moreover, the legislature had refused to adopt the one-drop rule in the 1920s when it was presented with two opportunities to do so. The uncertainty surrounding Rachel Knight's ancestry meant that the district attorney had not proven beyond reasonable doubt whether Davis Knight had more than one-eighth blood quantum of African ancestry.

And Attorney General Ethridge's brief pointed to another concern: the rising Black Freedom Movement. "I think this case would be a very dangerous one to be appealed to the Federal Supreme Court in view of the great agitation in many parts of the United States to break down racial segregation in schools, public conveyances and other public institutions and that there would be danger if this judgment is affirmed on the testimony in the record of it upsetting our policy of race segregation," Ethridge explained.[97] In other words, the state's case was so shaky that the US Supreme Court might take up the ruling—especially since it concerned a white veteran who had been sentenced to the penitentiary for marrying his sweetheart. Moreover, the California Supreme Court had just invalidated that state's law prohibiting interracial marriage as a violation of the Fourteenth Amendment.[98]

Quitman Ross merely had to build upon the foundation that the Mississippi attorney general had laid. Ross's brief focused on the fact that the state had not proven beyond a reasonable doubt that Davis had "one eighth or more Negro blood." Only one witness, Tom Knight, had demonstrably known Rachel and could testify to her skin color, and he had ulterior motives. Tom was full of "venom and anger" over his father, Newt Knight's, abandonment of his mother, Serena, when Newt had taken up with Rachel.[99] At the same time, two other white witnesses testified that Rachel was not a "full Negro." But, most powerfully, "the evidence of reputation was unquestionably untrue," Ross wrote. "If this man had been a negro, he would not have got a license from this clerk to marry the white woman who stood by said appellant when the license was issued."[100] Even the military officials at Camp Shelby had accepted Davis Knight as a white man. The evidence was overwhelming.

To conclude his argument, Ross performed a clever turnabout, concluding that what made a Black person Black was not racial math, but instead, sight alone. Ross concluded thus: "It is common sense and every day understanding that any person in Mississippi, not an idiot or blind, knows a negro on sight."[101] This was a calculated move: Ross transformed his skeptical insistence throughout the trial that anyone could possibly calculate Rachel Knight's blood quantum into an assertion of Blackness as a fact that "any person in Mississippi" would know if they saw it.

The Mississippi Supreme Court handed down its opinion in the *Knight* case in November 1949, less than a year after his conviction. With Ethridge's and Ross's briefs both arguing that they should overturn the jury's conviction of Davis Knight, the justices of the state's high court agreed that the evidence of Davis's racial identity was too weak to withstand scrutiny. The opinion was short, and it did not dwell on any of the loaded questions about race and heritage that the trial itself had raised. "We have carefully examined the record and we are convinced by it that the Attorney General was justified in making such admission and that the proof in this case does not establish beyond every reasonable doubt that the defendant had one-eighth or more Negro blood. The verdict is against the overwhelming weight of the evidence."[102] And with that, the court vacated Davis Knight's conviction.

Other historians have speculated that the Mississippi Supreme Court made its ruling based on the risk that, if they affirmed Davis's conviction, the federal courts might intervene.[103] (It appears they need not have worried, as the justices of the US Supreme Court avoided ruling in two other cases involving interracial marriages that were appealed to the high court in the following years.)[104] There is no question that Attorney General Ethridge took the national context seriously as a factor in writing his brief. At the same time, the court's decision in *Davis Knight v. State of Mississippi* was consistent with previous rulings involving interracial couples—especially *Dean v. State*, which had been decided nearly twenty-five years earlier. Both cases hinged on the problem of evidence that racial classifications created. In *Dean v. State*, too, the attorney general had concluded that the lower court's ruling should not stand. What made Davis Knight's case extraordinary is that the person accused of having African ancestry was a man.

The reversal of Davis's conviction may have been defensive, but it was also, in a sense, necessary to the maintenance of Jim Crow. Judges who upheld segregation laws were tasked with defining a concept that defied logic—that Blackness was inheritable but whiteness was not—so that those laws could be legally enforceable. They had to insist that the law was rational and its enforcement was not arbitrary. Viewed within a longer history of the prosecutions of interracial couples in Mississippi, these problems of evidence were not unique to Davis Knight's conviction. Judges and prosecutors had grappled with similar questions for decades, and not just in Mississippi, but across the South.[105] In this sense, Davis's case fit neatly within decades of legal struggles to apply racial classifications. This was something that courts had to take seriously, even if the judges might ascribe personally to a one-drop rule of racial inheritance. Their job was to apply the law. And in making the law seem rational and fair, they also protected Jim Crow. In Davis Knight's case, the evidence overwhelmingly pointed to his legal whiteness.

DAVIS AND JUNIE KNIGHT WERE FREE, BUT THEIR MARRIAGE WAS short-lived. The 1950 census, which was conducted the following spring, records Davis as living with his parents, and Junie with her sister.[106] By 1955, Junie had moved to Laurel.[107] Davis relocated to Harris County, Texas, where he tragically drowned while fishing in a reservoir in 1959. His death certificate identifies him as a white man.[108] His body was returned home to Mississippi, where he was interred in the Knight family cemetery—the same place his great-grandmother Rachel was buried. His father, Otho Knight, applied for and received a marble military headstone noting his World War II service in the US Navy.[109]

The national press had eagerly reported on the Davis Knight case. Black newspapers relished the opportunity to tell and retell the scandalous history of interracial sex and marriage in the South. The *Chicago Defender* used it as an opportunity to lift the veil on interracial relationships, noting that "in every city, regardless of size, there will be found individuals and couples who have stepped over the color line." Indeed, the *Defender* said, "The Davis Knight case, no doubt, has many southern whites, both men and women, trembling in their boots; for they too, have black blood in their veins." The article also repeated a quote that it attributed to "the late Huey Long, then governor of Louisiana, who in the midst of a fiery debate warned southerners about claiming a 'pure white background'": "Long said he could entertain 'all of the pure white men and women in Louisiana in his dining room' and he didn't have but six chairs in it. He further declared that a man was only as 'white as he looked.'"[110]

Other outlets emphasized the opposite point: that the trial of Davis Knight was notable primarily in its exceptionality. The *Minneapolis Star*, reprinting a story from *Newsweek*, reported that Davis's conviction was "the first miscegenation trial in the state's history."[111] It was nothing of the sort, but this was a convenient story for both Mississippians and outside observers to tell about the Knight case and why it mattered. If the Knight family of Jones County was so peculiar, so unusual as to have even the Mississippi Supreme Court perplexed by Davis's racial classification, then the case itself said nothing about the state's long history of interracial sex and marriage.

Much as Mississippi sought to project itself as a place wedded to segregation and racial separation, this rendering of the state's history demanded willful blindness to the protracted legal struggle for and against that separation. In this telling, there was no *Dean v. State*, in which the justices effectively declared Ralphine Burns and William Dean to have a legal marriage. Gone, too, were Pearl and Alex Miller, whose desire to remain together had forced them to flee the state. Isolated as an extraordinary case, the trial of Davis Knight could serve as the focus of white supremacist ire, leaving Davis standing alone as a person whose existence defied state law and custom. At the same time, these cases inadvertently created a detailed record of how the concept of strict separation of the races was a handy fiction that erased the complexity of southerners' lives.

CHAPTER 8

CRIMINAL AFFECTIONS

DAISY AND ELSIE

In 1957, the editorial page of the *Clarion-Ledger* of Jackson, Mississippi, warned that Black activists were "trying to establish racial equality in Chicago" through "miscegenation, mixed marriages, wholesale adultery, bastardy and mongrelization." The editor noted that the paper had obtained an "authentic report" of a meeting of the "Negro Improvement Association" that had details of a speech by the city's mayor, Richard Daley. The report—which is so absurd that it may well be satire—explained that Mayor Daley had given a speech touting a new initiative for white girls in city high schools: "Take a Negro Boy Home Tonight." White girls who participated by bringing young Black men home to dinner would "get higher marks and other privileges for promoting inter-racial harmony."[1]

Whether the *Clarion-Ledger*'s editors believed a word of this, or had simply printed it in jest, did not matter. Indeed, Chicago was hardly a racial utopia in the 1950s, when white mobs repeatedly attacked Black homeowners and tenants who attempted to move into segregated white neighborhoods.[2] That autumn, Black Chicagoans were reeling from an incident in which a white mob had attacked Black picnickers in Calumet Park on the city's far South Side. Mayor Daley had sent hundreds of police officers to patrol the area, fearing further outbreaks of violence and retaliation.[3] The story's appeal was unrelated to its accuracy: segregationists were obsessed with blaming outsiders for "miscegenation" in the wake of *Brown v. Board of Education*. The idea of a citywide effort to push "mongrelization" through the schools fit neatly into segregationist narratives about the dangers posed by the *Brown* decision.

Key among the defenses of segregation was the claim that desegregated schools would inevitably lead to "miscegenation."[4] The claim that the foremost goal of civil rights activists was to push Americans toward "amalgamation" spread like wildfire after the US Supreme Court issued its ruling in *Brown*. Circuit court judge Tom P. Brady delivered his infamous "Black Monday" speech, wedding school desegregation and interracial sex, in the wake of the *Brown* ruling. Among his assertions was the notion that interracial intimacy inevitably led to the downfall of empires. ("Cleopatra was a white woman," he wrote in a pamphlet distributed by the newly founded White Citizens Council. "The white man built the pyramids." It was only later that the "seepage of the negroid blood into the white blood" brought the downfall of the Egyptian kingdoms.)[5]

There were tangible benefits to segregated schooling for whites— namely, the white schools received the vast majority of the funding. But the NAACP had already begun to target funding inequities as proof that segregated schooling could never be separate and equal, as the old *Plessy v. Ferguson* logic claimed it would be.[6] White supremacists needed a different justification for the necessity of segregation to southern life. Thus, schools became the bulwark for the protection of white racial purity. This hysteria made contesting the color line especially dangerous throughout the South. People around the world were shocked by the lynching of fourteen-year-old Emmett Till in 1955 for allegedly whistling at a white woman, Carolyn Bryant.[7] Another international spectacle occurred two years later when President Dwight D. Eisenhower sent federal troops to protect the Little Rock Nine as they attempted to desegregate Central High School in September 1957. In the infamous 1958 "kissing case," police officers in Monroe, North Carolina, arrested and brutalized two young Black boys, an eight-year-old and a ten-year-old, for allowing a white girl to kiss their cheeks. A judge sentenced them to a juvenile detention facility for an "indeterminate" length of time.[8] As segregationists adopted a more aggressively defensive position, the public commitment to "white purity" raised the stakes for anyone who dared cross the color line.

THE GROWING HYSTERIA AMONG WHITE SUPREMACISTS ABOUT THE VUL-nerability of legal racial segregation in the South pushed state lawmakers to adopt a slew of new laws in the 1950s. The governor who oversaw the push to enhance Mississippi's segregation laws was James Plemon Coleman. Coleman was widely considered to be a "moderate" segregationist.[9] He held Theodore Bilbo's ostentatious and outrageous expressions of white supremacy in disdain, preferring practical solutions to the threat of desegregation. Coleman worried about the consequences of violent retaliation against civil rights activism and instead focused on legalistic solutions to the brewing crisis over federal intervention and grassroots activism.[10] He declined to seek the support of the White Citizens' Councils, which claimed to have a "respectable" membership—but this term only referred to their members' perception that they represented the middle class and thus a "better" category of people than those who joined the Ku Klux Klan.[11] The Citizens Councils used tactics of violence and intimidation to defend white supremacy even as they blamed the murders of Black Mississippians on "lower-class" whites—the "rednecks" who supported Bilbo and his ilk.[12] The organization was founded in Indianola, Mississippi, a city in the heart of the Delta, in the wake of the Supreme Court's decision in *Brown v. Board of Education*.[13] Prior to

Coleman's election as governor, in the early 1950s, he had served as the attorney general of Mississippi. In that role he had led the state's prosecution of Willie McGee, ensuring that both the state and federal courts would allow the execution to take place.[14] Such was the stance of a Mississippi "moderate."

During the 1956 session of the Mississippi Legislature, lawmakers turned back to the state's miscegenation laws. This session of the legislature was the third to convene since the US Supreme Court had issued its May 1954 ruling in *Brown v. Board of Education*. The following year, the justices had issued a second opinion, *Brown II*, calling for the desegregation of public schools to proceed "with all deliberate speed."[15] In these post-*Brown* sessions, members of the state legislature scrambled to draft new segregation laws and to sharpen the penalties for those already on the books. In accordance with his preference for legal means of defending segregation, Governor Coleman backed these efforts. One house bill sought to prohibit the "mixing of races in swimming pools, parks, etc."[16] Another wanted to require bus and train stations to racially segregate waiting areas and maintain "separate toilet facilities for races in intra-state travel."[17] Another major law proposed creating a centralized state agency to defend segregation. This proposed agency became the Mississippi State Sovereignty Commission, which not only surveilled and investigated civil rights activists but actively assisted white supremacists—including sharing information about location and license plate numbers, a policy that contributed to the murders of civil rights activists James Chaney, Andrew Goodman, and Michael Schwerner in Neshoba County in 1964.[18]

The legislature also focused its ire on those critical of segregation. Lawmakers aimed to revise the state's libel law to include slander and prohibit "libel of government institutions." The offense was made a felony punishable by a fine of up to $1,000 and a year in prison. The legal change was explained in the newspaper as "another weapon against integration of the races, apparently by cutting off bitter criticism of Mississippi by groups seeking integration." It would also make it a felony to "use words by telephone or any other method of communication" that were "obscene or indecent or as insults and calculated to lead to a breach of the peace."[19]

Another proposed bill would make it "unlawful" to advocate for "disobedience of state laws."[20] Schoolteachers would be required "to list all organizations to which they paid dues or belonged during the preceding five years." State legislative efforts to publicly identify the membership of organizations like the NAACP were an effective tool for culling participation. Being openly identified as a member of a civil rights organization made a Black person vulnerable to intimidation, harassment, and even lynching. In the late 1950s, the NAACP alone lost hundreds of local branches and nearly 50,000 members across the South.[21]

The 1956 Mississippi legislative session was consumed by these efforts to undermine any potential federal desegregation efforts and shore up the state's Jim Crow laws. What few legislators wanted to admit was that this action was necessary, in part, because the state's legal regime of segregation had never been terribly robust. This was especially true of the state's laws governing interracial marriage and sex. Common law marriages remained valid. Unlawful cohabitation was a mere misdemeanor, and there were no laws specifically criminalizing interracial sex. Those looking to bolster the legal foundation of segregation knew they would have to deal with these weaknesses in the laws governing the color line. And so legislators embarked on an effort to completely revise the marriage laws.[22]

On March 22, 1956, Representatives Joe Hopkins of Coahoma County and Thompson McClellan of Clay County introduced a revised version of the state's incest law. The law already prohibited "persons being within the degrees within which marriages are declared by law to be incestuous and void" from cohabiting. Should an incestuous couple cohabit, they faced a punishment of up to ten years in the state penitentiary. Hopkins and McClellan's innovation was to add a clause explicitly prohibiting interracial cohabitation. Interracial couples who cohabited would face the same harsh penalty that they faced for marrying: up to a decade of hard labor at Parchman Farm.[23] The law went even further to punish interracial sex: a person could be convicted under the law if he or she was found "guilty of a single act of adultery or fornication."[24] This was a dramatic departure from the status quo, though the legislature also kept the original unlawful cohabitation law in place with its requirement of "habitual sexual intercourse." For couples who fell into the same racial classification, unlawful cohabitation remained a misdemeanor. Same-race couples could not face criminal charges of fornication or adultery based on a single act of intercourse.[25]

The argument in favor of this new law was that the current legal code did not sufficiently address the problem of interracial cohabitation. Upon introducing the measure, Representative McClellan "read the House a letter from a district attorney who claimed a Negro and a white woman were living together and there was no statute under which they could be punished."[26] This was patently false. The unlawful cohabitation law was still in force. More likely, the district attorney felt that the punishment the law provided was woefully inadequate for what he viewed as such a serious violation of the color line. Six months in jail and a $500 penalty had never been enough to discourage all interracial couples from living together and forming families.

The bill sailed through both houses of the state legislature. H.B. 975 received the approval of the Committee of the Whole. It was read before the chamber three times, and then a vote was taken. Not a single member of the Mississippi House of Representatives voted against the bill.[27] The Senate soon followed with a unanimous vote.[28] On April 5, 1956, Governor Coleman announced that he had approved the new law.[29]

MEMBERS OF THE MISSISSIPPI LEGISLATURE WERE NOT FINISHED REVISING the state's laws governing interracial marriage and sex. Indeed, its 1956 session proved to be the most transformative in the state's history in regard to marriage law since Reconstruction and its overthrow.

Another bill aimed to require couples to obtain marriage licenses. But some members were hesitant to abolish common law marriage, revisiting the debates they had had over the issue in the early twentieth century. Representative Joe Wroten explained that, in his view, such a law would "take advantage of ignorant people."[30] Many Mississippians were accustomed to the legality of common law marriage; if they did not understand the legal change, they faced serious consequences. Children born after the abolition of common law marriage would not be considered legitimate offspring of their fathers. Widows would struggle to inherit the property of their common law husbands. Couples could face charges of unlawful cohabitation.

Critics of the change suggested providing a grace period that would give couples time to apply for licenses. Representative Joe Hopkins—one of the cosponsors of the cohabitation bill—argued that this was entirely unnecessary. In his view, abolishing common law marriage was an urgent matter. He added an evasive note to his colleagues concerning the importance of passing the law as quickly as possible: "You know the purpose of the bill." The *Clarion-Ledger*, covering the debate, observed, "Apparently, the House knew the purpose because it was never mentioned."[31] There was something about common law marriage and its relationship to segregation law that members of the legislature were unwilling to say aloud and put on the record.

The "purpose" that Hopkins alluded to was twofold. By outlawing common law marriages, the legislature made more couples legally unmarried. Southern lawmakers sought ways to get around *Brown v. Board of Education* that did not involve explicitly excluding Black children from white schools. One of these "loopholes" was excluding children on the basis of morality. Many white supremacists disparaged Black women as sexually immoral and prone to having children out of wedlock. Some made the case that the law could hinder efforts to desegregate schools. This argument presumed that many Black couples did not obtain marriage licenses—it was supposedly Black people, not white ones, who did not get marriage licenses—and the law would render the children of these informal marriages illegitimate.[32] The *Hattiesburg American* explained that the bill would be used "in bolstering the 1954 pupil assignment law based on health, morals and community welfare."[33] The state could argue that it segregated "illegitimate" (in other words, Black) children out of "moral" concerns rather than racial ones.[34]

There was a glaring hole in this argument: while the "morals" provision of the pupil assignment law might prevent some Black parents from filing desegregation suits, it would not do so until years into the future. The law abolishing common law marriage grandfathered in those unions that preceded the law's passage. The children who would be affected by this change had not yet been born, and although many Black children in Mississippi were identified as "illegitimate" at birth, most were not.[35] There was some other reason that Hopkins and other legislators used evasive language, to the frustration of their colleagues. Senator W. B. Alexander, one of the bill's opponents, said in exasperation, "I have repeatedly asked what possible benefit to maintaining segregation this bill will have and I have had no satisfactory answer. I feel as deeply as any man in this chamber about segregation but I have never been told how this will help."[36]

Newspaper reports about the purpose of the law struggled to explain clearly how abolishing common law marriage would protect racial segregation. The *Delta Democrat-Times* explained that it "was one of a block of bills recommended by the pro-segregation Legal Education Advisory Committee as a means of evading the U.S. Supreme Court decision outlawing segregation."[37] The *Biloxi Sun Herald* explained it as "another attempt to keep Negroes out of white society."[38]

There was another reason that requiring marriage licenses was an important bulwark in legal segregation: the history of interracial marriage. Some members of the legislature knew, as many other Mississippians did, that, historically, white men had cohabited with Black women. Some of these couples considered themselves married. The importance of abolishing common law marriage could not be explained without acknowledging this history—something legislators in the 1950s were wholly unwilling to do. Though governors and legislators of a previous generation had openly discussed the "problem" of white men cohabiting with Black women, by the 1950s the contours of acceptable public discourse had changed. No longer were many men—especially politicians—willing to put their real concerns on the record.

It was white men who were most likely to pursue interracial relationships—not Black men, as propagandists claimed. There was a long tradition of communities either accepting families headed by white men and Black women or looking the other way, subjecting them to punishment in the court of public opinion instead of legal prosecution. These couples might be treated as outcasts, but social ostracism was not adequate to deter white men and Black women from forming families. The children of these unions often had fairer complexions than their mothers; their racially ambiguous appearance similarly confounded claims that white Mississippians revered the separation of the races and the protection of white racial purity. This history was also partly the product of white legislators, judges, and juries who made and enforced the law. Admitting the truth of this history threatened to unmask segregation for what it truly was: a system that favored white men above all others, even so far as protecting their ability to cohabit with Black women. Mississippians did not have a long-standing commitment to segregation as strict separation. History showed that the opposite was true.

The confusion over the purpose of the law meant that the common law marriage bill faced greater resistance than the unlawful cohabitation law had. Legislators haggled over the wording of the bill. But in the end, the law prohibiting common law marriage passed the Mississippi House of Representatives by a vote of 117 to 5.[39] The state had finally abolished common law marriage, supposedly as a bulwark against desegregation.

Following the bill's passage, Governor Coleman called for even tighter restrictions on the ability to marry. He decried the state's "marriage mills," calling for blood tests, three-day waiting periods, and larger fees as well as a requirement to produce a birth certificate or other "documentary evidence of age." The tightened legal requirements would lessen the problems of "broken homes and homeless children," which he blamed on "quickie marriages." (He did not comment on the fact that, by creating further obstacles, these measures might increase the number of couples who simply did not marry at all.) Coleman also boasted that, since the legislature had outlawed common law marriage, "he had heard of no arrests made for co-habitation."[40]

Even if this was a true statement, this state of affairs would not last. In the legislators' haste to fortify segregation law, they had made some perplexing decisions that would cause them further trouble down the road once couples were arrested under the new law. Curiously, the amended bill that made interracial cohabitation a felony combined the anti-miscegenation provision with the legal prohibition of incest. The language of the law indicated that the interracial cohabitation provision applied only to those "persons whose marriage is prohibited by law by reason of race or blood *and* which marriage is declared to be incestuous and void" (emphasis added). The plain language of the law indicated that only interracial couples whose relationships were also incestuous could be convicted under the law.[41]

It seems that Hopkins and McClellan were not terribly attentive to their task as they drafted the amended law. The lawmakers' intent was, apparently, to make sentences harsher and more exacting. It seems that they borrowed the language of the 1880 law, which also had the same archaic use of "incestuous" buried inside it. That law, too, was written in a way that fused the incest and miscegenation provisions, even though the use of "incestuous" to refer to illicit sex had long fallen out of common speech. So instead of imposing a ten-year sentence on those convicted of incest *or* miscegenation, a contemporary observer might conclude that the law only applied to those convicted of both offenses.

The men who made and voted for the law may not have read it closely or listened carefully when the law was read three times before the final vote. But other people did.

MARY ROSE CONFESSED THAT SHE HAD BEEN DRINKING WHEN THE sheriff roused her from sleep in the early hours of February 14, 1958. This was the most convenient explanation for why a married white mother of four children ended up in a Black man's bed at four o'clock in the morning.[42] The home belonged to Joe Scott, one of the tenants who lived on the Rose family's property. Like Mary, Joe was married and had a child. When the sheriff pulled Mary out of bed and arrested her and Joe Scott, he didn't ask questions about what had transpired. The sheriff noted that Mary stunk of alcohol and seemed to be in a whiskey-induced stupor.[43] Mary had a reputation for drinking too much.[44]

Whether Mary and Joe had engaged in sexual intercourse was not a question that law enforcement officers seemed all that interested in answering. The sheriff took the pair to the Jones County jail but quickly split them up. Mary sobered up, and a highway patrolman drove her to the Forrest County jail in Hattiesburg.[45] She later testified that she was so intoxicated that she could not recall anything that happened while she was in her cell at the Jones County jail.[46] She did remember that, at one point, the sheriff asked her if she knew why she had been arrested. Mary answered that she did not. She recalled later that the sheriff explained her offense as "being in a colored person's home"—or something to that effect.[47]

Mary spent weeks in jail, where she was allowed to call her husband and speak to her daughter briefly. She assumed that her husband, Elmer, would post bond so that she could go home to await her trial. She also assumed that he would hire an attorney to defend her.[48] He did neither of these things. Mary remained in jail until her court hearing in late March.[49]

Perhaps Mary did not know that Elmer was the driving force behind her arrest. It was her own husband who had told the sheriff that Mary could be found in another man's bed, where the pair were found in a disheveled—but fully clothed—state.[50] The house was located only a few hundred yards from Mary and Elmer's home. Whatever transpired in the hours before Mary Rose passed out in Joe Scott's house, Elmer claimed that he knew all about it. He put his accusation of adultery in an affidavit that he filed with the justice of the peace in the hours before Mary was arrested, and Elmer rode along with the sheriff as he went to arrest Joe and Mary, his wife.[51]

In late March, after Mary and Joe had been jailed for five weeks, a Jones County grand jury indicted the pair for unlawful cohabitation under the revised state law that made interracial sex a felony.[52] The couple faced charges that could result in a sentence of up to ten years in the state penitentiary—the same penalty that applied to interracial marriage. Their indictment showed the consequences of the new law. Mary and Joe did not live together. Even the court's summary of their case did not explicitly say they were charged with having sexual intercourse—instead, it alleged that the pair did "wilfully, unlawfully and feloniously cohabit with each other."[53] Unlawful cohabitation now encompassed the offense of interracial sex.

The next time Mary Rose saw Joe Scott was when she was driven back to Jones County for their arraignment hearing. Because her husband had refused to hire a lawyer, she had no attorney to defend her when she finally had her day in court. On March 20, 1958, she pled guilty to the charge of unlawful cohabitation.[54] She later claimed she had been told to plead guilty by the Jones County sheriff, Fred Walters. He assured her that a trial would only lead to scandal, warning that if she did not plead guilty, "there will be a thousand eyes looking on you."[55] Mary Rose later acknowledged that she did not know the difference between a misdemeanor and a felony, or what, exactly, her punishment could entail, but her ignorance would not protect her from being sent to the penitentiary.[56]

Although couples charged with unlawful cohabitation in Mississippi had long received light sentences, this was no longer the legal terrain in which Mary and Joe found themselves. The judge sentenced Mary Rose to serve fifteen months at the notorious Parchman Farm. Joe Scott also had no attorney. By way of explanation of his own guilty plea, Joe told the court, "They told me not to dispute her word."[57] He received the same fifteen-month sentence.[58] Mary Rose was sent to the Hinds County jail to await transportation to Parchman. While she was there, Elmer sent her divorce papers.[59]

THE TREATMENT OF JOE SCOTT AND MARY ROSE REPRESENTED A RADI-cal break from the past. If this incident had taken place two years earlier, neither Joe nor Mary would have broken any laws. And, of course, the 1956 law only criminalized *interracial* sex. Same-race couples could not be charged under any Mississippi law for acts of sexual intercourse unless the acts were "habitual" and could be classed as unlawful cohabitation. No one claimed to have witnessed the pair having sexual intercourse, even though Scott lived in a one-room house and his wife and another man were present the evening that Mary Rose stumbled across their threshold.[60] The implication that Mary and Joe may have been intimate was enough to merit their harsh treatment.

After being sentenced, Mary Rose finally retained legal counsel. Within weeks she was represented by two white Jackson lawyers, Colin Stockdale and L. Percy Quinn.[61] By early April, Stockdale had filed a motion asking the court to allow Mary to withdraw her guilty plea. She had not understood the severity of the charge she had faced, he argued. Moreover, her arrest had been specifically engineered by her husband, who had wished "to procure a divorce from this defendant in order that he might marry another woman."[62] The couple had not lived together in some time. They shared ownership in a trucking business, which complicated their separation.[63] Stockdale implied that Elmer had wanted Mary Rose sent to jail so that he would not lose any money in a prolonged divorce. At the hearing, Mary testified that she had not understood the seriousness of the charges—nor had she and Joe had sexual intercourse that fateful night.[64] The court refused Stockdale's motion to set aside Mary's plea, however, declaring that she had not been deprived of any of her constitutional rights. The fact that she had had no lawyer at the time of her trial and conviction was a result of her own choice.[65]

Stockdale got to work crafting an appeal to the Mississippi Supreme Court on Mary's behalf. He did not struggle to find fault with the case against Mary Rose. Mary had not understood the gravity of the charges she faced. She pled guilty "to what she believed was a misdemeanor charge." She did this only because she wished "to protect the good name and reputation of her small children"—not because she was guilty of the alleged crime.[66]

The appeal encompassed a range of arguments about Mary's treatment by the circuit court judge. It focused on the unwillingness of the judge to allow Mary Rose to withdraw her guilty plea and be granted a new trial. She had asked her husband repeatedly to hire a lawyer, but he had refused to do so. And when she was finally charged in March after spending five weeks in jail, she was "wholly ignorant of the processes of law, having never been in court before upon any charge whatsoever." Had she had access to legal counsel, as she had requested, Mary would have pled not guilty and presented a "meritorious defense" to dispute the charges against her—that she and Joe had not engaged in sexual intercourse.[67]

The indictment read that the pair, "being persons prohibited by law from marrying each other by reason of race and blood and being persons whose marriage is declared to be incestious [sic] and void, The [sic] said Joe Scott being a member of the Negro race and the said Mary Rose being a member of the White race did wilfully, unlawfully and feloniously cohabit with each other."[68] But while Mary was a white woman and Joe was a Black man, the rest of the indictment made little sense given the facts of the case. Mary and Joe did not "cohabit." And the indictment said nothing about sexual intercourse—though, if it had, no one had witnessed the pair in the act. Moreover, the language of the 1956 law made the entire indictment sound peculiar: after all, there was certainly no evidence to suggest that Joe and Mary were related by blood.

Stockdale's brief also argued that the law itself was unconstitutional. By treating interracial sex and same-race sex differently, he alleged, the law violated the Fifth and Fourteenth Amendments to the US Constitution. The Mississippi law deprived people like Mary of the right to due process and equal protection of the law. And a law that mandated different penalties for the same crime depending on the race of the persons charged, he said, flew in the face of the spirit of the Fourteenth Amendment.[69]

What Stockdale was challenging was the precedent set by *Pace v. Alabama* in the 1880s. The US Supreme Court had not revisited this precedent since the nineteenth century. But in the post–*Brown v. Board of Education* era, and given the other civil rights cases of the 1940s and 1950s, Stockdale's brief suggested, the Supreme Court might revise its view of such laws, overturning them as it had other forms of segregation encoded in law as it chiseled away at the *Plessy* doctrine of "separate but equal."

After her lawyers filed their appeal, the court set bond at $2,500. Mary posted bond, and on April 15, 1958, two months after her arrest, she finally walked out of the Hinds County jail.[70] She was not free for long. Within months, Mary found herself back in court, charged with contributing to the delinquency of a minor. She had allegedly picked a sixteen-year-old girl up from school and persuaded her to drink a beer with Mary and a thirty-five-year-old white man at a motel. The court found her guilty, and Mary Rose was fined $50 and sentenced to serve four months in the county jail. She also lost custody of her children to Elmer.[71]

While Mary was out getting into even more legal trouble, Joe Scott was not able to post bond. Instead, that summer and autumn he toiled in the fields at Parchman Farm.[72]

WHILE MARY ROSE'S APPEAL WAS UNDERWAY, ANOTHER COUPLE WAS arrested for violating the new law criminalizing interracial sex. In this case, the judge came down even more harshly on those accused of breaking the law. But their convictions would turn the tide for the fate of both Mary Rose and Joe Scott.

Daisy Ratcliff was nearing fifty years old when she caught the eye of Elsie Arrington. Both Daisy and Elsie lived in Purvis, a tiny town southwest of Hattiesburg, halfway to Poplarville. (Theodore Bilbo's second cousin, the Lamar County superintendent of education Dewitt Bilbo, lived on Clark Street in Purvis, not far from Elsie and his father.)[73] Daisy worked as a cook; Elsie was a farmhand.[74] They lived down the street from one another, along the railroad tracks that cut through town. Eventually, Elsie began visiting Daisy regularly at her home. Their affair went on for a long time—perhaps five or six years, according to neighbors.[75] As Daisy was beyond childbearing age, their sexual relationship produced no children. It all might have amounted to nothing more than a bit of neighborhood gossip if it were not for the fact that Daisy Ratcliff was Black and Elsie Arrington was white.

One neighbor, Virillia Dickson, took notice of Elsie's frequent visits to Daisy's home. She blamed Daisy for the affair, claiming that she walked up and down the street in front of Elsie's home, trying to attract his attention.[76] Virillia went to the home of the town marshal and asked him to "go down to break that up."[77] He told her to give him a call if she saw Elsie go into Daisy's home again. Another neighbor, Eva Rouse, was also disturbed by the affair. She lived next door to Elsie and noted his regular visits to Daisy's home. Eva also ratted the couple out to the local sheriff.[78]

On the evening of July 2, 1958, Elsie and Daisy lay together quietly in bed in the dark. They were in their bedclothes: Elsie was clad in shorts and Daisy was dressed in her nightgown.[79] The sheriff, looking to catch the couple in an illegal act, silently crept up to the house and shone a flashlight through the window.[80] The town marshal and the deputy sheriff approached from the back.[81] Without warning—and lacking a search warrant—the sheriff barreled into the house and forced the pair out of bed. The sheriff ordered Elsie and Daisy to get dressed before he arrested them and took them to jail.[82]

Daisy Ratcliff was not a poor or defenseless woman. She owned her home and had the means to hire a lawyer and post the $500 bond.[83] Jesse Shanks, a local white attorney, took on Daisy's defense.[84] On the afternoon of July 12, Daisy was tried before a jury of six white men in the Purvis justice court. The local justice of the peace, Harvey Stewart, presided over the trial.[85] Some misdemeanor offenses could be tried in either a circuit court—which only met twice a year—or in the local justice court. Eva Rouse testified at the trial, though when asked if she had seen the pair engaged in sexual intercourse, she replied that she had not. After a short trial, the jury deliberated. They declared Daisy not guilty.[86]

Three days later, Daisy and Elsie were indicted by a grand jury in the Lamar County Circuit Court for unlawful cohabitation.[87] As before, Jesse Shanks defended Daisy against the charges. Shanks was a prominent Purvis attorney. He was a former state representative, having served in office during the 1940s. He was also no friend to the cause of civil rights or Black voting. When Republican US senators had demanded an inquiry into the voter suppression tactics lauded by Democrat Theodore Bilbo in 1946, Shanks had served as counsel to Bilbo. While running for lieutenant governor the following year, Shanks had decried the outside influence of "sinister forces" that would "pervert and destroy all the ideals and traditions of our great state and our southland and besmirch the rich heritage bequeathed to us by the blood, toil and tears of our forefathers."[88]

Despite his associations with Bilbo, Shanks was willing to go to bat for Daisy Ratcliff. He defended her vigorously, seemingly irritated at the overreach of local law enforcement officers and the abuses of the local courts for trying his client twice for the same crime. Before Daisy had her day in court for the second time, Shanks filed a demurrer to the indictment that argued, among other points, that the indictment was "vague and indefinite" and "duplicitous" and that it "charge[d] two separate offenses in the same count."[89] He also filed a motion arguing that the charges were a clear violation of Daisy Ratcliff's right to be protected against double jeopardy—a right enshrined in both the Mississippi and US Constitutions.[90]

Despite Shanks's protestations, Judge Sebe Dale allowed the district attorney to try Daisy again for unlawful cohabitation on July 24. This time, her case was argued before a jury of twelve white men. Many of the witnesses were the same—the three officers who arrested Daisy and Elsie on the night of July 2, and Eva Rouse, who was the source of much of the gossip about the couple's affair. But in the circuit court trial, Eva changed her story. She now insisted that she *had* witnessed Daisy and Elsie having sex as she glanced through the window of Elsie's home.[91] This was a boon for the prosecution. All the law required for interracial cohabitation was evidence of one single act of "fornication" or "adultery."

Daisy's lawyer worked doggedly to undermine Eva's story. Shanks called jurors from the first trial to the stand, attempting to show that Eva had changed her story. The district attorney objected to this line of questioning, and the judge agreed.[92] Shanks also attempted to have the testimony of the sheriff, the town marshal, and the deputy sheriff thrown out on the basis that they had not informed Daisy of the crime for which she was being arrested when they burst into her home.[93] Mississippi law only allowed an officer to trespass on private property and arrest a suspect without a search warrant if he witnessed someone in the act of committing a felony. Shanks argued that the sheriff had told Daisy and Elsie that they were being arrested under the misdemeanor unlawful cohabitation law, but he had not clearly said she would be charged with violating the felony cohabitation law.[94] Given that she was initially tried in justice court, this was a compelling argument, as justice courts could not try felony cases. In Shanks's view, the arrest itself was illegal.

These efforts were fruitless. Although the court's instructions to the jury indicate that one or more jurors may have been skeptical of the evidence, eventually the men returned with a unanimous verdict.[95] Daisy was proclaimed guilty. On July 24, 1958, the court sentenced her to the maximum penalty allowed under law: ten years at Parchman Farm.[96] This was a more severe sentence than even Davis Knight had faced after his conviction for marrying a white woman.

Elsie Arrington avoided prison. He was not tried for unlawful cohabitation in either court. Rather than being sent to Parchman, he was sent to the state mental hospital.[97] The message this disparate treatment sent was not subtle: Daisy's desire for Elsie was criminal. Elsie's affections for Daisy were evidence of mental illness. Daisy was the perpetrator in this scenario: a Black woman who had taken advantage of a dull-witted white man. She was the one who deserved to be punished.

DAISY'S LAWYER IMMEDIATELY APPEALED THE LAMAR COUNTY COURT'S ruling to the Mississippi Supreme Court, citing a range of defects with the trial and her conviction. The search conducted by the sheriff had been illegal. He had no warrant to enter Daisy's home, and she certainly did not invite him inside. Moreover, the sentence was excessive, and Daisy had been tried twice for unlawful cohabitation, violating her constitutional protection against double jeopardy.[98] Shanks also reluctantly noted that the felony interracial cohabitation law likely violated the Fourteenth Amendment's Equal Protection Clause. Shanks explained to the justices that he loathed having to discuss the potential unconstitutionality of the law, "but regardless of our personal feelings and in fulfilling our duty to our client," in his opinion the law violated not only the US Constitution but the Mississippi Constitution as well.[99]

An assistant attorney general for the state, G. Garland Lyell Jr., argued that Daisy had not, in fact, been tried twice for the same crime. In the justice court trial, he claimed, Daisy had been tried for violating the *old* statute on unlawful cohabitation—the misdemeanor offense. When she was tried in the circuit court, she had been charged with violating the new felony law. Therefore, she had not been tried for the same crime twice.[100] He implied that the not-guilty verdict in the justice court was the real source of the tragedy, as the maximum length of time she could have been incarcerated for violating the misdemeanor law was a mere six months in jail.

There was a major problem with this argument: if Daisy was initially charged with a misdemeanor, then Shanks was correct. Her arrest *was* illegal. The sheriff only found evidence of Daisy and Elsie sharing a bed once he had already trespassed on her property and shone a flashlight through her window. This invasion of her private property was only allowable if she was in the act of committing a felony.[101] Shanks also criticized Eva Rouse's testimony, implying that it had been unduly influenced by police or the prosecutor. "It is the firm opinion of this writer that between the time she testified in Justice Court and the time she testified in Circuit Court that someone, somehow, impressed upon her the necessity of proving at least one act of adultery," and that it was this pressure that had inspired Eva Rouse to make the claim that she had witnessed the couple having sex in Elsie's house.[102]

Finally, Shanks said, Daisy's conviction should be overturned based on the language of the law itself. "You can't tell whether it punishes you for miscegenous or for incestuous cohabitation," he wrote.[103] He then concluded the brief with an appeal to the racism of the justices of the state supreme court. Shanks explained that "Appellant is a Negro woman over 63 years of age, and is characteristic of so many of her race; that is, low mentality and ignorant, and accustomed all her life to working for 'white folks,' reared during a period of time when the morals of some of our white people were not of as high a standard as we in the South today believe we are." In other words, Daisy was a product of a different time, when white men were allowed dalliances with Black women. He continued, noting that "the thought occurs to this writer that, granting that the Appellant has been guilty of unlawful cohabitation with a white man, taking into consideration her status in society, the limits of her mental processes, and lack of educational background and opportunity and environment, her conduct is more 'unmoral' than 'immoral.'"[104]

Neither Elsie nor Daisy knew better. They had come of age in a different era of Jim Crow. The law had been different then, as had the customs of Mississippians, both Black and white. As Daisy and Elsie were people of "low mentality," the justices of the Mississippi Supreme Court should, at the very least, have mercy on them. Shanks clearly assumed that the justices would be receptive to a defense couched in insulting language about the supposed ignorance and reduced intellectual capacity of a Black woman.

WHILE THE MISSISSIPPI SUPREME COURT CONSIDERED THE APPEALS IN *State of Mississippi v. Daisy Ratcliff* and *State of Mississippi v. Mary Rose*, a third person was arrested and charged under the felony law. This arrest came amid reports about another shocking crime in rural Pontotoc County. On October 25, 1958, a white man named Howard Pritchard beat his wife so mercilessly that she later died of her injuries. Howard admitted to murdering his wife, who was the mother of their five children.[105]

But Howard offered the sheriff a rationale for his murderous rage: he claimed that his wife had had sexual intercourse with a Black man, David Lee Souter, while the three drank moonshine together that evening. *Jet* magazine, reporting on the case, offered a lurid tale. The article explained that Howard's wife had propositioned David Lee with her husband's permission. It was only after the two went off into "the bushes" that Howard changed his mind and was provoked to violence.[106] With this information, offered up as part of Howard's murder confession, the sheriff arrested David Lee and jailed him.[107] They did not disclose where he was incarcerated, anticipating that a lynch mob could appear.[108]

What happened next showed how dramatically the use of the state's unlawful cohabitation law had changed over the past three decades. In early December, a Pontotoc County grand jury indicted Howard Pritchard for murder and David Lee Souter for unlawful cohabitation. David Lee faced up to ten years in prison.[109]

Jet explained that "for most white Mississippians the case was one more piece of embarrassing proof that all relations between Negro men and white women (even in Mississippi) are not rape."[110] But this tragic case also demonstrated how the new law empowered law enforcement. Unshackled from the pesky technicalities of the old unlawful cohabitation law, state officials could charge individuals with a felony if they alleged even one instance of interracial sex. Even if that accusation came from the mouth of a confessed murderer.

Developments in the *Ratcliff* and *Rose* cases would shift David Lee Souter's fortunes dramatically. On December 15, 1958—less than a week after David Lee was formally charged with unlawful cohabitation—the Mississippi Supreme Court announced its rulings in both cases: the justices had decided to invalidate the convictions of both Daisy and Mary. The *Ratcliff* opinion came first. It was authored by Justice J. Gillespie, and it avoided any question of the constitutionality of the interracial cohabitation law. Instead, Gillespie identified "the sole question" in the case as whether the interracial cohabitation law "[made] it a crime for a white person and a Negro to cohabit, or live together as husband and wife, or be guilty of a single act of fornication." The felony law was, in fact, a derivative of the incest law. The state law clearly said that to be charged under the revised anti-miscegenation law, a couple had to be *both* interracial and related by blood. The relationship needed to be "miscegenistic" and "incestuous" to constitute a violation of the law. "A marriage between a white person and a negro would not be incestuous; it would be miscegenetic," Gillespie wrote. Moreover, the law prohibited cohabitation between "persons whose marriage is prohibited," implying that a couple needed to be legally wed to be prosecuted under the statute. "It is settled law that penal statutes must be strictly construed," the opinion concluded. Because the law had been so sloppily written, the justices had no choice but to deem it virtually unenforceable.[111]

Daisy Ratcliff's lawyer had done what might have seemed impossible: Jesse Shanks not only convinced the state's highest court to invalidate her conviction, but he also ensured that she could not be tried again under either statute. Daisy had been acquitted under the misdemeanor law, and the felony law was now unenforceable. Daisy Ratcliff would be free.

Conveniently, by voiding both convictions, the Mississippi justices did not need to worry that federal courts might review their decision and address the constitutionality of the law. The opinion sidestepped the question of whether the law violated the Fourteenth Amendment's Equal Protection Clause. Should the US Supreme Court revisit *Pace*, they might rule that such laws were, in fact, racially discriminatory.[112] And the Mississippi law was uniquely vulnerable: the state did not criminalize fornication between same-race couples. The discriminatory treatment that interracial couples faced was undeniable.

The state court's ruling in *Ratcliff* was a windfall for the beleaguered Mary Rose. The justices issued a short opinion in her case, referring to its ruling in *Ratcliff v. State*. As in Daisy's case, in Mary Rose's case, they said, "the State does not contend that any incestuous relationship is involved."[113] Mary Rose therefore should not have been convicted under the felony law. Mary—likely still jailed in Jones County—would not be sent to Parchman Farm after all.

Joe Scott, on the other hand, had already served eight months of his fifteen-month sentence in the state penitentiary. This was two months longer than the misdemeanor law allowed. Two days after the state supreme court had made its ruling in Mary's case, the Jones County district attorney had filed a petition to the circuit court arguing that "the sentence imposed by this court on the said Joe Scott is therefore void and of no effect and said void judgment and plea should be vacated and stricken from the minutes of this court." The motion noted that Joe had "already served a longer sentence than authorized by law" and asked that he "be restored to his liberty." The court sent an order to Parchman directing the warden to free Joe Scott.[114]

THE MISSISSIPPI SUPREME COURT'S RULINGS IN *RATCLIFF* AND *ROSE* did not go unnoticed by the press. Newspaper coverage of the decisions labeled the "faulty law" a mere "legislative goof."[115] The state legislature did not meet again for more than a year after the court issued the rulings, but in its next biennial session, the lawmakers once again took up the issue of unlawful cohabitation. Both houses introduced legislation to punish interracial couples. On January 13, 1960, state senators George Malone Yarbrough and Benjamin Franklin Hilbun Jr. introduced a new amendment to the cohabitation law that would separate the interracial and incest clauses.[116] Since *Ratcliff* and *Rose*, the felony law had been unenforceable. Couples could still face charges of unlawful cohabitation, but only as a misdemeanor. The bill faced no resistance in either house of the state legislature.[117] On February 24, 1960, Governor Ross Barnett signed the bill into law.[118] The state legislature closed the loophole that had allowed interracial couples to cohabit without fear of a felony prosecution. Once the new bill came into effect, the stakes were far higher for anyone in a domestic relationship with a person of a different race.

The revised anti-miscegenation law was put into use the same year it passed—but not to punish a consensual relationship. On Thanksgiving night in 1960, Mary Jean Lipsey, a Black teenager attending Okolona College in Chickasaw County, was raped by a white man, Thomas Hood. Thomas lured the young woman into his car by asking her to babysit his children. On the way to his home, he pulled the car over and raped her. Thomas might have assumed that no authority would punish him for assaulting a Black teenager. Southern prosecutors and juries had long been reluctant to charge and convict white men of rape when their victims were Black.[119] But if Thomas made this assumption, he was wrong. Mary Jean bravely reported the rape to the police despite the risk that they might not believe her. Thomas denied any wrongdoing, claiming that Mary Jean had consented to having sex with him.[120]

Local officials were hesitant to discuss the rape publicly, though they did note that Mary Jean had testified before the grand jury about what happened to her that evening. Despite this first-person account, the grand jury declined to indict Thomas for rape. Even though Mary Jean testified that Thomas had "used force," they determined there was not enough evidence under the state's rape statute. This doubt about Mary Jean's story leached into press coverage of the trial. The *Delta Democrat-Times* put "rape" in quotation marks in its headline, noting that according to the grand jury, "force was not apparent and therefore the crime was not rape."[121] In December 1960, the grand jury chose to charge Thomas Hood with violating the new interracial cohabitation law. This was perilous terrain for Mary Jean Lipsey: she, too, could be indicted. But the prosecutor opted not to prosecute Mary Jean and instead offered her immunity for her testimony.[122]

Local officials were likely anxious about the outrage that might follow in the wake of their treatment of the case. "It's a delicate proposition," the district attorney told one reporter, to charge a white man with fornication rather than rape. "There are a lot of folks who would like to make something of it."[123] The decision to charge Thomas with fornication was hugely consequential: rape remained a capital crime in Mississippi. A person convicted of rape could die in the electric chair, as Willie McGee had, or serve a life sentence in prison. The interracial cohabitation law, on the other hand, had a maximum penalty of ten years in Parchman Farm. And yet Thomas Hood did not feel the full force of the new law. *Jet* reported that Thomas received a two-year suspended sentence, though the magazine missed the rape allegation, reporting only that Thomas and Mary Jean "had relations." These reports made the encounter sound consensual. There was no mention of Mary Jean's assertion that Thomas had raped her.[124]

In Mary Jean Lipsey's case, the district attorney was clearly not motivated to pursue rape charges. This would not be the first instance of a white man being tried for the sexual assault of a Black woman in Mississippi: in May 1956, four white men had raped sixteen-year-old Annette Butler. The men were charged with "forcible ravishment and kidnap." Although Annette took the stand, only one of the men pled guilty; the others were acquitted or had charges dismissed after the jury deadlocked.[125] Ernest Dillon, who pled guilty to "assault with intent to rape," received a twenty-year sentence at Parchman Farm.[126] Just months after Mary Jean Lipsey's attacker would face no prison time, two white men in Yazoo County received life sentences for a heinous crime involving the rape of a Black woman and her daughter. Brothers Lewis and Charles

Coffee were convicted of raping the five-year-old girl.[127] A third white man, Bobby Smith, received only a five-year sentence for "assault and attempted rape" on the girl's mother.[128] Reporting on the case, the *New York Times* noted that "no white man has received the death penalty in the state for raping a Negro."[129] A report from the US Bureau of Prisons showed that across the nation, in 1956 alone, twelve Black men had been executed for rape. Not a single white man had faced the death penalty for this crime.[130]

Mississippi led the states in the use of capital punishment, including for rape. Since the execution of Willie McGee in 1951, another Black man convicted of raping a white woman had died in the state's new gas chamber. The state of Mississippi executed Mose Robinson on December 16, 1955.[131] In 1959, another accused Black man never made it to trial. After a white woman picked Mack Charles Parker out of a lineup, a white lynch mob seized him from the jail in Poplarville. Parker was viciously beaten before he was shot dead. His body was thrown in the Pearl River. The lynching caught the attention of national civil rights leaders and President Eisenhower. The FBI sent investigators, but no one was ever charged with a crime in the case.[132]

Law enforcement officers continued to use unlawful cohabitation laws in the service of white supremacy. In Holmes County, white officials had refused to allow Black voters to pay their poll taxes since 1956. In 1963, Hartman Turnbow, a local Black farmer, risked his life along with thirteen others to attempt to register at the county courthouse. The registrar refused to even allow most of the prospective voters to take the literacy test, but Hartman completed his. The registrar told him that not only had he failed the test, but "he was never going to pass." The local newspaper printed his name and labeled him an "integrationist." Less than a month later, someone threw a firebomb into Hartman's home while he slept. The arsonist then shot at Hartman when he ran outside. The sheriff, who reluctantly turned up six hours later, arrested Hartman for arson.[133] The grand jury declined to indict him. But they did indict Hartman and his common law wife for unlawful cohabitation—the first such prosecution in Holmes County since 1938.[134] Amid rising Black Freedom protests, law enforcement officers could use unlawful cohabitation laws for a new end: to target those seeking to register to vote.

The Mississippi Legislature refashioned its laws governing sex and marriage in ways that could be used to achieve dual purposes. The new felony interracial cohabitation law sent a strong message to the world that white Mississippians cared deeply about the notion of "racial purity." The fact that the law could not withstand the scrutiny of the state supreme court and was declared void and unenforceable within a year of its passage was beside the point. Unlawful cohabitation laws had never been effective at eliminating interracial sex or relationships. Instead, they had long served in practice to protect the prerogative of white men to choose their families, even across the color line even as arbitrary enforcement ensured these couples could never feel fully safe or secure. It was the need to defend racial segregation as a system of racial separation that required lawmakers to create this new and more punitive legal regime.

Indeed, another transformative result of the 1956 session of the legislature was the demise of common law marriage. Anyone growing up in this environment or observing it from afar would see interracial sex as one of the most serious crimes a person could commit. No doubt this shaped the generation that would come of age in the 1950s and 1960s, forging a particular view of segregation in their minds. This was a new era in the history of Jim Crow, but it was all too easy and tempting to rewrite the past.

CHAPTER 9

THE WHITE MAN'S WILL

SIM

There was one point on which all parties agreed: at the end of his life in 1952, Sim Burnside was rich. A wealthy man by most standards, Sim was especially fortunate compared to his neighbors, particularly the men and women who rented parcels of his land in the forests of eastern Mississippi. As the last living descendant of his father, Bill Burnside, Sim had inherited his impressive landholdings—hundreds of acres of densely forested land—from his older siblings as they passed away. He lived out his final days alone in late December 1952 on the expanse of Neshoba County that had belonged to his family for generations. It was the only home Sim had ever known.[1]

The Burnside family estate sat about six miles up the road from the county seat of Philadelphia and eighty miles northeast of the state capital at Jackson. Neshoba County is home to the headwaters of the Pearl River, which flows southeast into Jackson before meandering south, carving out the winding contours of Mississippi's western boundary before finally spilling into Lake Borgne at the marshy edges of the Gulf of Mexico. The Pearl River connected residents to Jackson, New Orleans, and beyond. The river once cut through the Burnside plantation and, after changing its course, left behind an oxbow lake. Locals called the enviable fishing hole Burnside Lake.[2]

Neshoba was a county of farmers—some rich but many poor—who clustered in tight-knit communities. In the decades since Sim's father and grandfather had laid claim to this stretch of woods in the 1840s, a small village had grown around the Burnside home. This was the kind of place that did not attract many outsiders. By the 1950s, many residents' great-great-grandfathers' names were printed among the lists of original patent-holders who had flooded in from the east after Indian Removal. They fished at Burnside Lake and gossiped about the bootlegging and gambling in the days when Sim's older brothers had run the store, before the railroad came through and the family made a respectable income from timber.[3] Friendships, rivalries, and business associations were carried down through the generations. Everybody knew everybody—and everybody in this part of Neshoba County seemed to know the Burnsides.

Over their century in Neshoba County, the Burnsides had accrued quite a bit of wealth. As the sole living heir, Sim owned more than 700 acres of land, including 350,000 feet of what an appraiser termed "merchantable timber."[4] Much of the family's fortune came from decades spent in the lumber business profiting off their land, which remained thickly wooded with pine, oak, and sweetgum trees. In the wake of the Civil War, the Burnsides had had land but not much else. When the timber industry boomed in the early twentieth century, the Burnside siblings profited handsomely, accruing most of their wealth after the death of their father.[5]

Beyond the land itself, the estate included the house where Sim and his siblings had lived, a store that had once served as the post office for the town of Burnside, and $64,167.17 in cash at the Citizens Bank of Philadelphia—a sum valued at more than $700,000 in today's dollars.

And the Burnsides were living in a well-furnished home: they had chairs, stools, tables, a stove, a hot plate, dishes, a wood box, an ice box, blankets, quilts, beds and bed frames, trunks, a dresser, an iron heater, a wash-stand, pictures, clocks, three double-barrel shotguns, and two rifles, as well as many modern conveniences, such as a refrigerator, a Singer sewing machine, and a radio. They had managed to hang on to a few relics from earlier decades of the twentieth century, including a Model Ford, a Victrola, and a "piana." Rounding out the estate was a cow, her calf, and a flock of chickens.[6]

In short, Sim Burnside had all the trappings of white wealth in mid-century Mississippi: he came from an influential family that traced its roots back to the town's origins, he had land, he had plenty of cash in the bank, and he was well-to-do enough to rent out land to both white and Black tenants.[7] In the final years of his life, Sim lived comfortably in his home with two sisters, Elizabeth and Mary, and a small household staff that cooked, cleaned, and cared for them and maintained the house and grounds.[8] But after Mary and Elizabeth died in 1951, Sim, having never married, became the last of the Burnsides. His longtime caretaker, a Black man named Everett Hudson, bathed him, lifted him into his wheelchair, and helped him around the house.[9]

After his sisters' deaths, Sim's health declined precipitously. He was a diabetic who was fond of whiskey, a combination that stressed his kidneys. He knew, in some sense, that the end was near. Facing his declining health and lacking a direct heir, like many men of means Sim Burnside sought out legal assistance. His lawyer, Dees Stribling, drew up Sim's last will and testament. On April 8, 1952, Sim called together a small group to witness the signing.[10] The witnesses—all white locals—included a deputy clerk from the chancery court in Philadelphia, Elizabeth Darby, and a longtime friend of Sim Burnside's, Ethel Beall. They were joined at the Burnside home by two men who had been appointed executors of the estate: Sim's business associate A. J. Pearson and his physician, Claude Yates.[11] Claude owned a hospital in Philadelphia.[12]

The will stipulated that upon his death, all the land, including the lake, would be converted into a nature preserve and park open to the public: a protected wildlife refuge for game, where anyone could come and appreciate the natural beauty of the forest. The preserve should be called "Burnside Memorial Park," Sim decided.[13] Just as he and his siblings had when they were young, visitors would be free to clamber through the woods, splash at the edges of the lake, and trawl for fish in its depths.

Ethel Beall later recalled the poignancy of the moment—an event he remembered clearly because he "had never seen a will in [his] life."[14] Ethel had known Sim and his family since he was a boy, and he had his own fond memories of fishing in Burnside Lake.[15] He recalled in detail how the document was prepared and formally read aloud for all to hear. Sim voiced his assent and signed the will. A Baptist minister, Ethel testified that the moment brimmed with meaning: watching a wealthy man turn over everything he had to the public good, leaving a precious gift for future generations.[16] Ethel recalled that Sim seemed overcome with emotion as the witnesses dwelled upon his remarkable act of generosity. As Ethel put it, "There were tears that come in his eyes."[17]

Not long after Sim took his final breath on New Year's Eve, 1952, the trouble began. It did not take long for word to spread that Burnside had left his sizable estate to the county—and not to his nearest living relatives, the descendants of his uncle John Burnside. John had died in the 1870s, but he had had an unusually large brood (even by country standards): over the course of his two marriages, he had fathered at least seventeen children.[18] Though John's children had mostly moved away from Neshoba County, his grandchildren and great-grandchildren knew of their moneyed cousin on the lake. They also knew that Sim had no children or any other direct heirs, and they likely had long anticipated that there would come a day when they could claim the estate for themselves.

Twenty-four of Sim's second cousins joined a lawsuit to contest the validity of the will. The legal battle that ensued set into motion a series of events that would culminate in the two most sensational trials Neshoba County had yet seen, trials that would expose profoundly conflicting narratives of who the Burnsides truly were. Both cases would eventually reach the Mississippi Supreme Court, which would decide once and for all the fate of the Burnside fortune, but not before dredging up a century of rumors and secrets that many had hoped would stay buried. Sim's second cousins were a far-flung group, scattered across the state of Mississippi and in southern states from Florida to Texas, but a few still lived in the county and were privy to details (and gossip) about Sim's decline and death.[19] The story that Sim's last will and testament was motivated by philanthropy quickly fell apart. Rumors abounded that someone had taken advantage of him.

The cousins argued that in his old age, Sim had lost his mind. Their complaint cited his recent illnesses, noting that he had "an impairment of body and mind" that "produced a mental incompetency to the extent that he could not execute a valid will."[20] They leveraged the fact that Sim was a diabetic and, most importantly, they claimed he was a drunk. They accused Sim's executor A. J. Pearson of supplying Sim with whiskey that clouded his mind. Instead of a generous bequest, they cast the signing of the will as a nefarious act completed through fraud and coercion. According to them, "by cunning and by the influence of intoxicating liquor," A. J. and other unnamed co-conspirators had "completely dethroned the mind and reason of Sim Burnside," plying him with booze to dupe him into robbing his second and third cousins of their rightful inheritance.[21] (No one seemed bothered by the fact that A. J. obviously could have coerced Sim for personal gain instead of creating a public park.) The cousins were certain: this was no act of goodwill—it was theft.

It was true that Sim Burnside had been ill, plagued by persistent problems with his kidneys. But even if sickness did temporarily "dethrone his mind and reason," it was not so easy to disregard a person's will under Mississippi law.[22] The cousins faced an uphill battle. There was no shortage of suits brought by disgruntled spouses, children, and siblings who had failed to persuade judges and juries to disregard the deceased's wishes. The courts had long established that a person could distribute his or her estate based on any motive, including "love, gratitude, partiality, prejudice, whim, or caprice."[23] In a 1937 challenge to a will brought by the spurned children of a wealthy woman, the Mississippi Supreme Court had reiterated that even "a person afflicted with general insanity may direct and make a valid will when in a lucid period."[24]

Breaking the will, in other words, would be no easy feat. And the distant cousins had already made enemies of A. J. Pearson and Pearl Cheatham—herself a distant cousin of Sim's—who rejected the claim that they had coerced Sim. Sim did not care much, if at all, for his distant cousins, A. J. and Pearl's lawyers argued. Their lawyers' response explained that Burnside "had no relatives for whom he had any affection." Leaving his fortune to the public was both a show of civic mindedness and a rebuke to his closest living relatives. As A. J. and Pearl's lawyers noted, "He cared nothing about them." In the end, "he did not want any of them to inherit any of his property at his death."[25] Sim had left out his distant cousins on purpose.

What went unsaid in the statement was that Sim may have willed his property to all the people of Neshoba County to avoid identifying his closest living kin. His bequest was an act of charity, but it may also have been a careful effort to submerge his family's history. Sim had been born the same year that Mississippi legalized interracial marriage, and one year after the ratification of the 1868 radical state constitution that formalized common law marriages. But as Sim grew, so did the effort to void and punish interracial marriage amid the rise of segregation law. By the time Sim was an old man, he had witnessed legislators' efforts to construct the color line, and, as the Black Freedom Struggle gained momentum, the cracks formed that would lead to the collapse of the entire edifice of legal segregation. Eighteen months after his death, the US Supreme Court would issue its ruling in *Brown v. Board of Education*, and white supremacists would launch their violent counteroffensive, leading to the fateful night that would put Neshoba County on the map: the kidnapping and murder of James Chaney, Andrew Goodman, and Michael Schwerner during the 1964 Freedom Summer campaign.

Of course, the faults in the legal structure of segregation were present from the start, even as lawmakers sought to patch them up: the problematic theory of the blood quantum, the refusal of neighbors to give evidence in cohabitation cases, the vague language of the unlawful cohabitation law, all compounded by the presence of a large class of people who could step over the color line with relative ease—a class that some whispered included Sim Burnside himself.

THE HEARING TO DETERMINE THE FATE OF SIM BURNSIDE'S WILL BEGAN on September 7, 1953, in Philadelphia before Chancellor Jerry Kindred Gillis. Over the following week, dozens of people weighed in on the mental competency of Sim Burnside, with locals competing to show just how intimately they knew the family. Undoubtedly, the prospect of a windfall also informed the eagerness of some witnesses to claim close, personal knowledge of its members.

Pearl Cheatham's sister, Annie Ellis, who rented a house on the Burnside property, claimed she had seen Sim weep and worry about his health, evidence to her that he was not in the proper state of mind to make a will.[26] Annie was particularly upfront about her view that the fortune properly belonged to the nearest kin—a group that included her mother. The cousins found no shortage of witnesses to testify to Sim's fondness for alcohol, and many of these witnesses also, perhaps not coincidentally, stood to benefit from the case. Jack Eubanks testified that he knew Burnside had drunk a fifth of whiskey every day.[27] (His grandmother was party to the suit.) Tim Fox, another relative, claimed that Burnside was "the worst drunk, doped up man I ever saw."[28]

The cousins recruited a physician who had never met Sim to testify that his diabetes could have led to "senile dementia."[29] A neighbor, Thomas McAdory, testified that he had heard Sim "raving" about people trying to cut down his timber, and that he was "crazy."[30] Others recalled Sim being caught in reveries, preoccupied with the past. A woman who had once worked for Sim's sister Elizabeth claimed she had heard him hallucinating and warning Elizabeth of "negroes coming in at the windows," Black women fishing in the lake, and "Mexicans" driving covered wagons through his woods "to take this country over."[31] Another witness described Sim as "living in the past." He had heard his long-dead mother "sing[ing] Spanish songs." He had conversed with the ghosts of his older brothers.[32]

Exasperated with all the gossip about Sim's sanity (or lack thereof), A. J. Pearson offered a radically different story of Burnside's final years, detailing his friendship with a man who had been an avid reader and who had kept up with the news via the radio and newspapers.[33] Born and raised in Winston County, just north of the Burnside community, Pearson was a well-known and respected lumberman who had often purchased timber from the Burnsides, and he was friendly enough with the family that he had assisted the elderly siblings when he could, running errands and cashing checks at the bank.[34] Sim had long been community-minded, he said, giving permission to neighbors and friends to fish at the lake and speaking of his plans to clear out the undergrowth to ready the land to become a public park.[35] Pearson also testified that Sim had purposely disinherited his relatives. Pearson explained that Sim's "heirs had never done anything for him nor come to see him, and he didn't want them to have anything of what he had." Instead, Sim "wanted the public to have what he had, no individual."[36] Other witnesses similarly testified to the resilience of Sim's mind. Lewis Jones, who ran the store owned by the Burnsides, said that Sim was lucid and had always been game to talk politics when they were not discussing hunting or fishing.[37] Marvin Henley, a tax collector and member of the Mississippi Legislature, testified that he considered Sim one of his "close, personal and political friends."[38]

Despite their differences of opinion on Sim's alleged drunkenness, everyone agreed that Sim Burnside had loved the land. One witness described how Sim had refused to sell the property to those who made offers, and how he had papered the walls with his prized collection of R. Hoe & Company calendars, which featured pastoral scenes of wildlife and national parks.[39] Joe Reese, one of the property's caretakers, testified that as Sim slipped in and out of consciousness in the last weeks of his life, he had been especially concerned about the calendars. He had spent decades collecting them and didn't want them to "be destroyed," Reese explained.[40]

Sim Burnside was either a paranoid, haunted old drunk or an upstanding citizen concerned about the natural world. Either way, he was not present to take the stand himself.

After an hour and ten minutes of deliberation, the jury returned with a startling verdict. By a vote of eleven to one, the jury had decided in favor of invalidating the will and distributing Sim Burnside's fortune among his distant cousins.[41] The relatives, no matter how distant, rightfully deserved a slice of the estate. The premise of the case also included a thinly veiled message about the wisdom of conservation: only a crazy person would leave so much land to the public and so much cash in the bank. Why else would the jury side with the distant cousins, who were so obviously motivated by self-interest? Why would they reject a gift so generously offered to the people of Neshoba County?

There was another reason the twelve white men who made up the jury might have sided with the second cousins. It is likely that they had heard other stories about Sim that may have colored their views about the kind of person Sim was—stories that no one was willing to mention on the witness stand. A secret that few wanted to say aloud even though everyone seemed to know it. Later, A. J. Pearson would testify before a different jury that before Sim's death, he had privately been warned that there would be "an awful mess" if Sim died without a will. There was something "about Sim's mother," Pearson said cryptically.[42] Perhaps questions about his family's past had provided another motive for Sim's decision to leave the property to the people of Neshoba County: he wanted to avoid a public contest over who might be his closest living relatives.

But not everyone was willing to stay quiet. Two crucial developments followed the jury's decision that ensured that these shocking secrets would spill out into the public. First, A. J. and Pearl's lawyers appealed the ruling to the Mississippi Supreme Court, and in February 1955 the state's high court upheld the jury's decision to invalidate the will.[43] The following month, a group claiming to be the *first* cousins of Sim Burnside filed suit in Philadelphia. The lawsuit challenged the second cousins who had broken the will and claimed these new seven plaintiffs were Sim's rightful heirs. This group did not make claims through Sim's father, Bill Burnside. Instead, they claimed to be the closest living kin of Sim Burnside through their relationship to his mother. All these Burnsides were Black.

Lee Prisock, a white lawyer with a practice in Jackson, represented the Black Burnsides. Prisock told the paper that he had done research on the Burnside family history and traced the migration of the Burnside brothers, including Sim's father, from South Carolina. Prisock had also been born and raised in the area, so he likely also had personal knowledge of the family. According to Prisock, on this westward journey Bill Burnside had "brought with him several slaves including a woman named Betsy who had a small daughter named Mariah." Betsy also had other children. After settling in Neshoba County, Bill Burnside had taken Mariah "as his wife," and she bore his eight children over the span of two decades. Sim's older brothers were born into slavery, but, as one of the youngest, Sim was born free in the 1870s. Mariah's siblings had families of their own. Prisock explained, "Seven of these children are still alive. It is this seven, who were first cousins of Sim, that we seek to recover the estate for."[44]

If these men and women were indeed Sim's first cousins, that meant they had a better claim to the estate than the white second and third cousins who had successfully broken the will. If the court agreed, the money and the land would go to these Black men and women and the white Burnsides would not receive a single cent.

The new claimants to the Burnside fortune told a story that spanned generations and, amid the segregationist violence that followed *Brown v. Board of Education*, defied the basic logic of Jim Crow. According to the Black Burnsides, Mariah and her children had crossed the color line a decade after the end of the Civil War. The family had adopted a white racial identity, and eventually the local white community had accepted them—or at least pretended not to know the truth. While she was enslaved, Mariah had given birth to at least five children, all of them fathered by Bill Burnside. After the war ended, Mariah had remained with Bill, and they had lived as a married couple. She had several more children in the decade following emancipation. Mariah's children, including Sim, had inherited Bill's estate upon Bill's death in 1891. They had become successful financially and socially, and they had maintained a white reputation for the rest of their lives. Mariah had outlived Bill by three and a half decades. She never remarried.[45]

By all legal and newspaper accounts from the twentieth century, Mariah and her children were white people. When Mariah died on July 6, 1925, her death certificate identified her as a ninety-one-year-old white widow, the daughter of an Irish father and a Spanish mother. Her cause of death was "acute indigestion and senility."[46] The *Winston County Journal* announced Mariah's death as the sad departure of "one of the best known citizens" of the Burnside village. In her final moments, her six living children gathered at her bedside, and the community mourned her death. As the obituary noted, "The deceased was loved and respected by all who knew her, as was attested by the large attendance at her funeral."[47] Mariah died a respected white woman. But where, and to whom, she had been born became the subject of heated debate.

The legal contest over Sim Burnside's fortune suddenly shifted from disagreements over Sim Burnside's sanity to a profound conflict over the history of Mississippi. For the Black Burnsides to succeed, they would have to force the court to admit that the color line was neither stable nor impermeable. Their claim to the Burnside estate told a very different story about the history of Neshoba County that upended the powerful racist narratives about the end of slavery and the Jim Crow era that had taken hold in the segregation era. As the case moved forward, the Black Burnsides would put history on trial.

News of the claims about Sim Burnside's secret racial past spread like wildfire. Even the local newspaper, usually reluctant to report on sensitive topics, could not resist detailing the new developments in the Burnside estate saga. The *Neshoba Democrat* called the lawsuit a "fantastic story" that had "elements to make it one of the most sensational court trials in the history of the state."[48] Outside Mississippi, only the Black press picked up the story. In a brief article on the lawsuit, *Jet* magazine reported that the Black Burnsides' lawyers "hinted that they would bare the strange story of the planter Burnside, who reportedly remained single because of his fear of violating the state ban on mixed marriage."[49]

The group of seven claimants to the estate included Robert Burnside, Nannie Burnside Jones, Maudie Johnson, Will Burnside, Tennessee Burnside, Ethel Burnside, and Cleveland Burnside. According to these Burnsides, Mariah's mother, Betsy, had five children whose biological father was a white slaveholder, Tom Talley. Mariah's siblings—Bill, Sarah, Dolphus, and Delia—had their own families, and their children were the claimants represented by Lee Prisock. They claimed that Mariah's mixed ancestry and her fair complexion had allowed her to identify as a white woman after emancipation even though she had been born enslaved.[50]

Sim's father had purchased Mariah more than a century ago. The children she bore him, including Sim, were even more fair than their mother and could identify as white. Eventually, the community accepted the Burnsides as white people. And the Black Burnsides had records—including census documents—that they argued proved that their story was true.

The 1870 census identifies Mariah and her five children as "mulatto," people of mixed white and African ancestry. William Burnside, on the other hand, is identified as "white."[51] In the 1860 census, Mariah was not listed at all, though the couple's three oldest sons were identified as living with William.[52] The 1860 "slave schedules"—censuses of enslaved people used to tabulate taxation and representation via the Three-Fifths Clause of the US Constitution—identify a twenty-five-year-old "mulatto" woman among the enslaved people who labored on Bill Burnside's plantation.[53] According to the Black Burnsides, this woman was Mariah.

The couple had a substantial age gap: in 1870, Bill was nearing sixty years old. The census identified Mariah as thirty-six. Their oldest son, Harry, was twenty years old in 1870, meaning that Mariah may have been as young as fifteen when she first became pregnant by a thirty-nine-year-old white man, who was quite possibly her enslaver. When the census-taker visited the family in the summer of 1870, Bill and Mariah had three boys—all born before the Civil War began—and two younger girls, Belle Dixie and Elizabeth. Sim and two more siblings, Samuel and Mary, were born after 1870. But by the time Sim and his siblings were identified in the 1880 census just ten years later, the entire family was racially identified as white.[54]

THE SITUATION ONLY GREW MURKIER WHEN ANOTHER GROUP OF BLACK cousins filed their own claims—and they had yet another story about Mariah's past. They claimed kinship through Tom Burnside, alleging Tom was the only brother of Mariah and insisting that Betsy was not Mariah's mother. The 1870 census lists a Thomas Burnside, aged forty-three, living in neighboring Winston County. Like Mariah, his race was noted as "mulatto," and his birthplace was given as South Carolina. Tom Burnside and his wife, Lucinda, had seven children.[55] By the 1880 census, their household had expanded to include eleven children, including daughters named Princey, Nancy, and Sallie—the women who now claimed to be Sim's closest living family members. Though Tom is again identified as "mulatto" in the 1880 record, his birthplace, curiously, is recorded as being Mexico.[56]

It was not at all surprising to find both Black and white families of Burnsides in Neshoba County. Many white families had Black counterparts and had for generations. There were white Moores and Black Moores, and white Tripletts and Black Tripletts. The county had scores of white and Black Tallys. The 1940 census records both a Black Tom Tally (aged sixty, employed as a laborer for a florist, never went to school) and a white Tom Tally (aged forty-six, employed as a farmer, had a seventh-grade education).[57] Both Tom Tallys had wives and children. There was even a Black Mariah Burnside who was born in 1871—the daughter of Tom Burnside, Sim's alleged uncle.[58]

According to white residents of Neshoba County, the existence of such families was merely the result of the process that followed emancipation. Formerly enslaved people often adopted the last names of their enslavers. Following the war, these families parted ways and lived separate lives in segregated worlds, sharing only a name and nothing more during the

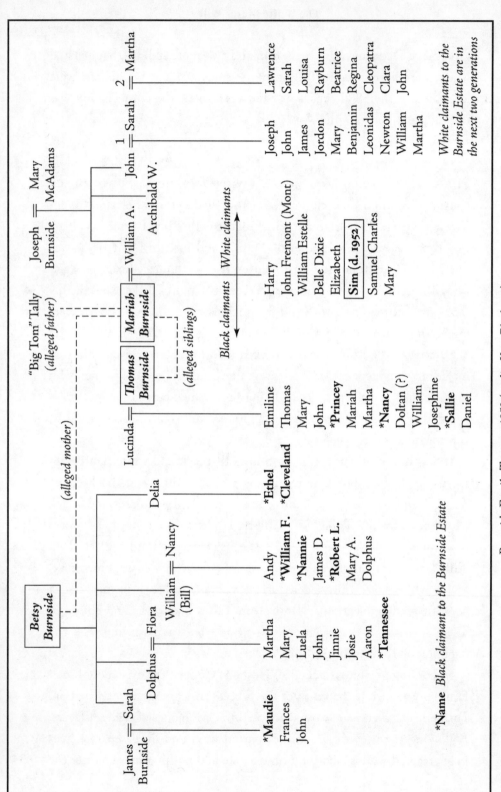

Burnside Family Tree, ca. 1952 (credit: Kate Blackmer).

Jim Crow era. To many, these new accounts of the Burnside family history were thoroughly scandalous—and unbelievable. The legal principle of segregation relied upon meaningful and stable racial categories. Black people were Black; white people were white. The two races did not mix. People did not simply step over the line, as Sim and his siblings were said to have done. But the Black Burnsides insisted on telling a very different story about how the color line was still and had always been far more porous than midcentury white Mississippians would admit.

On Thursday, May 20, 1954, the *Neshoba Democrat* carried a front-page story about the new claimants to the Burnside estate, but the main headline carried news of another, vastly more dramatic challenge to the color line. Reporting on the previous week's *Brown v. Board of Education* decision, the headline announced, "United States Supreme Court Rules Out Segregation by Unanimous Vote of the Nine Court Justices."[59] The second trial over Sim Burnside's estate began at 9:00 a.m. on May 9, 1955, a year after the Black Burnsides first filed their lawsuit. By this time, white southerners were in open revolt against the *Brown* decision.

The trial unfolded before an eager audience, with whites crowding the benches on the main floor and Black observers relegated to the segregated balcony. Lee Prisock, who represented Betsy's children, was the first attorney to present his case. One of his first witnesses was Nannie Burnside Jones, the daughter of one of Mariah's alleged brothers. Like many of the other witnesses, both Black and white, Nannie had grown up near Sim and his family.[60] She was close with her grandmother, Betsy, who had told her all about the family's history. Betsy had explained that she and her daughter had come to Mississippi when Mariah was twelve years old, and that after emancipation, Betsy unsuccessfully tried to reunite the family. But Mariah and her children stayed with Bill Burnside, keeping their ties to their Black cousins secret. Nannie explained, "They would tell us that they were kin to us, but they said they couldn't own it, because if they did they would be treated like we was, as colored folks, and that that was not going to be, because their father was a white man."[61]

In Nannie's recollection, Sim and his siblings were white enough to "pass," but Mariah was not. "She was a brown-skinned woman," Nannie explained, who avoided the gaze of white strangers who might ask unwanted questions. When visitors came to the home, she hid. The effort to keep Mariah in the background had a single purpose: to preserve the family's land and money. The siblings feared that if people knew of Mariah's African ancestry, "the white people would overrule them and take their property, and they wasn't going to stand for that."[62]

The lawyer for the white Burnsides, Leonard B. Melvin, had a different explanation for the Black Burnsides' lawsuit. Unlike Prisock, Melvin was not a local. His law practice was based in Laurel where in 1958 his son, Leonard B. Melvin Jr., would later participate in the prosecution of Mary Rose in his role as Jones County attorney.[63] Melvin questioned Nannie about how she had become involved in the suit in the first place, implying that someone more powerful must be manipulating these elderly Black people to get them to engage in this unfortunate spectacle. Upon cross-examination, Nannie Jones explained that "Mr. Weir and Mr. Hillman" from the FBI had come to visit her after the white cousins had broken Sim Burnside's will. The men, Nannie explained, just appeared on her doorstep one day. "They told me they were FBI men looking out for the colored part of the relatives to Sim Burnside," she said of the surprise visit, speaking to a packed courtroom. "They told me I had a right to my claim in the Burnside estate."[64] Melvin's purpose was to make Nannie look foolish and imply that someone—perhaps a lawyer looking for a payday—had planted the story in her head.

Nannie's brother Robert echoed her testimony, adding that "so many people now you see this day in time are going for colored people and they are not, and some calling themselves negroes, yet they ain't. They are spotted up so, our race is." In other words, not only did some white people have African ancestry, but some white people who did not have African ancestry were adopting Black identities when it was necessary or convenient to do so. His cousins at the lake were, as he put it, "white Negroes."[65] Robert's explanation of the family's history echoed the saga of Davis Knight of Jones County and the arguments that had persuaded the state legislature to reject the one-drop rule in the 1920s. Race was not determined by blood or ancestry. What decided a person's racial identity was how that person presented himself and whether the community agreed.

Prisock then called Walter Burnside, one of the white cousins who had successfully broken the will, to the stand. Walter had moved away from Neshoba County when he was young, but his family had occasionally returned to visit their cousins at the lake. His responses to Prisock's questions were measured—mostly. Walter described Mariah as a woman with "light hair" and "brown eyes" who "looked like anybody else."[66] He claimed not to know anything at all about her background or family. But when pressed on whether Mariah was "all white" or whether she "looked like a Spaniard," Walter snapped in response, "She was not perfectly white. Are you?"[67]

This exchange edged close to touching on the racial tension that underlay many of the witnesses' testimony. Walter's reply, implying that Prisock was not so white himself, was one note of a refrain that played time and again between the white Burnsides and the attorneys for the alleged Black cousins. Maybe the Burnsides had skeletons in their closets. But if that could be true, perhaps other white people should be worried that someone might go rummaging around in their own pasts. When one of Pearl Cheatham's sisters, Maude Moore, was asked by Lee Prisock whether she could identify a dark-skinned Black woman (alleged to be Betsy) in a photograph, she replied tartly, "It looks like your grandmaw."[68] Even as the white Burnsides waged a campaign based on the purity of the white race, they could not help indulging in the old southern tradition of casting doubt on an adversary's family tree.

The white Burnsides presented their own theory of Mariah's parentage—one that explained her family's absence from official records, though not necessarily her absence in the census before 1870. According to another of John Burnside's descendants, Cora, Mariah was an orphan, and Bill Burnside had rescued her from a convent in New Orleans. This narrative deprived Mariah of having any family history of her own. "She didn't have any folks," Cora explained. Bill's decision to take Mariah as

Mary Burnside (*left*) and unidentified woman, submitted as evidence in the *Burnside v. Burnside* trial (courtesy of the Archives and Records Services Division, Mississippi Department of Archives and History).

his wife was an act of benevolent charity bestowed upon a poor orphan. Cora insisted that there was no question that Mariah was white. "She was a little small, slender, tall woman, and she had the prettiest white, long hair that came down here, just as straight as it could be," Cora explained. Mariah's skin, she told the jury, "was whiter than mine."[69] Of course, Cora, born in 1899, never met her great-uncle Bill, and by the time she was old enough to know Mariah, her great-aunt was in her seventies.

THE THIRD BRANCH OF CLAIMANTS WOULD STIR THE POT THE MOST about the mixed-up history of the Burnside clan. Their lawyer R. W. Boydstun's questions were inflammatory, leading, and often drenched in racism. He asked Cora Talley whether Sim's sisters Elizabeth and Mary "had very thick lips and showed dark under the skin." He asked leading questions that implied that everyone knew the truth about the family's past. Wasn't it true, Boydstun asked Cora, that "back when we were young, the Burnsides were just a bunch of mean half negroes down on the lake?" Boydstun dug in, asking pointedly, "Isn't it a matter of common knowledge among all the Burnside family that the old man William A. Burnside went to New Orleans and bought her on the slave market?" Cora denied it.[70]

Boydstun was especially interested in airing the violent misdeeds of Sim's father and older brothers, who he claimed were rough and ruthless in the 1890s before soaring timber prices allowed them to buy their way into respectability. "Wasn't it part of the family history that old man Bill Burnside killed his brother about this yellow girl?" Boydstun prodded. "I never did hear nothing like that, Mr. Boydstun," Cora replied. Then she went for the jugular: "If we are bringing out skeletons, how about let's bring out some about your folks?"[71]

Boydstun wasn't deterred: he relished the opportunity to have the last word on the Burnsides' place in local history. He boasted that his intimate knowledge of the family dated back to 1890, when the whiteness of the Burnside siblings was much more tenuous. His father, he claimed, had grown up near the Burnside plantation; he and his siblings had sometimes stayed there; and since his boyhood he had sponged up the local gossip about the family at the lake. As Boydstun later explained in a legal brief to the court, "We have heard the matter of ancestry of the Burnside children discussed and re-discussed for many years."[72]

Boydstun's star witness was Pearl Cheatham, Sim's distant cousin and one of the white defendants in the first lawsuit over the will. Pearl, alongside A. J. Pearson, had been named in the lawsuit filed by Sim's white cousins as one of the people responsible for manipulating Sim and cheating her own family out of the estate. Pearl's mother, Sarah Butler Burnside, was the sister of Walter Burnside.[73] Pearl's testimony was particularly valuable to the descendants of Tom Burnside. She was not one of the greedy cousins who had initially sought to break the will, and so, unlike so many other witnesses, both Black and white, she did not have a direct financial stake in the outcome of the trial. Pearl had known and loved Sim Burnside and his sisters. She was a white woman who had lived near the Burnsides and worked for them practically her entire life. Her words, Boydstun argued, should hold more weight than anyone's—other than his own, of course.

Her testimony likely shocked everyone who heard it. Pearl testified that Tom Burnside was indeed Mariah's brother. She had heard it from Mariah herself. But Pearl's testimony diverged in a notable way from the other witnesses for the Black Burnsides: Pearl explained that both Mariah and Tom Burnside were white. The confusion lay in the fact that there were two Tom Burnsides: "One Tom Burnside was a slave, but this Tom Burnside I am talking about was not a slave. He was Irish and Spanish," Pearl explained. On this point, she was insistent. Mariah and her brother Tom "didn't have a drop of colored blood in them."[74]

Pearl's testimony offered more peculiar details about the family's history. She recalled hearing her parents describe how Bill Burnside had killed his brother following an argument over the legality of Bill and Mariah's marriage. According to Pearl, Bill Burnside's brother had questioned whether the couple had obtained a marriage license. The Neshoba County courthouse had burned, taking all the records with it. In Pearl's version of the story, the brothers went to see the justice of the peace, who confirmed that he had presided over the marriage of Bill and Mariah. But this answer did not satisfy the brother. "When they came back they had an argument, and he shot him. Uncle Billie shot Willison and said it was an accident," Pearl explained, blithely unconcerned as to *why* someone might be skeptical that the marriage was legal.[75] Others told a different story: Bill Burnside killed his brother Archibald, a Confederate veteran, after he denounced Bill's continued relationship with Mariah and his decision to make his biracial children his legal heirs.[76]

In Pearl's telling, Mariah and Tom had been orphaned. Their parents died of cholera when they were children, and Sim's grandfather Joseph Burnside invited the children's elderly aunt and uncle "to give him the little girl, Marie Emma, for his three old maid daughters." They agreed—but only if he also took in her brother. And this was how Mariah and

Tom came to live with the Burnside family when she was just eight and her brother was six.[77]

According to Pearl, there was only one Burnside who had crossed the color line. It was not Mariah. It was Mariah's brother, Tom. Pearl explained that Tom had "married a negro woman": "He was Irish and Spanish, but he said he was going to marry the blackest negro he could find, and he did it."[78] Tom's desire to marry a Black woman meant that he had to choose between his wife and his whiteness. As she described it, Tom adopted a Black identity to marry Lucinda.

The shocking nature of these stories being aired under oath in a Mississippi courtroom in the 1950s—by a white woman, no less—should not be underestimated. Lee Prisock, the lawyer for Betsy's Black descendants, pressed Pearl as to whether she had ever heard anyone refer to the Burnsides as "half-Negroes," and Pearl admitted that yes, she had. In fact, it was her own grandmother—a contemporary of Mariah and Bill who would have known them—who had said as much.[79]

Again, Pearl offered a rather implausible explanation. Her grandmother was "mad" and had used the term as a slur after Harry and her grandfather had fought. She had meant it as an insult, not a truthful descriptor. Pearl clarified, "She knew they didn't have any negro in them, but she called them half negro" in her anger. When asked by Prisock whether she had ever heard "any of the Burnside family, Sim or any of his brothers, resent being referred to as part negro," Pearl responded with a barely veiled threat: "I am telling you right now somebody that told them that, they would have hung them."[80] Once again, Pearl's testimony gave credence to the claims made by the Black Burnsides, who testified that Bill Burnside and his sons *had* violently responded when people accused them of being less than "all white." Their willingness to lash out at anyone who questioned their whiteness protected their poorly kept secret. Pearl did not reveal whether she had connected these dots, but certainly observers in the courtroom would have.

As his questioning continued, Prisock's exasperation with Pearl's testimony ballooned. Pearl explained that the Burnsides could not have been Black because they were, in fact, committed white supremacists. "Now, you say they had a real hatred for negroes?" Prisock asked, to which Pearl replied, "Yes, sir." Prisock asked again, "Isn't it a fact that the reason they were so badly against those negroes was the fact that everybody around here said they were half negro?" Pearl was aghast. Whether someone was white or not was not ambiguous. "I knew they were not negroes. Anybody can tell a negro from a white person. My goodness, you can tell them in the dark," she explained.[81]

Her final testimony took a truly bizarre turn. Pearl presented her family Bible as evidence. She explained that she had kept locks of hair from the Burnsides and recorded the names and birthdates of the family members, producing a sample of Mary Burnside's hair that she claimed had been tucked away in its pages "for years and years." The hair appeared auburn, but also seemed to have been treated with dye—perhaps recently, as a reddish stain had leached into the small paper envelope that enclosed the last relic of Mary Burnside.[82] Florence Mars, a local white woman

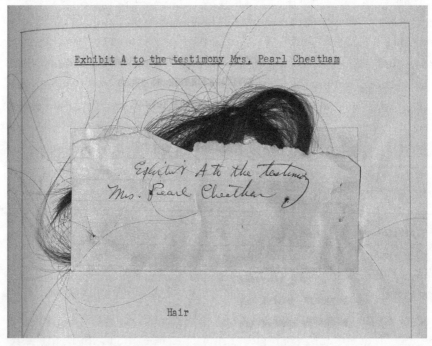

Alleged lock of hair from Mary Burnside submitted as evidence by Pearl Cheatham at the *Burnside v. Burnside* trial (courtesy of the Archives and Records Services Division, Mississippi Department of Archives and History).

who attended the trial, noted wryly that everyone in the courtroom could see that the lock of hair was a farce. The dye was still wet.[83]

What do we make of Pearl—who had nothing to gain from the trial—testifying so passionately that the Burnsides were "all white"? Pearl was closer to Sim than almost anyone else in his final days. As a white woman in Jim Crow Mississippi, the implication that she might have worked in service to a Black family outraged her. It inverted the southern social order. Black people waited on whites, not the other way around. If Sim Burnside was anything but white, that could shake the very foundations of her racial ideology and threaten her *own* reputation as a white woman.

And yet, a core part of Pearl's story about the tangled Burnside family tree was that the color line could be crossed voluntarily, as Tom Burnside had allegedly done. Pearl's story—that Mariah and Tom were brother and sister, but that neither of them had African ancestry—was echoed by other witnesses, though they offered different versions of this basic tale. Tom Burnside's grandson Henry Riddle described hearing his grandfather talk about his sister, Mariah. Riddle considered his grandfather to be "part Negro, at least." He did not know whether Tom had ever been enslaved, but he did recall hearing his grandfather speak multiple languages: an "Indian type" and a "Spanish type."[84] So perhaps Tom was Black. Or not. Maybe he was Choctaw. Or Mexican. Maybe he was both.

The most fantastical accounting of Mariah's origins came from one of Tom Burnside's granddaughters, Callie McKinley. Callie had been close to her grandfather when she was young, and she lived with him until she was eleven years old. Her grandfather, she recalled, was about five-foot-five with "straight hair." His skin was "real light," and he "had a fair complexion."[85] Her grandfather had told her about his sister—Mariah—and how he had left Neshoba County because there had been "a misunderstanding in the family about the color some way."[86] Callie testified that she had heard Tom tell stories about his childhood and his life. According to Callie, Mariah and Tom had been born somewhere in South America, and as teenagers they had found passage to New York on a ship in or around 1846. Tom had set off for the boat when he realized that Mariah had surreptitiously followed him for miles. Mariah begged Tom to take her with him to the United States, and he relented.[87] In New York City, Mariah and Tom found work in restaurants, but at some point, they sailed to New Orleans in search of new opportunities. In Louisiana, they labored in sugarcane fields until Tom heard that he could find work laying a railroad between Durant and Aberdeen, Mississippi. But when he arrived, there were no jobs, and so the pair "wandered" until they ended up in Neshoba County. This is how Mariah came to meet Bill Burnside.[88]

Upon cross-examination, Prisock picked at the plethora of inconsistencies in Callie's story. The part about working in the sugarcane fields was especially unbelievable. "Don't you know as a matter of fact the sugar cane plantations at that time didn't hire labor at all?" he asked Callie. "Don't you know at that time sugar cane plantations only had slave labor?" But Callie was defiant. Her grandfather "was not a slave," she insisted.[89]

Lafayette Wilkes, another Black grandchild of Tom Burnside, testified that he had visited the Burnsides at the lake and Mariah had greeted him warmly, treating him like he was one of her own children. The white Burnsides' lawyer, Leonard Melvin, balked at this story of familial closeness. On cross-examination, he asked, "And you tell this bunch of white folks here in Neshoba County, Mississippi that that white woman ran out there and grabbed you in her arms and hugged you up to her? Is that what you tell this court?" The lawyer R. W. Boydstun objected "to the attitude of counsel," but Judge Gillis overruled his motion.[90]

Boydstun then took the extraordinary step of calling himself as a witness to explain to the jurors why he had taken the case in the first place. "I will be seventy-one years old this coming July," Boydstun explained. "In my younger days, I knew Tom Burnside very well up until the time I was nearly twenty-one years old." Boydstun lived about halfway between Tom Burnside's home in Choctaw County and the Burnsides of Neshoba County. On one occasion, Boydstun was out in the field with his brothers when Tom rode by on his wagon. The men exchanged pleasantries, and Boydstun asked where Tom was going. "He told us his sister was Mariah Burnside at the Burnside Lake," Boystun testified. He did not know if Tom had African ancestry, explaining that "he didn't talk like a negro, and he didn't look like a negro." Boydstun elaborated, "He looked kind of like a Spaniard, and he stated in my presence that Mariah Burnside at the lake was his sister."[91] Under cross-examination, Boydstun revealed that he did, however, believe that both Tom and Mariah had been enslaved by Bill Burnside. This did not mean, however, that Mariah and Tom were Black. Here, he added his own implausible rationale: they must have been white people who had somehow become enslaved. Boydstun speculated that they were Mexican.[92]

DESPITE THE FACT THAT BETSY'S DESCENDANTS HAD A COMPELLING case and census evidence, the white Burnsides determinedly cobbled together testimony of Mariah's white identity. Almost every witness they called was white, and many of them were the cousins who had broken Sim's will.

The white Burnsides' witness Mary Johnson testified that Mariah had told her about her mother, Philace Wallace, who had come from Spain, and her father, John Dunne, who was Irish.[93] (No one commented that "Philace Wallace" would be a rather unusual name for a Spaniard.) Mariah had told Mary that she had been born in South Carolina—not South America. Tim Fox, who had grown up in the Burnside community and attended school with Sim and his siblings, testified that Mariah had immigrated from Spain to South Carolina, but that when she was young, her parents had died from yellow fever. Mariah had ended up in a convent in New Orleans, where she met Bill Burnside.[94] Upon cross-examination, Prisock prodded Fox about his motivations for testifying, relaying a conversation the two allegedly had had before the trial. Prisock asked, "I believe that the other day, down there the other day in Burnside when I stopped and talked with you, you told me that you were going to come up here and see that these negroes didn't get anything, didn't you?" Fox denied it, replying, "I never told you no such."[95]

Prisock continued his campaign to get white witnesses to testify about Sim Burnside's Black past, including James Duncan, a white farmer who had lived in Neshoba County his entire life. Duncan testified that he had known the Burnsides for five or six decades, and when asked about "the general reputation of the Burnsides as to whether they had negro blood in them," he responded, "They did."[96]

But even with the testimony of both Black and white witnesses, Prisock was fighting an uphill battle against the lethally enforced racial lines of 1950s Mississippi. If the Burnsides had managed to bury their African ancestry, their white neighbors were not keen on rooting it out—with the exception of Boydstun, perhaps, who seemed to have his own motivations. Instead, they seemed committed to covering it up, as if their own racial identities hinged upon the whiteness of the Burnsides. Jack Eubanks testified that he knew that Sim and his siblings were white people because only white people could shop at the Burnside store, and the siblings "went to the white polls to vote."[97] Jack's father, Barney, described the Burnsides as being "as white as me or you."[98]

The last witness called at the trial was perhaps one of the most compelling and important for the Black Burnsides. Murphy Cannon was one of the few witnesses who was not directly related to any of the alleged heirs, white or Black. He was a white man who had no clear stake in the outcome of the case, financial or otherwise. Murphy had, however, courted Mary Burnside when they were both young. Murphy had been smitten with Mary after they had first met at a Fourth of July picnic in 1885, and eventually he had proposed marriage. But he told the jury that Mary had turned him down. "I can't marry," he recalled her saying. "We are under a pledge to never marry." He pressed Mary for more information. Why would the siblings make a pact never to marry? "We are crossed up," he recalled Mary saying.[99]

With this, all sides rested.

THE OUTCOME OF THE TRIAL, UNSURPRISINGLY, WAS NOT IN THE BLACK Burnsides' favor. The court rejected their claims. Although there was no evidence to substantiate the story, Judge Jerry Gillis explained that Mariah had been born in South Carolina to Spanish and Irish parents, and that she had been an orphan girl in New Orleans when she met Bill Burnside. On the question of whether Mariah or her children had any

African ancestry, Gillis answered straightforwardly: "The court finds that there was no negro blood in Mariah Burnside, but that she was half Spanish and half Irish, and that the complexions of her children or some of them may have been swarthy, which would result from the Spanish blood they received from their mother."[100]

Both Prisock and Boydstun appealed the decision, but the Mississippi Supreme Court affirmed Judge Gillis's ruling.[101] The white Burnsides were the only heirs to Sim Burnside's fortune. The law had spoken—and had rewritten a family tree to conform to the beliefs about the impeachability of southern white lineages.

On Monday, September 30, 1957, Sim Burnside's land went up for auction at the Neshoba County Courthouse. Although newspapers had reported wildly different values of the estate—citing figures ranging from $100,000 to $750,000—a local oil distributor, Edgar Pope, purchased it for a paltry $48,200.[102] The whole affair ended with a whimper. In the end, each of Sim's distant white cousins received less than $2,000 from the sale of the land.

The ruling may have settled the lawsuit, but the trial had set forth multiple irreconcilable accounts of the Burnside family history, and these stories inverted accepted narratives about slavery and race. Mexicans were enslaved in Mississippi; white men became Black; a person's race was not necessarily knowable, and it was also potentially changeable through sheer force of will (and, for Sim's older brothers, an adequate supply of weapons). Only reputation and money mattered.

If race was so easily changeable—if someone could simply slip across the line without fanfare—then the color line itself was a farce. What was the point of separating white people from Black people if one could simply change the facts of one's life? And, perhaps most dangerously, if Black and white people could trace their family trees back to the same roots, what justified white supremacy? Black and white Mississippians were linked not just by history but by blood.

The Mississippi Supreme Court handed down its decision affirming Gillis's ruling in 1956, at the same time that state legislators were frantically attempting to change the state's laws governing interracial sex and marriage. Amid this effort to erase the history of interracial marriage, other white people admitted that there was more to the story. Florence Mars, a local white woman who later wrote a first-person account of the aftermath of the murders of James Chaney, Andrew Goodman, and Michael Schwerner, briefly sketched the history of the Burnside affair in her book *Witness in Philadelphia*. Her interest in the Burnside family spurred its own book project, which she eventually self-published as *The Lake Place Burnsides*.[103] Florence had a personal connection to the Burnside case. Her stepfather, Dees Stribling, had represented A. J. Pearson and Pearl Cheatham in the first trial. He also helped Sim draft his will. Judge Jerry Gillis, who presided over both trials, was related to Dees through marriage. Gillis's wife, Zelma, who had died in 1950, was a Stribling and a distant cousin of Dees, whose grandfather had been born in Pickens County, Alabama.[104] Cal Stribling, another of Dees's cousins, was a witness at the trial, where he testified that his family had associated with the Burnsides for generations. Both families had migrated first from South Carolina to Pickens County and then on to Neshoba County. When Bill Burnside had first headed west to Mississippi from Alabama, Cal Stribling's grandfather, Benjamin Franklin Quarles, had given him a place to stay.[105]

Dees was not involved with the second trial, but Florence sat in the audience, rapt. In *Witness in Philadelphia*, she turned a sharp eye to her community, a place steeped in evangelical Christianity and conservative "southern" values. Florence was deeply interested in how white Neshoba Countians had created a culture in which men could savagely murder civil rights workers in defense of white supremacy and get away with it. To her, the murders were evidence of an unforgivable strain of hypocrisy, since, as her grandfather, "Poppaw," had told her, in Neshoba County the color line was never inviolable. Florence's grandfather had told her about the history of illicit interracial sex when she was a young woman. She mused in the book about how he had said "that certain colored families were related to white families," and he had told her "the connection." But, she added, "he greatly disapproved of white men 'carrying on' with Negro women. The opposite [Black men with white women] was virtually unheard of."[106]

When Florence interviewed several of the Black Burnsides in the early 1970s, she concluded that the rightful heirs to the Burnside fortune were the children and grandchildren of Betsy, Mariah's alleged mother. Florence wrote that in 1846, Bill Burnside had "bought a beautiful mulatto girl named Mariah . . . on the auction block in Mobile." At the time, Mariah was just thirteen years old. Burnside was accompanied to the slave auction by "Boss" Tom Talley, who purchased Mariah's parents, Betsy Soom and Harry. Though they lived on different plantations, the family remained close. Everyone knew of the relation between the white and Black Burnsides. In the late nineteenth century, she wrote, "There was no question in the mind of the white community of Neshoba County that these children were Negro."[107] Within the span of a few decades, this sentiment shifted. By the early twentieth century, the Burnside children had acquired a "white" racial identity, and the family managed land and businesses around the Burnside community. To deter scrutiny, Florence explained, Sim and his siblings "made a pact among themselves never to marry." Realizing the limits of their whiteness, "They did not want to live as Negroes in Neshoba County and knew that though they looked white, their mixed blood made it both scandalous and illegal to marry whites."[108] And so Sim and his siblings remained single and childless. The marriage pact protected their history from public scrutiny—until Sim's death and the dispute over the will.

FLORENCE NEVER UNCOVERED DOCUMENTARY EVIDENCE OF MARIAH'S parentage, though she tried doggedly to get to the truth of the family's past. She found no deed documenting the sale of an enslaved girl matching Mariah's description. In the end, Florence had only the evidence presented at the trial and the stories told to her by other local people, including many of the Black Burnsides. But Mariah's genetic make-up is not what matters for our world today: what matters is how the stories about her came to be, explaining why white and Black Mississippians had very different memories of the demise of slavery and the rise of Jim Crow. Indeed, the world around Mariah and her children transformed several times over during their lives, each time redrawing the color line as needed to protect whiteness. Mariah was born into a world where slavery seemed immovable, but she would live through the Civil War and emancipation, eventually witnessing Reconstruction and its violent overthrow. Neither she nor Bill Burnside nor anyone else knew what would happen in the future. And few could have anticipated how radically Mississippi would change in the wake of emancipation and how consequential those transformations would be for families like the Burnsides, whose histories reveal a very different and complicated account of the color line than the one white Mississippians held so dear.

EPILOGUE

The Natchez City Cemetery sits high atop a bluff, perched among the emerald rolling hills at the city's northern edge. At the northeast corner of Plot Three, where a sloping hill meets the road, lie the final resting places of Ralphine Burns and William Sanders Dean. They are marked by a single gravestone hewn from red granite, with only their last names—"BURNS" and "DEAN"—etched for posterity in the polished stone face. Taken in isolation, it is unclear who is buried here. There are no first names, and no dates of life or death. In retrospect, this seems intentional: to lie together after death, they had to omit key information that would make it clear that their union was illegal during their lives.

I found Ralphine and William's gravestone on Memorial Day. It was sunny and bright, and even in the early evening, the heat and humidity were unrelenting. I stumbled upon it while looking for something else: the grave marker for Ralphine's father, William Burns Jr. As it turns out, Ralphine and William were buried in her family plot, between her father and her mother, Elmira, who died in 1901 at the age of thirty-nine. Ralphine was only a teenager when she lost her mother.[1] Although the state of Mississippi attempted to split them up twice during her lifetime, Ralphine refused to be separated from William even in death.

Ralphine was born two years after the Mississippi Legislature outlawed interracial marriage. She lived through the disfranchisement of Black men like her father, the rise of "redneck" politics, and the revival

245

of the Ku Klux Klan, and she lived to see the emerging Black Freedom Struggle. Her date of death is unclear, but the headstone resembles others made in the 1950s and early 1960s. Her lifetime nearly traced the arc of the entire Jim Crow era. And yet Ralphine and William managed to remain married and to be buried together. Their relationship spanned decades, produced nine children, and endured two legal prosecutions fifteen years apart. It seems fitting that their final resting place serves as one last rebuke to the people and the legal system that attempted to destroy their bond.

In the late afternoon, Ralphine and William's graves are shaded by the enormous entwined canopies of two trees that reach nearly a hundred feet into the sky. Just up the hill are a juniper and a pecan tree that, at some point in the past century, fastened themselves to one another at the base. From a distance, they appear to be a single tree. But up close, it is clear that they are different species, having grown together until they became conjoined. This process is called "inosculation," from the Latin word "to

Gravestone of Ralphine Burns and William S. Dean, Natchez City Cemetery (photo by the author).

Marriage tree overlooking the gravestone of Ralphine Burns and William S. Dean, Natchez City Cemetery (photo by the author).

kiss." Such trees are also called "marriage trees" or "husband and wife" trees. Together, they are magnificent, reaching toward the sun. At the base, the trunks have slowly broken through a wrought-iron fence. The symbolism of this tree in this place could not be more obvious.

ON JULY 14, 1958, TWELVE DAYS AFTER ELSIE ARRINGTON AND DAISY Ratcliff were roused from their shared bed by the sheriff in Purvis, Mississippi, a strikingly similar scene played out halfway across the country, in Carroll County, Virginia. This event would garner far more attention than Daisy's trials ever did. Like Elsie and Daisy, Richard and Mildred Loving had law enforcement officers burst into their home in the middle of the night. Mildred, a Black woman, and Richard, a white man, were arrested for violating Virginia's 1924 Racial Integrity Act. Nine years later, on June 12, 1967, the United States Supreme Court issued its ruling in the final appeal of their case. The justices declared in *Loving v. Virginia* that states could not prohibit interracial marriages. By barring couples from marrying across racial lines, the state had violated their fundamental right to marry.[2]

The struggle of Richard and Mildred Loving to keep their family together has been told in books, magazines, documentaries, and a major motion picture. One of the more moving aspects of their story is how ordinary the Lovings were. They simply wanted the state and its officers to leave their family alone. Their legal fight had consequences for families across the United States, including in Mississippi, where local newspapers covered some of the first post-*Loving* interracial marriages with keen interest.

In July 1970, two couples attempted to obtain marriage licenses but were foiled by the Southern National Party, a segregationist organization that purported to represent the interests of the "Anglo-Saxon Southerner." The party's leader obtained an injunction alleging that these marriages were unconstitutional and a violation of "the Southern way of life and white supremacy."[3] Vernon Davis, a Black factory worker from Canton, sought to marry Noreen V. Leary, a white social worker who hailed from Massachusetts.[4] The other couple, Berta Linson and Roger Mills, received far more attention. They met while working with the NAACP Legal Defense Fund. Berta, a Black woman, had grown up in Mississippi, but her white husband was an outsider. Both couples finally obtained licenses on an order from a federal district judge, who ruled that *Loving v. Virginia* did, in fact, apply to Mississippi. One irony of the entire affair was that the judge was Harold Cox, who had long been a vocal racist and opponent of civil rights.[5] The order came in hours before the Hinds County Circuit Court clerk's office closed, so Roger and Berta had to rush to get their license. They had a church wedding planned for that weekend. Newspapers from Rochester, New York, to Palm Beach, Florida, and to Washington state carried photos of the smiling bride and groom, kissing and cutting into their towering white wedding cake.[6] *Florida Today* explained the significance of the couple's wedding as the "end of Mississippi's anti-miscegenation laws, which dated back to slave days."[7]

Many observers, of course, knew this assessment was not fully accurate. Nor was it the whole story. Even Roger, the groom, said as much in interviews. "The only thing that is new is that this is the first time the state of Mississippi has ever sanctioned it," Roger told reporters. "For a great many years whites have been going through the back door and doing approximately the same thing without having the legal means to do it."[8] In its coverage of the story, *Jet* magazine nestled photographs of Berta and Roger next to an accompanying survey of the long history of interracial relationships in the state, including the marriage of Albert and Carrie Morgan. Quoting Lerone Bennett Jr.'s book *Before the Mayflower*, the article noted that interracial relationships continued even after they were outlawed, as "in communities like the Mississippi Delta some white men became so attached to Negro mistresses that they abandoned white society and 'went native!'"[9] Of course, enslaved Black people were not indigenous to Mississippi. Both slavery and Jim Crow were supported by racist laws that aimed to cleave ties of affection and blood.

By the 1970s, the memory of interracial families was mostly segregated by race. As University of Mississippi historian James Silver observed in 1964, "Like other Southerners, Mississippians are obsessed by their sense of the past, but this does not ensure the accuracy of their historical picture; they see legend rather than history."[10] This was true for the white descendants of interracial couples like Ralphine Burns and William Dean, who did not know of their family's history until genealogy websites made it easy to find census data filling in the silences of the stories families tell about themselves and their forebears. Some of Ralphine's children identified as white after leaving Natchez, a decision that expanded their employment horizons. Juel and Clarence settled in New Brunswick, New Jersey, after serving in World War II.[11] The father of Dorothy's children was white. Dorothy and her children eventually left Natchez and settled in Tennessee, where they lived as white people for the rest of their lives. Until recently, their descendants did not know of their family's long history on the other side of the color line.[12] Olga, another daughter, married Louis Sabine, a Black man, in Natchez.[13] Living on different sides of the color line did not sever family ties. At least three of Ralphine and William's children—Juel, Olga, and Ethel—are buried together in the Dean family plot in the Natchez City Cemetery, not far from the final resting place of their parents.

The efforts of segregationists to erase this past were not entirely successful. Black Mississippians held on to these memories and passed them down through generations. The son of assassinated civil rights leader Vernon Dahmer has long discussed his family's interracial past.[14] Vernon Jr. told a journalist that his grandfather, George Washington Dahmer, was a white man who had adopted a Black identity. George, as family lore had it, was a "white outcast who lived his entire life as a Black man."[15]

The details of George's life in the census shed some light on the Dahmer family's history. George was born in 1871 and adopted sometime thereafter by a Black man, Charles Craft. In 1880, the census shows a blended family headed by Charlie and Laura Craft.[16] George's father was a white man named Peter Dahmer. His mother, Laura, was a white woman who, according to family history, had been spurned by her family for having a child out of wedlock.[17] At some point, she had met Charlie Craft, and when a mob chased her and her son from their home, Charlie took them in. Thereafter, the Crafts lived in the Kelly Settlement, home to a community descended from a white slaveholder, John Kelly, and a Black woman, Sarah. Laura and George adopted Black identities.[18] During the 1870s, Laura and Charlie's relationship would not have been illegal. The family's complicated history of crossing the color line was something that survived in living memory, even if many white Mississippians were unaware that such a story could be true.

For decades, in literature and in interviews, Black Mississippians have openly discussed the state's complicated color line, though it has always been a fraught subject. Raylawni Branch, a descendant of Newton and Rachel Knight of Jones County, recalled how people referred to her family as "white Negroes." She explained in a 2015 interview with historian Emilye Crosby that she had inherited land from her white forebears. "That's one reason—because of a mixture of the races—that's why black people have so much land," she told Crosby. "Because they gave their children all that." But it was not only property that was passed through the generations. The toleration of white men crossing the color line also created trauma and suffering. Raylawni's grandmother had become pregnant after being raped by a white plantation owner. Raylawni's own childhood had been fraught with bullying and teasing about her fair complexion. The absurdity of the "one-drop" rule of Black racial inheritance was torture for her as a child. She felt like she did not truly belong on either side of the color line. She could not understand why Newt and Rachel Knight would bring children into the world who would be faced with "all of this hatred among both races." Of Mississippi's history, she sighed, "It was never black and white."[19]

It was not only children who found the sexual double standard infuriating. In Anne Moody's 1968 memoir, *Coming of Age in Mississippi*, she recalls understanding as a child in the 1950s that, while Emmett Till could be tortured and murdered for allegedly whistling at a white woman, everyone knew that white men fathered children with Black women.[20] Myrlie Evers, the widow of Medgar Evers, who was murdered for his activism, told historian Charles Payne that her husband was legendary for his even-keeled demeanor, but she did see him get angry once when he came across a Black woman kissing a white man in a parking lot.[21] Evers's frustration with a Black woman engaging in a relationship with a white man—who likely would not have openly embraced the equality of the races—was enough to boil over into outrage. In June 1963, Byron De La Beckwith, a white supremacist obsessed with the concept of white racial purity, shot Evers in the back in Evers's own driveway, killing him.[22]

Evers's anger is understandable. The openness with which a white man could cross the color line was yet another reminder that Jim Crow existed to create and sustain inequality. Not only have the histories of interracial couples been forgotten, but the memory of interracial relationships has been warped by criminalization and by attitudes casting them as illicit and shameful. Any such relationship could be subject to the terms set by other people: the policemen who investigated allegations, the juries who heard evidence about their neighbors, the judges who presided over trials of "unlawful cohabitation." All these people were white, and during the Jim Crow era they were almost always men. The way they enforced the law was not arbitrary: it typically reinforced their own rights and privileges at everyone else's expense. This is most obvious in the stark contrast between the lax treatment many interracial couples received when charged with unlawful cohabitation and the derision and mockery heaped upon Black widows and biracial children of white men when they asserted their claims to inherit. These individual stories typically do not reveal whether any of these actors were profoundly ideologically opposed to interracial sex or marriage, but they do tell us something important about white supremacy and its ultimate purpose. Laws prohibiting interracial marriage were not effective in preventing couples from forming families. They did, however, successfully protect white wealth. Any reckoning with this history must not only account for the people whose relationships were torn apart or disparaged as unlawful but also acknowledge the theft of Black wealth that underlay the entire system of Jim Crow.

ACKNOWLEDGMENTS

THIS BOOK WOULD NOT HAVE BEEN POSSIBLE WITHOUT TWO THINGS: archivists and money. I owe a deep debt of gratitude to the wonderful staff at the Mississippi Department of Archives and History (MDAH), who attempted to answer every question I could muster about their own holdings. They also pointed me in the direction of other archives and courthouses and helped me find some of the richest material in the book. Special thanks to Caroline Gray-Primer at MDAH, whose questions and suggestions propelled further research. Nicole Harris and Mimi Miller at the Historic Natchez Foundation showered me with generosity as they helped me find critical court records. Mimi is an endless font of knowledge about Natchez and the complicated histories of families who lived there, and Nicole helped me track down crucial court records from Adams County. Jennifer McGillan at Mississippi State University helped me navigate the Florence Mars Papers and pointed me toward the striking image of a woman with her children that appears in Chapter 6.

I benefited from the assistance of many helpful people staffing courthouse offices who took time out of their busy schedules to help a beleaguered historian find records that were often disorganized or stored offsite. The Adams County Circuit Court clerk, Eva Givens, and the staff allowed me to access the euphemistically named "storage annex"—really, a warehouse—where I found a bounty of records from early twentieth-century Natchez. Robert Coleman, the clerk of the Yazoo County Circuit Court, spent a morning helping me search rusty file cabinets in the courthouse basement. Gretta Myles and the staff at the Claiborne County Clerk's Office made me feel welcome as they graciously allowed me to use their library. Jay Driskell provided meticulous and thorough research assistance at the Library of Congress.

I was tremendously fortunate to receive a Public Scholar Award from the National Endowment for the Humanities, which allowed me to spend a year focused on completing the research and writing of this manuscript. The University of Oklahoma History Department provided funds that helped me get to Mississippi at a critical stage of the research process. A Junior Faculty Fellowship awarded by the Research Council of the University of Oklahoma Office of the Vice President for Research and Partnerships funded a pivotal early trip to Mississippi.

I am grateful for colleagues and friends in the United States and Australia who read and offered comments on drafts of the manuscript, including Julia Bowes, Jim Campbell, David Chappell, Frances Clarke, Clare Corbould, Laura Edwards, Susannah Engstrom, David Goodman, Jessica Lake, Patrick McGrath, Sarah Miller-Davenport, Celeste Moore, and Emily Remus. I am grateful for the feedback I received from presenting this research at the Notre Dame American Studies Workshop, the American Society for Legal History, the University of Oklahoma History Department Workshop, the Schusterman Center JuSt Lunch series, the University of Melbourne Brown Bag series, the University of Tasmania's "More Than a Story" webinar, and the University of Sydney History on Wednesday series. Thanks especially for insightful comments and questions from Pete Cajka, Kristin Collins, Jennifer Davis-Cline, Lauren Duval, Kat Ellinghaus, Korey Garibaldi, Alan Levenson, Josh Specht, and Thomas Tweed. Alan connected me to Mark Bauman, who shared a wealth of information on southern Jewish history. I am grateful to Jim Downs, Kate Masur, Gautham Rao, and the anonymous reviewers whose questions and suggestions on articles based on Chapters 1 and 5 in this book challenged me to think more deeply about the significance of this research. While writing this book, I began a new position at the University of Sydney. I cannot imagine a better place to land than the United States Studies Centre, where I have been welcomed by enthusiastic and generous colleagues, including Mike Green, Aaron Nyerges, Brendon O'Connor, Sabina Rahman, David Smith, and Rodney Taveira.

I was incredibly fortunate to meet Jim Campbell at an early stage of this project, as he was working on his own book on Neshoba County. Jim's generosity in sharing ideas, research, and his networks in Mississippi enriched this project in countless ways—especially the chapter on the Burnsides. Jim introduced me to many people and places in Jackson and Neshoba County and treated me to more than one wonderful dinner when my research funds were lacking (the company was, of course, always better than the food). Jeremy Chalmers and Dawn Lea Mars Chalmers welcomed me into their home. Rebecca Tuuri pointed me toward some key sources and stories about the Kelly Settlement. I am tremendously grateful to people who talked to me about their own family histories, including Gail Green, Richard Dean, and Olivia Roberts.

The encouragements of my wonderful editor Brandon Proia propelled me through the final stages of writing and revision. Lucy Cleland, agent extraordinaire, said yes to this book when it was in its infancy. Her questions and comments pushed me to expand the scope of my research and to ask more ambitious questions about what this story could truly be. Kate Blackmer did a superb job creating the map and the family trees that beautifully display the complicated and sometimes confusing stories told in this book. Katherine Streckfus provided meticulous and thoughtful copyediting for the manuscript. Kevin Butterfield went above and beyond to track down the wonderful image of John Roy Lynch at the Library of Congress. Andrew McNulty at MDAH and Gigi Broyles at the Bentley Historical Library offered crucial assistance in getting reproductions of images for Chapters 2 and 9.

It would be difficult to write a book about marriage and family without reflecting on your own and appreciating the love and sacrifice that accumulate over a lifetime. I am grateful every day for the unwavering support of my parents, Bill and Teresa Schumaker, who put their own dreams on hold so that their children could pursue theirs—even if it meant leaving town (and, in my case, the continent). My husband, Matthew, believed I could write this book before I ever did. He has been by my side, encouraging me to keep going at every step of the way. Thank you.

NOTES

Prologue

1. Clarence was born on March 14, 1924. Clarence William Dean, Box 1, Mississippi, in *U.S., World War II Draft Cards Young Men, 1940–1947*, National Archives and Records Administration (NARA) (via Ancestry.com).

2. Ralphine Burns, *1920 Federal Census*, Beat 5, Adams County, Mississippi, supervisor's district 7, enumeration district 6, p. 12A (via Ancestry.com).

3. Ralphine Burns, *1900 Federal Census*, Beat 4, Adams County, Mississippi, supervisor's district 7, enumeration district 8, p. 132-A; Ralphine Burns, *1920 Federal Census*, City of Natchez, Adams County, Mississippi, supervisor's district 7, enumeration district 6, p. 12A (via Ancestry.com).

4. "Circuit Court to Take Up Criminal Docket on Monday," *Natchez Democrat*, April 2, 1924.

5. On the context of Ralphine's first charge of unlawful cohabitation in 1909, see Chapter 4.

6. *State of Mississippi v. W. S. Dean and Ralphine Burns*, case no. 3787, Adams County Circuit Court, Minute Book I, p. 212, Historic Natchez Foundation, Natchez, Mississippi (hereafter HNF).

7. "An Act in Relation to Marriage and Divorce," Sec. 1147, Chap. 42, Miss. Code 1880; Sec. 2859, Chap. 90, Miss. Ann. Code (1892); Sec. 3244, Miss. Code 1906.

8. Peggy Pascoe, *What Comes Naturally: Miscegenation Law and the Making of Race in America* (New York: Oxford University Press, 2009), 21.

9. Pascoe, *What Comes Naturally*, 81, 168. On the legal prohibition of interracial marriage, see also Peter W. Bardaglio, "'Shamefull Matches': The Regulation of Interracial Sex and Marriage in the South Before 1900," in *Sex, Love, Race: Crossing Boundaries in North American History*, ed. Martha Hodes (New York: New York University Press, 1999); William D. Zabel, "Interracial Marriage and the Law," in *Interracialism: Black-White Intermarriage in American History, Literature, and Law*, ed. Werner Sollors (New York: Oxford University Press, 2000), 54–61; Peter Wallenstein, *Tell the Court I Love My Wife: Race, Marriage, and Law—an American History* (New York: Palgrave

Macmillan, 2002); Julie Novkov, *Racial Union: Law, Intimacy, and the White State in Alabama, 1865–1954* (Ann Arbor: University of Michigan Press, 2008).

10. Pascoe, *What Comes Naturally*, 19–20. On colonial prohibitions on interracial marriage and their relation to slavery, see Kathleen N. Brown, *Good Wives, Nasty Wenches, and Anxious Patriarchs: Gender, Race, and Power in Colonial Virginia* (Chapel Hill: University of North Carolina Press, 1996), 187–211; A. Leon Higginbotham and Barbara K. Kopytoff, "Racial Purity and Interracial Sex in the Law of Colonial and Antebellum Virginia," in Sollors, *Interracialism*; Jennifer Morgan, "*Partus Sequitur Ventrem*: Law, Race, and Reproduction in Colonial Slavery," *Small Axe* 22, no. 1 (March 2018): 1–17.

11. On the invention of the term "miscegenation," see Elise Lemire, *Miscegenation: Making Race in America* (Philadelphia: University of Pennsylvania Press, 2002).

12. My work is influenced by Barbara Fields, who argues that race is an ideology in the United States, that associations between physical characteristics and racial classifications are dependent on context, and that they can and do change over time. Barbara J. Fields, "Ideology and Race in American History," in *Region, Race, and Reconstruction: Essays in Honor of C. Vann Woodward*, ed. J. Morgan Kousser and James M. McPherson (New York: Oxford University Press, 1982), 143–177. Peggy Pascoe argues that laws prohibiting interracial marriage "made race" in the United States and were "the foundation for the larger racial projects of white supremacy and white purity." Pascoe, *What Comes Naturally*, 6.

13. On whiteness as a social, cultural, and historical construct, see David Roediger, *The Wages of Whiteness: Race and the Making of the American Working Class* (New York: Verso, 1991); Noel Ignatiev, *How the Irish Became White* (New York: Routledge, 1995); Matthew Frye Jacobson, *Whiteness of a Different Color: European Immigrants and the Alchemy of Race* (Cambridge, MA: Harvard University Press, 1998); Grace Elizabeth Hale, *Making Whiteness: The Culture of Segregation in the South, 1890–1940* (New York: Pantheon, 1998).

14. Ian Haney López, *White by Law: The Legal Construction of Race* (New York: New York University Press, 2006); Ariela J. Gross, *What Blood Won't Tell: A History of Race on Trial in America* (Cambridge, MA: Harvard University Press, 2008). On the history of interracial families in the United States, see Joshua D. Rothman, *Notorious in the Neighborhood: Sex and Families Across the Color Line in Virginia, 1787–1861* (Chapel Hill: University of North Carolina Press, 2003); Annette Gordon-Reed, *The Hemingses of Monticello: An American Family* (New York: W. W. Norton, 2008); Anne F. Hyde, *Born of Lakes and Plains: Mixed-Descent Peoples and the Making of the American West* (New York: W. W. Norton, 2020); R. Isabela Morales, *Happy Dreams of Liberty: An American Family in Slavery and Freedom* (New York: Oxford University Press, 2022); Amrita Chakrabarti Myers, *The Vice President's Black Wife: The Untold Life of Julia Chinn* (Chapel Hill: University of North Carolina Press, 2023).

15. "An Act in Relation to Marriage and Divorce," Sec. 1147, Chap. 42, Miss. Code 1880.

16. Sec. 263, Art. 14, Miss. Const. 1890.

17. *State v. Dean*, case no. 3787, Adams County Circuit Court, Minute Book I, p. 212, HNF.

18. *State v. Dean*, case no. 3787, Adams County Circuit Court, Minute Book I, p. 222, HNF.

19. *State v. Dean*, case no. 3787, Adams County Circuit Court, Minute Book I, p. 234, HNF.

20. *W. S. Dean and Ralphine Burns v. State of Mississippi*, 139 Miss. 515 (1925).

21. Ralphine Burns, *Polk's Natchez (Adams County, Miss.) City Directory* (Richmond, VA: R. L. Polk & Co., 1947), 64.

22. "Circuit Court Proceedings," *Natchez Democrat*, April 19, 1908.

23. Terence Finnegan writes, "Many whites could not conceive of a social order that tolerated African American independence and autonomy, and lynching enabled whites to dispel their anxieties and fears in a cauldron of bloodshed that they hoped would restore order and security to southern society." Terrence Finnegan, *A Deed So Accursed: Lynching in Mississippi and South Carolina, 1881–1940* (Charlottesville: University of Virginia Press, 2013), 3. See also Ida B. Wells, *Southern Horrors: Lynch Law in All Its Phases* (New York: New York Age Print, 1892); Martha Hodes, *White Women, Black Men: Illicit Sex in the Nineteenth-Century South* (New Haven, CT: Yale University Press, 1997), 176–208; Crystal Feimster, *Southern Horrors: Women and the Politics of Lynching* (Cambridge, MA: Harvard University Press, 2009).

24. The preamble to the 1691 Virginia law prohibiting interracial marriage—the first to apply equally to men and women regardless of racial classification—specifically described the undesirability of "negroes, mulattoes, and Indians intermarrying with English, or other white women." On the 1691 Virginia law, see Brown, *Good Wives, Nasty Wenches*, 187–211; Higginbotham and Kopytoff, "Racial Purity and Interracial Sex in the Law of Colonial and Antebellum Virginia"; Wallenstein, *Tell the Court I Love My Wife*; Pascoe, *What Comes Naturally*, 19–21. On the inheritability of slavery, see Morgan, "*Partus Sequitur Ventrem*"; Brooke N. Newman, "Blood Fictions, Maternal Inheritance, and the Legacies of Colonial Slavery," *Women's Studies Quarterly* 48, nos. 1/2, Special Issue: Inheritance (Spring/Summer 2020): 27–44.

25. On the sexual abuse and rape of Black women by white men after emancipation, see Danielle McGuire, *At the Dark End of the Street: Black Women, Rape, and Resistance—a New History of the Civil Rights Movement from Rosa Parks to the Rise of Black Power* (New York: Knopf, 2010); Wilma King, "'Prematurely Knowing of Evil Things': The Sexual Abuse of African American Girls and Young Women in Slavery and Freedom," *Journal of African American History* 99, no. 3 (Summer 2014): 173–196.

26. Timothy Tyson, *Radio Free Dixie: Robert F. Williams and the Roots of Black Power* (Chapel Hill: University of North Carolina Press, 1999), 94.

27. Neil McMillen's history of Black Mississippians, for example, describes most relationships between white men and Black women as "casual and commercial in character." Neil McMillen, *Dark Journey: Black Mississippians in the Age of Jim Crow* (Urbana: University of Illinois Press, 1990), 17.

28. Martha Hodes notes that Reconstruction marked a turning point in the politics of miscegenation law, with greater political focus shifting to relationships between white women and Black men, and considerably less concern for interracial sex between white men and Black women—thus preserving white control over the sexuality of both Black men and women. Hodes, *White Women, Black Men*, 147–175. Other scholars have found

the same pattern of what Peggy Pascoe terms the "engendering" of miscegenation law in the Reconstruction-era South. Pascoe, *What Comes Naturally*, 24–46; Charles Robinson, *Dangerous Liaisons: Sex and Love in the Segregated South* (Fayetteville: University of Arkansas Press, 2003), 69–72.

29. I agree with Julie Novkov, who argues in her study of Alabama that segregation laws sought to privilege and protect white families to bolster white supremacy, but in this book I challenge her assertion that southern lawmakers and jurists viewed interracial relationships as "most dangerous when they most closely approximated familial relations." Novkov, *Racial Union*, 5.

30. Brief of Appellees, *Dean v. State*, 139 Miss. at 517.

31. In 1919, the Bureau of War Risk Insurance published a study of marriage law in the United States and its territories noting the widespread validity of common law marriage. Even in some states that had recently passed legislation requiring couples to obtain marriage licenses, including Illinois (1905) and Arizona (1913), those laws did not void the validity of preexisting common law marriages. In other parts of the United States, including Connecticut and Washington, DC, the validity of common law marriage was unclear. US Bureau of War Risk Insurance, *Digest of the Law Relating to Common Law Marriage in the States, Territories, and Dependencies of the United States* (Washington, DC: US Government Printing Office, 1919).

32. Robert E. Dillon, *Common Law Marriage* (Washington, DC: Catholic University Press, 1942), 10–11.

33. Jennifer Thomas, "Common Law Marriage," *Journal of the American Academy of Matrimonial Lawyers* 22, no. 1 (2009): 151–168.

34. For examples of the destruction of county courthouse records, see Mississippi Genealogical Society, *Survey of Records in Mississippi Court Houses* (Jackson: Mississippi Genealogical Society, 1957); Bryan F. McKown and Michael E. Stauffer, "Destroyed County Records in South Carolina, 1785–1872," *South Carolina History Magazine* 97, no. 2 (April 1996): 149–158; Martha Doty Freeman, "Preservation of Texas's Public Records, a Vital Work in Progress," *Information and Culture* 49, no. 1 (2014): 90–107.

35. On the central importance of gender to southern politics, see Peter Bardaglio, *Reconstructing the Household: Families, Sex, and the Law in the Nineteenth-Century South* (Chapel Hill: University of North Carolina Press, 1995); Laura F. Edwards, *Gendered Strife and Confusion: The Political Culture of Reconstruction* (Urbana: University of Illinois Press, 1997); Amy Dru Stanley, *From Bondage to Contract: Wage Labor, Marriage, and the Market in the Age of Slave Emancipation* (New York: Cambridge University Press, 1998).

36. On common law marriage, see Michael Grossberg, *Governing the Hearth: Law and the Family in Nineteenth-Century America* (Chapel Hill: University of North Carolina Press, 1985), 73–75, 86–100; Edwards, *Gendered Strife*, 60–61; Nancy F. Cott, *Public Vows: A History of Marriage and the Nation* (Cambridge, MA: Harvard University Press, 2000), 32–33; Joanna L. Grossman and Lawrence Friedman, *Inside the Castle: Law and the Family in 20th Century America* (Princeton, NJ: Princeton University Press, 2011), 78–89; Tera Hunter, *Bound in Wedlock: Slave and Free Black Marriage in the Nineteenth Century* (Cambridge, MA: Harvard University Press, 2017), 279–282.

37. Discrimination against illegitimate children was a key feature of the British common law, which labeled bastards as *filius nullis*, "child and heir of no one." American states reformed their bastardy laws in the nineteenth century, allowing illegitimate children to inherit from their mothers and to be legitimated by the marriage of their parents. It was not until the 1970s that states began to acknowledge the rights of illegitimate children to inherit from their fathers. See Harry D. Krause, *Illegitimacy: Law and Social Policy* (Indianapolis: Bobbs-Merrill, 1971); Grossberg, *Governing the Hearth*, 196–233; Martha T. Zingo and Kevin E. Early, *Nameless Persons: Discrimination Against Non-Marital Children in the United States* (Westport, CT: Praeger, 1994); Serena Mayeri, "Marital Supremacy and the Constitution of the Nonmarital Family," *California Law Review* 5 (2015): 1277–1352.

38. Sec. 1381 and 1383, Miss. Ann. Code 1917.

39. Sec. 1387, Miss. Ann. Code 1917.

40. "Board of Police," *Natchez Daily Courier*, April 13, 1853; Rachel Burns, *1850 Federal Census*, City of Natchez, Adams County, Mississippi, p. 12A (via Ancestry.com).

41. "Death of William Burns," *Natchez Daily Courier*, October 19, 1849.

42. It is not clear when Charles and Delia's relationship began, though they had a son, Edward, in 1857. Charles Lacoste and Delia Berthe, *1860 Federal Census*, Central Township, St. Louis County, Missouri, p. 56; Charles Lacoste and Delia White, *1870 Federal Census*, Central Township, St. Louis County, Missouri, p. 67; Charles Lacoste and Delia White, *1880 Federal Census*, Central Township, St. Louis County, Missouri, supervisor's district 1, enumeration district 175, p. 32D; Edward Lacoste, *1900 Federal Census*, St. Louis, Missouri, supervisor's district 11, enumeration district 206, p. 12A (via Ancestry.com).

43. This story is told most fully in a property dispute that took place in the 1890s between Ralphine's father, William Burns Jr., and her uncle, Randolph Burns. *William Burns et al. v. Randolph Burns et al.*, case no. 1350, Adams County Chancery Court Records, Natchez, MS (via Ancestry.com).

44. "Descent of Estate of Inheritance in Lands, Etc.," Sec. 50, Art. 2, Chap. 44, Miss. Code 1848. This story is also told in a biography of Louise Berthe's daughter, social reformer Lugenia Burns Hope. There is no footnote in the book, indicating that the story was likely passed on to the author (who died several years ago) via oral history interviews with Louise and Lugenia's descendants. Jacqueline Anne Rouse, *Lugenia Burns Hope: Black Southern Reformer* (Athens: University of Georgia Press, 1989).

45. On the material value of whiteness, see Cheryl Harris, "Whiteness as Property," *Harvard Law Review* 106, no. 8 (June 1993): 1707–1791.

46. Here I draw from Adolph Reed's work on the memory of Jim Crow. Adolph Reed Jr., *Jim Crow and Its Afterlives* (New York: Verso, 2022).

47. Historians have long recognized the contingent nature of Jim Crow as a political, cultural, and legal regime. As Glenda Gilmore, Jane Dailey, and Bryant Simon write, white supremacy was "a precarious balancing act, pulled in all directions by class, gender, and racial tensions." Glenda Gilmore, Jane Dailey, and Bryant Simon, eds., *Jumpin' Jim Crow: Southern Politics from Civil War to Civil Rights* (Princeton, NJ: Princeton University Press, 2000), 4. See also Hale, *Making Whiteness*; Stephen A. Berrey, *The*

Jim Crow Routine: Everyday Performances of Race, Civil Rights, and Segregation in Mississippi (Chapel Hill: University of North Carolina Press, 2015).

48. Steven Mintz, *Huck's Raft: A History of American Childhood* (Cambridge, MA: Belknap Press of Harvard University Press, 2004); Jennifer Ritterhouse, *Growing Up Jim Crow: How Black and White Southern Children Learned Race* (Chapel Hill: University of North Carolina Press, 2006).

49. Tera Hunter, *To 'Joy My Freedom: Southern Black Women's Lives and Labors After the Civil War* (Cambridge, MA: Harvard University Press, 1997).

50. Saidiya Hartman, *Scenes of Subjection: Terror, Slavery, and Self-Making in Nineteenth-Century America* (New York: Oxford University Press, 1997).

51. There is a voluminous literature on the establishment of separate Black institutions, including churches and schools, as well as Black separatist movements in the nineteenth and twentieth centuries. See, e.g., Evelyn Brooks Higginbotham, *Righteous Discontent: The Women's Movement in the Black Baptist Church* (Cambridge, MA: Harvard University Press, 1993).

52. Karlos K. Hill, *The 1921 Tulsa Race Massacre: A Photographic History* (Norman: University of Oklahoma Press, 2021); Michael Pierce and Calvin White Jr., eds., *Race, Labor and Violence in the Delta: Essays to Mark the Centennial of the Elaine Massacre* (Fayetteville: University of Arkansas Press, 2022). Grace Elizabeth Hale argues that acts of violence, including lynchings, were essential to maintaining the culture of segregation, as they reminded Black southerners that everything could be taken from them at any time. Hale, *Making Whiteness*, 8–9.

53. On the struggle against Jim Crow as a class struggle, see Robin D. G. Kelley, *Race Rebels: Culture, Politics, and the Black Working Class* (New York: Free Press, 1996); Henry M. McKiven Jr., *Iron and Steel: Class, Race, and Community in Birmingham, Alabama, 1875–1920* (Chapel Hill: University of North Carolina Press, 1995); Charles C. Bolton, *The Hardest Deal of All: The Battle over School Integration in Mississippi, 1870–1980* (Jackson: University Press of Mississippi, 2005).

54. On inequitable segregated schooling, see James D. Anderson, *The Education of Blacks in the South, 1860–1935* (Chapel Hill: University of North Carolina Press, 1988); Blair L. M. Kelley, "Bearing the Burden of Separate but Equal in the Jim Crow South," in *A New History of the American South*, ed. W. Fitzhugh Brundage, Laura F. Edwards, and Jon E. Sensbach (Chapel Hill: University of North Carolina Press, 2023). On extralegal violence, including lynching, see Feimster, *Southern Horrors*; Margaret A. Burnham, *By Hands Now Known: Jim Crow's Legal Executioners* (New York: W. W. Norton, 2022).

55. On the public nature of marriage, see Cott, *Public Vows*; Hendrik Hartog, *Man and Wife in America* (Cambridge, MA: Harvard University Press, 2000); Hunter, *Bound in Wedlock*.

56. Linda K. Kerber, *No Constitutional Right to Be Ladies: Women and the Obligations of Citizenship* (New York: Hill and Wang, 1998).

57. On women's access to birth control, see Linda Gordon, *The Moral Property of Women: A History of Birth Control Politics in America* (Urbana: University of Illinois Press, 1974), 286–291; on credit, see Lizabeth Cohen, *A Consumer's Republic: The Politics of Mass Consumption in Postwar America* (New York: Knopf, 2003), 143–148.

58. The only southern state that compelled women's jury service was North Carolina, and the US Supreme Court unanimously upheld women's exclusion from jury service in its 1961 decision *Gwendolyn Hoyt v. State of Florida*, 368 U.S. 57 (1961). This opinion was not overturned until 1975 in *Billy J. Taylor v. State of Louisiana*, 419 U.S. 522 (1975). See Kerber, *No Constitutional Right to Be Ladies*, 124–220; Gretchen Ritter, "Jury Service and Women's Citizenship Before and After the Nineteenth Amendment," *Law and History Review* 20, no. 3 (Autumn 2002): 479–515; Jennifer L. Brinkley, "Dorothy Kenyon and Pauli Murray: Their Quest for Sex Equality in Jury Service," *Tennessee Journal of Race, Gender and Social Justice* 12, no. 2 (2022): 1–49.

59. The first Black woman elected to the Mississippi state legislature was Alyce Clarke, who, as of 2023, also became the state's longest-serving woman legislator. "Black Woman Wins Election to Legislature," *Hattiesburg (MS) American*, March 26, 1985; Emily Wagster Pettus, "Mississippi's 1st Black Woman Legislator Won't Seek New Term," Associated Press, February 1, 2023; Kari Frederickson, "The South and the State in the Twentieth Century," in Brundage et al., *A New History of the American South*, 398.

60. "Delinquent Poll Tax Payers for the Fiscal Year 1910," *Natchez Weekly Democrat*, March 8, 1911.

61. Kathleen M. Blee, *Women of the Klan: Racism and Gender in the 1920s* (Berkeley: University of California Press, 1991); Elizabeth Gillespie McRae, *Mothers of Massive Resistance: White Women and the Politics of White Supremacy* (New York: Oxford University Press, 2018); Rebecca Brückmann, *Massive Resistance and Southern Womanhood: White Women, Class, and Segregation* (Athens: University of Georgia Press, 2021).

62. Some of Albert and Lucinda's children moved to Chicago and adopted the Bunckley surname. Given that Ralph and Clarence were born eighteen years apart, it seems more likely than not that Albert fathered all of Lucinda's children. Ralph Bunckley, in *U.S. World War II Draft Cards Young Men, 1940–1947*, NARA; Clarence Bunckley, *1950 Federal Census*, Chicago, Cook County, Illinois, enumeration district 103–298, p. 16 (via Ancestry.com).

63. "Turley Appeal up to Supreme Court," *Memphis Commercial Appeal*, October 24, 1913.

64. *In the Matter of the Last Will and Testament of August Bourgeois, Sr.*, case no. 1567, Hancock County Chancery Court files, microfilm reel 37912, Mississippi Department of Archives and History, Jackson, Mississippi (hereafter MDAH).

65. On interracial inheritance under slavery, see Bernie D. Jones, *Fathers of Conscience: Mixed-Race Inheritance in the Antebellum South* (Athens: University of Georgia Press, 2009).

66. Dylan Penningroth, *The Claims of Kinfolk: African American Property and Community in the Nineteenth Century* (Chapel Hill: University of North Carolina Press, 2003).

67. Jane Dailey, *White Fright: The Sexual Panic at the Heart of America's Racist History* (New York: Basic Books, 2020).

68. The study of "law on the ground," which this book's methodology employs, is also referred to by historians and legal scholars as "legal culture." See Hendrik Hartog, "Pigs and Positivism," *Wisconsin Law Review* 1985, no. 4 (1985): 899–936; Laura

F. Edwards, *The People and Their Peace: Legal Culture and the Transformation of Inequality in the Post-Revolutionary South* (Chapel Hill: University of North Carolina Press, 2009); Kimberly Welch, *Black Litigants in the Antebellum South* (Chapel Hill: University of North Carolina Press, 2018); Dylan Penningroth, *Before the Movement: The Hidden History of Black Civil Rights* (New York: Liveright, 2023).

69. During the Jim Crow era, Mississippi had the highest per capita rate of lynchings of Black people in the nation, and, as historian Joseph Crespino puts it, in the 1950s and 1960s white Mississippians "committed some of the most ghastly, high-profile acts of racial violence." Joseph Crespino, *In Search of Another Country: Mississippi and the Conservative Counterrevolution* (Princeton, NJ: Princeton University Press, 2007), 5; Finnegan, *A Deed So Accursed*, 4. See also McMillen, *Dark Journey*; Timothy B. Tyson, *The Blood of Emmett Till* (New York: Simon and Schuster, 2017).

Chapter 1: Inheritances

1. G. and L. Dickerson, *1860 Federal Census—Slave Schedules*, Coahoma County, Mississippi, pp. 12–13; Ann Yellow, *1870 Federal Census*, Friars Point, Coahoma County, Mississippi, p. 20 (via Ancestry.com).

2. Bill of Complaint, July Term 1871, Coahoma County Chancery Court, *Susan Dickerson et al. v. W. N. Brown et al.* case file, Mississippi Department of Archives and History, Jackson, Mississippi (hereafter MDAH).

3. Edwin P. Harman, *1860 Federal Census*, Township 13, Range 5, Attalaville, Attala County, Mississippi, p. 232; E. P. Harman, in *US, Compiled Service Records of Confederate Soldiers Who Served in Organizations from the State of Mississippi, 1861–1865*, RG 109, roll 0214, publication M269, State: MS, National Archives and Records Administration (hereafter NARA) (via Ancestry.com). The name on the Confederate service file is "Edward P. Harman," but biographical details correspond to Edwin P. Harman, so "Edward" is likely a typographical error. Most of the individual records in the file refer to "E. P. Harman."

4. Judgment, July 26, 1871, Coahoma County Chancery Court, *Dickerson v. Brown* case file, MDAH.

5. *Dickerson v. Brown*, 49 Miss. 357 (1873).

6. *In the Matter of the Estate of Susan and Oliver Dickerson, Minors*, Coahoma County Chancery Court Minutes, vol. I, p. 546, *Mississippi Probate Records, 1781–1930* (via FamilySearch.org).

7. On freedwomen in the Mississippi Delta during the emancipation era, see Nancy Bercaw, *Gendered Freedoms: Race, Rights, and the Politics of Household in the Delta, 1861–1875* (Gainesville: University Press of Florida, 2003).

8. Noralee Frankel, *Freedom's Women: Black Women and Families in Civil War Era Mississippi* (Bloomington: Indiana University Press, 1999), 110–112.

9. Bill of Complaint, July 8, 1871, *Dickerson v. Brown* case file, MDAH.

10. On Black women and the sexual economy of slavery, see Deborah Gray White, *Ar'n't I a Woman? Female Slaves in the Plantation South* (New York: W. W. Norton, 1985); Thelma Jennings, "'Us Colored Women Had to Go Through a Plenty': Sexual Exploitation of African-American Slave Women," *Journal of Women's History* 1, no. 3 (Winter 1990): 45–74; Jennifer L. Morgan, *Laboring Women: Reproduction and Gender in New*

World Slavery (Philadelphia: University of Pennsylvania Press, 2004); Brenda Stevenson, "What's Love Got to Do with It? Concubinage and Enslaved Women and Girls in the Antebellum South," *Journal of African American History* 98, no. 1, Special Issue: Women, Slavery, and the Atlantic World (Winter 2013): 99–125; Wilma King, "'Prematurely Knowing of Evil Things': The Sexual Abuse of African American Girls and Young Women in Slavery and Freedom," *Journal of African American History* 99, no. 3 (Summer 2014): 173–196.

11. Alexandra Finley, *An Intimate Economy: Enslaved Women, Work, and America's Domestic Slave Trade* (Chapel Hill: University of North Carolina Press, 2020).

12. Black feminist scholars have emphasized the importance of using critical analysis to examine sexual relationships between enslaved women and their enslavers rather than labeling them as either fully consensual or coerced. This approach requires taking into consideration the limits of archival records that reveal the interiority of such women's lives and the complexities of their existences and choices. See Marisa Fuentes, *Dispossessed Lives: Enslaved Women, Violence, and the Archive* (Philadelphia: University of Pennsylvania Press, 2016); Daina Ramey Berry and Leslie M. Harris, eds., *Sexuality and Slavery: Reclaiming Intimate Histories of the Americas* (Athens: University of Georgia Press, 2018); Emily A. Owens, *Consent in the Presence of Force: Sexual Violence and Black Women's Survival in Antebellum New Orleans* (Chapel Hill: University of North Carolina Press, 2022).

13. James McPherson, *Battle Cry of Freedom: The Civil War Era* (New York: Oxford University Press, 1988), 421–422.

14. On Black women's self-emancipation during the Civil War, see Frankel, *Freedom's Women*, chaps. 1 and 2; Stephanie M. H. Camp, *Closer to Freedom: Enslaved Women and Everyday Resistance in the Plantation South* (Chapel Hill: University of North Carolina Press, 2004), chap. 5; Chandra Manning, "Working for Citizenship in Civil War Contraband Camps," *Journal of the Civil War Era* 4, no. 2 (June 2014): 172–204.

15. Ann Yellow, *1870 Federal Census*, Friars Point, Coahoma County, Mississippi, p. 20 (via Ancestry.com).

16. On slavery and marriage, see, generally, Tera Hunter, *Bound in Wedlock: Slave and Free Black Marriage in the Nineteenth Century* (Cambridge, MA: Harvard University Press, 2017).

17. Tera Hunter describes this as "perhaps the harshest written law" governing the marriages of free Black people in the South. Hunter, *Bound in Wedlock*, 102.

18. Sec. 1, Art. 1, Miss. Const. 1865; Eric Foner *Reconstruction: America's Unfinished Revolution, 1863–1877* (New York: Harper and Row, 1988), 193–194.

19. Mississippi Constitutional Convention, *Journal of the Proceedings and Debates in the Constitutional Convention of the State of Mississippi, August 1865* (Jackson, MS: Yeager, 1865), 110, 125.

20. Linda K. Kerber, *No Constitutional Right to Be Ladies: Women and the Obligations of Citizenship* (New York: Hill and Wang, 1998), 51–67. On vagrancy law, see Risa Goluboff, *Vagrant Nation: Police Power, Constitutional Change, and the Making of the 1960s* (New York: Oxford University Press, 2016).

21. Amy Dru Stanley, *From Bondage to Contract: Wage Labor, Marriage, and the Market in the Age of Slave Emancipation* (New York: Cambridge University Press, 1998),

101–115; Kate Masur, *Until Justice Be Done: America's First Civil Rights Movement, from the Revolution to Reconstruction* (New York: W. W. Norton, 2021), 4–12.

22. Geo. D. Stewart and Mary E. Stewart, in Natchez, Mississippi, Register of Payments to Claimants, vol. 227, April 28 to October 20, 1868; roll 37, M1907, Records of the Field Offices, *U.S., Freedman's Bureau Records, 1865–1878*, NARA (via Ancestry .com); Barbara Brooks Tomblin, *The Civil War on the Mississippi: Union Sailors, Gunboat Captains, and the Campaign to Control the River* (Lexington: University Press of Kentucky, 2016), 126–127.

23. Marriage certificate, George D. Stewart and Mary E. Olive, April 15, 1865, Freedmen's Marriage Certificates, 1865–1869, Washington Headquarters, M1875, in *U.S. Freedmen's Bureau Marriage Records*, NARA (via Ancestry.com).

24. "Inaugural Address of Gov. Benjamin G. Humphreys," *New York Times*, October 28, 1865.

25. "Mississippi Legislature: Third Day," *Jackson (MS) Daily Clarion*, October 20, 1865.

26. On the Black laws, see Masur, *Until Justice Be Done*.

27. Masur, *Until Justice Be Done*, 309.

28. Foner, *Reconstruction*, 199–200.

29. "The Vagrant Act," November 24, 1865, reprinted in Edward McPherson, ed., *The Political History of America During the Period of Reconstruction, from April 15, 1865 to July 15, 1870*, 2nd ed. (Washington, DC: Solomans and Chapman, 1875), 30.

30. "An Act to Confer Civil Rights on Freedmen, and for Other Purposes," November 25, 1865, in McPherson, *Political History*, 31.

31. Stanley, *From Bondage to Contract*, 48–52; Hunter, *Bound in Wedlock*, 213–218.

32. The analogy between slavery and marriage was one that some nineteenth-century women's rights activists used to critique coverture, a common law concept that justified sex discrimination via marriage. See Stanley, *From Bondage to Contract*, chap. 5.

33. On ex-slaves' ideas of marriage, see Frankel, *Freedom's Women*, 79–122.

34. "An Act to Confer Civil Rights on Freedmen," in McPherson, *Political History*, 31.

35. On the history of Black women and the sexual economy of slavery, see White, *Ar'n't I a Woman?*; Jennings, "'Us Colored Women Had to Go Through a Plenty'"; Morgan, *Laboring Women*; King, "Prematurely Knowing of Evil Things"; Finley, *An Intimate Economy*.

36. The Mississippi Legislature voted to ratify the Thirteenth Amendment in 1995 but failed to transmit official notice to the US archivist. The legislature did not notice or fix the error until 2013—after Steven Spielberg's film depicting the ratification process, *Lincoln*, was a box office and critical success. Jerry Mitchell, "Historic Miss. Oversight Corrected," *Jackson (MS) Clarion-Ledger*, February 17, 2013.

37. Foner, *Reconstruction*, 230–240.

38. On the history of birthright citizenship in the United States, see Martha Jones, *Birthright Citizens: A History of Race and Rights in Antebellum America* (New York: Cambridge University Press, 2018).

39. Masur, *Until Justice Be Done*, 313.

40. *Statutes at Large*, 39th Cong., 1st sess., April 9, 1866, p. 27.

41. *Vicksburg Journal,* April 28, 1866.

42. Masur, *Until Justice Be Done,* 324.

43. "Miscegenation," *Hinds County (MS) Gazette,* August 17, 1866.

44. *Jackson (MS) Clarion-Ledger,* September 13, 1866.

45. "Practical Miscegenation," *Hinds County (MS) Gazette,* June 22, 1866.

46. "Practical Miscegenation," *Hinds County (MS) Gazette,* June 22, 1866.

47. "Civil Rights Bill Won't Stand," *Natchez Weekly Courier,* July 2, 1866.

48. "Practical Miscegenation," *Hinds County (MS) Gazette,* June 22, 1866.

49. Joel Bishop was the leading proponent of common law marriage. On Bishop's views, see Joel Prentiss Bishop, *Commentaries on the Law of Marriage and Divorce, and Evidence in Matrimonial Suits,* 3rd ed. (Boston: Little, Brown, 1859), chap. 3, sec. 36. On the judicial debates over common law marriage, see Michael Grossberg, *Governing the Hearth: Law and the Family in Nineteenth-Century America* (Chapel Hill: University of North Carolina Press, 1985), 89–90; Lawrence Friedman, *Private Lives: Families, Individuals, and the Law* (Cambridge, MA: Harvard University Press, 2004), 18–24.

50. Nelson Salter, *1880 Federal Census,* District 2, Wayne County, Mississippi, supervisor's district 2, enumeration district 128, p. 21A (via Ancestry.com).

51. The *Survey of Records* identifies no extant Wayne County records from before the 1892 fire. Mississippi Genealogical Society, *Survey of Records in Mississippi Court Houses* (Jackson: Mississippi Genealogical Society, 1957), 167.

52. *Vicksburg Herald,* September 22, 1869.

53. Nelson Salter, *1880 Federal Census,* District 2, Wayne County, Mississippi, supervisor's district 2, enumeration district 128, p. 21A (via Ancestry.com).

54. On the politics of anti-miscegenation law in the Reconstruction era, see Peter Bardaglio, *Reconstructing the Household: Families, Sex, and the Law in the Nineteenth Century South* (Chapel Hill: University of North Carolina Press, 1995), 153–155; Peggy Pascoe, *What Comes Naturally: Miscegenation Law and the Making of Race in America* (New York: Oxford University Press, 2009), 22–46; Julie Novkov, *Racial Union: Law, Intimacy, and the White State in Alabama, 1865–1954* (Ann Arbor: University of Michigan Press, 2008), 29–37.

55. On concubinage, sexuality, and slavery, see Fuentes, *Dispossessed Lives*; Lisa Ze Winters, *The Mulatta Concubine: Terror, Intimacy, Freedom, and Desire in the Black Transatlantic* (Athens: University of Georgia Press, 2016); Stevenson, "What's Love Got to Do with It?"; Owens, *Consent in the Presence of Force.*

56. On Richard Johnson and Julia Chinn, see Chakrabarti Myers, *The Vice President's Black Wife: The Untold Life of Julia Chinn* (Chapel Hill: University of North Carolina Press, 2023).

57. James Kent, *Commentaries on American Law,* vol. 2 (New York: O. Halsted, 1827).

58. *John L. Hargroves, Adm'r., &c. v. William I. Thompson,* 31 Miss. 211 (1856).

59. Grossberg, *Governing the Hearth,* 73–75.

60. *James Campbell's Adm'r. and Heirs v. Sarah A. Gullatt,* 43 Ala. 57 (1869).

61. *Holmes v. Holmes,* 6 La. 463 (1833).

62. On political ideology and antebellum southern households, see Stephanie McCurry, *Masters of Small Worlds: Yeoman Households, Gender Relations, and the Political*

Culture of the Antebellum South Carolina Lowcountry (New York: Oxford University Press, 1997).

63. See Annette Gordon-Reed, *Thomas Jefferson and Sally Hemings: An American Controversy* (Charlottesville: University of Virginia Press, 1997); Annette Gordon-Reed, *The Hemingses of Monticello: An American Family* (New York: W. W. Norton, 2008).

64. Adrienne Davis, "The Private Law of Race and Sex: An Antebellum Perspective," *Stanford Law Review* 51, no. 2 (January 1999): 221–288; Bernie D. Jones, *Fathers of Conscience: Mixed-Race Inheritance in the Antebellum South* (Athens: University of Georgia Press, 2009).

65. Richard L. Hume, "Carpetbaggers in the Reconstruction South: A Group Portrait of Outside Whites in the 'Black and Tan' Constitutional Conventions," *Journal of American History* 64, no. 2 (September 1977): 315.

66. John Roy Lynch, *The Facts of Reconstruction* (New York: Arno Press, 1968), 19.

67. According to Google's Ngram Viewer, usage of the term *black and tan* first spiked in popularity in the 1850s—in references to the dog breed—but spiked again in the Reconstruction era, when it was applied to interracial politics. See, e.g., "About Dogs," *Ballou's Dollar Monthly Magazine* 13, no. 1 (January 1861): 109–111.

68. Mississippi Constitutional Convention, *Journal of the Proceedings of the Constitutional Convention of the State of Mississippi, 1868* (Jackson, MS: E. Stafford, 1871), 3.

69. Mississippi Constitutional Convention, *Journal of the Proceedings of the Constitutional Convention of the State of Mississippi, 1868*, 29.

70. Draft Bill of Rights, *Proceedings of the Convention*, 83–84.

71. *Proceedings of the Convention*, 199.

72. *Proceedings of the Convention*, 211.

73. *Proceedings of the Convention*, 212.

74. *Proceedings of the Convention*, 313.

75. Sec. 2, Art. 7, Miss. Const. 1868.

76. Sec. 1, Art. 8, Miss. Const. 1868.

77. Sec. 22, Art. 12, Miss. Const. 1868.

78. On the ratification of the 1868 constitution, see James Henry Garner, *Reconstruction in Mississippi* (New York: Macmillan, 1901), 237–248; Richard L. Hume and Jerry B. Gough, *Blacks, Carpetbaggers, and Scalawags: The Constitutional Conventions of Radical Reconstruction* (Baton Rouge: Louisiana State University Press, 2008), 74–96.

79. "Official Proceedings of the Vicksburg Military Commission," *Natchez Democrat*, October 19, 1868. The paper notes that the liquid was either "coal tar or turpentine," though other papers report that Stewart was "tarred."

80. *Vicksburg Herald*, October 8, 1868.

81. "Sentenced to the Penitentiary," *Canton (MS) American Citizen*, October 17, 1868.

82. Minnie and George Stewart, *1870 Federal Census*, City of Natchez, Adams County, Mississippi, p. 245 (via Ancestry.com).

83. Mary E. Stewart, widow of George D. Stewart, August 15, 1891, in *U.S., Civil War Pension Index: General Index to Pension Files*, NARA (via Ancestry.com).

84. "Appointments to Be Made by Gov. Alcorn," *Vicksburg Herald*, March 19, 1870.

85. "An Act to Repeal Certain Laws Relating to Slaves, Free Negroes and Mulattoes and Freedmen, and for Other Purposes," Chap. 10; "An Act to Repeal Certain Portions of an Act Entitled 'An Act to Amend the Vagrant Laws of This State,'" Chap. 20; Mississippi Legislature, *Laws of the State of Mississippi, Passed at a Regular Session of the Mississippi Legislature* (Jackson, MS: Kimball, Raymond and Company, 1870), 73, 95.

86. Sec. 2486, Art. III, Chap. 58, Miss. Rev. Code 1871.

87. Pascoe, *What Comes Naturally*, 40–46.

88. "Judge Fisher in a New Role," *Jackson (MS) Clarion-Ledger*, October 10, 1872.

89. "Amalgamation," *Vicksburg Herald*, October 4, 1872.

90. "Adultery and Fornication," Sec. IV, Art. 8, Chap. LXIV, Miss. Rev. Code 1857.

91. Sec. 2486, Art. 3, Chap. 58, Miss. Rev. Code 1871.

92. Victoria Bynum, *Unruly Women: The Politics of Social and Sexual Control in the Old South* (Chapel Hill: University of North Carolina Press, 1992), 93.

93. Sec. 2488, Art. 3, Chap. 58, Miss. Rev. Code 1871.

94. Bill of Complaint, July 8, 1871, p. 2, *Dickerson v. Brown* case file, MDAH. In 1860, when Levin and his brother George had eighty people enslaved, Peter had fourteen slaves on his plantation. George died in 1861. Pete also owned less real estate and personal property as reported on the 1860 census. P. C. Dickerson, *1960 Federal Census—Slave Schedules*, Coahoma County, Mississippi, p. 13; L. P. Dickerson, *1860 Federal Census*, Friars Point, Coahoma County, Mississippi, p. 13 (via Ancestry.com).

95. Abstract of Appellant, July 8, 1871, *Dickerson v. Brown* case file, MDAH.

96. Bill of Complaint, July 8, 1871, pp. 2–3, *Dickerson v. Brown* case file, MDAH.

97. Bill of Complaint, July 8, 1871, p. 3, *Dickerson v. Brown* case file, MDAH.

98. Bill of Complaint, July 8, 1871, p. 4, *Dickerson v. Brown* case file, MDAH.

99. Handy resigned in 1867 in protest of the military occupation of Mississippi during the early years of Reconstruction. The High Court of Errors and Appeals was replaced by the supreme court via the 1868 constitution. Dunbar Rowland, *Courts, Judges, and Lawyers of Mississippi, 1798–1935* (Jackson, MS: State Department of Archives and History, 1935), 80.

100. Rowland, *Courts, Judges, and Lawyers of Mississippi*, 111.

101. Bryan Steel Wills, *The River Was Dyed with Blood: Nathan Bedford Forrest and Fort Pillow* (Norman: University of Oklahoma Press, 2014), 127.

102. Jones, *Fathers of Conscience*, 99–100.

103. "Democratic-Conservative Mass Meetings," *Jackson (MS) Weekly Clarion*, August 4, 1875.

104. On white lawyers who represented Black clients during Reconstruction, see Melissa Milewski, *Litigating Across the Color Line: Civil Cases Between Black and White Southerners from the End of Slavery to Civil Rights* (New York: Oxford University Press, 2018), 58–60; Dylan Penningroth, *Before the Movement: The Hidden History of Black Civil Rights* (New York: Liveright, 2023), chap. 3.

105. Transcript of Proceedings, Coahoma County Chancery Court, July Term 1871, p. 15, *Dickerson v Brown* case file, MDAH.

106. David F. Alcorn's father was R. W. Alcorn of Livingston County, Kentucky, who was likely a sibling of James Lusk Alcorn's father, James Aristides Alcorn. David F. Alcorn, *1870 Federal Census*, Friars Point, Coahoma County, Mississippi, p. 10; David Alcorn, *1850 Federal Census*, Livingston County, Kentucky, p. 64 (via Ancestry.com).

107. Argument for Appellants, *Dickerson v. Brown*, 49 Miss. at 359.

108. Abstract of Appellant, July 8, 1871, p. 2, *Dickerson v. Brown* case file, MDAH.

109. On the "widow's thirds" in American law, see Marylynn Salmon, *Women and the Law of Property in Early America* (Chapel Hill: University of North Carolina Press, 1986), 141–184.

110. Jackson Clifton, *1870 Federal Census*, Friars Point, Coahoma County, Mississippi, p. 19 (via Ancestry.com).

111. Argument for Appellants, *Dickerson v. Brown*, 49 Miss. at 362 (1873).

112. Argument for Appellees, *Dickerson v. Brown*, 49 Miss. at 365–366 (1873).

113. Argument for Appellants, *Dickerson v. Brown*, 49 Miss. at 362 (1873).

114. *Dickerson v. Brown*, 49 Miss. 357 (1873).

115. *Dickerson v. Brown*, 49 Miss. 357 (1873).

116. "A Strange Case with a Moral," *Jackson (MS) Weekly Clarion*, March 19, 1874.

117. *In the Matter of the Estate of Susan and Oliver Dickerson, Minors*, Coahoma County Chancery Court Minutes, vol. I, p. 546, *Mississippi Probate Records, 1781–1930* (via FamilySearch.org).

118. S. A. Caldwell, *1900 Federal Census*, South and East Riverside Branch, Beat 2, Coahoma County, Mississippi, supervisor's district 3, enumeration district 22, p. 6B (via Ancestry.com).

119. *Madora Rundle v. G. G. Pegram, Adm'r.*, 49 Miss. 751 (1874).

Chapter 2: Strategies of Survival

1. Albert T. Morgan, *Yazoo; Or on the Picket Line of Freedom in the South* (Washington, DC: A. T. Morgan, 1884), 346–347.

2. Morgan, *Yazoo*, 17; Mississippi Constitutional Convention, *Journal of the Proceedings in the Constitutional Convention of the State of Mississippi, 1868* (Jackson, MS: E. Stafford, 1871), 749.

3. *1860 Federal Census*, City of Syracuse, Seventh Ward, Onondaga County, New York, p. 68; Charles Highgate, 185th Infantry, *New York, U.S. Civil War Muster Roll Abstracts, 1861–1900* (via Ancestry.com).

4. Morgan, *Yazoo*, 345.

5. Morgan, *Yazoo*, 354; "Marriage Extraordinary," *Jackson (MS) Clarion-Ledger*, August 11, 1870.

6. Mississippi Constitutional Convention, *Journal of the Proceedings in the Constitutional Convention of the State of Mississippi, 1868*, 748–749.

7. "Marriage Extraordinary," *Jackson (MS) Semi-Weekly Clarion*, August 5, 1870; "Morgan Once More," *Vicksburg Weekly Commercial Herald*, September 10, 1870.

8. Edmonia Highgate to Gerrit Smith, September 2, 1870, reprinted in Dorothy Sterling, ed., *We Are Your Sisters: Black Women in the Nineteenth Century* (New York: W. W. Norton, 1984), 303. Edmonia had been in a relationship with a white poet named John Henry Vosburg, who was married to a woman who had been committed to

a mental institution. Edmonia tragically died following a botched abortion just a month after writing this letter. Following her death, Albert Morgan wrote that he believed Edmonia had pursued the abortion because John Henry's family had threatened to cut him off if he continued the relationship. A. T. Morgan to Gerrit Smith, October 21, 1870, reprinted in Sterling, *We Are Your Sisters*, 304.

9. On the overthrow of Reconstruction in Mississippi, see Eric Foner, *Reconstruction: America's Unfinished Revolution, 1863–1877* (New York: Harper and Row, 1988), 558–563; Steven Hahn, *A Nation Under Our Feet: Black Political Struggles in the Rural South from Slavery to the Great Migration* (Cambridge, MA: Belknap Press of Harvard University Press, 2003), 295–302. See, generally, Nicholas Lemann, *Redemption: The Last Battle of the Civil War* (New York: Farrar, Straus, and Giroux, 2006).

10. Morgan, *Yazoo*, 382–384.

11. "The Conflict in Yazoo," *Hinds County (MS) Gazette*, January 14, 1874; "The Yazoo Tragedy," *Jackson (MS) Clarion-Ledger*, January 15, 1874.

12. Morgan, *Yazoo*, 318.

13. Morgan, *Yazoo*, 344–345.

14. Henry Garner, *Reconstruction in Mississippi* (New York: Macmillan, 1901), 175.

15. Foner, *Reconstruction*, 342.

16. Kidada E. Williams, *I Saw Death Coming: A History of Terror and Survival in the War against Reconstruction* (New York: Bloomsbury, 2023).

17. Hahn, *Nation Under Our Feet*, 282.

18. Testimony of O. C. French, *Report of and Testimony Taken by the Joint Select Committee to Inquire into the Condition of Affairs in the Late Insurrectionary States*, 13 vols. (Washington, DC: US Government Printing Office, 1872), 11:9–10.

19. Martha Hodes, *White Women, Black Men: Illicit Sex in the Nineteenth-Century South* (New Haven, CT: Yale University Press, 1997), 149–168.

20. Testimony of Hampton L. Jarnagin, *Report of and Testimony Taken by the Joint Select Committee*, 11:514.

21. *Report of and Testimony Taken by the Joint Select Committee*, 11:469–470.

22. Testimony of James Rives, *Report of and Testimony Taken by the Joint Select Committee*, 11:548.

23. Testimony of A. Orr, *Report of and Testimony Taken by the Joint Select Committee*, 12:704–705.

24. Testimony of James Rives, *Report of and Testimony Taken by the Joint Select Committee*, 11:560.

25. "Legal Intelligence: United States Circuit Court and District Court," *Weekly Mississippi Pilot*, February 6, 1875.

26. Indictment, Hinds County Circuit Court, January Term 1879, *H. W. Kinard v. State of Mississippi* case file, Mississippi Department of Archives and History, Jackson, Mississippi (hereafter MDAH).

27. Warrant and arrest record, January 17, 1879, pp. 7–8, *Kinard v. State* case file, MDAH.

28. Judgment, case no. 885, Hinds County Circuit Court, July Term 1879, pp. 10–12, *Kinard v. State* case file, MDAH.

29. Testimony of Erwin Barlow, July 17, 1879, pp. 14–15, *Kinard v. State* case file, MDAH.

30. Testimony of Erwin Barlow, July 17, 1879, pp. 14–15, *Kinard v. State* case file, MDAH.

31. Testimony of Edmund Falconer, July 17, 1879, p. 16, *Kinard v. State* case file, MDAH.

32. Testimony of Shed Donaldson, July 17, 1879, pp. 17–18, *Kinard v. State* case file, MDAH.

33. Testimony of James Bell, July 17, 1879, p. 18, *Kinard v. State* case file, MDAH.

34. Testimony of William Kinard, July 17, 1879, p. 20, *Kinard v. State* case file, MDAH.

35. Testimony of William Kinard, Charles Turner, H. W. Prisock, and J. M. Chiles, July 17, 1879, pp. 19–21, *Kinard v. State* case file, MDAH.

36. Testimony of James Bell, July 17, 1879, p. 18, *Kinard v. State* case file, MDAH.

37. Judgment, case no. 885, Hinds County Circuit Court, July Term 1879, pp. 10–12, *Kinard v. State* case file, MDAH.

38. Instructions to the jury, July 17, 1879, pp. 21–22, *Kinard v. State* case file, MDAH.

39. *Joe Carotti et al. v. State of Mississippi*, 42 Miss. R., 334 (1868).

40. *Carotti v. State*, 42 Miss. R., 334 (1868).

41. *Carotti v. State*, 42 Miss. R., 334 (1868).

42. Instructions to the jury, July 17, 1879, pp. 23–24, *Kinard v. State* case file, MDAH.

43. Brief, *Kinard v. State*, 57 Miss. 132 (1879).

44. Appellee's brief, *Kinard v. State*, 57 Miss. 132 (1879).

45. *Reports of Cases in the Supreme Court for the State of Mississippi* (Boston: Little, Brown, 1880), iii.

46. *Kinard v. State*, 57 Miss. 132 (1879).

47. On the persistence of the concept of "concubinage" in the post-emancipation South, see Alecia P. Long, *The Great Southern Babylon: Sex, Race, and Respectability in New Orleans, 1865–1920* (Baton Rouge: Louisiana State University Press, 2005).

48. *Kinard v. State*, 57 Miss. 132 (1879).

49. Foner, *Reconstruction*, 538–539.

50. William Alexander Mabry, "The Disfranchisement of the Negro in Mississippi," *Journal of Southern History* 4, no. 3 (August 1938): 318–333; Vernon Lane Wharton, *The Negro in Mississippi, 1865–1890* (Chapel Hill: University of North Carolina Press, 1947), 181–198; Foner, *Reconstruction*, 558–563; Hahn, *Nation Under Our Feet*, 297–302.

51. Hamilton H. Chalmers, "The Effects of Negro Suffrage," *North American Review* 132, no. 292 (March 1881): 240.

52. Chalmers, "Effects of Negro Suffrage," 247.

53. *L. B. Adams, Admr. v. Susan Adams*, 57 Miss. 267 (1879).

54. *Adams v. Adams*, 57 Miss. 267 (1879).

55. Wharton, *Negro in Mississippi*, 199–203.

56. "An Act in Relation to Marriage and Divorce," Chap. 42, Sec. 1147, Code of 1880.

57. "An Act in Relation to Marriage and Divorce," Chap. 42, Sec. 1147, Code of 1880.

58. *Oxford English Dictionary*, s.v. "incest (n.), Etymology," September 2023, https://doi.org/10.1093/OED/1015613921.

59. *Mark Stewart and Hattie Brown v. State of Mississippi*, 64 Miss. 626 (1887).

60. *Stewart and Brown v. State*, 64 Miss. 626 (1887).

61. It seems that the society was short-lived based on a dearth of advertising after 1882. *Jackson (MS) Clarion-Ledger*, September 20, 1882.

62. *Stewart and Brown v. State*, 64 Miss. 626 (1887).

63. *Stewart and Brown v. State*, 64 Miss. 626 (1887).

64. *1880 Federal Census*, City of Brookhaven, Lincoln County, Mississippi, supervisor's district 3, enumeration district 28, p. 22 (via Ancestry.com).

65. "Circuit Court—Cases Disposed of First Week," *Brookhaven (MS) Semi-Weekly Leader*, August 7, 1884.

66. "Circuit Court—Second Week," *Brookhaven (MS) Semi-Weekly Leader*, August 14, 1884.

67. "Circuit Court," *Brookhaven (MS) Semi-Weekly Leader*, February 5, 1885.

68. "Batesville Circuit Court—May Term, 1884," *Panola (MS) Weekly Star*, May 17, 1884.

69. "Batesville Court," *Panola (MS) Weekly Star*, May 15, 1886.

70. "Circuit Criminal Court," *Vicksburg Evening Post*, June 15, 1885.

71. *Panola (MS) Weekly Star*, July 16, 1881; *Liberty (MS) Southern Herald*, May 17, 1889.

72. "The Legislature," *Vicksburg Herald*, January 29, 1888; "The Legislature," *Vicksburg Herald*, February 24, 1888.

73. "State Legislature," *Jackson (MS) Clarion-Ledger*, March 1, 1888; Mississippi Legislature, *Journal of the Senate of the State of Mississippi* (Jackson, MS: R. H. Henry, 1888), 387.

74. *Senate Journal* (1888), 443, 507.

75. "Capt. Tho's. Kirkman's Tragic Death, and Reflections Growing Out of It," *Grenada (MS) Sentinel*, August 12, 1882.

76. "Mass Meeting," *Grenada (MS) Sentinel*, August 26, 1882.

77. "A Horrible Affair near Grenada," *Jackson (MS) Clarion-Ledger*, August 9, 1882.

78. "Terrible Tragedy: Seven Miles North-East of Grenada!" *Grenada (MS) Sentinel*, August 5, 1882.

79. "Capt. Tho's. Kirkman's Tragic Death, and Reflections Growing Out of It," *Grenada (MS) Sentinel*, August 12, 1882.

80. "Capt. Tho's. Kirkman's Tragic Death, and Reflections Growing Out of It," *Grenada (MS) Sentinel*, August 12, 1882.

81. "The Kirkman Tragedy," *New Orleans Times-Democrat*, August 7, 1882.

82. On the trope of the "tragic mulatto" in American literature, see, generally, Werner Sollors, *Neither Black nor White yet Both: Thematic Explorations of Interracial Literature* (Cambridge, MA: Harvard University Press, 1999).

83. Albert D. Kirwan, *Revolt of the Rednecks: Mississippi Politics, 1876–1925* (Lexington: University Press of Kentucky, 1951), 58–59.

84. B. F. Jones, letter to the editor, *Jackson (MS) Clarion-Ledger*, May 8, 1890.

85. Wharton, *Negro in Mississippi*, 204–209; Stephen Cresswell, *Multiparty Politics in Mississippi, 1877–1902* (Jackson: University Press of Mississippi, 2007).

86. Glenda Gilmore, *Gender and Jim Crow: Women and the Politics of White Supremacy* (Chapel Hill: University of North Carolina Press, 1996); Jane Dailey, *Before Jim Crow: The Politics of Race in Postemancipation Virginia* (Chapel Hill: University of North Carolina Press, 2000); James M. Beeby, ed., *Populism in the South Revisited: New Interpretations and New Departures* (Jackson: University Press of Mississippi, 2012).

87. Mississippi Constitutional Convention, *Journal of Proceedings of the Constitutional Convention of the State of Mississippi* (Jackson, MS: E. L. Martin, 1890), 3–9.

88. "Notice," *Yazoo (MS) Democrat*; "Democratic Convention," *Yazoo (MS) Democrat*, July 30, 1859; "Judge S. S. Calhoon," *Jackson (MS) Clarion-Ledger*, August 28, 1890.

89. "Death of Judge S. S. Calhoon," *Jackson (MS) Daily News*, November 11, 1908.

90. "Judge Calhoon's Views," *Jackson (MS) Clarion-Ledger*, March 4, 1890.

91. US Constitution, Art. IV, sec. 4.

92. "Discussion Continues," *Jackson (MS) Clarion-Ledger*, September 18, 1890.

93. "The Convention: A Complete Record of the Proceedings," *Jackson (MS) Clarion-Ledger*, August 14, 1890.

94. "Marriage," Chap. 90, Sec. 2859, *Annotated Code of the General Statute Laws of the State of Mississippi* (1892).

95. Miss. Code Annotated (1892) Sec. 460.

96. "The Marriage Law," *Vicksburg Evening Post*, May 21, 1894.

97. *Brookhaven (MS) Semi-Weekly Leader*, June 5, 1894; *Biloxi (MS) Herald*, June 2, 1894; *Winston County (MS) Journal*, July 20, 1894; *Grenada (MS) Sentinel*, May 26, 1894.

98. *Jackson (MS) Clarion-Ledger*, June 26, 1894.

99. H.B. 382, Mississippi Legislature, *Journal of the House of Representatives of the State of Mississippi* (Nashville: Brandon Printing Company, 1904), 845; Mississippi Legislature, *Journal of the Senate of the State of Mississippi* (Nashville: Brandon Printing Company, 1904), 852.

100. Sec. 3249, Chap. 96, Miss. Rev. Code 1906; "Gossip of the Legislature," *Jackson (MS) Daily News*, April 5, 1906; "Proceedings of the Legislature," *Jackson (MS) Clarion-Ledger*, April 12, 1906.

101. Sec. 3244, Miss. Rev. Code 1906.

102. John McAlpine and Matilda Gibson, *1870 Federal Census*, Grand Gulf, Claiborne County, Mississippi, p. 2 (via Ancestry.com).

103. *1880 Federal Census*, Claiborne County, Mississippi, supervisor's district 31, enumeration district 66, p. 43 (via Ancestry.com).

104. Last Will and Testament of John R. McAlpine, Claiborne County Wills, 1828–1928, Book 3, pp. 154–155 (via FamilySearch.org).

105. *Estate of Jno. R. McAlpine, Decd.*, case no. 1243, Claiborne County Chancery Court, Final Record, vol. Y, p. 213 (via FamilySearch.org).

106. Court order, April 17, 1894, *Estate of Jno. R. McAlpine, Decd.*, case no. 1243, Claiborne County Chancery Court case files 1892–1897 (via FamilySearch.org).

107. Sven Beckert, *Empire of Cotton: A Global History* (New York: Vintage, 2015), 311.

108. *Estate of Jno. R. McAlpine, Decd.*, case no. 1243, Claiborne County Chancery Court case files 1892–1897 (via FamilySearch.org).

109. *Estate of Jno. R. McAlpine, Decd.*, case no. 1243, Claiborne County Chancery Court, Final Record, vol. Y, p. 213 (via FamilySearch.org).

110. *Estate of Jno. R. McAlpine*, case no. 1243, Claiborne County Chancery Court case files 1892–1897 (via FamilySearch.org).

111. Last Will and Testament of S. R. Stiles, October 5, 1904, *In re Estate of S. R. Stiles*, case no. 1827, Claiborne County Chancery Court, *Mississippi, U.S., Wills and Probate Records, 1780–1982* (via Ancestry.com).

112. *In re Estate of S. R. Stiles*, case no. 1827, Claiborne County Chancery Court, *Mississippi, U.S., Wills and Probate Records, 1780–1982* (via Ancestry.com).

113. Matilda Gibson, *1910 Federal Census*, Beat 1, Claiborne County, Mississippi, supervisor's district 7, enumeration district 33, p. 4A (via Ancestry.com).

114. H. W. Kinard, *1900 Federal Census*, Beat 4, Washington County, Mississippi, supervisor's district 137, enumeration district 88, p. 4A (via Ancestry.com).

115. Alex Kinard, *1900 Federal Census*, Beat 4, Washington County, Mississippi, supervisor's district 137, enumeration district 88, p. 4A (via Ancestry.com).

116. Wharton, *Negro in Mississippi*, 162–163.

117. US House of Representatives, *Testimony in the Contested Election Case of John R. Lynch and James R. Chalmers, from the Sixth Congressional District of Mississippi* (Washington, DC: US Government Printing Office, 1881).

118. John R. Lynch, *Reminiscences of an Active Life* (Chicago: University of Chicago Press, 1970), 9–13.

119. On Mississippi, the best example of this work, dubbed the "Dunning School" of history after a Columbia historian who pioneered this interpretation of Reconstruction, is Garner, *Reconstruction in Mississippi*.

120. Garner, *Reconstruction in Mississippi*, 5–6.

121. John R. Lynch, *The Facts of Reconstruction* (New York: Arno Press, 1968), 240.

122. Lynch, *Facts of Reconstruction*, 241.

123. Lynch, *Facts of Reconstruction*, 242–243.

124. Lynch, *Facts of Reconstruction*, 244.

125. Lynch, *Facts of Reconstruction*, 248–249.

126. A. T. Morgan, *1880 Federal Census*, Washington, DC, enumeration district 60, p. 332C (via Ancestry.com).

127. Lynch, *Reminiscences*, 309–320; Justin Behrend, "Facts and Memories: John R. Lynch and the Revising of Reconstruction History in the Era of Jim Crow," *Journal of African American History* 97, no. 4 (Fall 2012): 436–437.

128. *1900 Federal Census*, Sugarneck Township, Boone County, Indiana, supervisor's district 9, enumeration district 21, p. 6 (via Ancestry.com).

129. Lucia E. Hogg, *1910 Federal Census*, City of Brockton, Ward 2, Precinct A, Plymouth County, Massachusetts, p. 6 (via Ancestry.com).

130. Angela Morgan Obituary, *Chicago Tribune*, January 25, 1957.

Chapter 3: Concubines and Wives

1. Transcription, vol. II, p. 413, *Mary Covington et al. v. Godfrey Frank et al.* (1898) case file, Mississippi Department of Archives and History, Jackson, Mississippi (hereafter MDAH).

2. Deposition of Mary Covington, September 13, 1894, vol. II, p. 396, *Covington v. Frank* (1898) case file, MDAH.

3. Bill of Complaint, January 22, 1892, vol. I, p. 7, *Covington v. Frank* (1898) case file, MDAH.

4. Deposition of Albert McGee, August 15, 1894, vol. I, pp. 154–155, *Covington v. Frank* (1898) case file, MDAH.

5. Exhibit G, Mortgage Contract, April 16, 1889, vol. I, pp. 17–21, *Covington v. Frank* (1898) case file, MDAH.

6. Answer to Bill of Complaint, September 27, 1892, vol. I, pp. 41–43, *Covington v. Frank* (1898) case file, MDAH.

7. Mary Covington claimed a homestead exemption on the property. Sec. 1970 and 1975, Miss. Ann. Code, 1892.

8. Answer to Bill of Complaint, September 27, 1892, vol. I, p. 39, *Covington v. Frank* (1898) case file, MDAH.

9. Sec. 1543, Miss. Ann. Code, 1892.

10. Deposition of Fred Braker, June 6, 1894, vol. II, p. 358, *Covington v. Frank* (1898) case file, MDAH.

11. Marriage record, J. W. J. Niles and Margaret Hume, September 2, 1852, Record of Marriage, 1838–1883, Monroe County, Tennessee, p. 163, *Tennessee, U.S., Compiled Marriages, 1851–1900* (via Ancestry.com).

12. Deposition of Mary Covington, September 13, 1894, vol. II, pp. 402–403, *Covington v. Frank* (1898) case file, MDAH.

13. Deposition of Mary Covington, September 13, 1894, vol. II, pp. 386–387, *Covington v. Frank* (1898) case file, MDAH.

14. Deposition of Mary Covington, September 13, 1894, vol. II, pp. 406–407, *Covington v. Frank* (1898) case file, MDAH.

15. The indictment was confirmed by the Bolivar County Circuit Court clerk, who identified the case as *State of Mississippi v. W. A. Covington and Mary Richardson*, case no. 411, April Term, 1868, recorded in Minute Book C, p. 349, vol. III, pp. 455–456, *Covington v. Frank* (1898) case file, MDAH.

16. Deposition of N. L. Glass, August 15, 1894, vol. 1, pp. 173–174, *Covington v. Frank* (1898) case file, MDAH.

17. Deposition of J. B. Griffin, October 30, 1900, p. 28, *W. A. Covington Jr. et al. v. Godfrey Frank et al.* (1901) case file, MDAH.

18. Record of Bolivar County Circuit Court, April Term, 1868, as transcribed in vol. III, p. 455, *Covington v. Frank* (1898) case file, MDAH.

19. Deposition of N. L. Glass, August 15, 1868, vol. I, pp. 169–170, *Covington v. Frank* (1898) case file, MDAH.

20. Deposition of Mary Covington, September 13, 1894, vol. II, p. 389, *Covington v. Frank* (1898) case file, MDAH.

21. Deposition of Mary Covington, September 13, 1894, vol. II, p. 387, *Covington v. Frank* (1898) case file, MDAH.

22. Deposition of Mary Covington, September 13, 1894, vol. II, pp. 388–389, *Covington v. Frank* (1898) case file, MDAH.

23. Deposition of Cornelia Miller, vol. III, p. 416, *Covington v. Frank* (1898) case file, MDAH.

24. Answer to Bill of Complaint, vol. I, p. 30, *Covington v. Frank* (1898) case file, MDAH.

25. Deposition of Cornelia Miller, November 9, 1893, vol. III, p. 425, *Covington v. Frank* (1898) case file, MDAH.

26. Deposition of Cornelia Miller, November 9, 1893, vol. III, p. 417, *Covington v. Frank* (1898) case file, MDAH.

27. Deposition of Albert McGee, August 15, 1894, vol. I, pp. 154–155, *Covington v. Frank* (1898) case file, MDAH.

28. Deposition of E. Beard, June 6, 1894, vol. II, p. 337, *Covington v. Frank* (1898) case file, MDAH.

29. See Thomas C. Kennedy, *A History of Southland College: The Society of Friends and Black Education in Arkansas* (Fayetteville: University of Arkansas Press, 2009).

30. Segregated Black schools in the South tended to be one-room schoolhouses, and few rural Black students had access to high school education. The Mound Bayou Normal School was not completed until the 1890s. James D. Anderson, *The Education of Blacks in the South, 1860–1935* (Chapel Hill: University of North Carolina Press, 1988), 186–187, 204.

31. Deposition of Mary Covington, September 13, 1894, vol. II, p. 392, *Covington v. Frank* (1898) case file, MDAH.

32. Deposition of Mary Covington, September 13, 1894, vol. II, p. 394, *Covington v. Frank* (1898) case file, MDAH.

33. Deposition of Samuel Fitzpatrick, January 20, 1895, vol. II, pp. 373–374, *Covington v. Frank* (1898) case file, MDAH.

34. Deposition of Samuel Fitzpatrick, January 20, 1895, vol. II, p. 374, *Covington v. Frank* (1898) case file, MDAH.

35. Deposition of Mariah Slaughter, June 6, 1894, vol. II, p. 193, *Covington v. Frank* (1898) case file, MDAH.

36. Testimony of Louis Stubbefield, August 14, 1894, vol. I, p. 139, *Covington v. Frank* (1898) case file, MDAH.

37. Eric Foner, *Reconstruction: America's Unfinished Revolution, 1863–1877* (New York: Harper and Row, 1988), 357; Vernon Lane Wharton, *The Negro in Mississippi* (Chapel Hill: University of North Carolina Press, 1947), 203.

38. Neil McMillen, *Dark Journey: Black Mississippians in the Age of Jim Crow* (Urbana: University of Illinois Press, 1989), 186.

39. Norman L. Crockett, *The Black Towns* (Lawrence: University of Kansas Press, 2021), 96–97.

40. Neil McMillen, *Dark Journey*, 187.

41. Howard N. Rabinowitz, "Three Reconstruction Leaders: Blanche K. Bruce, Robert Brown Elliott, and Holland Thompson," in *Black Leaders of the Nineteenth*

Century, ed. Leon Litwack and August Meier (Urbana: University of Illinois Press, 1988), 195.

42. On Bruce's life as a member of the Black bourgeoisie, see Willard B. Gatewood Jr., *Aristocrats of Color: The Black Elite, 1880–1920* (Bloomington: Indiana University Press, 1990).

43. McMillen, *Dark Journey*, 120–121; William F. Holmes, "Whitecapping: Agrarian Violence in Mississippi," *Journal of Southern History* 35, no. 2 (May 1969): 166–167.

44. On rising violence toward Black Mississippians, see McMillen, *Dark Journey*.

45. Deposition of Cornelia Miller, June 6, 1894, vol. III, pp. 417, 425, *Covington v. Frank* (1898) case file, MDAH.

46. A. W. Greely, "The Mississippi Floods," *North American Review* 150, no. 402 (May 1890): 626.

47. "Surging Floods," *Daily Memphis Avalanche*, March 9, 1882.

48. Greely, "Mississippi Floods," 625.

49. Mark Twain, *Life on the Mississippi* (Boston: James R. Osgood and Company, 1883), 290–291.

50. The 1897 floods reached greater heights than the 1882 floods, but improvements to the levee system after 1882 meant the floods were less devastating. Committee on Commerce, US Senate, *Report on the Mississippi River Floods* (Washington, DC: US Government Printing Office, 1898), v–vi.

51. E. A. Sherman, "What Forests Can Do for the Mississippi River," *Annals of the American Academy of Political and Social Science* 135 (January 1928): 45–49.

52. Deposition of John H. Griffin, August 16, 1900, p. 37; Application for Life Insurance, May 6, 1886, pp. 42–48, *Covington v. Frank* (1901) case file, MDAH.

53. Deposition of Cornelia Miller, June 6, 1894, vol. III, p. 425, *Covington v. Frank* (1898) case file, MDAH.

54. Deposition of Cornelia Miller, June 6, 1894, vol. III, p. 419, *Covington v. Frank* (1898) case file, MDAH.

55. Deposition of Cornelia Miller, June 6, 1894, vol. III, p. 425, *Covington v. Frank* (1898) case file, MDAH.

56. W. A. Covington to Cornelia Miller, January 4, 1891, Gunnison, Mississippi, vol. II, p. 281, *Covington v. Frank* (1898) case file, MDAH.

57. W. A. Covington to Cornelia Miller, December 22, 1891, Gunnison, Mississippi, vol. II, p. 283, *Covington v. Frank* (1898) case file, MDAH.

58. Deposition of N. L. Glass, August 15, 1894, vol. I, p. 178, *Covington v. Frank* (1898) case file, MDAH.

59. Deposition of N. L. Glass, August 15, 1894, vol. I, p. 173, *Covington v. Frank* (1898) case file, MDAH.

60. Deposition of William Johnson, August 16, 1894, vol. I, p. 183, *Covington v. Frank* (1898) case file, MDAH.

61. Deposition of William Johnson, August 16, 1894, vol. I, p. 184, *Covington v. Frank* (1898) case file, MDAH.

62. J. T. Butt, Affidavit, June 14, 1894, vol. I, p. 63, *Covington v. Frank* (1898) case file, MDAH. Bruce died in 1898, before the conclusion of the case. Wharton, *Negro in Mississippi*, 161.

63. Deposition of J. W. Fulton, January 20, 1895, vol. II, pp. 369–370, *Covington v. Frank* (1898) case file, MDAH.

64. Deposition of J. W. Fulton, January 20, 1895, vol. II, p. 371; Deposition of Charles Trumper, vol. II, p. 351, *Covington v. Frank* (1898) case file, MDAH.

65. Deposition of Fred Braker, June 6, 1894, vol. II, p. 359, *Covington v. Frank* (1898) case file, MDAH.

66. Deposition of Fred Braker, June 6, 1894, vol. II, p. 363, *Covington v. Frank* (1898) case file, MDAH.

67. Deposition of J. W. Fulton, January 20, 1895, vol. II, p. 368, *Covington v. Frank* (1898) case file, MDAH.

68. Kennedy, *History of Southland College*, 108.

69. Deposition of Albert McGee, August 15, 1894, vol. I, pp. 156–157, *Covington v. Frank* (1898) case file, MDAH.

70. Deposition of Albert McGee, August 15, 1894, vol. I, p. 156, *Covington v. Frank* (1898) case file, MDAH.

71. Trumper stated in his deposition that the fire took place in December 1889, but it in fact took place one year prior. Deposition of Charles Trumper, June 6, 1894, vol. II, p. 344, *Covington v. Frank* (1898) case file, MDAH.

72. "Fifteen Lives Lost," *New Orleans Times-Picayune*, December 24, 1888; "Twenty-Three Lives Lost," *New York Times*, December 24, 1888.

73. "Thirty or More Drowned," *Chicago Inter-Ocean*, December 24, 1888.

74. Deposition of Charles Trumper, June 6, 1894, vol. II, p. 351, *Covington v. Frank* (1898) case file, MDAH.

75. Deposition of Charles Trumper, June 6, 1894, vol. II, pp. 348–349, *Covington v. Frank* (1898) case file, MDAH.

76. Deposition of Charles Trumper, June 6, 1894, vol. II, pp. 349–350, *Covington v. Frank* (1898) case file, MDAH.

77. Brief for Appellees, filed December 4, 1899, p. 42, folder 1, *Covington v. Frank* (1898) case file, MDAH.

78. Brief for Appellees, filed December 4, 1899, p. 38, folder 1, *Covington v. Frank* (1898) case file, MDAH.

79. Deposition of H. C. Arnold, February 14, 1895, vol. III, p. 479, *Covington v. Frank* (1898) case file, MDAH.

80. Interrogatories propounded to P. A. Shelton, October 19, 1900, p. 32, *Covington v. Frank* (1901) case file, MDAH.

81. Exhibit 1, Application to Manhattan Life Insurance Company, May 6, 1886, p. 42, *Covington v. Frank* (1901) case file, MDAH.

82. Deposition of H. C. Arnold, February 14, 1895, vol. III, pp. 479–480, *Covington v. Frank* (1898) case file, MDAH.

83. Deposition of L. M. Hunter, February 12, 1895, vol. III, p. 465, *Covington v. Frank* (1898) case file, MDAH.

84. Deposition of Jacob Frank, July 27, 1900, pp. 11–12, *Covington v. Frank* (1901) case file, MDAH.

85. Deposition of Jacob Frank, July 27, 1900, p. 13, *Covington v. Frank* (1901) case file, MDAH.

86. Deposition of Jacob Frank, July 27, 1900, p. 16, *Covington v. Frank* (1901) case file, MDAH.

87. Deposition of Jacob Frank, July 27, 1900, p. 14, *Covington v. Frank* (1901) case file, MDAH.

88. Deposition of Jacob Frank, July 27, 1900, p. 19, *Covington v. Frank* (1901) case file, MDAH.

89. Deposition of W. R. Shepherd, October 26, 1900, pp. 25–26, *Covington v. Frank* (1901) case file, MDAH.

90. Deposition of J. R. Peterson, October 14, 1900, p. 103, *Covington v. Frank* (1901) case file, MDAH.

91. Deposition of J. R. Peterson, October 14, 1900, p. 105, *Covington v. Frank* (1901) case file, MDAH.

92. Deposition of J. R. Peterson, October 14, 1900, p. 107, *Covington v. Frank* (1901) case file, MDAH.

93. Deposition of Mrs. M. J. Wise, undated, pp. 112–113, *Covington v. Frank* (1901) case file, MDAH.

94. Deposition of William Arnold, October 22, 1900, pp. 117–118, *Covington v. Frank* (1901) case file, MDAH.

95. Deposition of James C. McGee, undated, p. 123, *Covington v. Frank* (1901) case file, MDAH.

96. Deposition of James C. McGee, undated, p. 126, *Covington v. Frank* (1901) case file, MDAH.

97. *Covington v. Frank*, 77 Miss. 606 (1900).

98. Cornelia Miller, *1900 Federal Census*, Ward 34, Hyde Park Township, Cook County, Illinois, supervisor's district 1, enumeration district 1097, p. 9B (via Ancestry .com).

99. Filing, October 29, 1900, p. 4, *Covington v. Frank* (1900) case file, MDAH.

100. Mary Craig Sinclair, *Southern Belle* (New York: Crown, 1957), 20–21.

101. A. M. C. Kimbrough, *1900 Federal Census*, City of Greenwood, Leflore County, Mississippi, supervisor's district 4, enumeration district 53, p. 1-B (via Ancestry .com).

102. Albert D. Kirwan, *Revolt of the Rednecks: Mississippi Politics, 1876–1925* (Lexington: University Press of Kentucky, 1951), 160–161.

103. Sinclair, *Southern Belle*, 14.

104. Sinclair, *Southern Belle*, 3.

105. Sinclair, *Southern Belle*, 10.

106. Order, February 23, 1901, Bolivar County Chancery Court, pp. 160–161, *Covington v. Frank* (1901) case file, MDAH.

107. Sinclair, *Southern Belle*, 14.

108. Cornelia Miller, *1900 Federal Census*, Hyde Park Township, Chicago, Illinois, supervisor's district 1, enumeration district 1097, p. 9 (via Ancestry.com).

109. "Murzynka dostanie $50,000," *Dziennik Chicagoski*, December 18, 1895.

110. "Claimed by an Old Slave," *Chicago Chronicle*, November 13, 1895.

111. "A Romantic Story," *Vicksburg Daily Commercial Herald*, December 10, 1895.

112. "A Romantic Story," *Vicksburg Daily Commercial Herald*, December 10, 1895.

113. "She Was His Legal Wife," *Chicago Chronicle*, December 18, 1895.

114. "She Was His Legal Wife," *Chicago Chronicle*, December 18, 1895.

115. "Verdict for $50,000," *Chicago Inter-Ocean*, November 23, 1895.

116. *William J. Laurence v. Maria Evans Laurence*, 164 Ill. at 377.

117. Appellant's brief, *Laurence v. Laurence, Reports of Cases at Law and in Chancery Argued and Determined in the Supreme Court of Illinois* 164, p. 368.

118. "Was Dr. Henry Lawrence's Wife," *Chicago Tribune*, December 18, 1895.

119. "She Was His Legal Wife," *Chicago Chronicle*, December 18, 1895.

120. *Laurence v. Laurence*, 164 Ill. 367 (1896).

121. Maria Evans, *1910 Federal Census*, Cook County Infirmary, Cook County, Illinois, supervisor's district 1, enumeration district 67, p. 13-B (via Ancestry .com).

122. On the Cook County Infirmary and paupers' burials in Chicago, see Michael K. Rosenow, *Death and Dying in the Working Class, 1865–1920* (Urbana: University of Illinois Press, 2015), 48–49.

Chapter 4: "The Law Is a Grinning Corpse"

1. "The Moral Movement," *Port Gibson (MS) Reveille*, December 12, 1907.

2. "The Moral Movement," *Port Gibson (MS) Reveille*, December 12, 1907.

3. Ed Polk Douglas, *Architecture in Claiborne County, Mississippi: A Selective Guide* (Jackson: Mississippi Department of Archives and History, 1974); Henry Stolzman and Daniel Stolzman, *Synagogue Architecture in America: Faith, Spirit, and Identity* (Mulgrave, Australia: Images Publishing, 2004), 127.

4. This quote is probably apocryphal. I was unable to identify an original source for it.

5. "Where Only Man Is Vile," *Vicksburg American*, January 4, 1908.

6. "Circuit Court," *Port Gibson (MS) Reveille*, January 23, 1908; "Judge Bush's Jury Strictures," *Port Gibson (MS) Reveille*, July 2, 1908.

7. Verdict, *State of Mississippi v. J. A. Regan and Kittie Harper*, June 26, 1908, case no. 1169, Claiborne County Circuit Court, Minute Book 12, June 1902 to June 1908, p. 612, Claiborne County Courthouse, Port Gibson, Mississippi.

8. "Judge Bush's Jury Strictures," *Port Gibson (MS) Reveille*, July 2, 1908.

9. Peggy Pascoe, *What Comes Naturally: Miscegenation Law and the Making of Race in America* (New York: Oxford University Press, 2009), 63.

10. On Norwood's political and legal career, see William Harris Bragg, "The Junius of Georgia Redemption: Thomas M. Norwood and the 'Nemesis' Letters," *Georgia Historical Quarterly* 77 (Spring 1993): 86–122.

11. Thomas M. Norwood, "Address on the Negro: On Retiring from the Bench," *Vardaman's Weekly*, April 11, 1908.

12. Norwood, "Address on the Negro."

13. Norwood, "Address on the Negro."

14. "Do We Need a New Constitution?" *Vardaman's Weekly*, February 1, 1908.

15. "Vardaman to Fight Negro Appointment," *Pascagoula (MS) Chronicle-Star*, October 3, 1913.

16. Albert D. Kirwan, *Revolt of the Rednecks: Mississippi Politics, 1876–1925* (Lexington: University Press of Kentucky, 1951), 122–135.

17. On the decline of third-party politics and the consolidation of Democratic power, see Stephen Cresswell, *Multiparty Politics in Mississippi, 1877–1902* (Jackson: University Press of Mississippi, 1995).

18. Kirwan, *Revolt of the Rednecks*, 131.

19. *Smith v. Allwright*, 321 U.S. 649 (1944). See Darlene Clark Hine, *Black Victory: The Rise and Fall of the White Primary in Texas*, 2nd ed. (Columbia: University of Missouri Press, 2003).

20. See, generally, William F. Holmes, *The White Chief: James Kimble Vardaman* (Baton Rouge: Louisiana State University Press, 1970).

21. The literature on Progressivism as a national phenomenon is voluminous. See, generally, Richard Hofstadter, *The Age of Reform* (New York: Knopf, 1955); Michael McGerr, *A Fierce Discontent: The Rise and Fall of the Progressive Movement in America, 1870–1920* (New York: Free Press, 2003). On southern Progressivism and politics, see Dewey W. Grantham, *Southern Progressivism: The Reconciliation of Progress and Tradition* (Knoxville: University of Tennessee Press, 1983); William A. Link, *The Paradox of Southern Progressivism, 1880–1930* (Chapel Hill: University of North Carolina Press, 1992); Edward Ayers, *Promise of the New South: Life After Reconstruction* (New York: Oxford University Press, 1992); Glenda Gilmore, *Gender and Jim Crow: Women and the Politics of White Supremacy in North Carolina* (Chapel Hill: University of North Carolina Press, 1996).

22. Pascoe, *What Comes Naturally*, chap. 5; Elizabeth Gillespie McRae, *Mothers of Massive Resistance: White Women and the Politics of White Supremacy* (New York: Oxford University Press, 2018), chap. 2. Edward Larson argues that "southern eugenicists were also preoccupied with race, but at least initially they worried more about the deterioration of the Caucasian race than about any threat from the African race." Edward Larson, *Sex, Race, and Science: Eugenics in the Deep South* (Baltimore: Johns Hopkins University Press, 1995).

23. Jere Nash, "Edmund Favor Noel (1908–1912) and the Rise of James K. Vardaman and Theodore G. Bilbo," *Journal of Mississippi History* 81, nos. 1 and 2 (2019): 10.

24. Kirwan, *Revolt of the Rednecks*, 146–147.

25. Joseph A. Regan, *1910 Federal Census*, Beat 3, Claiborne County, Mississippi, supervisor's district 7, enumeration district 37, p. 2A; George P. Emerick, *1900 Federal Census*, Beat 3, Claiborne County, Mississippi, supervisor's district 7, enumeration district 160, p. 2 (via Ancestry.com).

26. "Earnest Meeting: Anti-Miscegenation League Is Formed," *Vicksburg Herald*, July 11, 1907.

27. "Dr. Warner on Vice," *Vicksburg American*, December 3, 1907.

28. "'Miscegenation Is Touched On as Charge," *Vicksburg Evening Post*, July 1, 1907.

29. On the history of racial ambiguity and the problem of the color line, see Joel Williamson, *New People: Miscegenation and Mulattoes in the United States* (New York: Free Press, 1980); Ariela J. Gross, *What Blood Won't Tell: A History of Race on Trial in America* (Cambridge, MA: Harvard University Press, 2008); Pascoe, *What Comes Naturally*.

30. "An Individual Duty," *Vicksburg American*, July 18, 1907.

31. William F. Holmes, "Whitecapping: Anti-Semitism in the Populist Era," *American Jewish Historical Quarterly* 63, no. 3 (March 1974): 244–261; Terence Finnegan, "Lynching and Political Power in Mississippi and South Carolina," in *Under Sentence of Death: Lynching in the South*, ed. Fitzhugh Brundage (Chapel Hill: University of North Carolina Press, 1997), 206–207.

32. "Wilkinson's Successor," *Natchez Evening Post*, August 2, 1906.

33. D. Clayton James, *Antebellum Natchez* (Baton Rouge: Louisiana State University Press, 1968), 260–261.

34. On free Black people in the Natchez District, see Nik Ribianszky, *Generations of Freedom: Gender, Movement, and Violence in Natchez, 1779–1865* (Athens: University of Georgia Press, 2021); Kimberly Welch, "Black Litigiousness and White Accountability: Free Blacks and the Rhetoric of Reputation in the Antebellum Natchez District," *Journal of the Civil War Era* 5, no. 3 (September 2015): 372–398.

35. William Johnson, *William Johnson's Natchez: The Ante-bellum Diary of a Free Negro* (Ann Arbor: University of Michigan Press, 1951); Edwin Adams Davis and William Ransom Hogan, *The Barber of Natchez* (Baton Rouge: Louisiana State University Press, 1973).

36. Aaron Zerkowsky, *1860 Federal Census*, Amite County, Mississippi, p. 28 (via Ancestry.com).

37. Jack E. Davis, *Race Against Time: Culture and Separation in Natchez Since 1930* (Baton Rouge: Louisiana State University Press, 2001), 105.

38. "Notice to the Public," *Natchez Democrat*, March 10, 1910.

39. "Board of Aldermen," *Natchez Democrat*, August 28, 1903; "Board of Aldermen," *Natchez Democrat*, April 7, 1908.

40. *New Orleans Times-Democrat*, April 27, 1909.

41. *State of Mississippi v. Charles Zerkowsky and Ella Carter*, October 4, 1909, case no. 2099, Sheriff's Docket Book, p. 31, Adams County Courthouse Storage Facility, Natchez, Mississippi.

42. *1910 Federal Census*, City of Natchez, Ward 1, Adams County, Mississippi, supervisor's district 7, enumeration district 4, p. 5B (via Ancestry.com).

43. Mattie Holmes, Eddie Zerkowsky, and Princess Zerkowsky, *1920 Federal Census*, City of Natchez, Ward 3, Adams County, Mississippi, supervisor's district 7, enumeration district 9, p. 17A (via Ancestry.com). Mattie and Seaman were arrested for unlawful cohabitation in 1924. Their case is discussed in Chapter 6 of this book.

44. *New Orleans Times-Democrat*, February 12, 1899; *Memphis Commercial Appeal*, August 22, 1901.

45. "With Circuit Court," *Natchez Democrat*, April 25, 1909.

46. On southern antisemitism, see Leonard Dinnerstein, *The Leo Frank Case* (New York: Columbia University Press, 1968); David Goldfield, "A Sense of Place: Jews, Blacks, and White Gentiles in the American South," *Southern Cultures* 3, no. 1 (Spring 1997): 58–79; Edward S. Schapiro, "Antisemitism: Mississippi Style," in *A Unique People in a Unique Land: Essays on American Jewish History* (Boston: Academic Studies Press, 2022). There is a robust debate about the relative whiteness of southern Jews. See Leonard Rogoff, "Is the Jew White? The Racial Place of the Southern Jew," *American Jewish History* 85, no. 3 (September 1997): 195–230; Karen Broadkin, *How Jews Became White*

Folks and What That Says About Race in America (New Brunswick, NJ: Rutgers University Press, 1998); Matthew Frye Jacobson, *Whiteness of a Different Color: European Immigrants and the Alchemy of Race* (Cambridge, MA: Harvard University Press, 1998), 171–199; Eric Goldstein, *The Price of Whiteness: Jews, Race, and American Identity* (Princeton, NJ: Princeton University Press, 2006).

47. On how the ethnic and religious identities of Jewish, Italian, and Slavic people positioned them on the margins of whiteness in the late nineteenth and early twentieth centuries, see Matthew Frye Jacobson, *Whiteness of a Different Color: European Immigrants and the Alchemy of Race* (Cambridge, MA: Harvard University Press, 1998).

48. Nancy MacLean, "The Leo Frank Case Reconsidered: Gender and Sexual Politics in the Making of Reactionary Populism," *Journal of American History* 78, no. 3 (December 1991): 917–948.

49. *State of Mississippi v. William Paul and Emmaline Miller*, April 21, 1909, case no. 2115, Adams County Circuit Court, Minute Book H, p. 32, Historic Natchez Foundation, Natchez, Mississippi (hereafter HNF).

50. *State v. Paul and Miller*, April 21, 1909, case no. 2115, Adams County Circuit Court, Minute Book H, p. 33, HNF.

51. *State v. Paul and Miller*, April 30, 1909, case no. 2115, Adams County Circuit Court, Minute Book H, p. 50, HNF.

52. *Natchez Democrat*, November 1, 1909. They did not, evidently, send it to the governor for approval. I did not find a record of the petition among those in the governor's files at the Mississippi Department of Archives and History (MDAH).

53. *State of Mississippi v. J. N. Ratcliff and Mamie Joseph*, April 22, 1909, case no. 2117, Adams County Circuit Court, Minute Book H, pp. 33–34, HNF.

54. "With Circuit Court," *Natchez Democrat*, May 2, 1909.

55. Carrie Rowan, Ella Stanton, *1910 Federal Census*, City of Natchez, Ward 2, Adams County, Mississippi, supervisor's district 1, enumeration district 6, p. 4A (via Ancestry.com).

56. Carrie Rowan and Henry Hunter, *1900 Federal Census*, City of Natchez, Ward 3, Adams County, Mississippi, supervisor's district 7, enumeration district 9, p. 13B (via Ancestry.com).

57. Charles Zerkowsky, *1920 Federal Census*, Beat 4, Adams County, Mississippi, supervisor's district 4, enumeration district 16, p. 2A (via Ancestry.com).

58. Mamie Godbolt, *1910 Federal Census*, City of Natchez, Ward 4, Adams County, Mississippi, supervisor's district 7, enumeration district 10, p. 21A (via Ancestry.com).

59. Mamie Godbolt, *1900 Federal Census*, Beat 1, Adams County, Mississippi, supervisor's district 7, enumeration district 1, p. 1A (via Ancestry.com).

60. *Natchez Democrat*, May 14, 1909.

61. "Three More," *Natchez Democrat*, May 13, 1909.

62. L. H. Clapp, *1900 Federal Census*, City of Natchez, Ward 4, Adams County, Mississippi, supervisor's district 7, enumeration district 10, p. 15 (via Ancestry.com).

63. *State of Mississippi v. Henry Hunter*, April 22, 1909, case no. 2107, Adams County Circuit Court, Minute Book H, p. 36, HNF.

64. *State of Mississippi v. R. Lee Parker*, April 22, 1909, case no. 2105, Adams County Circuit Court, Minute Book H, p. 36, HNF.

65. *State of Mississippi v. Cora Poter*, October 16, 1909, case no. 2105, Adams County Circuit Court, Minute Book H, p. 73, HNF.

66. *State of Mississippi v. Nap Lisso*, April 29, 1909, case no. 2110, Adams County Circuit Court, Minute Book H, p. 47, HNF.

67. *State of Mississippi v. Carrie Rowan*, October 12, 1909, case no. 2102, Adams County Circuit Court, Minute Book H, pp. 58–59, HNF.

68. *State of Mississippi v. William Sanders and Mamie Godbolt*, case no. 2103; *State of Mississippi v. Lee Richardson and Eliza White*, case no. 2111; *State of Mississippi v. John Rutherford*, case no. 2092, October 12, 1909, Adams County Circuit Court, Minute Book H, pp. 58–59, HNF.

69. *State of Mississippi v. L. H. Clapp and Mary Dent*, October 13, 1909, Adams County Circuit Court, Minute Book H, pp. 65–66, HNF.

70. *State of Mississippi v. Charles Zerkowsky*, case no. 2099, October 12, 1909, Adams County Circuit Court, Minute Book H, p. 61; *State of Mississippi v. Caleb Weir and Ella Stanton*, case no. 2106, April 19, 1910, Adams County Circuit Court, Minute Book H, p. 94, HNF.

71. *State of Mississippi v. Fred Passbach and Barbara Rouff*, case no. 2109, October 12, 1909, Adams County Circuit Court, Minute Book H, p. 60, HNF.

72. Adams County Circuit Court, April 19, 1910, Minute Book H, pp. 92–94, HNF.

73. "Peach Tree King Is Now Taking Orders," *Natchez Democrat*, September 23, 1917.

74. "Chamber of Commerce," *Natchez Democrat*, January 18, 1911.

75. Brief and Argument for Appellant, pp. 1–2, *R. F. Wilson v. State of Mississippi* case file, Mississippi Department of Archives and History (hereafter MDAH).

76. "Supreme Court Sitting," *Jackson (MS) Daily News*, May 4, 1908.

77. "Greenwood Man Defends Manship—Excoriates Noel for Wilson Pardon," *Hattiesburg (MS) Daily News*, May 26, 1908.

78. "Ask Pardon for Woman," *Jackson (MS) Daily News*, November 21, 1908.

79. "Ask Pardon for Woman," *Jackson (MS) Daily News*, November 21, 1908.

80. "Mississippi Matters," *New Orleans Times-Democrat*, April 26, 1911.

81. "Has Skipped Again: Negro School Teacher Whose Wife Is in the Pen," *Jackson (MS) Weekly Clarion-Ledger*, April 2, 1908.

82. Telisha Dionne Bailey, "'Please Don't Forget About Me': African American Women, Mississippi, and the History of Crime and Punishment in Parchman Prison, 1890–1980" (PhD diss., University of Mississippi, 2015), 33.

83. Letter, J. B. Webb to Governor E. F. Noel, June 5, 1909, Suspensions and Pardons Correspondence, 1908–1912, series 863, box 1234, folder 41, MDAH.

84. Letter, M. H. Wilkinson to Governor E. F. Noel, July 2, 1909, Suspensions and Pardons Correspondence, 1908–1912, series 863, box 1234, folder 41, MDAH.

85. On the history of Parchman Farm, see David Oshinsky, *Worse Than Slavery: Parchman Farm and the Ordeal of Jim Crow Justice* (New York: Free Press, 1996); William Banks Taylor, *Down on Parchman Farm: The Great Prison in the Mississippi Delta* (Columbus: Ohio State University Press, 1999).

86. Susie Perkins, *Parchman Prison Convict Register*, Book G, p. 179, Microfilm no. 13788, MDAH.

87. Charles Cade, *1910 Federal Census*, City of Port Gibson, Claiborne County, Mississippi, supervisor's district 7, enumeration district 33, p. 22B; Ella Killian, *1900 Federal Census*, City of Port Gibson, Claiborne County, Mississippi, supervisor's district 7, enumeration district 156, p. 3A (via Ancestry.com).

88. *State of Mississippi v. Charles Cade*, case no. 1233, June 29, 1909, Claiborne County Circuit Court, Minute Book 13, p. 120, Claiborne County Courthouse, Port Gibson, Mississippi.

89. Samuel Thames, *1880 Federal Census*, City of Crawfordville, Lowndes County, Mississippi, supervisor's district 1, enumeration district 104, p. 2 (via Ancestry .com).

90. *State vs. Regan and Harper*, case no. 1169, June 26, 1908, Claiborne County Circuit Court, Minute Book 12, p. 612, Claiborne County Courthouse, Port Gibson, Mississippi.

91. Indictment, June 27, 1909, *State v. Cade* case file, p. 6, MDAH; Testimony of Ed Johnson, June 30, 1909, trial transcript, *State v. Cade* case file, p. 26; Testimony of William Brown, June 30, 1909, trial transcript, *State v. Cade* case file, pp. 28–29, MDAH.

92. Testimony of Cary Murry, June 30, 1909, trial transcript, *State v. Cade* case file, p. 30, MDAH.

93. Testimony of Tom Rowan, June 30, 1909, trial transcript, *State v. Cade* case file, p. 22, MDAH.

94. Remarks to the jury, June 30, 1909, trial transcript, *State v. Cade* case file, pp. 32–33, MDAH.

95. Trial transcript, June 30, 1909, *State v. Cade* case file, p. 34, MDAH. The stenographer, T. M. DeLoach, may have been a cousin of the Thames brothers.

96. Instructions to the jury, trial transcript, *State v. Cade* case file, p. 40, MDAH.

97. Verdict, trial transcript, July 1, 1909, *State v. Cade* case file, p. 45, MDAH.

98. "Judge Bush Returns from Claiborne County Court," *Vicksburg American*, July 2, 1909; *State v. Cade*, case no. 1233, Claiborne County Circuit Court, Minute Book 13, September 1908 to September 1913, Claiborne County Courthouse, Port Gibson, Mississippi.

99. *Charles Cade v. State of Mississippi*, 96 Miss. 434 (1910).

100. Verdict, July 1, 1909, *State v. Cade*, case no. 1233, Claiborne County Circuit Court, Minute Book 13, p. 212, Claiborne County Courthouse, Port Gibson, Mississippi.

101. Sentence, *State of Mississippi v. L. P. DeJean and Eva Lewis*, January 30, 1914, trial transcript, p. 22, *L. P. DeJean and Eva Lewis v. State of Mississippi*, case file, MDAH.

102. Appellant Brief, pp. 1–2, *DeJean and Lewis v. State* case file, MDAH.

103. Testimony of R. J. Burgdorf, January 28, 1914, trial transcript, pp. 38, 40–41, *DeJean and Lewis v. State* case file, MDAH.

104. Testimony of R. J. Burgdorf, January 28, 1914, trial transcript, *DeJean and Lewis v. State* case file, p. 39, MDAH.

105. Testimony of R. J. Burgdorf, January 28, 1914, trial transcript, *DeJean and Lewis v. State* case file, pp. 35–36, MDAH.

106. Testimony of L. P. DeJean, January 28, 1914, trial transcript, *DeJean and Lewis v. State* case file, pp. 80–81, MDAH.

107. Brief for the State, *DeJean and Lewis v. State* case file, p. 6, MDAH.

108. *DeJean and Lewis v. State*, 108 Miss. 146 (1914).

109. "Louis P. DeJean Expires Suddenly," *Biloxi (MS) Sun Herald*, July 15, 1915.

110. Lawrence H. Clapp, *1910 Federal Census*, City of Natchez, Ward 4, Adams County, Mississippi, supervisor's district 7, enumeration district 10, p. 16B (via Ancestry.com).

111. Last Will and Testament of Charles Zerkowsky, filed October 18, 1930, Adams County Chancery Court, *Record of Wills*, no. 7, pp. 364–365 (via Ancestry.com).

112. First Annual Account of the Executors, August 5, 1931, *In the Matter of the Estate of Charles Zerkowsky, Deceased*, Adams County Chancery Court, *Administrators, Guardians, and Executors Accounts Allowed*, vol. 20, *1919–1932*, p. 367 (via Ancestry.com).

113. Davis, *Race Against Time*, 94.

114. Napthalia Lisso and Christine Williams, September 13, 1917, *Cook County, Illinois, U.S. Marriages Index, 1914–1942*, p. 6126 (via Ancestry.com).

115. Christine W. Lisso, January 5, 1929, *Cook County, Illinois Death Index, 1908–1988*, file no. 6000671; marriage registration, Napthalia Lisso and Carrie L. Washington, September 13, 1917, *Indiana, U.S., Marriages, 1810–2001* (via Ancestry.com).

116. Napthalia and Carita Lisso, *1930 Federal Census*, Chicago, Ward 19, Cook County, Illinois, enumeration district 16741, supervisor's district 7, p. 12B (via Ancestry.com).

117. Napthalia Lisso, *Cook County, Illinois Death Index, 1908–1988*, file no. 6002962; Carrie Lisso, *1940 Federal Census*, Chicago, Cook County, Illinois, supervisor's district 27, enumeration district 1031310, p. 2B (via Ancestry.com).

118. Mamie Godbolt and Willie Sanders, *1920 Federal Census*, Palestine Precinct, Adams County, Mississippi, supervisor's district 3, enumeration district 13, p. 8A (via Ancestry.com).

119. William Sanders and Mamie Godbolt, *1930 Federal Census*, Beat 5, Warren County, Mississippi, enumeration district 75–22, supervisor's district 6, p. 11B (via Ancestry.com).

120. William Sanders and Mamie Godbolt, *1940 Federal Census*, City of Natchez, Adams County, Mississippi, supervisor's district 7, enumeration district 1–5, p. 15B (via Ancestry.com).

121. State Directory Co., *Natchez, Mississippi, City Directory, 1941*, vol. 2 (Gulfport, MS, and Parsons, KS: State Directory Co., 1941), 358.

Chapter 5: "One Drop"

1. On the history of cohabitation laws, see Mary Frances Berry, "Judging Morality: Sexual Behavior and Legal Consequences," *Journal of American History* 78, no. 3 (December 1991): 838–842; Victoria Bynum, *Unruly Women: The Politics of Social and Sexual Control in the Old South* (Chapel Hill: University of North Carolina Press, 1992);

JoAnne Sweeny, "Undead Statutes: The Rise, Fall, and Continuing Uses of Adultery and Fornication Criminal Laws," *Loyola University Chicago Law Journal* 46 (2014): 127–173.

2. "Circuit Court News," *Bay St. Louis (MS) Sea Coast Echo*, October 19, 1912.

3. "Hancock Co. Circuit Court Proceedings—Spring Term," *Bay St. Louis (MS) Sea Coast Echo*, March 23, 1913.

4. On the history of the blood quantum, see Lauren L. Basson, *White Enough to Be American? Race Mixing, Indigenous People, and the Boundaries of State and Nation* (Chapel Hill: University of North Carolina Press, 2017); Ariela Gross, *What Blood Won't Tell: A History of Race on Trial in America* (Cambridge, MA: Harvard University Press, 2008); Ian Haney López, *White by Law: The Legal Construction of Race* (New York: New York University Press, 1996); Katherine Ellinghaus, "The Benefits of Being Indian: Blood Quanta, Intermarriage, and Allotment Policy on the White Earth Reservation, 1889–1920," *Frontiers* 29, no. 2–3 (2008): 81–105.

5. US Census Bureau, *1910 Census*, vol. 2, *Population, Reports by States, with Statistics for Counties, Cities, and Other Civil Divisions* (Washington, DC: US Census Bureau, 1913), 1029.

6. Ora H. Keller, "A Trip Through Southland," *Bay St. Louis (MS) Sea Coast Echo*, September 7, 1895.

7. "Beautiful Gulf Coast Country," *Bay St. Louis (MS) Sea Coast Echo*, January 31, 1914; "Wilson Leaves Pass Christian," *Los Angeles Times*, January 11, 1914.

8. Louisa Jourdan and Vincent Covacevich, *Mississippi Compiled Marriage Index, 1776–1935* (via Ancestry.com). Louisa is sometimes identified as "Louise Jourdain," and Vincent's surname has many alternate spellings. Many of the names of individuals in this chapter vary between the census and other records (i.e., Covacevich is sometimes "Covasovich" or "Kovacevich"), including on marriage certificates and in church records. For clarity, I have standardized the spellings of the family name to "Covacevich," which is the version present on the family headstone where Clara Grandich and Victor Covacevich are buried.

9. Land tax receipt, December 30, 1879, Sheriff's Office, Hancock County, Mississippi; land tax receipt, December 16, 1885, Sheriff's Office, Hancock County, Mississippi; land tax receipt, October 19, 1892, Sheriff's Office, Hancock County, Mississippi; *Southern Pine Company v. E. P. and S. S. Webb*, case no. 803, Hancock County Chancery Court case files, 1901, microfilm reel 37899, Mississippi Department of Archives and History, Jackson, Mississippi (hereafter MDAH).

10. Map, 1829, St. Stephens Meridian (East of Pearl River), Mississippi, in *U.S., Indexed Early Land Ownership and Township Plats, 1785–1898* (via Ancestry.com).

11. *Succession of Noel Jourdan*, 1845, Orleans Parish Estate Files, Louisiana, in *Louisiana, U.S. Wills and Probate Records, 1756–1984* (via Ancestry.com).

12. Vincent and Louisa Covacevich, *1900 Federal Census*, Jordan River, Hancock County, Mississippi, supervisor's district 6, enumeration district 26, p. 5A (via Ancestry.com).

13. Records from Our Lady of the Gulf have been transcribed and preserved digitally through the Hancock County Historical Society in Bay St. Louis. Many original records from the church were destroyed by Hurricane Katrina. *Catholic Church Records*

(1847–1911), Hancock County Historical Society, hancockcountyhistoricalsociety.com (hereafter HCHS).

14. Marriage record, Victor Covacevich and Louise Albertine Young, December 4, 1911, *New Orleans Marriage Records Index, 1831–1964* (via Ancestry.com).

15. Clyde L. MacKenzie Jr., "History of Oystering in the United States and Canada, Featuring the Eight Greatest Oyster Estuaries," *Marine Fisheries Review* 58, no. 4 (1996): 2.

16. *State of Louisiana v. State of Mississippi*, 202 U.S. 1 (1906). The Mississippi Legislature allowed oystermen to dredge the oyster beds with sheets of iron chains, whereas Louisiana banned the practice to prevent overharvesting.

17. "Mayor Indorsed [*sic*] Negro," *Washington Post*, January 17, 1903.

18. Matthew Frye Jacobson explains the position of Slavic and Italian immigrants as a process of both becoming American and becoming white; even as they received the legal protection of whiteness, they still struggled for inclusion in a sense of "social whiteness." Matthew Frye Jacobson, *Whiteness of a Different Color: European Immigrants and the Alchemy of Race* (Cambridge, MA: Harvard University Press, 1998), 46–62. Jessica Barbata Jackson argues that Italians enjoyed a wider range of social acceptance in the South prior to the 1890s than they did as the decade progressed, and that anti-Italian sentiment rose sharply during that time period. Jessica Barbata Jackson, *Dixie's Italians: Sicilians, Race, and Citizenship in the Jim Crow Gulf South* (Baton Rouge: Louisiana State University Press, 2020). See also Karel D. Bicha, "Hunkies: Stereotyping the Slavic Immigrants, 1890–1920," *Journal of American Ethnic History* 2, no. 1 (Fall 1982): 16–38.

19. Rebecca Scott, *Degrees of Freedom: Cuba and Louisiana After Slavery* (Cambridge, MA: Belknap Press of Harvard University Press, 2005), 158.

20. On the lynchings and Italians in New Orleans, see Alan G. Gauthreaux, "An Inhospitable Land: Anti-Italian Sentiment and Violence in Louisiana, 1891–1924," *Louisiana History* 51, no. 1 (Winter 2010): 41–68; Jackson, *Dixie's Italians*, 17–42.

21. Stefano Luconi, "Tampa's 1910 Lynching: The Italian-American Perspective and Its Implications," *Florida Historical Quarterly* 88, no. 1 (Summer 2009): 30–53.

22. Jackson, *Dixie's Italians*, 118–145.

23. *1910 Federal Census*, vol. 1, *Population: General Report and Analysis* (Washington, DC: US Government Printing Office, 1913), chap. 2.

24. US Census Bureau, *Instructions to Enumerators, Thirteenth Census of the United States* (Washington, DC: US Government Printing Office, 1910), 28.

25. On the role of the census in the legislative process surrounding the Johnson-Reed Act, see Mae Ngai, *Impossible Subjects: Illegal Aliens and the Making of Modern America* (Princeton, NJ: Princeton University Press, 2004), chap. 1.

26. Antonio Grandich, *1910 Federal Census*, City of Bay St. Louis, Ward 1, Hancock County, Mississippi, supervisor's district 6, enumeration district 30, p. 1A (via Ancestry.com).

27. Marriage license, Antonio Grandich and Clara Covacevich, October 7, 1889, p. 149, Volume F, Microfilm Reel 9445, MDAH.

28. Vincent and Louisa Covacevich, *1900 Federal Census*, Jordan River, Hancock County, Mississippi, supervisor's district 6, enumeration district 26, p. 5A (via Ancestry.com).

29. Marriage record, George Remetich and Victoria Covacevich, July 21, 1898, Our Lady of the Gulf Catholic Church, HCHS.

30. Clara Louise Remetich, born April 20, 1899, baptized July 2, 1899, baptismal record, Our Lady of the Gulf Catholic Church, HCHS.

31. George and Clara Remetich, *1910 Federal Census*, City of Bay St. Louis, Ward 2, Hancock County, Mississippi, supervisor's district 6, enumeration district 30, p. 1B (via Ancestry.com).

32. Declaration of Intention, November 6, 1918, US Department of Labor, Naturalization Service, *Mississippi, US, Naturalization Records, 1907–2008* (via Ancestry.com).

33. "Enrico Breghenti Dies," *Biloxi (MS) Sun Herald*, December 11, 1946.

34. *1910 Federal Census*, City of Bay St. Louis, Hancock County, Mississippi, supervisor's district 6, enumeration district 30, p. 2-A (via Ancestry.com).

35. "A Rootin' Tootin' Time Had by Some 500 Favre Descendants," *Bay St. Louis (MS) Sea Coast Echo*, April 28, 1991, Vertical Files, HCHS.

36. Simon Favre family tree, Vertical Files, HCHS.

37. Daniel H. Usner Jr., "The Frontier Exchange Economy of the Lower Mississippi Valley in the Eighteenth Century," *William and Mary Quarterly* 44, no. 2 (April 1987): 177–178.

38. Simon Favre family tree, Vertical Files, HCHS.

39. Last Will and Testament of Simon Favre, 1812, Vertical Files, HCHS.

40. Mary and Victor Pouyadou, *1910 Federal Census*, Beat 5, City of Bay St. Louis, Hancock County, Mississippi, supervisor's district 6, enumeration district 30 (via Ancestry.com).

41. Victor Pouyadou, *1900 Federal Census*, Beat 5, City of Bay St. Louis, Hancock County, Mississippi, supervisor's district 6, enumeration district 28 (via Ancestry.com).

42. Mary Favre, *1900 Federal Census*, Beat 5, City of Bay St. Louis, Hancock County, Mississippi, supervisor's district 6, enumeration district 28 (via Ancestry.com).

43. Georgeann Spadoni and Saverino Melito, *Louisiana, US, Compiled Marriage Index, 1831–1964* (via Ancestry.com).

44. Sam and Georgeann Melito, *1910 Federal Census*, City of Bay St. Louis, Ward 1, Hancock County, Mississippi, supervisor's district 6, enumeration district 30, p. 15A (via Ancestry.com).

45. George Spadoni, naturalization card, *U.S., Naturalization Record Indexes, 1791–1992* (via Ancestry.com).

46. Willie Fulton and Madalena Eurissa, May 9, 1912, *New Orleans Marriage Index, 1831–1964*; Lena and Willis Fulton, *1920 Federal Census*, City of Moss Point, Jackson County, Mississippi, p. 7B (via Ancestry.com).

47. Marriage record, Adele Nicaise and Peter Cospelich, February 26, 1871, *Mississippi, US, Compiled Marriage Index, 1776–1935* (via Ancestry.com).

48. Adele and Peter Cospelich, *1880 Federal Census*, Beat 5, Hancock County, Mississippi, supervisor's district 2, enumeration district 150, p. 43 (via Ancestry.com).

49. The family does not appear in the 1870 census as it appears on Ancestry.com. There are some pages missing from the scanned files of Hancock County, so they may have been listed on those pages. Alternately, it is possible that the family briefly moved

away, though marriage records note that the couple was wed in Hancock County in 1871.

50. Peter Cospelich, *1840 Federal Census*, Hancock County (via Ancestry.com).

51. Adele and Peter Cospelich, *1880 Federal Census*, Beat 5, Hancock County, Mississippi, supervisor's district 2, enumeration district 150, p. 43 (via Ancestry.com).

52. Mrs. F. Pergolis, *1880 Federal Census*, New Orleans, Orleans Parish, Louisiana, supervisor's district 1, enumeration district 39, p. 14B (via Ancestry.com); marriage record, Nicholas Cospelich and Angeline Pergolis, October 16, 1886, HCHS; marriage record, Stephen Cospelich and Frances (Christina) Pergolis, August 13, 1888, HCHS.

53. Peter Cospelich, *1900 Federal Census*, City of Bay St. Louis, Hancock County, Mississippi, supervisor's district 6, enumeration district 27, p. 11 (via Ancestry.com).

54. Peter and Emma Cospelich, *1910 Federal Census*, City of Bay St. Louis, Ward 1, Hancock County, Mississippi, supervisor's district 6, enumeration district 30, p. 12B (via Ancestry.com).

55. Emma Cospelich, *1920 Federal Census*, New Orleans, Ward 13, Orleans Parish, Louisiana, supervisor's district 8138, enumeration district 221, p. 5B (via Ancestry.com).

56. Adele Cospelich, *1900 Federal Census*, City of Bay St. Louis, Beat 5, Hancock County, Mississippi, supervisor's district 6, enumeration district 27, p. 10A (via Ancestry.com).

57. Adele Cospelich, *1910 Federal Census*, Beat 5, Hancock County, Mississippi, supervisor's district 6, enumeration district 29, p. 11A (via Ancestry.com).

58. Joseph Cospelich, *1900 Federal Census*, City of Bay St. Louis, Hancock County, Mississippi, supervisor's district 6, enumeration district 27, p. 11A (via Ancestry.com).

59. Charles Cade, *1900 Federal Census*, Beat 5, Hancock County, Mississippi, supervisor's district 6, enumeration district 27, p. 12B (via Ancestry.com).

60. Richard Optime and Hettie Valsin, *1900 Federal Census*, City of Bay St. Louis, Hancock County, Mississippi, supervisor's district 6, enumeration district 28, p. 6 (via Ancestry.com).

61. August Bourgeois, *1910 Federal Census*, Beat 5, Hancock County, Mississippi, supervisor's district 6, enumeration district 29, p. 26A (via Ancestry.com).

62. Mary Wilhemina Cospelich was the daughter of Angeline Pergolis and Nicholas Cospelich. Nicholas was a son of Peter and Adele Cospelich. Angeline was the daughter of Frank Pergolis and Sara Jourdan, the sister of Louise Jourdan. Marriage record, Nicholas Cospelich and Angeline Pergolis, October 16, 1886, Our Lady of the Gulf Catholic Church, HCHS; Mary Wilhemina Cospelich, born April 2, 1889, baptized June 16, 1889, baptismal record, Our Lady of the Gulf Catholic Church, HCHS.

63. After Leduc's death in 1897, he was succeeded by a Mississippi-born priest, J. M. Prendergast, who presided over some interracial marriages, including that of George Remetich and Victoria Covacevich. Marriage record, George and Victoria Remetich, July 21, 1897, HCHS; H. Leduc, *1880 Federal Census*, City of Bay St. Louis, Hancock County, Mississippi, supervisor's district 2, enumeration district 150, p. 1A; J. M. Prendergast, *1910 Federal Census*, City of Bay St. Louis, Ward 3, Hancock County, Mississippi, supervisor's district 6, enumeration district 30, p. 21A (via Ancestry.com).

64. Ellis Anderson, *Under Surge, Under Siege: The Odyssey of Bay St. Louis and Hurricane Katrina* (Jackson: University Press of Mississippi, 2010).

65. "Report of Hancock County Grand Jury—14 True Bills," *Bay St. Louis (MS) Sea Coast Echo*, March 15, 1913.

66. On the problems posed by racial classifications in miscegenation trials, see Gross, *What Blood Won't Tell*; and Peggy Pascoe, *What Comes Naturally: Miscegenation Law and the Making of Race in America* (New York: Oxford University Press, 2009).

67. Some marriage records from Hancock County have been preserved on microfilm in the Mississippi Department of Archives and History.

68. "Coast Editor Dies from Sudden Heart Attack at Home," *Bay St. Louis (MS) Sea Coast Echo*, November 29, 1941.

69. Charles Moreau's wife, Angeline, had her own interesting history. Angeline's father, Henry Picaluga, claimed Italian heritage, though the census records his birthplace as Jamaica or, alternately, Mexico. Angeline Moreau, *1900 Federal Census*, City of Bay St. Louis, Hancock County, Mississippi, supervisor's district 6, enumeration district 28, p. 6 (via Ancestry.com).

70. Board of Trustees Minutes, Exhibit A, p. 14, *Moreau* case file, MDAH.

71. Gross, *What Blood Won't Tell*, 5.

72. Lena and Willis's son, John Fulton, was born in or around 1915. Lena and Willis Fulton, *1920 Federal Census*, City of Moss Point, Jackson County, Mississippi, p. 7B (via Ancestry.com). Mary's husband, Victor Pouyadou, died in 1914. In 1920, Mary and all of the children are once again classified racially as "mulatto." *1920 Federal Census*, Beat 5, Hancock County, Mississippi supervisor's district 6, enumeration district 35, p. 7A (via Ancestry.com).

73. "First Communion Service," *Bay St. Louis (MS) Sea Coast Echo*, June 1, 1912.

74. *Bay St. Louis (MS) Sea Coast Echo*, October 17, 1914.

75. Petition for Mandamus, April 19, 1915, Case No. 1403, *Charles G. Moreau et al., Board of Trustees v. Antonio and Clara Grandich* case file, MDAH.

76. US Department of the Army, *Grand Isle and Vicinity, Louisiana: Report of the Chief of Engineers* (Washington, DC: US Government Printing Office, 1964), 63.

77. "Fear 260 Perished in Gulf Hurricane," *Washington Post*, October 2, 1915; US Department of the Army, *Grand Isle and Vicinity*, 23.

78. As Peggy Pascoe and Ariela Gross describe, such bodily inspections were common in racial trials in the early twentieth century. Pascoe explains, "Whenever they could, lawyers relied on the jury's visual scrutiny to determine the race of the plaintiff or defendant who appeared in the courtroom before them. . . . [T]his technique had the considerable advantage of appearing to rest on the common sense of jurors rather than legal strategy and thus appearing to be no technique at all." Pascoe, *What Comes Naturally*, chap. 4; Gross, *What Blood Won't Tell*, chap. 1.

79. Testimony of Louisa Covacevich, March 22, 1916, pp. 18–19, *Moreau v. Grandich* case file, MDAH.

80. Testimony of Louisa Covacevich, March 22, 1916, p. 20, *Moreau v. Grandich* case file, MDAH.

81. Testimony of Clara Grandich, March 22, 1916, p. 22, *Moreau v. Grandich* case file, MDAH.

82. Testimony of Louisa Covacevich, March 22, 1916, p. 25, *Moreau v. Grandich* case file, MDAH.

83. Deposition of Celine Clouatre, undated, p. 60, *Moreau v. Grandich* case file, MDAH.

84. Deposition of Lucien Thibodaux, undated, p. 65, *Moreau v. Grandich* case file, MDAH.

85. Deposition of Camille Blouin, undated, p. 77, *Moreau v. Grandich* case file, MDAH.

86. Deposition of Camille Blouin, undated, p. 80, *Moreau v. Grandich* case file, MDAH.

87. Deposition of Nora Francoise, undated, p. 82, *Moreau v. Grandich* case file, MDAH.

88. Deposition of Mrs. M. J. Robinson, undated, p. 25, *Moreau v. Grandich* case file, MDAH.

89. Deposition of Mrs. M. J. Robinson, undated, p. 37, *Moreau v. Grandich* case file, MDAH.

90. Victor Jourdan, *1850 Federal Census*, Eastern District, St. James Parish, Louisiana (via Ancestry.com).

91. Deposition of Jules Dugas, undated, p. 51, *Moreau v. Grandich* case file, MDAH.

92. Deposition of Jules Dugas, undated, p. 48, *Moreau v. Grandich* case file, MDAH.

93. Deposition of Jules Dugas, undated, p. 56, *Moreau v. Grandich* case file, MDAH.

94. Judgment, March 23, 1916, p. 93, *Moreau v. Grandich* case file, MDAH.

95. Brief for Appellees, p. 3, *Moreau v. Grandich* case file, MDAH.

96. *State of Louisiana v. Octave Treadway*, 126 La. 300 (1909).

97. *Moreau v. Grandich*, 114 Miss. 560 (1917).

98. "Antonio Grandich," "Find a Grave," www.findagrave.com/memorial/40069567/antonio-grandich.

99. Clara Grandich, *1920 Federal Census*, New Orleans, Ward 7, Orleans Parish, Louisiana, supervisor's district 1, enumeration district 126, p. 7B (via Ancestry.com).

100. Marguerite Cobb, *1920 Federal Census*, New Orleans, Ward 7, Orleans Parish, Louisiana, supervisor's district 1, enumeration district 126, p. 20B (via Ancestry.com).

101. Rita Davis, *1920 Federal Census*, Baton Rouge, Ward 2, East Baton Rouge Parish, Louisiana, supervisor's district 6, enumeration district 26, p. 16B (via Ancestry.com).

102. Interview with Gail Green, August 24, 2021.

103. Ildebrandi Brighenti, *1920 Federal Census*, Beat 5, City of Bay St. Louis, Hancock County, Mississippi, supervisor's district 6, enumeration district 36, p. 3B (via Ancestry.com).

104. Helen Saucier, *1930 Federal Census*, New Orleans, Orleans Parish, Louisiana, supervisor's district 11, enumeration district 36–271, p. 13B (via Ancestry.com).

105. Helen Brighenti, *1940 Federal Census*, City of Bay St. Louis, Hancock County, Mississippi, supervisor's district 6, enumeration district 23–5, p. 17A (via Ancestry.com).

106. Louisa Covacevich, *1940 Federal Census*, City of Bay St. Louis, Hancock County, Mississippi, supervisor's district 6, enumeration district 23–5, p. 17A (via Ancestry.com).

Chapter 6: Myths of Racial Integrity

1. See, e.g., Elliott M. Rudwick, *Race Riot at East St. Louis, July 2, 1917* (Carbondale: Southern Illinois University Press, 1964); William Tuttle, *Race Riot: Chicago in the Red Summer of 1919* (Urbana: University of Illinois Press, 1996); Grif Stockley, *Blood in Their Eyes: The Elaine Race Massacres of 1919* (Fayetteville: University of Arkansas Press, 2001).

2. See, e.g., Patrick Renshaw, "The IWW and the Red Scare, 1917–1924," *Journal of Contemporary History* 3, no. 4, "1918–19: From War to Peace" (October 1968): 63–72; Mark Ellis, "J. Edgar Hoover and the 'Red Summer' of 1919," *Journal of American Studies* 28, no. 1 (April 1994): 39–59; John M. Barry, *The Great Influenza: The Epic Story of the Deadliest Plague in History* (New York: Viking, 2004).

3. On the boll weevil's effect on Mississippi cotton agriculture, see James C. Giesen, *Boll Weevil Blues: Cotton, Myth, and Power in the American South* (Chicago: University of Chicago Press, 2011).

4. On the rise of the Second Ku Klux Klan, see Leonard Joseph Moore, *Citizen Klansman: The Ku Klux Klan in Indiana, 1921–1928* (Chapel Hill: University of North Carolina Press, 1991); Nancy MacLean, *Behind the Mask of Chivalry: The Making of the Second Ku Klux Klan* (New York: Oxford University Press, 1994); Felix Harcourt, *Ku Klux Kulture: America and the Klan in the 1920s* (Chicago: University of Chicago Press, 2017); Linda Gordon, *The Second Coming of the KKK: The Ku Klux Klan of the 1920s* (New York: Liveright, 2017). On the influence of eugenics thought in the 1920s, see Laura Briggs, *Reproducing Empire: Race, Sex, Science and U.S. Imperialism in Puerto Rico* (Berkeley: University of California Press, 2002); Wendy Kline, *Building a Better Race: Gender, Sexuality, and Eugenics from the Turn of the Century to the Baby Boom* (Berkeley: University of California Press, 2005); Paul Lombardo, *Three Generations, No Imbeciles: Eugenics, the Supreme Court, and* Buck v. Bell (Baltimore: Johns Hopkins University Press, 2008).

5. On the influence of Stoddard's work among white intellectuals, see Matthew Frye Jacobson, *Whiteness of a Different Color: European Immigrants and the Alchemy of Race* (Cambridge, MA: Harvard University Press, 1998), 91–135; Thomas C. Leonard, *Illiberal Reformers: Race, Eugenics, and American Economics in the Progressive Era* (Princeton, NJ: Princeton University Press, 2016), 112–117.

6. David Mark Chalmers, *Hooded Americanism: The History of the Ku Klux Klan* (Durham, NC: Duke University Press, 1987), 270–271.

7. Lothrop Stoddard, *The Revolt Against Civilization: The Menace of the Under Man* (New York: Scribner, 1923), 5–6.

8. Stoddard, *Revolt Against Civilization*, 10.

9. Stoddard, *Revolt Against Civilization*, 71–72.

10. "Worse Than Death," *Vardaman's Weekly*, November 17, 1921.

11. "The Paramount Problem of the Age," *Vardaman's Weekly*, April 7, 1921; "Pernicious Mischief," *Vardaman's Weekly*, November 3, 1921.

12. Testimony of Sam A. Winn, undated, trial transcript, p. 32, *Mollie Kemp v. State of Mississippi* case file, Mississippi Department of Archives and History, Jackson, Mississippi (hereafter MDAH).

13. Testimony of Jerry Lindsay, undated, trial transcript, pp. 1–3, *Kemp v. State* case file, MDAH.

14. Testimony of Sam A. Winn, undated, trial transcript, p. 33, *Kemp v. State* case file, MDAH.

15. Testimony of O. J. Turner, undated, trial transcript, pp. 33–34, *Kemp v. State* case file, MDAH.

16. Indictment, May 1, 1919, *Kemp v. State* case file, MDAH.

17. *Kemp v. State* case file, p. 57, MDAH.

18. *Kemp v. State*, 121 Miss. 589 (1920).

19. Testimony of Paul Hudson, undated, trial transcript, p. 37, *Kemp v. State* case file, MDAH.

20. Testimony of Jerry Lindsay, undated, trial transcript, p. 14, *Kemp v. State* case file, MDAH.

21. Testimony of Paul Hudson, undated, trial transcript, p. 37, *Kemp v. State* case file, MDAH.

22. Trial transcript, undated, p. 35, *Kemp v. State* case file, MDAH.

23. Testimony of Mike G. Griffin, trial transcript, p. 31, *Kemp v. State* case file, MDAH.

24. "Judge O'Brien Wants Full Investigation," *Vicksburg Herald*, July 8, 1919.

25. On the Second Klan's founding, see Wyn Craig Wade, *The Fiery Cross: The Ku Klux Klan in America* (New York: Simon and Schuster, 1988), chap. 4.

26. MacLean, *Behind the Mask of Chivalry*; Moore, *Citizen Klansman*; James H. Madison, *The Ku Klux Klan in the Heartland* (Bloomington: Indiana University Press, 2020).

27. S.B. 198, Mississippi Legislature, *Journal of the Senate of the State of Mississippi* (Jackson, MS: Tucker Printing House, 1920), 363–364.

28. S.B. 198, *Journal of the Senate* (1920), 989; Mississippi Legislature, *Journal of the House of Representatives of the State of Mississippi* (Jackson, MS: Tucker Printing House, 1920), 1501–1502.

29. *Journal of the Senate* (1920), 1320.

30. Annotated Mississippi Code Supplement of 1921, Chap. 15, Sec. 1142e.

31. The Espionage and Sedition Acts were upheld by the US Supreme Court in *Abrams v. United States*, 250 U.S. 616 (1919). On free speech and labor activism in the early twentieth century, see Laura Weinrib, *The Taming of Free Speech: America's Civil Liberties Compromise* (Cambridge, MA: Harvard University Press, 2016).

32. *Gitlow v. New York*, 268 U.S. 652 (1925).

33. Chap. 15, Sec. 1142f, Miss. Ann. Code Supp. 1921.

34. "The People's Forum," *Natchez Democrat*, July 9, 1922.

35. "Six White Robed Ku Klux Enter Council's Hospital Meet, Give Woman $1000," *Winona (MS) Times*, April 28, 1922.

36. "Taxes of Aged Widow Paid by Ku Klux Klan," *Brookhaven (MS) Semi-Weekly Leader*, March 8, 1922.

37. "Speech of Hon. John E. Rankin of Mississippi in House of Representatives," *Jackson (MS) Clarion-Ledger*, February 15, 1922.

38. "Speech of Hon. John E. Rankin of Mississippi in House of Representatives," *Jackson (MS) Clarion-Ledger*, February 15, 1922.

39. "Lincoln League of Women Voters," *Brookhaven (MS) Semi-Weekly Leader*, November 16, 1921.

40. "War on Cohabitation," *Jackson (MS) Daily News*, September 13, 1922.

41. "Court Opens Fall Session Monday," *Brookhaven (MS) Semi-Weekly Leader*, September 6, 1922.

42. "Miss. Votes Uninstructed Unit," *Winona (MS) Times*, June 6, 1924.

43. "Percy and Mrs. Yates Cross Up," *Winona (MS) Times*, June 20, 1924.

44. Albert D. Kirwan, *Revolt of the Rednecks: Mississippi Politics, 1876–1925* (Lexington: University Press of Kentucky, 1951), 224–225.

45. On LeRoy Percy, see William Alexander Percy, *Lanterns on the Levee: Recollections of a Planter's Son* (Baton Rouge: Louisiana State University Press, 1973).

46. "Circuit Court to Take Up Criminal Docket on Monday," *Natchez Democrat*, March 30, 1924.

47. "Sentences Given by Judge Corban," *Natchez Democrat*, April 11, 1924.

48. *State of Mississippi v. Fritz Meyer and Ella Ford* case file, MDAH.

49. Indictment, March 31, 1924, *State v. Meyer and Ford* case file, MDAH.

50. Ella Ford, *1920 Federal Census*, Palestine District, Adams County, supervisor's district 34, enumeration district 14, page 2B (via Ancestry.com).

51. *State v. Meyer and Ford*, April 1, 1924, case no. 3793, Adams County Circuit Court, Minute Book I, p. 167, Historic Natchez Foundation, Natchez, Mississippi (hereafter HNF).

52. "Court Continues Cases of Former County Officers," *Natchez Democrat*, April 8, 1924.

53. "Civil Case Takes Up Court Session," *Natchez Democrat*, April 9, 1924.

54. *State v. Meyer and Ford*, April 9, 1924, case no. 3793, Adams County Circuit Court, Minute Book I, p. 181, HNF.

55. Brief on behalf of defendants, May 24, 1924, p. 2, *State v. Meyer and Ford* case file, MDAH.

56. Brief on behalf of defendants, May 24, 1924, p. 4, *State v. Meyer and Ford* case file, MDAH.

57. *State v. Meyer and Ford*, 135 Miss. 882 (1924).

58. *State v. Meyer and Ford*, March 30, 1925, case no. 3793, Adams County Circuit Court, Minute Book I, p. 258, HNF.

59. Circuit Court Minutes, Adams County Circuit Court, Minute Book I, p. 222, HNF. Both Bennett and Burns are identified as carpenters in the Natchez City Directory (1925).

60. *State of Mississippi v. W. S. Dean and Ralphine Burns*, 139 Miss. 518 (1925).

61. *State v. Dean and Burns*, November 25, 1924, case no. 3787, Adams County Circuit Court, Minute Book I, p. 212, HNF.

62. Elizabeth Stampley, *1930 Federal Census*, City of Natchez, Ward 2, Adams County, Mississippi, enumeration district 1–2, supervisor's district 10, p. 1B (via Ancestry.com).

63. *State of Mississippi v. Peter Burns and Lizzie Stampley*, November 20, 1924, case no. 3795, Adams County Circuit Court, Minute Book I, p. 213, HNF.

64. *1880 Federal Census*, City of Natchez, Ward 2, Adams County, Mississippi, supervisor's district 3, enumeration district 49, p. 18B (via Ancestry.com).

65. *State of Mississippi v. J. M. Crawford and Millie Brooks*, March 30, 1924, case no. 3796, Adams County Circuit Court, Minute Book I, p. 258, HNF.

66. *State of Mississippi v. Seaman Zerkowsky and Mattie Holmes*, case no. 3790; *State of Mississippi v. Geo. Niblock and Ethel Garrett*, case no. 3792; *State of Mississippi v. Ed Hunter*, case no. 3794; *State of Mississippi v. Henry Steir, alias Buddy Steir*, case no. 3799; *State of Mississippi v. Annie Weis*, case no. 3791, April 3, 1925, all in Adams County Circuit Court, Minute Book I, pp. 271–272, HNF.

67. Brief for Appellants, *Dean et al. v. State of Mississippi*, 139 Miss. 517 (1925).

68. *Dean v. State*, 139 Miss. 518 (1925).

69. *Dean v. State*, 139 Miss. 518 (1925).

70. Adams County Circuit Court, Minute Book I, HNF.

71. On the history of the Virginia Racial Integrity Act, see Peter Wallenstein, *Tell the Court I Love My Wife: Race, Marriage, and Law—an American History* (New York: Palgrave Macmillan, 2002); Peggy Pascoe, *What Comes Naturally: Miscegenation Law and the Making of Race in America* (New York: Oxford University Press, 2009); Lombardo, *Three Generations*.

72. H.B. 74, Mississippi Legislature, *Journal of the House of Representatives of the State of Mississippi* (Jackson: Hederman Brothers, 1926), 203.

73. J. Douglas Smith, "The Campaign for Racial Purity and the Erosion of Paternalism in Virginia, 1922–1930: 'Nominally White, Biologically Mixed, and Legally Negro,'" *Journal of Southern History* 68, no. 1 (February 2002): 73.

74. "Miscegenation Bill Is Coming: Yazoo Representative to Offer Measure to Preserve Separate Races," *Jackson (MS) Clarion-Ledger*, January 10, 1926.

75. Pascoe, *What Comes Naturally*, 142.

76. "Governor Urges Sanctity of Race: Recommends Legislature Adopt Stringent Miscegenation Measure," *Jackson (MS) Clarion-Ledger*, February 5, 1926.

77. "Governor Urges Sanctity of Race: Recommends Legislature Adopt Stringent Miscegenation Measure," *Jackson (MS) Clarion-Ledger*, February 5, 1926.

78. "Governor Urges Sanctity of Race: Recommends Legislature Adopt Stringent Miscegenation Measure," *Jackson (MS) Clarion-Ledger*, February 5, 1926.

79. "Governor Urges Sanctity of Race: Recommends Legislature Adopt Stringent Miscegenation Measure," *Jackson (MS) Clarion-Ledger*, February 5, 1926.

80. "Mississippians Fight Breakdown of Color Line," *Chicago Defender*, June 5, 1926.

81. James R. Grossman, *Land of Hope: Chicago, Black Southerners, and the Great Migration* (Chicago: University of Chicago Press, 1989), 74–89.

82. *House Journal* (1926), 1921.

83. Gideon and Emma Brown, *1920 Federal Census*, City of Bay Springs, Jasper County, Mississippi, supervisor's district 5, enumeration district 18, p. 1A (via Ancestry .com).

84. "Mrs. Emma A. Brown Dies, Rites Friday," *Jackson (MS) Clarion-Ledger*, August 3, 1951.

85. Gideon and Emma Brown, *1910 Federal Census*, City of Bay Springs, Jasper County, Mississippi, supervisor's district 4, enumeration district 18, p. 1B (via Ancestry .com).

86. On the Ainsworth family's history, see Victoria E. Bynum, *The Long Shadow of the Civil War: Southern Dissent and Its Legacies* (Chapel Hill: University of North Carolina Press, 2010), 119–123.

87. Mariah Ainsworth, *1900 Federal Census*, Antioch Precinct, Jasper County, Mississippi, supervisor's district 1, enumeration district 49, p. 12B; Mariah Ainsworth, *1910 Federal Census*, Kenedy Town, Karnes County, Texas, supervisor's district 9, enumeration district 112, p. 10A (via Ancestry.com).

88. Family trees on Ancestry.com identify Mary/Mariah as "L. M. Poole" in the 1860 federal census; another child in the home, a sister named M. E. Poole, is later identified as living in Jasper County as "Mariah E. Pool" in the 1870 census. Racial classifications are not marked on the 1860 census, though Mariah E. Pool is identified as white in 1870. Mariah Ainsworth and Mariah E. Pool are two different people, though according to Ancestry.com trees, they are sisters. L. M. Poole, *1860 Federal Census*, North Division of Choctaw County, Alabama, p. 11; Mariah E. Pool, *1870 Federal Census*, Center Beat, Jasper County, Mississippi, p. 34 (via Ancestry.com).

89. James L. and Mariah Ainsworth, *1910 Federal Census*, Precinct 4, Kenedy, Karnes County, Texas, supervisor's district 9, enumeration district 112, p. 10A (via Ancestry.com).

90. The bill initially had support, but late in the session the Mississippi Senate voted to postpone debate on the bill indefinitely. H.B. 74, Mississippi Legislature, *Journal of the Senate of the State of Mississippi* (Jackson: Hederman Brothers, 1926), 2253–2254.

91. "Great Homecoming in Rankin County," *Newton (MS) Record*, July 9, 1925.

92. "Sermon Delivered by Rev. A. M. Ayers at Presbyterian Church, Sunday July 9," *Vicksburg Evening Post*, July 10, 1922.

93. "New House Bills," *Jackson (MS) Clarion-Ledger*, February 2, 1928.

94. "In the House," *Jackson (MS) Clarion-Ledger*, April 4, 1928.

95. "Solons Provide for Own Salary," *Greenwood (MS) Commonwealth*, June 25, 1929.

96. "Death Calls Yazoo County Legislator," *Yazoo (MS) Herald*, September 11, 1928.

97. "Murphree Charges Bilbo Deliberately Falsified Record About Cost of Calling Troops," *Jackson (MS) Clarion-Ledger*, July 27, 1927.

98. On the Great Migration, see Alferdteen Harrison, *Black Exodus: The Great Migration from the American South* (Jackson: University Press of Mississippi, 1992); Grossman, *Land of Hope*; Isabelle Wilkerson, *The Warmth of Other Suns: The Epic Story of America's Great Migration* (New York: Vintage, 2010).

Chapter 7: Exiling the Past

1. Last Will and Testament of Pearl Mitchell Miller, filed November 18, 1944, pp. 76–77, *Alex D. Miller v. James Lucks et al.* case file, Mississippi Department of Archives and History, Jackson, Mississippi (hereafter MDAH).

2. *1940 Federal Census*, Chicago, Ward 4, Block 6, Cook County, Illinois.

3. Bill of Appraisement of the Estate of Pearl M. Miller, February 25, 1946, p. 88, *Miller v. Lucks* case file, MDAH.

4. Demurrer, Answer and Cross-Bill of Respondent, June 17, 1946, p. 9, *Miller v. Lucks* case file, MDAH.

5. Petition to Establish Heirs of Deceased, January 3, 1946, *In re: Pearl Mitchell Miller, Deceased*, pp. 3–5; marriage license, Pearl Mitchell and Alex Miller, filed July 31, 1939, Cook County, Illinois, *Miller v. Lucks* case file, MDAH.

6. Pearl Mitchell, *1910 Federal Census*, Beat 5, City of Jackson, Hinds County, Mississippi, supervisor's district 8, enumeration district 28, p. 8B; *1920 Federal Census*, City of Jackson, Hinds County, Mississippi, supervisor's district 8, enumeration district 17, p. 8A; *1930 Federal Census*, Chicago, Ward 3, Cook County, Illinois, supervisor's district 8, enumeration district 16–2414, p. 2A (via Ancestry.com); death certificate, Pearl Mitchell Miller, filed September 17, 1945, Chicago Board of Health, p. 70, *Miller v. Lucks* case file, MDAH.

7. Demurrer, Answer, and Cross-Bill of Alex D. Miller, Respondent, June 17, 1946, pp. 8–13, *Miller v. Lucks* case file, MDAH.

8. Transcript, Theodore Bilbo campaign speech, May 7, 1946, Pontotoc, Mississippi, MDAH, https://da.mdah.ms.gov/vault/projects/OHtranscripts/AU1008_120959.pdf.

9. On Bilbo's Senate trials and investigations, see Zachary L. Wakefield, "'The Skeleton in America's Own Cupboard': Mississippi's Theodore Bilbo and the Shaping of Racial Politics, 1946–1948" (PhD diss., Auburn University, 2017).

10. On moderate segregationists' responses to the Black Freedom Struggle, see Joseph Crespino, *In Search of Another Country: Mississippi and the Conservative Counterrevolution* (Princeton, NJ: Princeton University Press, 2007); Anders Walker, *The Ghost of Jim Crow: How Southern Moderates Used* Brown v. Board of Education *to Stall the Civil Rights Movement* (New York: Oxford University Press, 2009).

11. Last Will and Testament of Pearl Mitchell Miller, filed November 18, 1944, *Miller v. Lucks* case file, p. 77, MDAH.

12. Sec. 459, Miss. Code 1942.

13. Amended Petition of James Lucks and Eddie May White to Establish Heirs of Deceased, February 6, 1946, *Miller v. Lucks* case file, p. 39, MDAH.

14. Supplemental Cross-Bill, August 13, 1946, *In re: Pearl Mitchell Miller, Deceased*, p. 24, *Miller v. Lucks* case file, MDAH.

15. Demurrer, Answer and Cross-Bill of Respondent, June 17, 1946, p. 12, *Miller v. Lucks* case file, MDAH.

16. Demurrer, Answer and Cross-Bill of Respondent, June 17, 1946, p. 12, *Miller v. Lucks* case file, MDAH.

17. Petition, Cook County Probate Court, November 26, 1945, pp. 72–73, *Miller v. Lucks* case file, MDAH.

18. Stipulation and agreement as to facts, June 13, 1947, *In re: Pearl Mitchell Miller, Deceased*, Hinds County Chancery Court, p. 98, *Miller v. Lucks* case file, MDAH.

19. Hearing transcript, June 13, 1947, *In re: Pearl Mitchell Miller, Deceased*, p. 93, *Miller v. Lucks* case file, MDAH.

20. Hearing transcript, June 13, 1947, *In re: Pearl Mitchell Miller, Deceased*, p. 95, *Miller v. Lucks* case file, MDAH.

21. Hearing transcript, June 13, 1947, *In re: Pearl Mitchell Miller, Deceased*, p. 94, *Miller v. Lucks* case file, MDAH.

22. Hearing transcript, June 13, 1947, *In re: Pearl Mitchell Miller, Deceased*, p. 95, *Miller v. Lucks* case file, MDAH.

23. Final Decree, June 25, 1947, *In re: Pearl Mitchell Miller, Deceased*, case no. 33,494, Hinds County Chancery Court, pp. 100–103, *Miller v. Lucks* case file, MDAH.

24. "State Supreme Court Rules White Husband Inherits Property of Negro Wife," *Jackson (MS) Advocate*, June 26, 1948.

25. US Constitution, Art. IV, sec. 1.

26. On comity, see Hendrik Hartog, *Man and Wife in America* (Cambridge, MA: Harvard University Press, 2000), 269–275.

27. On "migratory divorces," see Hartog, *Man and Wife*, 277–282; Laura Oren, "No-Fault Divorce Reform in the 1950s: The Lost History of the 'Greatest Project' of the National Association of Women Lawyers," *Law and History Review* 36, no. 4 (November 2018): 859–862.

28. *Succession of Caballero (Mrs. Conte) v. the Executor et al.*, 24 La. 573 (1872); *State of North Carolina v. Pink Ross and Sarah Ross*, 76 NC 242 (1877); *State of North Carolina v. Isaac Kennedy and Mag Kennedy*, 76 NC 251 (1877); *Josephine Whittington v. R. E. L. McCaskill*, 65 Fla. 162, 61 So. 236 (1913).

29. *Miller v. Lucks*, 203 Miss. 824 (1948).

30. Johnpeter Horst Grill and Robert L. Jenkins, "The Nazis and the American South in the 1930s: A Mirror Image?," *Journal of Southern History* 58, no. 4 (November 1992): 667–694; James Q. Whitman, *Hitler's American Model: The United States and the Making of Nazi Race Law* (Princeton, NJ: Princeton University Press, 2017).

31. On the Black Freedom Struggle during World War II, see, generally, Patricia Sullivan, *Days of Hope: Race and Democracy in the New Deal Era* (Chapel Hill: University of North Carolina Press, 1996); Barbara Ransby, *Ella Baker and the Black Freedom Movement: A Radical Democratic Vision* (Chapel Hill: University of North Carolina Press, 2003); Charles Payne, *I've Got the Light of Freedom: The Organizing Tradition and the Mississippi Freedom Movement* (Berkeley: University of California Press, 2007).

32. Robin D.G. Kelley, *Hammer and Hoe: Alabama Communists During the Great Depression* (Chapel Hill: University of North Carolina Press, 1990).

33. On the labor cases, see Risa Goluboff, *The Lost Promise of Civil Rights* (Cambridge, MA: Harvard University Press, 2007).

34. On A. Philip Randolph's role in the Black Freedom Struggle, see Eric Arnesen, *Brotherhoods of Color: Black Railroad Workers and the Struggle for Equality* (Cambridge, MA: Harvard University Press, 2001).

35. Mary L. Dudziak, *Cold War Civil Rights: Race and the Image of American Democracy* (Princeton, NJ: Princeton University Press, 2000), 18–23.

36. See Payne, *I've Got the Light of Freedom*, 29–66.

37. Ransby, *Ella Baker*, 108. On the postwar growth of the NAACP, see Patricia Sullivan, *Lift Every Voice: The NAACP and the Making of the Civil Rights Movement* (New York: New Press, 2009).

38. *Missouri ex rel. Gaines v. Canada*, 305 U.S. 337 (1938). On the Gaines case, see James W. Endersby and William T. Horner, *Lloyd Gaines and the Fight to End Segregation* (Columbia: University of Missouri Press, 2016). On the NAACP Legal Defense Fund, see Mark Tushnet, *The NAACP's Legal Strategy Against Segregated Education, 1925–1950* (Chapel Hill: University of North Carolina Press, 1987).

39. Michael J. Klarman, *From Jim Crow to Civil Rights: The Supreme Court and the Struggle for Racial Equality* (New York: Oxford University Press, 2004).

40. Gary M. Lavergne, *Before* Brown: *Heman Marion Sweatt, Thurgood Marshall, and the Long Road to Justice* (Austin: University of Texas Press, 2010).

41. Kari Frederickson, *The Dixiecrat Revolt and the End of the Solid South, 1932–1968* (Chapel Hill: University of North Carolina Press, 2001).

42. Chap. 541, House Concurrent Resolution No. 22, *General Laws of the State of Mississippi* (1948).

43. James Silver, *Mississippi: The Closed Society* (Jackson: University Press of Mississippi, 1964), 6–8. See, generally, Clive Webb, ed., *Massive Resistance: Southern Opposition to the Second Reconstruction* (New York: Oxford University Press, 2005).

44. See Wakefield, "'Skeleton in America's Own Cupboard.'"

45. Testimony of Theodore Bilbo, *Investigation by the Senate of the State of Mississippi of the Charges of Bribery in the Election of a United States Senator* (Jackson, 1910), 49.

46. Testimony of Theodore Bilbo, *Investigation by the Senate*, 52.

47. Chester M. Morgan, *Redneck Liberal: Theodore G. Bilbo and the New Deal* (Baton Rouge: Louisiana State University Press, 1985), 28.

48. Morgan, *Redneck Liberal*, 60.

49. Morgan, *Redneck Liberal*, 34.

50. Morgan, *Redneck Liberal*, 60–61.

51. Resolution No. 4, *Investigation by the Senate of the State of Mississippi of the Charges of Bribery in the Election of a United States Senator* (Jackson, 1910), 6.

52. "Senate Repudiates Bilbo; Demands His Resignation," *Natchez Democrat*, April 15, 1910.

53. Morgan, *Redneck Liberal*, 35.

54. William Alexander Percy, *Lanterns on the Levee: Recollections of a Planter's Son* (Baton Rouge: Louisiana State University Press, 1973), 149.

55. On Bilbo's support for Black colonization, see Michael W. Fitzgerald, "'We Have Found a Moses': Theodore Bilbo, Black Nationalism, and the Greater Liberia Bill of 1939," *Journal of Southern History* 63, no. 2 (May 1997): 293–320.

56. Theodore G. Bilbo, *Take Your Choice: Separation or Mongrelization* (Poplarville, MS: T. G. Bilbo, 1947).

57. House Concurrent Resolution 27, Chap. 544, *General Laws of the State of Mississippi*, 1948.

58. Craig Zaim, "Trial by Ordeal: The Willie McGee Case," *Journal of Mississippi History* 65, no. 3 (Fall 2003): 216–217.

59. Zaim, "Trial by Ordeal," 219.

60. Zaim, "Trial by Ordeal," 220–222.

61. Leandra Zarnow, "Braving Jim Crow to Save Willie McGee: Bella Abzug, the Legal Left, and Civil Rights Innovation, 1948–1951," *Law and Social Inquiry* 33, no. 4 (Fall 2008): 1003–1041.

62. John N. Popham, "Mississippi Arrests 41 at Capitol as Willie McGee Plea Is Studied," *New York Times*, May 7, 1951.

63. "Willie McGee Dies in Electric Chair," *Jackson (MS) Clarion-Ledger*, May 8, 1951.

64. "Mississippi Whites Roar Approval as Willie McGee Dies in the Electric Chair," *Chicago Defender*, May 19, 1951.

65. Testimony of Mrs. Hannon Graves, trial transcript, p. 4, *State of Mississippi v. Davis Knight* case file, MDAH.

66. The trial of Davis Knight is told most fully in Victoria Bynum, "'White Negroes' in Segregated Mississippi: Miscegenation, Racial Identity, and the Law," *Journal of Southern History* 64, no. 2 (May 1998): 247–276.

67. F. A. Behymer, "The Tragic Story of Davis Knight," *St. Louis Post-Dispatch*, January 9, 1949.

68. Arrest warrant, June 22, 1948, p. 5, *State v. Knight* case file, MDAH.

69. Circuit court indictment, June 22, 1948, p. 4, *State v. Knight* case file, MDAH.

70. Judgment, December 17, 1948, p. 26, *State v. Knight* case file, MDAH.

71. Victoria Bynum reads the Davis Knight case as a clear example that white Mississippians adhered to the one-drop standard, even though it was not the legal definition of Blackness. See Bynum, "'White Negroes'"; Victoria E. Bynum, *The Long Shadow of the Civil War: Southern Dissent and Its Legacies* (Chapel Hill: University of North Carolina Press, 2010), 123.

72. The trial took place over several days during the week of December 13, 1948, though the specific dates of witness testimony are not noted in the transcript. Testimony of J. M. Powell, trial transcript, p. 82, *State v. Knight* case file, MDAH.

73. Testimony of Mrs. Hannon Graves, trial transcript, pp. 7–8, *State v. Knight* case file, MDAH.

74. Victoria E. Bynum, *The Free State of Jones: Mississippi's Longest Civil War* (Chapel Hill: University of North Carolina Press, 2003); Rudy H. Leverett, *Legend of the Free State of Jones* (Jackson: University Press of Mississippi, 2009); Sally Jenkins and John Stauffer, *The State of Jones* (New York: Doubleday, 2009).

75. On the complicated Knight family tree, see Bynum, *Long Shadow*, 117–135.

76. Bynum, *Long Shadow*, 125.

77. Rachel died in 1889. Brief for Appellant, *Davis Knight v. State of Mississippi*, 207 Miss. at 565 (1949).

78. Testimony of Tom Knight, trial transcript, p. 12, *State v. Knight* case file, MDAH.

79. Testimony of Tom Knight, trial transcript, pp. 21–22, *State v. Knight* case file, MDAH.

80. Testimony of D. H. Valentine, trial transcript, p. 30, *State v. Knight* case file, MDAH.

81. Testimony of D. H. Valentine, trial transcript, pp. 31–32, *State v. Knight* case file, MDAH.

82. Testimony of D. H. Valentine, trial transcript, p. 32, *State v. Knight* case file, MDAH.

83. Testimony of D. H. Valentine, trial transcript, p. 36, *State v. Knight* case file, MDAH.

84. Trial transcript, pp. 28–29, *State v. Knight* case file, MDAH.

85. Testimony of Wiley McHenry, trial transcript, pp. 55–56, *State v. Knight* case file, MDAH.

86. Testimony of H. V. Welch, trial transcript, p. 67, *State v. Knight* case file, MDAH.

87. Testimony of Mrs. Bertis Ellzey, trial transcript, p. 71, *State v. Knight* case file, MDAH.

88. Testimony of Oscar Williams, trial transcript, p. 77, *State v. Knight* case file, MDAH.

89. Testimony of J. W. Stringer, trial transcript, p. 84, *State v. Knight* case file, MDAH.

90. Testimony of J. W. Stringer, trial transcript, p. 89, *State v. Knight* case file, MDAH.

91. Testimony of J. W. Stringer, trial transcript, pp. 90–91, *State v. Knight* case file, MDAH.

92. Testimony of Henry Knight, trial transcript, p. 96, *State v. Knight* case file, MDAH.

93. Testimony of W. W. Jackson, trial transcript, pp. 109–110, *State v. Knight* case file, MDAH.

94. Trial transcript, pp. 111–112, *State v. Knight* case file, MDAH.

95. "Davis Knight Found Guilty in Jones," *Jackson (MS) Clarion-Ledger*, December 19, 1948.

96. "Race 'Mix-Up' Case Upturns White South," *Chicago Defender*, January 1, 1949.

97. Brief for Appellee, p. 13, *State v. Knight* case file, MDAH.

98. On the California case, *Andrea D. Perez v. W. G. Sharp*, see Peggy Pascoe, *What Comes Naturally: Miscegenation Law and the Making of Race in America* (New York: Oxford University Press, 2009), 205–223.

99. Brief of Appellant, *Knight v. State*, 207 Miss. at 565 (1949).

100. Appellant brief, p. 17, *State v. Knight* case file, MDAH.

101. Appellant brief, p. 18, *State v. Knight* case file, MDAH.

102. *Knight v. State*, 207 Miss. 564 (1949).

103. This is the argument made by Victoria Bynum and Peggy Pascoe. See Bynum, "'White Negroes'"; Pascoe, *What Comes Naturally*, 224–225.

104. Peggy Pascoe termed the US Supreme Court's treatment of the two appealed cases involving interracial couples, *Linnie Jackson v. State of Alabama* and *Han Say Naim v. Ruby Elaine Naim*, as exercises in "the art of judicial ducking." Pascoe, *What Comes Naturally*, 225–231.

105. Ariela Gross compares the Knight family to other racially ambiguous communities in Virginia, Tennessee, and Kentucky, whose members often claimed Native American (rather than African) ancestry. Ariela J. Gross, *What Blood Won't Tell: A History of Race on Trial in America* (Cambridge, MA: Harvard University Press, 2008), 111–139.

106. Davis Knight, *1950 Federal Census*, Beat 4, Jasper County, Mississippi, enumeration district 31–20, p. 28; Junie L. Knight, *1950 Federal Census*, Beat 3, Jones County, Mississippi, enumeration district 34–42, p. 71 (via Ancestry.com).

107. Junie Lee Spradley, *Polk's Laurel (Jones County, Miss.) City Directory, 1955* (Richmond: R. L. Polk and Company, 1955), 295.

108. Death certificate, Davis Knight, September 1, 1959, in *Texas, U.S., Death Certificates, 1903–1982* (via Ancestry.com).

109. Application for headstone or marker, US, Headstone Applications for Military Veterans, 1925–1963, M1916, M2113, National Archives and Records Administration (NARA) (via Fold3.com).

110. "Dustin' Off the News: We Get Some More Nonsense from Mississippi," *Chicago Defender*, January 1, 1949.

111. "Mississippi Court Reverses Rumor, Rules Veteran Is White Man, Legally Wed," *Minneapolis Star*, November 28, 1949.

Chapter 8: Criminal Affections

1. "As It Now Is in Chicago," *Jackson (MS) Clarion-Ledger*, October 6, 1957.

2. On the Chicago housing riots, see Arnold R. Hirsch, *Making the Second Ghetto: Race and Housing in Chicago, 1940–1960* (Chicago: University of Chicago Press, 1983).

3. Hirsch, *Making the Second Ghetto*, 65–66.

4. On the panic over desegregation and miscegenation, see, generally, Jane Dailey, *White Fright: The Sexual Panic at the Heart of America's Racist History* (New York: Basic Books, 2020).

5. Tom P. Brady, "A Review of Black Monday," p. 3, *Pamphlets and Broadsides*, Citizens Councils Collection, University of Mississippi, https://egrove.olemiss.edu /citizens_pamph/3.

6. On the equalization strategy, see Mark Tushnet, *The NAACP's Legal Strategy Against Segregated Education, 1925–1950* (Chapel Hill: University of North Carolina Press, 1987).

7. See Timothy B. Tyson, *The Blood of Emmet Till* (New York: Simon and Schuster, 2017).

8. On the "kissing case," see Timothy Tyson, *Radio Free Dixie: Robert F. Williams and the Roots of Black Power* (Chapel Hill: University of North Carolina Press, 2001), 92–101.

9. On Coleman's career as a moderate segregationist, see Joseph Crespino, *In Search of Another Country: Mississippi and the Conservative Counterrevolution* (Princeton, NJ: Princeton University Press, 2007), 19–30; Anders Walker, *The Ghost of Jim Crow: How Southern Moderates Used* Brown v. Board of Education *to Stall the Civil Rights Movement* (New York: Oxford University Press, 2009), 11–48.

10. Crespino, *In Search of Another Country*, 18–19.

11. On the White Citizens' Councils, see Walker, *Ghost of Jim Crow.*

12. Crespino, *In Search of Another Country*, 26–27.

13. Crespino, *In Search of Another Country*, 19–20.

14. Walker, *Ghost of Jim Crow*, 18.

15. *Brown v. Board of Education*, 349 U.S. 294 (1955).

16. Mississippi Legislature, *Journal of the House of Representatives of the State of Mississippi* (Jackson: Hederman Brothers, 1956), 390.

17. H.B. 12, *House Journal* (1956), 409. These bills became Sec. 2351.5 and Sec. 2351.7, Miss. Ann. Code 1942.

18. Jerry Mitchell, "State Spied on Schwerner 3 Months Before Death," *Jackson (MS) Clarion-Ledger*, September 10, 1989. See, generally, Yasuhiro Katagiri, *The Mississippi State Sovereignty Commission: Civil Rights and States' Rights* (Jackson: University Press of Mississippi, 2001).

19. "Criminal Libel Bill Aims at Integration," *Jackson (MS) Clarion-Ledger*, January 18, 1956.

20. H.B. 119, *House Journal* (1956), 84.

21. Charles Payne, *I've Got the Light of Freedom: The Organizing Tradition and the Mississippi Freedom Movement* (Berkeley: University of California Press, 2007), 43.

22. "Racial Bills Await Action in Legislature," *Hattiesburg (MS) American*, January 23, 1956.

23. *House Journal* (1956), 685.

24. This bill became Sec. 2000, Miss. Rev. Code 1942.

25. As of 2024, the unlawful cohabitation law remains on the books. Sec. 97–29–1, Miss. Code 2019.

26. "Senate Votes to Keep Cattle off Highways," *Hattiesburg (MS) American*, March 23, 1956.

27. H.B. 975, *House Journal* (1956), 713.

28. H.B. 975, *House Journal* (1956), 981; Mississippi Legislature, *Journal of the Senate of the State of Mississippi* (Jackson: G. R. and J. S. Fall, 1956), 836.

29. H.B. 975, *House Journal* (1956), 1072.

30. "Ask Common Law Marriage Ban," *Greenwood (MS) Commonwealth*, February 17, 1956.

31. Douglas Starr, "House Passes New Segregation Bill," *Jackson (MS) Clarion-Ledger*, February 17, 1956.

32. On the use of morals clauses in pupil assignment laws to avoid desegregation, see Walker, *Ghost of Jim Crow*, 20–22, 41–43.

33. "Kill Common Law Marriage Bill," *Hattiesburg (MS) American*, March 1, 1956.

34. "Record Budget Waits Gov. Coleman's OK," *Hattiesburg (MS) American*, April 3, 1956.

35. Walker, *Ghost of Jim Crow*, 41.

36. "State Common-Law Marriages Banned by Senate's Action," *Jackson (MS) Clarion-Ledger*, March 31, 1956.

37. "Bill Outlawing Common-Law Ties Approved by House," *Delta Democrat-Times*, April 1, 1956.

38. "Delay Work on Absentee Voting Bill," *Biloxi (MS) Sun Herald*, February 17, 1956.

39. *House Journal* (1956), 624.

40. "Gov. Coleman Hits at Marriage Mills," *Jackson (MS) Clarion-Ledger*, November 27, 1956.

41. Chapter 241, H.B. 975, Mississippi Legislature, *Laws of the State of Mississippi* (Jackson: Langdon, 1956).

42. Testimony of Fred Walters, hearing transcript, p. 34, *Mary Rose v. State of Mississippi* case file, Mississippi Department of Archives and History, Jackson, Mississippi (hereafter MDAH). Details of Mary's arrest were offered by witnesses at a hearing to withdraw her guilty plea, which took place during the March 1958 term of the circuit court. The exact date of this hearing is not given in the record.

43. Testimony of Fred Walters, hearing transcript, pp. 26–27, *Rose v. State* case file, MDAH.

44. Testimony of Fred Walters, hearing transcript, p. 35, *Rose v. State* case file, MDAH.

45. Court order, April 11, 1958, p. 19, *Rose v. State* case file, MDAH.

46. Testimony of Mary Rose, hearing transcript, p. 22, *Rose v. State* case file, MDAH.

47. Testimony of Mary Rose, hearing transcript, p. 9, *Rose v. State* case file, MDAH.

48. Testimony of Mary Rose, hearing transcript, pp. 11–12, *Rose v. State* case file, MDAH.

49. Testimony of Mary Rose, hearing transcript, p. 4, *Rose v. State* case file, MDAH.

50. Testimony of Fred Walters, hearing transcript, p. 40, *Rose v. State* case file, MDAH.

51. Testimony of Fred Walters, hearing transcript, pp. 31–33, *Rose v. State* case file, MDAH.

52. Indictment, March 18, 1958, p. 6, *Rose v. State* case file, MDAH.

53. Commitment of Mary Rose, March 20, 1958, p. 10, *Rose v. State* case file; Commitment of Joe Scott, p. 9, *Rose v. State* case file, MDAH.

54. Judgment, March 20, 1958, p. 7, *Rose v. State* case file, MDAH.

55. Motion to Set Aside Plea, pp. 12–13, *Rose v. State* case file; Testimony of Mary Rose, trial transcript, p. 5, *Rose v. State* case file, MDAH.

56. Testimony of Mary Rose, hearing transcript, p. 3, *Rose v. State* case file, MDAH.

57. "White & Negro Plead Guilty; Get Pen Terms," *Laurel (MS) Call Leader*, March 26, 1958.

58. Judgment, March 20, 1958, *State of Mississippi v. Mary Rose*, case no. 1988; Judgment, March 20, 1958, *State of Mississippi v. Joe Scott*, case no. 1988; *Rose v. State* case file, pp. 7–8, MDAH.

59. Exhibit A, trial transcript, p. 21, *Rose v. State* case file, MDAH.

60. Testimony of Fred Walters, hearing transcript, p. 33, *Rose v. State* case file, MDAH.

61. Letter, Colin Stockdale to Jones County Circuit Clerk, April 4, 1858, p. 11, *Rose v. State* case file, MDAH.

62. Motion to Set Aside Plea, April 4, 1948, pp. 12–13, *Rose v. State* case file, MDAH.

63. Elmer and Mary Rose, *1950 Federal Census*, City of Laurel, Jones County, Mississippi, enumeration district 34–36, p. 71 (via Ancestry.com).

64. Testimony of Mary Rose, hearing transcript, pp. 3–5, *Rose v. State* case file, MDAH.

65. Court order, April 11, 1958, pp. 19–21, *Rose v. State* case file, MDAH.

66. Motion to Set Aside Plea, April 4, 1958, pp. 25–26, *Rose v. State* case file, MDAH.

67. Assignment of Error and Brief of Appellant, November 17, 1958, pp. 6–8, *Rose v. State* case file, MDAH.

68. Indictment, March 18, 1958, p. 4, *Rose v. State* case file, MDAH.

69. Assignment of Error and Brief of Appellant, November 17, 1958, pp. 9–10, *Rose v. State* case file, MDAH.

70. Appearance Bond, April 15, 1958, pp. 30–32, *Rose v. State* case file, MDAH.

71. "Laurel Pair Convicted in Delinquency Case," *Jackson (MS) Clarion-Ledger*, October 7, 1958.

72. "Man Serving Prison Term for Unlawful Cohabitation with White Woman Freed by Judge," *Laurel (MS) Call Leader*, December 17, 1958.

73. "George W. Bilbo Buried; Cousin of Sen. Bilbo," *Jackson (MS) Clarion-Ledger*, May 2, 1939; Dewitt Bilbo, *1950 Federal Census*, City of Purvis, Lamar County, Mississippi, enumeration district 37-1, p. 12 (via Ancestry.com).

74. Elsie Arrington and Daisy Ratcliff, *1950 Federal Census*, City of Purvis, Lamar County, Mississippi, enumeration district 37-1, pp. 14, 26 (via Ancestry.com).

75. Testimony of Eva Rouse, July 24, 1958, trial transcript, pp. 70–71, *Daisy Ratcliff v. State of Mississippi* case file, MDAH.

76. Testimony of Virillia Dickson, July 24, 1958, trial transcript, p. 73, *Ratcliff v. State* case file, MDAH.

77. Testimony of W. R. Campbell, July 24, 1958, trial transcript, p. 34, *Ratcliff v. State* case file, MDAH.

78. Testimony of Eva Rouse, July 24, 1958, trial transcript, pp. 68–69, *Ratcliff v. State*, MDAH.

79. Testimony of C. H. Hickman, July 24, 1958, trial transcript, p. 47, *Ratcliff v. State* case file, MDAH.

80. Testimony of W. R. Campbell, July 24, 1958, trial transcript, p. 38, *Ratcliff v. State* case file, MDAH.

81. Testimony of J. O. Baker, July 24, 1958, trial transcript, pp. 42–43, *Ratcliff v. State* case file, MDAH.

82. Testimony of J. O. Baker, July 24, 1958, trial transcript, p. 61, *Ratcliff v. State* case file, MDAH.

83. Testimony of W. R. Campbell, July 24, 1958, trial transcript, p. 34, *Ratcliff v. State* case file, MDAH.

84. Appearance bond, Daisy May Ratcliff, principal, July 3, 1958, p. 24, *Ratcliff v. State* case file, MDAH.

85. Venire facias, July 12, 1958, p. 26, *Ratcliff v. State* case file, MDAH. The transcript of the justice court trial is included in the later circuit court trial transcript as pp. 20–31.

86. Plea of Former Acquittal, July 22, 1958, p. 16, *Ratcliff v. State* case file, MDAH; Jury decision, July 12, 1958, p. 31, *Ratcliff v. State* case file, MDAH.

87. Indictment, July 15, 1958, p. 3, *Ratcliff v. State* case file, MDAH.

88. "Jesse Shanks Opens Campaign at Purvis," *Jackson (MS) Clarion-Ledger*, June 7, 1947.

89. Demurrer to indictment, July 22, 1958, p. 15, *Ratcliff v. State* case file, MDAH.

90. Plea of Former Acquittal, July 22, 1958, p. 16, *Ratcliff v. State* case file, MDAH; Sec. 22, Miss. Const. 1890; US Constitution, Fifth Amendment.

91. Testimony of Eva Rouse, July 24, 1958, trial transcript, pp. 69–70, *Ratcliff v. State* case file, MDAH.

92. Testimony of Pitts Ladner, July 24, 1958, trial transcript, pp. 80–82, *Ratcliff v. State* case file, MDAH.

93. Motion, trial transcript, July 24, 1958, pp. 40–41, *Ratcliff v. State* case file, MDAH.

94. Testimony of C. H. Hickman, July 24, 1958, pp. 48–49, *Ratcliff v. State* case file, MDAH.

95. Instructions to the jury, July 24, 1958, pp. 92, 94, *Ratcliff v. State* case file, MDAH.

96. Verdict and court order, July 24, 1958, pp. 95–96, *Ratcliff v. State* case file, MDAH.

97. "Negro Woman Appeals Sentence," *Delta Democrat-Times*, November 25, 1958.

98. Brief for Appellant, November 11, 1958, pp. 8–21, *Ratcliff v. State* case file, MDAH.

99. Brief for Appellant, November 11, 1958, pp. 18–20, *Ratcliff v. State* case file, MDAH.

100. Brief for Appellee, November 21, 1958, pp. 6–7, *Ratcliff v. State* case file, MDAH.

101. Brief for Appellant, November 21, 1958, pp. 15–17, *Ratcliff v. State* case file, MDAH.

102. Brief for Appellant, November 21, 1958, p. 11, *Ratcliff v. State* case file, MDAH.

103. "High Court Disagrees on Meaning of Term," *Jackson (MS) Clarion-Ledger*, November 25, 1958.

104. Brief for Appellant, November 21, 1958, p. 20, *Ratcliff v. State* case file, MDAH.

105. "Name Negro Youth in Mixed Love Slaying," *Jackson (MS) Advocate*, November 1, 1958.

106. "Miss. White Man Watches Act Then Beats Wife to Death," *Jet*, November 13, 1958.

107. "Pontotoc Man in Jail, Admits Killing Wife," *Jackson (MS) Clarion-Ledger*, October 30, 1958; "Dairyman Faces Murder Charge in Death of His Wife," *Delta Democrat-Times*, October 27, 1958.

108. "Miss. White Man Watches Act Then Beats Wife to Death," *Jet*, November 13, 1958.

109. "Jury Indicts Two in Death of Woman," *Jackson (MS) Clarion-Ledger*, December 11, 1958.

110. "Miss. White Man Watches Act Then Beats Wife to Death," *Jet*, November 13, 1958.

111. *Ratcliff v. State*, 234 Miss. 724 (1958).

112. *Pace v. Alabama*, 106 U.S. 583 (1883).

113. *Rose v. State*, 234 Miss. 731 (1958).

114. "Man Serving Prison Term for Unlawful Cohabitation with White Woman Freed by Judge," *Laurel (MS) Call Leader*, December 17, 1958.

115. "Three Go Free Because of Faulty Law," *Hattiesburg (MS) American*, December 18, 1958; "Legislative Goof: Knocks Out State Race-Mix Penalty," *Hattiesburg (MS) American*, December 15, 1958.

116. S.B. 1509, Mississippi Legislature, *Journal of the Senate of the State of Mississippi* (Jackson: Hederman Brothers, 1960), 28.

117. S.B. 1509, Mississippi Legislature, *Journal of the House of Representatives of the State of Mississippi* (Jackson: Hederman Brothers, 1960), 143; S.B. 1509, *Senate Journal* (1960), 78.

118. S.B. 1509, *Senate Journal* (1960), 169.

119. On prosecutions of white men who raped or sexually assaulted Black women, see Danielle McGuire, *At the Dark End of the Street: Black Women, Rape, and Resistance—a New History of the Civil Rights Movement from Rosa Parks to the Rise of Black Power* (New York: Knopf, 2010), 131–155; Estelle Freedman, *Redefining Rape: Sexual Violence in the Era of Suffrage and Segregation* (Cambridge, MA: Harvard University Press, 2013), 276–281.

120. "'Rape' of Negro Coed Clouded in Confusion," *Delta Democrat-Times*, December 7, 1960.

121. "'Rape' of Negro Coed Clouded in Confusion," *Delta Democrat-Times*, December 7, 1960.

122. "Chickasaw Man First to Face Prosecution," *Jackson (MS) Clarion-Ledger*, December 8, 1960.

123. "'Rape' of Negro Coed Clouded in Confusion," *Delta Democrat-Times*, December 7, 1960.

124. "Miss. White Man Gets Suspended Term in Sex Case," *Jet*, December 29, 1960.

125. McGuire, *Dark End of the Street*, 117–119.

126. McGuire, *Dark End of the Street*, 118.

127. "Two Get Life for Rape," *New York Times*, February 10, 1960.

128. "Yazoo City Man Is Sentenced in Rape Attempt," *Hattiesburg (MS) American*, February 16, 1961.

129. "3 Indicted for Rape," *New York Times*, February 8, 1961.

130. "Mississippi Had Most Executions During Last Year," *Delta Democrat-Times*, February 25, 1957.

131. "Negro Executed in Belzoni Rape Case," *Greenwood (MS) Commonwealth*, December 16, 1955.

132. See Howard Smead, *Blood Justice: The Lynching of Mack Charles Parker* (New York: Oxford University Press, 1986).

133. *United States v. Holmes County*, 385 F.2d 145 (1967).

134. *United States v. Holmes County*, 385 F.2d 145 (1967).

Chapter 9: The White Man's Will

1. Mrs. Sidney B. Schamber, "Burnside," p. 1, folder 8, box A206, Mississippi Counties: Neshoba, State Guide File, WPA Federal Writers Project, Library of Congress, Washington, DC.

2. Schamber, "Burnside," p. 2.

3. Reply Brief of Sally Price, Nannie Macon, and Princie Montgomery, Appellants, pp. 10–11, folder 1, *Tennessee Burnside et al. v. Walter A. Burnside et al.* case file, Mississippi Department of Archives and History, Jackson, Mississippi (hereafter MDAH).

4. "Report of Appraisers," trial transcript, vol. I, p. 38, *Mrs. Pearl Cheatham et al. v. W. A. Burnside et al.* case file, MDAH.

5. Testimony of A. J. Pearson, trial transcript, vol. II, p. 307, *Cheatham v. Burnside* case file, MDAH. Testimony took place over several days, beginning on September 7, 1953.

6. "Report of Appraisers," trial transcript, vol. I, p. 38, *Cheatham v. Burnside* case file, MDAH.

7. The 1940 census reveals that most of the Burnsides' neighbors were renters, and witnesses at the later trials indicate that some of these renters lived on the Burnside property. *1940 Federal Census*, Beat 5, Neshoba County, Mississippi, supervisor's district 5, enumeration district 50-20B, p. 3A (via Ancestry.com).

8. Testimony of A. J. Pearson, trial transcript, vol. II, p. 322; Testimony of Annie Ellis, trial transcript, vol. I, p. 52, *Cheatham v. Burnside* case file, MDAH.

9. Testimony of Barney Eubanks, trial transcript, vol. III, p. 445 *Burnside v. Burnside* case file, MDAH.

10. Testimony of A. J. Pearson, trial transcript, vol. II, p. 315, *Cheatham v. Burnside* case file, MDAH.

11. Brief of Appellants, filed December 9, 1954, vol. I, p. 1, *Cheatham v. Burnside* case file, MDAH.

12. Claude Yates Obituary, *Jackson (MS) Clarion-Ledger*, January 20, 1953.

13. "Burnside Will Thrown Out by Neshoba Jurors," *Neshoba (MS) Democrat*, September 17, 1953.

14. Beall is sometimes also mistakenly identified as "Ethel Bell" or "Edith Beall" in court documents related to *Cheatham v. Burnside* and *Burnside v. Burnside*. Testimony of Ethel Beall, trial transcript, vol. III, p. 494, *Cheatham v. Burnside* case file, MDAH.

15. Testimony of Ethel Beall, trial transcript, vol. III, p. 490, *Cheatham v. Burnside* case file, MDAH.

16. Testimony of Ethel Beall, trial transcript, vol. III, p. 489, *Cheatham v. Burnside* case file, MDAH.

17. Testimony of Ethel Beall, trial transcript, vol. III, p. 515, *Cheatham v. Burnside* case file, MDAH.

18. John Burnside, *1850 Federal Census*, Neshoba County, Mississippi, p. 23; *1870 Federal Census*, Beat 2, Neshoba County, Mississippi, p. 27 (via Ancestry.com).

19. Bill of Complaint, trial transcript, vol. I, p. 46, *Cheatham v. Burnside* case file, MDAH.

20. Bill of Complaint, trial transcript, vol. I, p. 46, *Cheatham v. Burnside* case file, MDAH.

21. Bill of Complaint, trial transcript, vol. I, p. 49, *Cheatham v. Burnside* case file, MDAH.

22. Answer to Bill of Complaint, trial transcript, vol. I, p. 63, *Cheatham v. Burnside* case file, MDAH.

23. *R. R. Moore et al. v. Cordelia E. Parks et al.*, 122 Miss. 301 (1920).

24. *Harris Gholson et al. v. Marion C. Peters et al.*, 180 Miss. 256 (1937).

25. Answer to Bill of Complaint, trial transcript, vol. I, p. 60, *Cheatham v. Burnside* case file, MDAH.

26. Testimony of Annie Ellis, trial transcript, vol. I, p. 64, *Cheatham v. Burnside* case file, MDAH.

27. Testimony of Jack Eubanks, trial transcript, vol. II, p. 102, *Cheatham v. Burnside* case file, MDAH.

28. Testimony of Tim Fox, trial transcript, vol. II, p. 122, *Cheatham v. Burnside* case file, MDAH.

29. Testimony of Shedhill Caffey, trial transcript, vol. II, p. 281, *Cheatham v. Burnside* case file, MDAH.

30. Testimony of Thomas McAdory, trial transcript, vol. I, pp. 46–48, *Cheatham v. Burnside* case file, MDAH.

31. Testimony of Maude Moody, trial transcript, vol. II, p. 173, *Cheatham v. Burnside* case file, MDAH.

32. Testimony of Bob Byars, trial transcript, vol. II, pp. 147–148, *Cheatham v. Burnside* case file, MDAH.

33. Testimony of A. J. Pearson, trial transcript, vol. II, p. 310, *Cheatham v. Burnside* case file, MDAH.

34. Testimony of A. J. Pearson, trial transcript, vol. II, pp. 305–307; testimony of Vernon Gamblin, trial transcript, vol. II, pp. 259–260, *Cheatham v. Burnside* case file, MDAH.

35. Testimony of A. J. Pearson, trial transcript, vol. II, p. 314, *Cheatham v. Burnside* case file, MDAH.

36. Testimony of A. J. Pearson, trial transcript, vol. II, p. 349, *Cheatham v. Burnside* case file, MDAH.

37. Testimony of Lewis Jones, trial transcript, vol. III, p. 439, *Cheatham v. Burnside* case file, MDAH.

38. Testimony of Marvin Henley, trial transcript, vol. I, p. 15, *Cheatham v. Burnside* case file, MDAH.

39. Testimony of Jack Eubanks, trial transcript, vol. II, p. 103, *Cheatham v. Burnside* case file, MDAH.

40. Testimony of Joe Reese, trial transcript, vol. III, pp. 422–425, *Cheatham v. Burnside* case file, MDAH.

41. "Burnside Will Thrown Out by Neshoba Jurors," *Neshoba (MS) Democrat*, September 17, 1953.

42. Testimony of A. J. Pearson, trial transcript vol. IV, pp. 676–677, *Burnside v. Burnside* case file, MDAH.

43. *Cheatham v. Burnside*, 222 Miss. 872 (1955).

44. "Fantastic Story Unfolds as Negroes Seek to Inherit an Estate White Cousins Want," *Neshoba (MS) Democrat*, March 11, 1954.

45. "Fantastic Story Unfolds as Negroes Seek to Inherit an Estate White Cousins Want," *Neshoba (MS) Democrat*, March 11, 1954.

46. Death certificate, Mariah Burnside, July 6, 1925, exhibit E, vol. IV, *Burnside v. Burnside* case file, MDAH.

47. "Old Citizen Gone," *Winston County (MS) Journal*, July 17, 1925.

48. "Fantastic Story Unfolds as Negroes Seek to Inherit an Estate White Cousins Want," *Neshoba (MS) Democrat*, March 11, 1954.

49. "Miss. Negroes Seek 'White' Man's $1/4 Million Estate," *Jet*, March 31, 1955, 7.

50. Amended Petition for Adjudication of Heirs, vol. I, p. 12, *Burnside v. Burnside* case file, MDAH.

51. Mariah Burnside, *1870 Federal Census*, Beat 2, Neshoba County, Mississippi, p. 27 (via Ancestry.com).

52. W. A. Burnside, *1860 Federal Census*, Township 12, Range 11, Neshoba County, Mississippi, p. 100 (via Ancestry.com).

53. W. A. Burnside, *1860 Federal Census—Slave Schedules*, Township 12, Range 12, Neshoba County, Mississippi, p. 19 (via Ancestry.com).

54. W. A. and Mariah Burnside, *1880 Federal Census*, Beat 5, Neshoba County, Mississippi, supervisor's district 3, enumeration district 61, p. 21 (via Ancestry.com).

55. Thomas Burnside, *1870 Federal Census*, Township 13, Range 10, Winston County, Mississippi, p. 6 (via Ancestry.com).

56. Thomas Burnside, *1880 Federal Census*, Beat 5, Winston County, Mississippi, supervisor's district 2, enumeration district 168, p. 10B (via Ancestry.com).

57. Tom Talley, *1940 Federal Census*, Beat 1, City of Philadelphia, Neshoba County, Mississippi, supervisor's district 5, enumeration district 50–2, p. 20B; Tom Jeff Talley, *1940 Federal Census*, Beat 5, Neshoba County, Mississippi, supervisor's district 5, enumeration district 50–20A, p. 15A (via Ancestry.com).

58. Mariah Burnside, *1880 Federal Census*, Beat 5, Winston County, Mississippi, supervisor's district 2, enumeration district 168, p. 10B (via Ancestry.com).

59. "United States Supreme Court Rules Out Segregation by Unanimous Vote of the Nine Court Justices," *Neshoba (MS) Democrat*, May 24, 1954.

60. The 1900 Census for Beat 5 includes Mariah and her children on the first page and several other witnesses on subsequent pages, including Cora Talley's family and

Nannie Burnside Jones. *1900 Federal Census*, Beat 5, Neshoba County, Mississippi, supervisor's district 5, enumeration district 46, pp. 1A–2B (via Ancestry.com).

61. Testimony of Nannie Burnside Jones, trial transcript, vol. I, p. 37, *Burnside v. Burnside* case file, MDAH.

62. Testimony of Nannie Burnside Jones, trial transcript, vol. I, p. 41, *Burnside v. Burnside* case file, MDAH.

63. Trial transcript, p. 1, *Mary Rose v. State of Mississippi* case file, MDAH.

64. Testimony of Nannie Burnside Jones, trial transcript, vol. I, p. 71, *Burnside v. Burnside* case file, MDAH.

65. Testimony of Robert Burnside, trial transcript, vol. II, pp. 191–192, *Burnside v. Burnside* case file, MDAH.

66. Testimony of Walter Burnside, trial transcript, vol. I, p. 5, *Burnside v. Burnside* case file, MDAH.

67. Testimony of Walter Burnside, trial transcript, vol. I, p. 16, *Burnside v. Burnside* case file, MDAH.

68. Testimony of Maude Moore, trial transcript, vol. IV, p. 639, *Burnside v. Burnside* case file, MDAH.

69. Testimony of Cora Talley, trial transcript, vol. I. pp. 19–20, *Burnside v. Burnside* case file, MDAH.

70. Testimony of Cora Talley, trial transcript, vol. I, pp. 25–26, *Burnside v. Burnside* case file, MDAH.

71. Testimony of Cora Talley, trial transcript, vol. I, p. 28, *Burnside v. Burnside* case file, MDAH.

72. Reply Brief of Sally Price, Nannie Macon, and Princie Montgomery, Appellants, p. 15, folder 1, *Burnside v. Burnside* case file, MDAH.

73. Testimony of Pearl Cheatham, vol. II, p. 251, *Burnside v. Burnside* case file, MDAH.

74. Testimony of Pearl Cheatham, vol. II, pp. 231–232, *Burnside v. Burnside* case file, MDAH.

75. Testimony of Pearl Cheatham, vol. II, pp. 233–234, *Burnside v. Burnside* case file, MDAH.

76. Assignment of Errors and Brief of Sally Price, Nannie Macon, and Princie Montgomery, Appellants, March 25, 1956, p. 1, *Burnside v. Burnside* case file, MDAH.

77. Testimony of Pearl Cheatham, vol. II, p. 238, *Burnside v. Burnside* case file, MDAH.

78. Testimony of Pearl Cheatham, vol. II, p. 238, *Burnside v. Burnside* case file, MDAH.

79. Testimony of Pearl Cheatham, vol. II, p. 249, *Burnside v. Burnside* case file, MDAH

80. Testimony of Pearl Cheatham, vol. II, p. 244, *Burnside v. Burnside* case file, MDAH.

81. Testimony of Pearl Cheatham, vol. II, p. 250, *Burnside v. Burnside* case file, MDAH.

82. The lock of hair is preserved along with other evidence in vol. IV of the *Burnside v. Burnside* case file, MDAH.

83. Florence Mars, *Witness in Philadelphia* (Baton Rouge: Louisiana State University Press, 1977), 51.

84. Testimony of Henry Riddle, trial transcript, vol. II, p. 329, *Burnside v. Burnside* case file, MDAH.

85. Testimony of Callie McKinley, trial transcript, vol. II, p. 273, *Burnside v. Burnside* case file, MDAH.

86. Testimony of Callie McKinley, trial transcript, vol. II, pp. 274–275, *Burnside v. Burnside* case file, MDAH.

87. Testimony of Callie McKinley, trial transcript, vol. II, p. 267, *Burnside v. Burnside* case file, MDAH.

88. Testimony of Callie McKinley, trial transcript, vol. II, p. 269, *Burnside v. Burnside* case file, MDAH.

89. Testimony of Callie McKinley, trial transcript, vol. II, p. 280, *Burnside v. Burnside* case file, MDAH.

90. Testimony of Lafayette Wilkes, trial transcript, vol. III, pp. 370–372, *Burnside v. Burnside* case file, MDAH.

91. Testimony of R. W. Boydstun, trial transcript, vol. III, pp. 378–379, *Burnside v. Burnside* case file, MDAH.

92. Testimony of R. W. Boydstun, trial transcript, vol. III, p. 387, *Burnside v. Burnside* case file, MDAH.

93. Testimony of Mary Johnson, trial transcript, vol. III, p. 544, *Burnside v. Burnside* case file, MDAH.

94. Testimony of Tim Fox, trial transcript, vol. III, p. 581, *Burnside v. Burnside* case file, MDAH.

95. Testimony of Tim Fox, trial transcript, vol. III, p. 582, *Burnside v. Burnside* case file, MDAH.

96. Testimony of James A. Duncan, trial transcript, vol. IV, p. 671, *Burnside v. Burnside* case file, MDAH.

97. Testimony of Jack Eubanks, trial transcript, vol. III, p. 433, *Burnside v. Burnside* case file, MDAH.

98. Testimony of Barney Eubanks, trial transcript, vol. III, p. 438, *Burnside v. Burnside* case file, MDAH.

99. Testimony of Murphy Cannon, trial transcript, vol. IV, pp. 678–679, *Burnside v. Burnside* case file, MDAH.

100. Opinion of the Court, trial transcript, vol. IV, pp. 683–684, *Burnside v. Burnside* case file, MDAH.

101. *Burnside v. Burnside*, 228 Miss. 180 (1956).

102. "Oil Distributor Buys Estate of Neshoba Recluse," *Delta Democrat-Times*, October 2, 1957.

103. Florence Mars, *The Lake Place Burnside Family: A Neshoba County Story* (Philadelphia, MS: F. Mars, 1995).

104. "Mrs. Zelma Gillis Dies in New Orleans," *Jackson (MS) Clarion-Ledger*, November 27, 1950.

105. Testimony of Cal Stribling, trial transcript, vol. III, pp. 525–526, *Burnside v. Burnside* case file, MDAH.

106. Mars, *Witness in Philadelphia*, 16.

107. Mars, *Witness in Philadelphia*, 45.

108. Mars, *Witness in Philadelphia*, 46.

Epilogue

1. Ralphine Burns, *1900 Federal Census*, Beat 4, Adams County, Mississippi, supervisor's district 7, enumeration district 8, p. 2A (via Ancestry.com).

2. On *Loving v. Virginia*, see Peter Wallenstein, *Tell the Court I Love My Wife: Race, Marriage, and Law—an American History* (New York: Palgrave Macmillan, 2002); Phyl Newbeck, *Virginia Hasn't Always Been for Lovers: Interracial Marriage Bans and the Case of Richard and Mildred Loving* (Carbondale: Southern Illinois University Press, 2004); Sheryll Cashin, *Loving: Interracial Intimacy in America and the Threat to White Supremacy* (Boston: Beacon Press, 2017).

3. "Interracial Couples File Federal Complaint," *McComb (MS) Enterprise-Journal*, July 29, 1970; "Southern National Party Rebuke Political Apathy," *Jackson (MS) Clarion-Ledger*, January 22, 1970; "Now Will You Join the Southern National Party," *Jackson (MS) Clarion-Ledger*, July, 21, 1981.

4. Leroy Morganti, "District Court Action: 2 Interracial Couples May Obtain Licenses," *Shreveport (LA) Times*, August 1, 1970.

5. A former director of the NAACP Legal Defense Fund called Cox "possibly the most racist judge ever to sit on the federal bench." Jack Greenberg, *Crusaders in the Courts: How a Dedicated Band of Lawyers Fought for the Civil Rights Revolution* (New York: Basic Books, 1994), 321.

6. "Wed in Mississippi," *Palm Beach (FL) Post*, August 3, 1970; "Names in the News," *Tri-City Herald* (Kennewick, WA), August 3, 1970; *San Francisco Examiner*, August 9, 1970; "Mixed-Race Marriage Ends Mississippi Ban," *Rochester (NY) Democrat and Chronicle*, August 3, 1970.

7. "Romance Integrated," *Florida Today*, August 3, 1970.

8. Valerie Jo Bradley, "Mississippi's First Mixed Marriage Since 1890: Whites 'Going Through Back,'" *Jet*, August 20, 1970, 24–25.

9. "Mississippi Has History of Interracial Dates, Marriages," *Jet*, August 20, 1970, 26–27.

10. James Silver, *Mississippi: The Closed Society* (Jackson: University Press of Mississippi, 1964), 5.

11. Juel and Clarence Dean, *1950 Federal Census*, City of New Brunswick, Middlesex County, New Jersey, enumeration district 12–121, p. 72 (via Ancestry.com).

12. Correspondence between the author and Richard Dean, 2023.

13. Olga Sabine, *1940 Federal Census*, City of Natchez, Ward 2, Adams County, Mississippi, supervisor's district 7, enumeration district 1–5, p. 12B (via Ancestry.com).

14. On the murder of Vernon Dahmer Sr., see Jerry Mitchell, *Race Against Time: A Reporter Reopens the Unsolved Murder Cases of the Civil Rights Era* (New York: Simon and Schuster, 2020); Curtis Wilkie, *When Evil Lived in Laurel: The "White Knights" and the Murder of Vernon Dahmer* (New York: W. W. Norton, 2021).

15. Mitchell, *Race Against Time*, 162.

16. Charlie and Laura Craft, *1880 Federal Census*, Covington County, Mississippi, Beat 5, supervisor's district 2, enumeration district 124, p. 40 (via Ancestry.com).

17. Transcript, oral history of Vernon Dahmer Jr., conducted with Emilye Crosby, December 1, 2015, Hattiesburg, Mississippi, Civil Rights History Project, Southern Oral History Program, Smithsonian Institution, National Museum of African American History and Culture and the Library of Congress, www.loc.gov/item/2016655405.

18. Mitchell, *Race Against Time*, 162. This story is told most fully on the *Renegade South* blog. Wilmer Watts Backstrom and Yvonne Bivins, "The Family Origins of Vernon F. Dahmer, Mississippi Civil Rights Activist," *Renegade South* blog, https://renegadesouth.wordpress.com/tag/kelly-settlement.

19. Transcript, oral history of Raylawni G. Branch and Jeannette Smith, conducted by Emilye Crosby, December 1, 2015, Hattiesburg, Mississippi, Civil Rights History Project, Southern Oral History Program, Smithsonian Institution, National Museum of African American History and Culture and the Library of Congress, www.loc.gov/item/2016655403.

20. Anne Moody, *Coming of Age in Mississippi* (New York: Random House, 1968), chaps. 10 and 11.

21. Charles Payne, *I've Got the Light of Freedom: The Organizing Tradition and the Mississippi Freedom Movement* (Berkeley: University of California Press, 2007), 52.

22. On the murder of Medgar Evers, see Mitchell, *Race Against Time*, 47–53.

INDEX

Index

Index

KATHRYN SCHUMAKER is Senior Lecturer of American Studies at the University of Sydney. The author of *Troublemakers: Students' Rights and Racial Justice in the Long 1960s*, she lives in Australia.